MW00893791

Everything is Possible

A Nurse's Memoir

Sylvia Kleiman Fields

All of the case histories in this memoir are based on real people and actual events over my eighty year history. However, the first and last names of all patients and professionals have been considered for change to prevent any possible invasion of privacy.

Archway Publishing books may be ordered through booksellers or by contacting:

Archway Publishing
1663 Liberty Drive
Bloomington, IN 47403
www.archwaypublishing.com
1 (888) 242-5904

ISBN: 978-1-4808-2263-4 (sc)
ISBN: 978-1-4808-2262-7 (hc)
ISBN: 978-1-4808-2264-1 (e)

Library of Congress Control Number: 2015918338

Print information available on the last page.

Archway Publishing rev. date: 1/8/2016

In memory of my parents
Frieda Berkowitz Kleiman and Isidor Irving Kleiman

And to my brother Norman, my lifetime friend, may he live to be 120

Dedication

This book is dedicated to my dearest friend, mentor and *supporter who made my doctoral study in the 1970's and this Memoir possible in 2015:*

Georgie Labadie, EdD, RN. Emeritus Professor of Nursing and Associate Dean, University of Miami School of Nursing and former Associate Professor of Nursing Education, Department of Nursing Education, Teachers College, Columbia University, New York, N.Y.

And to my beloved children and grandchildren:

Melissa Ellen, Andrew Gregory, and Elizabeth Carrie, who survived me, and blessed me with the "most beautiful and brilliant" grandchildren:

Alix Sara, Courtney Danielle, Samuel Mathew, Rachel Emily, Jonathan Zachery, and Gabriella Madison

They continue to make it all worthwhile.

Contents

Preface

I have often been asked how I happened to become a professional nurse, and I usually say it was an accident, maybe a fluke. In the beginning of 1950, when I entered my last semester at James Madison High School in Brooklyn, New York, I was not yet sixteen and I had no clear goals. World War II was over, most of the GI's who had come home and gone to college under the GI Bill and had quickly looked to marry their girlfriends, start families and move to the suburbs. Meanwhile there was war in Korea so the draft continued. My brother and most of his friends and our male cousins who were too young for World War II were now in uniform; marriage for this generation would be delayed. For young girls like me who were thinking about college there were only a few options. Most of us were probably thinking of teaching, *temporarily*. The other option was probably nursing, but I did not know any nurses and had never thought about it. While a few of my classmates had professional goals and were considering universities outside New York City, especially those within the New York State System like Cornell or Buffalo, most were not leaving the City. Some of my classmates were already engaged and thinking about their weddings soon after graduation; they were looking locally to Hunter or Brooklyn College. I assumed I would follow that route. Meanwhile, I could fantasize about love and marriage, but that was all it could be since I had no serious young man "on my dance card."

My ideas for my life came out of fantasies in my head through the novels I had read, the Broadway musicals I had seen, and the romantic movie dramas I would watch on the big screen. I didn't want what I had seen at home: life in a tiny Brooklyn apartment and work in the garment industry. I wanted something different; I wanted an adventure. It wasn't that I was searching for freedom and professional identity. (It would be another ten years before Betty Friedan wrote her international best seller, "*The Feminine Mystique*" that has been credited with triggering the women's movement.) A career in nursing was nowhere in the picture.

The actual trigger for my studying nursing had much to do with not wanting to take *trigonometry* in my last semester of high school. "No more Mathematics," I pleaded. I only needed a half- credit course to meet graduation requirements, so my advisor, Mrs. Weiner, suggested a course called, "Home Nursing." She thought it would be an easy way for me to get an "A," and although I knew nothing about the course I agreed, as long as it wasn't math. That's where it started, but it also had very much to do with the Holocaust in Europe and a "sofa bed" that I will explain later.

Well, I took the home nursing course and drove the teacher and the other girls in the class crazy with all my questions. It was unlike any academic course I had taken so far in school; it wasn't boring! And I wanted more. Half way through the course, Mrs. Quinn, the instructor, called me aside and said, "Sylvia, you are smart and caring and I think you would make a very good nurse." When I told her I understood seventeen was the required age for admission to hospital diploma schools, and I was only sixteen, she suggested I look at Adelphi College in Garden City on Long Island, a small private liberal arts school I had never heard of. I did not know anything about nursing and did not know any nurses other than Mrs. Quinn. None of my close friends ever expressed interest in becoming nurses. No one seemed to know much about nursing education, except that usually you went to a hospital training school modeled after the school designed by Florence Nightingale in England and not to college. Several of my classmates in the home nursing course had already applied to Kings County and Mary Immaculate, local hospital schools in Brooklyn. But I wanted to go to college and I wanted something different after college. In the movies all the colleges had campuses with dormitories, yet I knew my religious parents would not let me move to an out- of town school. I would have to commute to a New York City public school like Brooklyn or Hunter

College in Manhattan that were then essentially free. However, neither of those schools had a nursing program at that time.

When I came home and told my family what Mrs. Quinn said, my father said "I don't think that's a good idea. Nursing is hard work. Jewish girls don't become nurses." "That is a myth," I shouted. "What about the midwives in the Bible?[1] Mrs. Quinn told us about a very famous Jewish American nurse, Lillian Wald,[2] a graduate of New York Hospital School of Nursing. During the 1890s she started the Henry Street Settlement House for poor sick immigrants from Eastern Europe in the lower east side of Manhattan. She is known all over the country for public health nursing and the world for the important community services she organized." My father didn't give up. "We wanted you to become a dress designer and work with us in the garment industry. Remember how you used to play with the paper dolls I brought home for you. You spent hours alone cutting-out their clothes, mixing and matching." (My brother Norman, who was five years older, laughed.) I looked at my father and said, "Don't be ridiculous, I was five or six years old then. I can't draw, and I couldn't even sew a button on straight in home economics in Cunningham junior high school."

"I want to do something different, and I like the idea of studying more biology and psychology. Most of all, I want to do something worthwhile; I want to be able to help people as you have always taught me." My mother said, "It is true, your stitches in the apron you made in the seventh grade were terrible, but I thought you wanted to be a teacher. You always liked to play "school" in your room with your friends Nancy and Selma when we lived in Philadelphia. " "Yes, that is true" I said, "but

---

1 There were indeed ancient Jewish precepts related to healing and Jewish women in Nursing since biblical days, as well as Jewish women among our American nursing leaders in history and today. See Benson, E.R.(2001) "As We See Ourselves: Jewish Women in Nursing." Indianapolis, Indiana: Center Nursing Publishing.

2 Lillian Wald, (1867-1940), the German-Jewish nurse who founded the Henry Street Settlement, grew within her lifetime into a figure of legend, known on every street of the Lower East Side of New York City. (Howe, I (1976) "World of Our Fathers," New York: Harcourt Brace Jovanovich. pp: 91-94.

I haven't had my own room since we left Philadelphia seven years ago and moved to Brooklyn. I don't have a quiet place of my own to read or study, or talk with my friends. I'm stuck on the sofa bed in the hallway sleeping across from Norman."

My mother changed her voice, "Maybe nursing is a good idea, it will come in handy when you marry and have children." And she was right. But it was much more than any of us could know then, for I kept asking questions, looking for answers and setting goals in my mind. I wanted to finish college and move out of Brooklyn; I wanted to become independent. But I also knew I wanted to have a family and a real home. Eventually I was prepared by my Adelphi education and subsequent years of graduate education and clinical accomplishments for all the challenges I have had to face in my professional and my personal life.

I became a nurse first, and then I did become a teacher, and I married and raised children. It was never easy; I struggled, particularly at home. My learning experiences continued while my profession kept moving along in new directions. One after the next, as one door closed, new ones opened. Meanwhile I survived many disappointments: disappointment and unfulfilled love, failed marriages, mental and economic depression and much more. I was fortunate to always find people who recognized my skills, supported my efforts and encouraged me. So, I just kept asking questions, seeking answers, setting goals, and offering service. And I kept smiling as I made new friends.

Along the way I raised questions about life and death, about God, the faith I was born into and religion generally. I have searched and studied informally and over time, I found some answers for myself; not all, but enough. There is a passage in the Bible somewhere I took to heart, "*Live each day so that at the end of the day, you can say, my day has been worthwhile.*"

I am proud to be a nurse first, a member of the most ethical and respected profession in society according to all the polls. And to this day, in the sunset of my life, my career has given me significant personal satisfaction in the value of the life I have lived.

There are two large posters on the wall of my office that speak to my philosophy of life. They have been there for many years. The first shows a bird on the beach looking out to the sunset over the blue waves.

"To be what we are and to become all we are capable of becoming, is the only end in life." (From Spinoza)

The next poster shows a skier sliding down the snow-covered mountain, followed by a friend. There is no author or artist.

"Life is a daring adventure or nothing at all."[3]

When I told my stories, friends, colleagues, students and strangers frequently said, "You should write a book!"

Here it is - the story of my adventure through sixty years in healthcare.

Everything is Possible

---

3 *(*Sometimes attributed to Helen Keller.*)*

Baruch or Benedict Spinoza

Baruch Spinoza was a 17th century philosopher of Sephardic heritage who used 'reason' to challenge mystical Jewish thought in the secularizing climate of Amsterdam that became the beginning of modern Judaism.

Spinoza insisted on rationalism even in the sanctioned unreason of religion.

He challenged the authority of priests in interpreting "revelation" and championed free thought. "Applying the process of scientific inquiry Spinoza produced the theory of God as infinite substance, creator and created, present in every phenomenon and physical object." Virtue, to Spinoza was the freedom of the sage to think and therefore to apply his wisdom to an informed love of God....

"The body of his true work has served to sharpen the intellectual eye of mankind for all time."[4]

---

4 Evslin, Bernard, (Editor). The Spirit of Jewish Thought (1969) New York & Canada: Grosset & Dunlop, Inc, and Rutledge Books, Inc. pp: 125-129. Ruderman, D.B. (2005) Between Cross and Crescent: Jewish Civilization from Mohammed to Spinoza. Chantilly, Va. The Teaching Company.

Introduction

My story begins with the history of my family and the world I was born into in 1934. I believe these very early influences provided a foundation for the person I became and led to the career I chose. There was much unrest all around the globe in the 1930s, and a serious economic depression in the United States. Of course I didn't understand anything about what was happening around me then. The one thing I remember clearly from my childhood was being told often when I was only about three or four years old was, *"eat up, finish your food, the children in Europe are starving."*[5]

As a child of Eastern European immigrants who were engrained with a spiritual base, a strong work ethic, and a mission to rescue extended family members trying to escape the impending war against the Jews, I was frequently told that I needed to be compassionate and caring for those who were less fortunate than me. Observing God's commandments according to our Jewish faith and trying to do good deeds every day was important in our family. While this was not translated directly into an early goal as a young girl to become a professional nurse, I know I was sensitized by my immediate family experience to Judeo-Christian values through education and exposure to the arts: music, art and literature.

My parents left Europe for the United States as teenagers soon after World War I was over. Before the war their homes had been part of the Austria-Hungarian Empire in an area known for the Carpathian Mountains. They lived miles apart so they did not know each other then, but much of their heritage as observant Jews was similar. My father came from Munkács, a large industrial city in Czechoslovakia with a significant Jewish population and important centers for Jewish learning in the late 19th and early 20th centuries. Most of the Jews, political activists, gypsies,

---

5 Some of my friends recall hearing as a child *"eat up, clean your plate, remember the starving Armenians."*

and homosexuals were killed locally or taken to Auschwitz and other concentration camps during World War II. Only a few survivors returned to the city which was taken over by communists after the war. Today the city is in southern Ukraine, just over the border with Hungary. (I visited the area about fifteen years ago. It was dilapidated and depressing. There were tremendous differences between the roads and housing in Munkacs from what we saw while driving up from Budapest through Hungary. There were very few Jews who either returned from the concentration camps at the end of World War II or left the Soviet Union when it broke up. During my visit I found Helen, a survivor I was personally looking for and a new developing Jewish Learning Center supported by American organizations. (Steve a California cousin of mine who had survived Auschwitz had visited Munkacs the previous year and found Helen, another survivor he knew in the camp. Steve asked me to give her fifty dollars in cash that would be confiscated if sent through the mail. Helen cried and hugged me when I gave her the money. I learned later she had used the money towards travel to a sister she had located in Israel soon after I left.) With the current political situation in the Ukraine, I am not sure that the one Center I experienced during my visit exists today, or that any Jews remain in Munkacs.

From the time I was about ten years old, I was aware of how lucky I was. *"There, but for the grace of God, go I"* [6]was a belief I lived with throughout my life about the fate I might have shared with so many young Jewish victims during the "War Against the Jews" had my parents not come to America when they did.

I may have thought it was an accident that led me to study nursing in college, but in retrospect, I had the foundation at home and in school all along. Although I was not thinking of a lifelong career in the beginning,

---

[6] John Bradford, English Reformer had supposedly said these words in reference to his observation of a group of prisoners about to be burned at the stake. Later as a martyr, he was imprisoned in the Tower of London for alleged crimes against Mary Tudor. He was punished and died in 1555 for the same crimes. In modern times, this proverbial phrase is sometimes used to express empathetic compassion and a sense of good fortune realized by avoiding hardship. (Wikipedia: https.//en.Wikipedia org/)

once I was exposed to the challenge of the healing arts as a student within the profession of nursing, I felt good about myself and the purpose it brought to my life. My interest in a full professional role soon took root. I have never lost that enthusiasm and I know now it was always in the plan for me.

Image of Author's family at her parents' wedding November 20, 1927. Author's Parents: Frieda Berkowitz and Irving Kleiman; Grandparents, Miriam and Simcha Berkowitz; Frieda's Brother Jack Berg and his wife, Sonia Berg; Frieda's Sister and her husband, Ida and Moshe (Morris) Heisler and their two sons, Irving and Stanley. (Author's Personal Family Collection)

Author as Infant, age nine months, Brooklyn, New York

1

The Early Years

"Eat up; finish your food, the children in Europe are starving."

When I was little we lived in a six-room row house in North Philadelphia, one house attached to the next, all the same on both sides of the street. Each house had a white porch up several steps from the sidewalk, with a small patch of rolling green grass surrounded all the way around by thick hedges. I remember jumping rope and playing hopscotch in the street. It was a quiet street, few cars passed; people went to work or school and stayed in their homes. Our house, which my parents rented for $37.50 a month, had three bedrooms and only one bath upstairs. My parents' bedroom was in the front of the house and my Brother Norman's room, which was almost as large as theirs, was in the back overlooking an alleyway. He had a desk where he could do his homework and a metal worktable where he put together model airplanes in balsawood from kits. The finished models hung from the ceiling with wires. Norman also cut out and painted decorative wooden animals (often copied from old coloring books of mine) and wooden flowers for the lawn in front of the house. He managed to sell some of his wooden sculptures to neighbors so many figures in different colors were found on the street.

My bedroom was in the middle of the second floor next to the bathroom and the smallest, but I had a little dresser, space for my tiny doll cradle, and a closet all my own. There was also a small desk where I could read and write my schoolwork or color or cut out paper dolls near the window overlooking the driveway in the back. Sometimes I played "school" with one or two of my friends. We would take turns being teacher while the others sat on pillows on the floor.

My mother washed our clothes and linens in a tub in the basement with a hand-held scrubbing board and hung them to dry on a line stretched from wall to wall when the weather wouldn't allow drying on a pole outside in the back of the house. There was a coal stove for heating in the basement where sometimes my father broiled hamburgers or lamb chops, as we might do today outside on a charcoal or gas grill. I went to Birney Public School on the next street and although I was frequently in trouble for talking too much, I loved school and did well. I was a happy child then.

As mentioned earlier, I had a very loving family whose mission it was, much like that of many Jewish families at that time, to get our relatives out of war-torn Europe. For as long as I can remember I was responsible for putting a penny into a small box on the kitchen table labeled The Jewish National Fund to help save the family in Europe and later to assist the few relatives who survived the war and the displacement camps. It was 1939 and I was about five years old when my father's niece Ruthie, who was about eighteen, came from Czechoslovakia to live with us for a while and slept with me in my bed. In the evening she went to Birney School to learn English until my father arranged a job for her in a Lakewood, New Jersey resort hotel where she lived and worked as a waitress. (After the war, Ruthie married a nice man who had survived Auschwitz.) A few other family members were able to leave Czechoslovakia as late as 1939, but were denied entry into the United States due to the rigid quotas, so some of the extended family were in Havana, Cuba, while others were in Bogota, Colombia.

My mother, who was a skilled seamstress, supplemented the family income by working part time in the factory downtown where my father worked. Sometimes she brought her very precise hand-sewing work home. Mother made all her own clothes and mine as well. If she wasn't working on the Singer sewing machine with a foot pedal in her bedroom, she was often found crocheting, embroidering, or needle pointing on linens while we all listened to the radio in the living room downstairs after dinner. (When later we moved to New York mother showed me the chest filled with beautiful crocheted doilies, embroidered tablecloths and pillowcases, as well as hand towels she had embroidered with our family initial, "K." She said they would all be mine once I married.)

I remember Geneva, an African-American woman, who stayed with me when my mother went downtown to work before I started school and later on school holidays. She was the first black person I ever talked to, and I never thought much about the color of her skin; I loved her. Sometimes Geneva brought her daughter Maddy to play with me while she cleaned. Maddy was a little older than me, and she liked to play school too, but she always wanted to be the teacher. I let her. I don't remember any African-American people living on our street or going to my school in Philadelphia.

We used to drive to New York from Philadelphia in my father's 1937 black Dodge with a running board, to see our grandparents and the rest of the family who lived on the Lower East Side of Manhattan. My parents would wrap me in a blanket while I slept and put me in the back seat with my brother Norman. We would leave about 3 a.m. on Friday night. Dad usually drove all night and went through the Holland Tunnel, but it was a long ride in those days, about six hours. Norman and I would usually wake up as we came near to New York City. When I was recovering from a long bout of whooping cough, the doctor said I would benefit from a trip to the ocean, so I had my first visit to the boardwalk at Atlantic City. I loved that trip. Although I continued to cough for weeks, my parents thought the sea air did help, so on the next trip to New York City, Dad took the ferry from Hoboken, New Jersey instead of the tunnel. After that I always pleaded for the ferry ride. It took a little bit longer, but it was so much more interesting than the tunnel.

Ours was theoretically a religious family that observed the commandments of the traditional Jewish family, and there were many rules to follow. We said short prayers before and after meals. We ate only kosher food (no pork or shellfish; no dairy foods with meat meals so no milk, just tea or water to drink with supper if we were having chicken or meat). No work, travel or entertainment was supposed to take place on the Sabbath, which began at sunset on Friday and ended at sunset on Saturday. In our immediate family there was flexibility with the rules about a few things, especially for children or there was illness. No one in the family ever said anything about our driving on the Sabbath when we traveled on the weekends from Philly to New York; they were just happy to see us come. I certainly did not know all the rules but my parents tried to follow the significant ones.

Grandpa was aging poorly and couldn't work anymore, so in 1940 he and Grandma moved in with my mother's older sister, Aunt Eta, and her husband Uncle Moshe. They lived on Norfolk Street in a small sixth-floor apartment with only one bathroom. I only saw one bedroom, but maybe there was another one in the back for my cousins Stanley and Irving, who were at least five years older than Norman. There was an elevator in the building, unlike most of the nearby Lower Eastside buildings, which were walk-ups. The apartment was crowded and uncomfortable, and I remember clearly walking through the tiny kitchen to the bathroom and after, washing my hands in the kitchen sink when I came out because there was no sink in the bathroom, although there was a bath tub. To this day I cannot figure out where they all slept. When we came to visit I remember sleeping on two stuffed armchairs put together while my parents slept on the pull-out couch in the living room. Uncle Jack, my mother's brother, and Aunt Sonia with their son Saul, who was a year younger than my brother, lived in an even smaller apartment on the third floor. Norman slept there with Saul in the living room. Sometimes I had that privilege too, on a quilt on the floor. Saul was my favorite cousin, because he always teased me and kept me up laughing all night. I saw him recently in Florida after many years. He still has a wonderful smile and sense of humor; he always makes me laugh. Saul told my friend visiting with me that I was his favorite cousin too, because I laughed at all his jokes. I couldn't help it. He hardly had to say anything, and there I was laughing at him.

We loved our visits to New York City in those years. The neighborhood was so exciting; there were crowds of people and pushcarts on the street loaded with all kinds of stuff: clothing, linens, pots and pans, toys, books, tools, food – and the smells! My favorite activity was our stop at

Bernstein's delicatessen for corned beef sandwiches on seeded rye bread, with a sour pickle out of a barrel. And their hot dogs were the famous Hebrew National frankfurters. I loved them with mustard and sauerkraut from the barrel; they were the best. There was nothing like it where we lived in what was then probably considered suburban Philadelphia. In later years when I traveled for business by plane if there was a Nathan's hot dog stand in the airport, (which I think were actually kosher style,) I had to stop and have one. Of course, although I might suffer later, I had to have it with mustard and sauerkraut. It was the closest thing to the strictly kosher hot dogs I remember from those early childhood days visiting New York City.

As part of our visits to New York as we got older, Norman and I wanted to visit my Uncle Moshe's necktie store on Allen Street, just a few blocks away from the apartment. The store was closed on the Sabbath and open on Sunday, although there wasn't very much business. Aunt Eta and one or two young refugee girls were sewing ties on machines in the back room of the store and when we came my mother helped out with her fine hand stitching. If there were no shoppers in the store, Uncle Moshe would let Norman and me play *tie store.* We would take turns being the salesperson or the buyer. "Can I help you, sir?" Norman would say in his most sophisticated voice, and I would answer proudly, "I am interested in that design over there," pointing to a large tan-colored box among dozens on the shelves, with one end of a tie hanging over the edge of the closed box, just enough to show the design. He would pull out the box, open it, and show a pack of six ties of similar design in different colors bound together. I would say, "No, I don't think this will do." Norman would then take out one tie, wrap it around his fingers like we had seen Uncle Moshe do, and show how it would look in front of a shirt. "This is a wonderful new design. You won't see this design anywhere else and look at the quality of the silk…for this price it is a steal," Norman would say in a strong, aristocratic voice. "Well you are right, young man, I will take six dozen, one in each color," I would say. This was a preview of Norman's charm and talent. I loved playing along with him. He had a great smile and sense of humor and became a salesman who could literally sell you ice in the wintertime. Wherever he went everyone liked Norman; they still do.

For my fifth birthday my grandpa bought me my first real doll. I had paper dolls to cut out and dress, and a little baby doll, but this was my first doll with real hair. It was a Shirley Temple doll and she had beautiful light brown curls all over her head just like the child actress Shirley Temple. The doll had big brown eyes that opened and closed and, round pink cheeks with dimples, and a red mouth. I can just see her now wearing a white organdy dress with tiny red rick-rack all around the Peter Pan collar, the bottom of the skirt, and the short puffy sleeves. There were tiny red buttons from the collar to the waist and a stiff petticoat under the dress to make it stand out. I remember the fine white panties, white socks, and little black Mary Jane shoes. I loved that doll, and I loved my grandpa even more for finding a way to buy it for me. I didn't have that doll too long before my brother, who just had to fool around, decided one day to give her a haircut. I cried hysterically and when my father came home my mother couldn't protect Norman from the beating with the belt. It was neither the first nor the last for him.

Saturday Matinee at the Movies

The rest of Norman's punishment was to have to take me to the movies on Saturday afternoon along with his friends, where there were games and yo-yo contests before the main feature. Norman, at ten years of age, was a local yo-yo hero so taking me along was really an embarrassment for him. But I was proud to be with him. Sometimes there was a cowboy picture with Gene Autry or Roy Rogers, and always cartoons with Mickey and Minnie Mouse or Popeye. I remember being really frightened when we first saw *The Wizard of Oz*, but then I couldn't wait to see it again; it made me want to dance and sing like Judy Garland. Norman wasn't too happy when he had to take me to see the Shirley Temple movie, *Little Miss Broadway*, but later he admitted it was "OK." He then started singing and tap dancing like Shirley. The night after seeing that movie, when my mother washed my hair, I made her put it up into pin curls, just like Shirley's. The curls didn't last very long because we did not have hair spray in those days, but every time I had a special occasion, my mother fixed my hair in those same curls.

I never got over the loss of my Shirley Temple doll. Many years later when my first daughter Melissa was five, I asked my parents to buy her a Shirley Temple doll. Sadly they told me they couldn't find such a doll, at least one that was affordable, so some other doll with hair was substituted. It didn't make a difference to Melissa, but it made a difference to me. Anyway, it did not take long before Barbie dolls were the new rage and Barbie invaded our house. Several years ago I saw an advertisement on TV for Shirley Temple videos. My husband thought I was crazy, but I bought the whole collection to share with my grandchildren. (It seems there was some kind of family tragedy in each of those films that "Shirley" was able to overcome.) Except for the tap dancing, I don't think my grandchildren appreciated Shirley as much as I thought I did.

I have a lifelong love of cinema. I think it's in my blood. My mother was hooked on the movies from the day she came to this country in 1921. She told us that it was through the movies that she really learned English. Mom said, "After work I went to school two evenings a week to learn how to read and write in English and to prepare for citizenship, but it wasn't enough. It was the movies that made a difference." Mom told us how she worked ten hours a day, six days a week. The only day she had free was Saturday, our Sabbath, the day movie matinees were shown. No unnecessary work, travel, entertainment, or handling of money was permitted on the Sabbath. But after synagogue on Saturday mornings Mom and her younger brother Jack wanted to go to the movies. "Grandpa knew how important it was for us to learn English," Mom said. Many of the workers in the garment industry were immigrants and they tended to speak their native language during work so they didn't improve their speech. As observant as he was, Grandpa bent the rules slightly, since there was no disrespectful work involved. He went to the movie house near the apartment on Friday afternoon after work before sundown and paid the manager for the Saturday tickets so mom and her brother could go to the matinee. Mom loved the actors, their clothes, the beautiful country homes and furnishings she saw. She was enchanted with the music and dancing and the dramatic love stories. Although I was supposed to be named in Hebrew after two great-grandmothers I never knew, she named me after one of her favorite movie actresses, Sylvia Sydney.

Tea with Mrs. Roosevelt

My mother hadn't been able to finish her citizenship preparation until the family moved to Philadelphia and she could attend classes at night at Birney Public School, the same school my brother and I attended. There were about fifteen other immigrants in the class, mostly of Italian backgrounds, and Mom made some new friends. One evening she came home all excited. The teacher announced that the class was going by bus to visit the Capitol and the White House in Washington, DC. They had been invited to have tea with the first lady, Eleanor Roosevelt. Mom couldn't believe it was going to happen and was afraid of the bus expense, but Dad reassured her it was too important to miss. Mom's teacher had told the class to be prepared to introduce themselves and tell about their background and families. It was fun listening to Mom practicing her introduction. She was very nervous on the day of the trip, but I knew she was prepared, even with her accent. Geneva came to stay with us and she was as excited as all of us were. We couldn't wait until Mom came home to hear about her experience, and I couldn't wait to tell my class at school the next day. I think it was a life-changing experience for my mother; she told us how warm and friendly Mrs. Roosevelt was to everyone, and all about the beautiful rooms in the White House and the lovely china tea cups and cookies served. Mom did complete her citizenship requirements soon after, and we were all very proud of her when she received her certificate.

Common Family and Personal Illness

It wasn't long before we learned that Grandpa, who had become blind from glaucoma, was dying with cancer of the esophagus, but of course I didn't know what that was. Everyone was very sad. There was no treatment for glaucoma then, and not much more for cancer, which was considered hopeless; the word itself was rarely mentioned within families. Health care around the world was still pretty primitive in the 1930s and there was practically no health insurance. Many people suffered from complications or died prematurely from diseases readily prevented or treated today.

My brother and I had frequent ear infections, often at the same time. There were no immunizations other than against smallpox and no antibiotics for treatment. One serious episode that turned into mastoiditis was treated by the only treatment available, surgery to drain the area. Norman and I had tonsillectomy surgery and the ear problems seemed to subside for a while, but we both have had continuing problems over the years and Norman has significant hearing loss. (So far I am managing without hearing aids.) One week both of us were sick at the same time with different infections, Norman with measles and I with mumps. My mother evidently did a good job of nursing us because we did not get each other's disease. One of my cousins caught scarlet fever as a baby and was quarantined in the hospital for a week behind glass windows. Her parents could not hold her; they could just look through the glass during limited visiting hours, one hour a day. We rarely hear of scarlet fever anymore.

One night I was the only one who heard a loud noise from the bathroom. I got up to see what it was and found my father on the floor unconscious; there was blood in the sink and all around on the floor, but he was breathing. I ran to get my mother, who called the family doctor's emergency number, and an ambulance came. My father spent several weeks in historic Pennsylvania Hospital downtown, the first hospital in the country, being treated for a bleeding peptic ulcer by famous Dr. Henry J. Tumen, one of the few gastrointestinal specialists in the country at that time. Since my parents had no hospital insurance I think they paid the bills a little each month over the year. Dad was treated with the Sippy diet of milk and cream through a tube feeding. I remember visiting him and watching his dinner flow from a bottle hanging on a stand next to the bed through the tube in his nose. At that time emotional stress and stomach acid were believed to be the cause of ulcers. Milk was considered soothing and all spices, as well as strong flavored and heavy foods, were to be eliminated. My dad lived for months on a very bland diet without meat, fruits (except applesauce), or vegetables, and no coffee, chocolate, or alcohol, with only bicarbonate of soda as an antacid. That was still the treatment 20 years later when I was a student nurse in the 1950s. It wasn't accepted in the United States until the 1990s that the cause of most ulcers was a bacterium and antibiotics were the treatment of choice. My father, a long-time smoker, had also been told firmly by Dr. Tumen to absolutely stop smoking. Dad was so frightened that he became a virulent antismoker, never drank alcohol except a small amount of sweet red ritual wine, ate carefully avoiding spicy foods, and did not return to a hospital for over fifty years until prostate problems appeared at age seventy five.

"December 7, 1941: A Date That Will Live in Infamy"

Franklin Delano Roosevelt,
President of the U.S.A.

In 1941, Norman turned thirteen, and it was time for his Bar Mitzvah in the small Orthodox synagogue in Philadelphia not too far from our house. My grandpa had passed away, but my grandmother and the rest of the family came by train to hear him sing the prayers, read from the Torah, and make a speech in Yiddish on Saturday morning that I barely understood. Norman, who had a wonderful trained voice from singing in the synagogue choir on the High Holy days, had studied hard for this event, and we were all very proud of him. Grandma and my mother and a "kosher catering lady" had cooked and baked for days before, so after the service and the congregation had blessed him with a prayer over wine, and according to the tradition the children threw candy at Norman, the party was to begin. Family and friends walked back to the house for more wine, challah, and traditional Hungarian Jewish foods such as chopped liver, stuffed cabbage, sweet kugel (noodle pudding), dried fruits and nuts, and lots of homemade honey cake and cookies. The New York family came on Friday afternoon and stayed over, some sleeping with nearby friends and neighbors, or in our beds, while Norman and I slept on quilts on the floor in my parent's bedroom.

Other orthodox friends and some family could not make it to the synagogue on Saturday, so the party continued on Sunday. The house was quieting down in the afternoon and most people had already left when my dad turned on the radio to get the news as he did every Sunday afternoon. It was December 7, 1941 and we heard the announcement that the Japanese had bombed the American fleet in Pearl Harbor. Everything stopped. My cousins Stanley and Irving, who were already in the service and in uniform, quickly packed up and Dad drove them to the train station to get back to New York. The party was over.

I did not understand what all this meant. The next day President Roosevelt announced on the radio that we had declared war against Japan in response to the bombing at Pearl Harbor. We knew a little about the events in Europe because we had listened to the news and had seen the newsreels on Saturday in the movies with pictures of the marching German soldiers. But I was less than eight years old, too young to really understand that when my parents spoke in Hungarian, rather than English, about family members still in Europe, they were trying to protect us. We had no TV or the Internet in those days to inform us about all the politics in Europe and Asia. No one expected the little island of Japan to start a war with the great United States. Supposedly peace discussions were taking place in Washington, DC.

At home, the days succeeding the Japanese attack on Pearl Harbor led to frequent air raid drills and blackouts. In school when the sirens sounded we silently marched out into the hall, sat on the floor, bent down, and covered our heads with our arms. We were told that with the Navy Yard in Philadelphia, our city was particularly vulnerable to attacks, and we heard rumors of German submarines in the Atlantic close to our shores.

My father became an auxiliary policeman, and received training and an assignment in the neighborhood during the blackouts. We were warned that there would be food shortages, so my mother and brother planted a victory garden in a small patch in front of the house. I think radishes were the first seeds they planted because my mother liked radishes, and they came up very quickly. (She got them all; my father, brother, and I would not eat them, not then and not to this day.) There were cucumbers and some beans too. Soon sugar and meat were rationed and worst of all gasoline. When we went to the movies on Saturday afternoon there was a new tax, so the price of admission went up from ten cents to twelve cents, and the cartoons gave way to the newsreels of the battles, especially in the Pacific. It was a while before full-length movies about the war were produced, but we learned many strange-sounding names of places we never heard of before: Bataan, Corregidor, Iwo Jima, and later, places in Africa like Casablanca or Tobruk. For a long time it seemed that we were losing the war, and the lists of casualties frightened us. With the fighting going on all over the world, as young as I was, I learned in school to locate the places on a large wall map in the back of our classroom. Geography became one of my best subjects, but we know now how dynamic geography is as the result of changing political alliances and wars for independence. There is very little resemblance between the maps in the 1930s and '40s and the maps today.

An English girl as a pen-pal

One day in 1942 my mother brought me a children's magazine she had found on the bus coming home from work. It was a small international magazine named *Children's Playmate* with stories, cartoons and letters from children around the world looking for pen-pals. I responded to a letter from a young girl in England named Joan Carter, who was two years older than I. Joan wrote about the bombing in London and having to move into the countryside after her family's home was destroyed. I'm sure my letters were not as interesting as hers. At the age of fourteen, Joan, who was not slotted for university education, had to leave school and go to work in an office. We corresponded, even after I moved from Philadelphia to Brooklyn, for about six years and then lost contact when I started college. I always kept a photo of Joan, a very attractive and mature looking young girl at fourteen, in my album. Almost forty years later, a letter from Joan arrived for me as my parents were packing to move from Brooklyn to Augusta, Georgia. It was amazing. I was long gone from that Brooklyn address and had moved many times. The chances of the letter from England being forwarded were pretty slim. We resumed our correspondence, but it was clear our lives had taken very different routes. I eventually visited England several years after and met Joan, but there was no resemblance to the lovely young girl whose photo I saved and we were worlds apart.

By the end of 1942, my father realized he wouldn't be able to get enough gas to go anywhere so he sold the 1937 Dodge that he loved. That was the end of our trips to New York and my innocent happy life.

Joan Carter, my British "pen-pal" from 1942-1950 at age fourteen posed seductively in London, England. We finally met fifty years later. (See Chapter 12.)

The Move to Brooklyn

My mother missed her family and felt guilty that she could not help her aging parents more. In addition she was convinced that my father's job was in danger, so she pressured him to look for a position in New

York City. He finally got the call, and we had to move quickly. There was a serious shortage of apartments in New York; many were being held for wounded veterans, and there was little time to look for one in an unfamiliar neighborhood. My mother did not want to move to the teeming crowded Lower East Side of Manhattan near her family, and rents elsewhere in Manhattan were beyond the family budget.

In January 1943 Mother announced that she had found an apartment in the same area of Brooklyn she and my father had lived in when I was born at Maimonides Hospital, and we would move in a few weeks. She said there were shops and movies we could walk to and the elevated line of the BMT subway was just a few blocks away, so we could easily go downtown to see family in Manhattan, and south to Brighton Beach and Coney Island by train. I was excited and looking forward to the move, but when I visited the actual apartment for the first time, I was in shock; I hadn't been warned. True, it was in a very nice section of Brooklyn, near Kings Highway and Ocean Parkway in Flatbush in a relatively new six-story pre-war elevator building, but it was a small one-bedroom apartment in the back of the building, facing another brick building, so it was dark. To this day, I remember running around and around crying, "But, where is my room? Where is my room?" There was no room for me alone as before, not for my brother, and not for me.

I slept next to Norman on a studio couch that opened into two beds in the entrance foyer. I had a drawer in my parents' dresser and hung my clothes in their closet. I had to do my reading and homework at the kitchen table or sprawled across my parents' bed, where at least I could close the door. There was a desk in the foyer but the drawers were filled with my parents' important papers, and someone was always walking through, to the kitchen, the bedroom, or the bathroom. At least there were a few built-in shelves in the foyer, over my head for family books; the encyclopedia and prayer books. My mother had set aside one shelf for me, but I did not have much other than my class books each semester until I started buying Nancy Drew and other mystery series books with money I earned by babysitting.

We were on the fourth floor and looked out across the living room and bedroom windows over a barren courtyard to the windows of another brick building; it was always dark. There were no trees, no lawn, and no birds. I was miserable and angry. I lived in that apartment for ten years, from the fourth grade through junior high and high school and two years of college. Above anything else, I guess what motivated me in life most was the loss of my own space. I wanted my own room again and I wanted out of Brooklyn.

I was in the middle of the fourth grade when we moved to Brooklyn and started at the new school, P.S. 153. Although I was anxious in the beginning, I was soon befriended by a few girls of different faiths: (Adele, Marcia, Virginia, and Felicia.) Marcia was assigned by the teacher to help me get settled when I arrived since she lived the closest. We met on the corner to walk to school in the morning and home together after school. We all became good friends. (Years later we rode rented bicycles on the Shore Parkway along the Atlantic Ocean). Although Marcia went to Hunter College after high school and married after the first year, we stayed in touch for many years, until we both left Brooklyn. I met another girl who came to our school in the 5th grade, Millicent who also went to Hunter College after high school graduation. Millicent and I lived near to each other in Old Bethpage and despite family changes over the years have maintained our very close friendship.

Meanwhile back to Brooklyn and the fourth grade, I learned how to cope with my loss of privacy. Without space for myself at home, I turned to my love of reading. The public library, two streets away on the second floor above a series of stores, became my salvation. I could read a book there in the afternoon after school and take out two books and return them a few days later. I discovered the Nancy Drew and Bobbsey Twins Mystery Series, hardcover books for young girls. I could buy my own books for sixty cents and read them over and over. I was hooked. (Too bad I didn't discover the Cherry Ames nursing series at that time; recently they have been republished by Springer Publishing.) I became a babysitter for a family with two little boys in our apartment building. Richard was four years old, and Aaron was 18 months. They were really sweet boys, and I was able to earn the money for my books at twenty five cents an hour, usually on Friday or Saturday evenings. Sometimes I got a call to sit with other children across the street. When the children were asleep it was quiet, and I could concentrate on reading, but there weren't many families with young children until the war was over. Young couples with babies wanted more space than the tiny Brooklyn apartments in that neighborhood. At the end of the war, a veteran could buy his own home in Levittown on Long Island with plenty of space inside and outside for children to play, with trees and grass all around and room for birds to fly, for $5,900. For years I had begged my parents to look for a larger apartment in our apartment building so I wouldn't have to sleep across from my brother. Supposedly there never were two bedroom vacancies in the building. I showed the newspaper ads of new houses for veterans in Levittown on Long Island to my parents and begged them to think about buying such a house. I was reminded that my father was not a veteran, and anyway there were no New York City subway stops nearby in Levittown; destroying my fantasy for the day.

Music Lessons and Hebrew School

My father loved music, and every Saturday afternoon after he went to the synagogue and came home for Sabbath lunch, I turned on the radio for him so he could hear the Metropolitan Opera of the Air at 2 P.M. on WQXR. (It was against the Sabbath rule for adults.) To my surprise when my grandmother came to stay with us, she did not say a word against the music, as observant as she was. At my mother's request, I also turned on the lights and pushed the elevator button when grandmother came, that was supposedly against the Sabbath rule. I never understood the rules against the lights and music. (In the olden days in Europe it was work to light the fire so it was forbidden. Playing music other than the sacred hymns and prayers was not considered serious religious study according to the Orthodox Jewish Code my parents tried to abide by, but this was the 1940s in America). I could not understand these rules; none of my friends who were Jewish followed such rules in or outside their homes. I complained. It was the beginning of my rebellion against the superstitions of my and all religions.

Dad also loved listening to cantorial music. He had large records by Richard Tucker, Jan Pierce and Robert Merrill who were famous Jewish Metropolitan Opera Singers and former Hebrew cantors. He also had accumulated many small tapes he had recorded himself at concerts my parents attended downtown.

I started music lessons when I was ten, first the violin at my father's insistence. Hungarians love string instruments and gypsy music and since my uncle Jack had a violin he brought from Europe he offered it to me. I struggled with the violin, but could not seem to find pleasure in the squeaky sounds I produced. I also did not like the elderly European man hired to teach me; it was very hard for me to understand his accent. After a year I cried and pleaded with my parents to stop the lessons. My parents finally gave in, agreeing to give me piano lessons like most of my friends. After a few months of going to the piano teacher's studio for lessons and practicing next door in our neighbor's apartment, my teacher told my parents about a small baby grand piano she found that would enable me to practice at home. As crowded as it was in that apartment, I loved that piano; it made the living room look elegant. I progressed slowly to playing some Chopin, but when I started college the music lessons had to stop; there was no way I could find the time to practice. Eventually my three children all took lessons on that piano and at least one continues to play to this day. It is tremendous pleasure for me when occasionally we are together and he plays for me.

At about ten years of age I also started Hebrew School at the Orthodox synagogue (Etz Chaim) two days a week in the afternoon after public school. The synagogue was on the next street from our apartment and where my parents attended services on the Sabbath and holydays. There were about twenty five boys, and I was one of three girls in the class. (Theoretically, among Orthodox families there should not have been girls and boys together in the same class room, but in the 1940's with few Orthodox Jewish families in our neighborhood, it was commonly found.) There was no Bat Mitzvah service for any girls in those days. I knew one girl who went to the Reform Temple nearby for religious classes for about a year. When she turned thirteen she had a confirmation, but I had no idea what she learned. My parents did not accept the concept of modern Reform Judaism so that possibility for our family was never discussed.

I learned bible history, to read and write in Hebrew, and to recite or sing prayers and songs in Hebrew. (It was a good thing there were some accompanying English translations for I never understood but a few words of the language then.) What I loved most was the music. My father came from a family of "Kohanim," who were supposed to be descendants of the Hebrew kings in the bible and he had been trained as a young boy in Europe; he was very skilled and important during the service wherever he attended orthodox services, so he was happy in that synagogue. He taught us at home to sing the prayers in Hebrew. It is still what I enjoy most about religious services. However, my brother and I did not enjoy attending services in that synagogue; the men were downstairs and the women upstairs. It was all in Hebrew or Yiddush. Several years later, when my grandmother was not able to come to our apartment for special services or holiday events anymore, my brother and I begged to go to the conservative synagogue around the corner where the men and women sat together, the prayer book included English translated from Hebrew, and the rabbi gave his sermon in English. My mother liked it better too so the battle was over; my father joined us and from then on we enjoyed the services together.

Meanwhile, I was miserable with the family-required Hebrew School because some of the boys always tried to tease us girls. (I don't know why since this did not seem to happen in the public school.) By eleven I was starting to develop and was very aware that I looked older as my body was changing. There was no place to run to when some 'smart aleck' boy would try to touch me when the teacher wasn't looking. When I complained to my mother she took me to buy a bra, but gave me a strict warning, "don't ever let a boy touch your breasts." She didn't give me much other instruction, just warnings. Some of my friends had been prepared early for the physical changes to expect as we got into the teen years but my mother had not told me anything. Fortunately most of the girls had more modern American born mothers or older sisters and a few pieces of information about what we could expect were shared. When my cousin Frances, who was attending Brooklyn College, came to visit one weekend I pressured her into a conversation. She was taking a biology course, and was happy to tell me what she had already learned. I received "the whole story," but when I tried to confirm what I had learned with my mother, all I received were more religious superstitions and forbiddance. For certain, I would have to remain "a virgin" or God would punish me.

The war seemed like it would never end. We kept hearing about the casualties all over the Pacific, and soon in Africa, Italy, and then during and after the invasion at Normandy. That is when the war came closer. Our family was informed of the worst news: my cousin Alfred, age nineteen, son of Uncle Bill, who had brought my mother and the rest of her family to this country, was killed in Belgium during the Battle of the Bulge in 1944. The whole family mourned. Uncle Bill, the handsome and distinguished patriarch of the family whom everyone adored, was never the same. (Between December 1941 and December 1946, there were almost a half million American military deaths resulting from battles and other causes. Every family was affected.)

Holocaust Survivors in Our Home

Finally in 1945 the war was over, but it took months before there was any specific information about family members who survived the concentration camps and were in displacement camps. My parents were sending clothing packages and money to surviving family members through the International Rescue Committee, a refugee relief organization. Later in 1946 and in 1947, we welcomed a series of family members who had survived the camps to stay with us temporarily until jobs and an apartment were found. It seemed like our tiny apartment was a railroad station, with people coming and going. I was sleeping on quilts on my parent's bed room floor, until finally my mother bought two convertible chairs for my brother and me to sleep on in the living room. Most of the time the refugees spoke in Yiddish or Hungarian; I didn't understand much of what was being said, and they didn't understand me. Fortunately, the women and some of the men knew how to sew; my father had a small contracting business for women's clothing so he would arrange a few jobs at his factory or with friends who were clothing manufacturers. Then when a small apartment was found and used furniture purchased, our guests could move on.

One cousin – Adina – had lost her boyfriend as well as most of her hair due to starvation and typhus in the Bergen-Belsen Camp. She was ashamed of her looks so she kept a scarf on her head all day until she got into bed. I thought it was because she was religious, but that was not the case; it was because she did not like the way she looked. Her future seemed dim. Apparently she had lost her faith and trust in God. She looked much older than she was, and she had put on much weight after the starvation in the camp. She refused to go to synagogue on the Sabbath even when my mother offered to take her. When my mother bought Adina a really nice natural looking wig, we all had fun together styling it for her. What a difference it made; she was finally ready to smile again. Although it was summer when she lived with us, Adina always wore a blouse with long sleeves to cover up the tattooed numbers on her arm; she was ashamed. I didn't notice it until that day we fixed her hair and she lifted her arms to feel the hair on her head; the sleeve rode up. It was the first time I had seen such a scar and I could understand how embarrassed Adina was. I tried not to look at the numbers because they made me uncomfortable and embarrassed for her. Then I felt terribly guilty for complaining about not having my own room. I thought, it could have been me in that concentration camp.

Adina left us after a few months to live permanently with another relative who had a house with a room for her in Detroit. She was also going to be able to go to school there to learn English there. Adina was happy in Detroit, it was not so crowded. Eventually she was introduced to another refugee and married but unfortunately as a result of her illness or treatments in the concentration camp she was never able to have children.

My father's nephew David had lost his wife and two daughters in Auschwitz; one daughter was evidently close to my age. My father remembered seeing the baby when he visited his mother in the summer of 1934; he told me Dave's wife was a really beautiful young woman and they were very happy. When Dave came to our apartment and met me he started to cry. I didn't understand at first why he did not want to stay with us and asked to leave right away until my father told me the story. My father said I probably looked like one of his daughters.

Dave was a very handsome man with blue eyes and steel grey hair. He had been a very successful and influential business man in Munkács and had thought he was safe, but it did not seem to make a difference, for late in 1944 he was sent to a labor camp and then to Auschwitz Concentration Camp. He survived, but his family did not; in the end he lost everything. After a few months the matchmaking started; Dave was introduced to a nice Jewish American woman who had never been married before. She was able to help Dave to improve his English which was necessary for him to get a job or start a business. They married and before long she had a set of twins. With help from my parents and the rest of our family Dave started a small textile business downtown, first on a pushcart on Orchard Street, then in a small store. After a few years he prospered in larger offices with several employees. But even after many years the depression always showed on Dave's face, and I learned later he had been admitted to a psychiatric facility for electric shock therapy. Dave never fully recovered but fortunately he did have much pride with the success of his American born children.

When I had looked at the sad faces of our surviving family members and saw the numbers tattooed on their arms, I remembered the awful pictures we had seen in the newsreels. I felt guilty for being angry about my lost bed room. I also realized that had my parents not come to this country in the 1920s, I might have been born in Europe, and I could have been sent to the camps like our guests. I just couldn't understand how God allowed this horrible war to take place and so many millions to be killed. I didn't understand why there was so much hatred for the Jews. I knew I should thank God for sparing me, but somehow I was not sure what to believe. Through the years, perhaps out of habit or guilt, I have thanked God for the life I have been able to have.

World War II Movies

The War and the Holocaust have been a rich source of artistic creation in literature, both in fiction and nonfiction, spawning hundreds of books and films dealing with the lead-up to the war, the actual fighting, the events surrounding the Holocaust, and the aftermath. It didn't take long for Hollywood to produce wonderful films, like *Casablanca*, in 1942, considered one of the greatest American films of all time. While the movie is fictional, it helped to illustrate how the war touched unique individuals in places around the globe that had seemed like sanctuaries. That same year, *Mrs. Miniver* focused on the home front for the British under Nazi bombardment. It had a powerful impact and won six Oscars. In 1946, *The Best Years of Our Lives* demonstrated the impact of the war on veterans returning home from the fighting. The films never cease to be produced, even sixty years after the war ended. Several have been Academy Award winners, such as *Schindler's List* produced and directed by Steven Spielberg 1993. This R-rated film, based on a true story of a German businessman who saved the lives of more than a thousand mostly Polish Jews during the Holocaust by employing them in his factories, vividly shows the barbaric cruelty of the Nazis under Hitler. The publication of books and production of movies has continued all over the world to this day. A few weeks ago we saw an excellent, although vividly depressing new German movie, "The Phoenix." It may very well be a candidate for an Oscar Award.

My General Education

When I entered Cunningham Junior high school for the seventh grade I was placed in the Rapid Advance program, which meant that I would skip the first half of the eighth grade, so by 1948 I was at James Madison High School, a much larger school for the tenth grade. It was a big adjustment. Since the seventh grade we had been with the same group of students but were now integrated with students from several other junior high schools. I felt alone in some of my classes, unsure of myself, and hesitant to reach out to make new friends. I did not excel in anything, and I did not consider myself pretty; boys were not interested in me while many of my old friends soon had boyfriends.

During those years after the war I became enthralled with my brother's favorite sport, baseball. He often played with his high school friends at Marine Park and sometimes I went along to watch. But once he took me to see our professional team, the Brooklyn Dodgers play, I was hooked. I was not able to go to the games often, but I listened to the games on the radio for hours at a time keeping box scores. I also read about the Dodger's personal lives in the newspaper. When Jackie Robinson started to play in 1947, he was very exciting to watch. He was known for trying to steal second base after a hit or a walk and it was amazing how successful he was. We were proud that Jackie, the first Negro to play in the major leagues, had been brought to Brooklyn. (I always kept up with the sport and was terribly disappointed when the Dodgers left for Los Angeles. When Roger Kahn published the book, "*The Boys of Summer*" in 1970, and Doris Kearns Goodwin later published "*Wait Till Next Year*" in 1997, I just had to buy each of those books.

One day in 1946 we learned that Morris Hoffman, my mother's cousin and his wife, whom he had married in a resettlement camp after the Auschwitz concentration camp were on the ship *Exodus* waiting in the harbor off Cyprus to get into Palestine. We listened to the news anxiously every night to hear word of the ship and hopefully the Hoffmans' arrival in Palestine. It didn't happen so fast. The British stopped the ship, took the refugees off, and sent them back to Hamburg, Germany. It was a nightmare; they were in a resettlement camps again and our world was upset with the cruelty of the British. The Hoffmans eventually did make it to the new State of Israel established in 1948, right after the first Israeli-Arab war. About twenty years later I visited the family in the beautiful seaside city of Natanya on the Mediterranean; their son Danny, born in Israel, proudly wore the uniform of the Israeli Air Force.

Setting a Career Goal

As I reached the last semester of high school I needed to think about my future. I wanted to go to college, but an out-of-town school was not in the plan for me: I knew my parents could not afford the expense. I was slated for a subway ride to Brooklyn College or Hunter College in Manhattan. Many of the girls in my James Madison High School class of 1950 were engaged and planning to be married soon after graduation, aiming for family life in suburbia even if they talked about college. I had the same dreams, but since I had not dated very much and there was no one special, my choices were limited. I wanted to go to college, probably to be a teacher, but if not teaching, work at what? Anyway, high school graduation had to come first. I needed an additional one-half credit to complete my academic diploma requirements, and trigonometry was on the schedule. I wasn't the greatest math student; literature and history were my preferences. I pleaded for an alternate subject and Mrs. Weiner, my advisor, suggested the "Home Nursing" course. Thinking it might be helpful when I did marry and have children, I signed up.

The course was different from all the other academic courses I had taken. There was a casual atmosphere in the class that made it possible for me to ask questions, lots of questions. I was the reader in the group and always needed to know "why?" and asked for more. Mrs. Quinn, the former Army nurse who was the instructor, liked my questions, believed they were "insightful" and helped introduce different perspectives. One day she called me aside and told me she thought I would make a good nurse in a college setting. At sixteen, I was too young for the local hospital diploma programs, so Mrs. Quinn recommended the Adelphi College[7] baccalaureate nursing program in Garden City, Long Island, established a few years before as a cadet nursing program. Adelphi, once an all-girls school with less than 1,000 students, had been able to increase the overall college enrollment significantly when the first dormitories

---

[7] Adelphi College was established first in Brooklyn, as a private non-sectarian Academy in 1863, chartered by the New York State Board of Regents as a Liberal Arts College in 1896, and as a Women's College in 1912. The school moved to Garden City in 1922. In 1963 the Regents granted Adelphi University Status.

were built in 1943 with federal support under the Hill-Burton Act, and men were able to be enrolled. Afterward the male enrollment increased significantly by World War II veterans bringing their GI benefits.

My brother Norman, who had been drafted for the Korean War and was home on leave from Camp Gordon, agreed to take the train wearing his uniform to see the Adelphi campus with me. He had dropped out of Brooklyn College when drafted and was curious about the College too. I was enthralled with the beautiful campus and the surrounding homes as we walked from the railroad station. We did not have an appointment, but the dean of nursing, Dr. Margaret T. Shay, was in her office and invited us in to talk about the program. Small private schools like Adelphi were looking for students in those years; unfortunately the federal program of subsidies for nursing students was over. Norman always had a way of charming women, young and old, and Dr. Shay seemed impressed with us. Of course I never told her why I took the home nursing course. I just explained the reality of my Holocaust family stories. In any event, once I learned about the full Adelphi program I knew Adelphi was what I wanted. I was determined to go there.

The nursing program in 1950 was a five-year program compressed into four calendar years; it was not on an academic year. At the end of the sophomore year, nursing students left the Garden City campus and moved into the nurses' residences of Nassau County Medical Center, (then known as Meadowbrook Hospital) and other affiliating hospitals for most classes and clinical experience. We would live in the Nurses Residence at the hospital. That was the clincher. If I went to Adelphi I would finally have a room of my own!

The tuition of $250 a semester, compared to no tuition at Hunter or Brooklyn College, was difficult to explain to my hardworking parents. My father said, "Nursing is not easy work. You don't need to go to college for that; why don't you become a dress designer?" Norman and I looked at each other; he knew where my skills and interests were. Even though I had played with cut-out paper dolls as a little girl, dressing and undressing them, I could not draw. I could not sew a button on straight to satisfy my perfectionist mother and I definitely did not want to be in the garment industry like the rest of our family. Obsessed with Hollywood movies and the English and American novels I devoured, I wanted something "different." I wanted an adventure, and I wanted to be "out of that apartment and out of Brooklyn." Norman became my champion. He suggested to my parents, "Why don't you call your cousin, Dr. Julius and ask him what he thinks?" Well it worked. Julius, who was American born, at least ten years younger than my father and whose room my father shared when he came to America, told my father he thought it was a very good education. That clinched it. The deal was made. I would enter Adelphi in the fall.

I was not really thinking that much about a career then or education for a lifetime. I thought whatever nursing was, how hard could it be? I didn't realize I had not taken chemistry and physics or enough mathematics in high school, and *that* would make it really hard. I did not think about the traveling every day either. The trip to Adelphi was much further and more expensive than Hunter College. I knew my parents would not let me move into the dormitory at Adelphi as it would cost too much. If I went to Hunter or Brooklyn I would be riding the BMT anyway. But I forgot about the monthly $30 railroad commuter ticket and subway fare I would need to get to Garden City, in addition to tuition cost, books and other incidental expenses later such as uniforms.

I had no idea what I was up against because all I kept thinking about was that room of my own at the end of the second year. It was a good thing I did not think too long, because I might have changed my mind. I could never have imagined how difficult the program was or the challenges I would face. All I thought about was the opportunities nursing education might offer me. I had no idea of the possibilities to come, the doors that would open, the supporters who would make it all possible, and the new adventures I would pursue year after year.

Brother Norman, age five years riding a pony. (1934) A similar photo taken in 1939 of the author at age five did not survive the years well enough to include.

Author as a small girl. I remember hating those white high top shoes from "*The Coward Company*" and later appreciating my first pair of black patent leather "Mary Jane" shoes.

Norman after his Bar Mitzvah (December, 6 1941) in front of our house in Philadelphia with cousin Stanley Heisler, who enlisted in U.S. Navy in 1940 at the age of eighteen. A student at the Manhattan College of Music N.Y.C, Stanley played the trumpet and spent the war years with the U.S. Navy Band.

I am a young girl of about twelve years with my parents and brother in a Catskills Mountain resort during the Passover Holidays.

Here I am at age sixteen with parents in our Brooklyn apartment. Baby grand piano is seen in the background. There is a small photo of my father as a yeshiva student in Czechoslovakia.

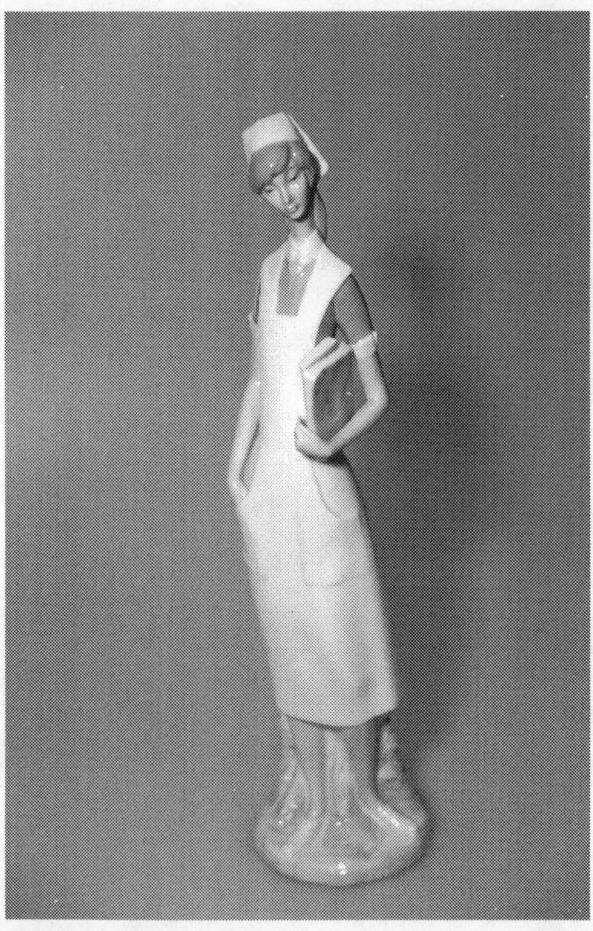

Historical Image of Nursing Student LLadro Porcelain Figurine. (Author's Personal Art Collection)

2

Becoming a College-Educated Nurse at Adelphi on Long Island

"TO BE WHAT WE ARE AND TO BECOME WHAT WE ARE CAPABLE OF BECOMING, IS THE ONLY END IN LIFE"

FROM BARUCH SPINOZA, 17TH CENTURY PHILOSOPHER ALSO, ROBERT LOUIS STEVENSON, 19TH CENTURY WRITER)

FOUNDATIONS OF NURSING

After graduating from James Madison High School, I started Adelphi's unique baccalaureate nursing curriculum in the fall of 1950. As mentioned before, at that time it was a five-year program condensed into four calendar years, with only six weeks annual vacation, six weeks that rarely came together or during the summer. The program was a foundation of liberal education applied to the traditional hospital training program for development of a patient-centered professional role in community health care, not just the hospital. The first two years focused on the basic liberal arts and science courses: English composition and literature, anatomy and physiology, chemistry and physics, microbiology, and social sciences including general and developmental psychology, family relationships, and sociology. There was also an overview of the history of the nursing and medical professions within the context of social, political, economic, and cultural backgrounds including philosophy, religion, ethics, from the Greeks and Romans, Hebrews, Christians, etc., to modern times. We learned about the evolution of professional nursing through wars as demonstrated by Florence Nightingale during the Crimean War, and how she saved lives with her focus on the environment: air quality, cleanliness, and nourishment. Often called the "Mother of Nursing," or the "Lady with a Lamp", Florence Nightingale started the first modern school of nursing in England, the model for the early nursing schools at hospitals in Philadelphia, Boston, and New York in the 1870s.

Although there was little opportunity for humanities electives in the tightly structured curriculum, four quarters of physical education courses were required. My choices were golf, tennis, and even fencing, everything I knew nothing about, except through the novels and movies I devoured. Fortunately I was able to select more literature and took courses beyond the required English Literature in Shakespeare and American Literature Studies.

Life was not much fun for me in those days. Throughout the first two years, I commuted on the Brighton Beach subway express to Atlantic Avenue, where I changed for the Long Island Railroad to Nassau Boulevard and then walked almost a mile to the Adelphi campus. My parents paid the $250 semester tuition, but I had to earn my expenses for travel and books and extras by babysitting in the evenings, and working in Loesser's department store on Thursday nights and Saturdays. No clubs, no sororities, no sports, or any other extracurricular activities for me; I had to catch the train. I was studying while sitting on my mother's bed in the only room in our apartment that had a door I could close. There was a desk in the entrance foyer I might use to write on when no one was home, but it was a hallway, and most of the time family sounds made it difficult to concentrate. I couldn't afford a typewriter in the beginning, so although I had learned to type in seventh grade, every course paper was handwritten.

The first year was especially hard. There was a nursing department policy that required a minimum of a "C" in all the science and nursing courses. I did very well in anatomy and physiology, memorizing enormous amounts of content, for example the names of all the bones, the origin and insertion of most muscles, and even the cranial nerves. There were all kinds of mnemonics used to facilitate memory for exams. To this day I can still recite this mnemonic for the cranial nerves, (***"On Old Olympus' Towering***

Tops A Finn And German Viewed Some Hops,") [8] although Google informs me that there have been many other versions created through the years, some considerably more racy.

I loved the course; it was fascinating. We dissected cats in the laboratory and one of my classmates worked on a cat that had been pregnant. She was able to preserve the fetus in formaldehyde, and kept it in her dorm room all through school. Our instructor, Dr. Heim, also taught anatomy to Cornell University medical students in Manhattan. She arranged field trips for our class, which included physical education majors, so we could observe the medical students during their human anatomy dissection lab. There was so much to learn. Of course we later had a rebellion when Dr. Heim tried to test us on the origin and insertion of all the muscles. She gave in and limited the requirement for the nurses to the specific muscles we would need to know in practice, such as the sites for massage in the back for patients on bed rest and intramuscular injections in the deltoid on the upper outer arm and gluteus maximus muscles in the buttocks.

Unfortunately I hadn't planned to study science in college, and had taken Earth Science instead of chemistry in high school. In Earth Science we learned about the planets, the sun, the moon, and the stars, and about weather. I enjoyed the course, but it did not do me much good in chemistry class. Had I realized how hard the nursing curriculum would be without knowledge of high school chemistry, I would have registered for a chemistry course in summer school at James Madison before starting college. However, I needed money for school expenses and had taken a job as a mother's helper for a family with two little boys I used to babysit for in our apartment building. The job was in a bungalow colony in Mount Freedom, New Jersey, and offered a chance to get away from the summer heat of New York City. I earned $500 towards books and train fare in the fall and made some wonderful friends among the other nannies that summer.

---

8 I Olfactory, II Optic, III Occulomotor, IV Trochlear, V Trigeminal, VI Abducens, VII Facial, VIII Accustic IX Glossopharyngeal, X Vagus, XI Spinalaccessory, XII Hypoglossal

Towards the end of the first semester I knew I was in trouble. After the last class before final exam week, I went to speak to Dr. Atlas, the chemistry professor. I told him I was afraid I was going to fail the final exam and pleaded with him not to give me a "D." I would be humiliated, forced out of the program, and have to wait a year to be readmitted, "I told him. At first Dr. Atlas advised me to hire a tutor, (which I should have done long before), but when I told him how difficult it would have been for me earlier as a commuter with my part-time jobs after school, he offered to review all my exams with me. He gave me a set of questions to review that night and we sat for two hours the following afternoon and then the next. He showed me where I had messed up on the earlier exams, explaining the information I really had not understood. I stayed up all night before the final exam to study and dozed off on the train in the morning, almost missing my stop. Thankfully, I managed to get a 75 on the final exam and ended up with a C– in the course instead of a D. The next semester I had more confidence. It was organic and biochemistry, which I found more interesting. I passed without special help, and Dr. Atlas told me he was proud of me.

In the second year, we started the Nursing Arts course, also known as Fundamentals of Nursing Care, in a campus laboratory equipped with hospital beds and supplies for practice on a manikin or on each other. Soon we received our student uniforms, a bright yellow starched long dress practically down to my ankles, with white collar and cuffs and an embroidered Adelphi emblem on the left breast pocket. A name pin with large letters sat just above the pocket; "Miss S. Kleiman," it announced. I liked it, I was really proud to have reached this level! My professional identity was being established further by the white rounded starched cap packed with the uniforms – there was no official capping ceremony at Adelphi like those in the hospital schools. I was grateful that the cap made me look much taller than my 5 feet 2 inches. In addition we were fitted for a pair of very professional and healthful looking white laced oxfords, "the Clinic Shoe" which we wore with white stockings. No jewelry was allowed, makeup was restricted, and our hair had to be neat and short, above the uniform collar, or a hair net was required.

Despite the classic look it gave, we all hated that yellow uniform and the taunts we received when out in public, which was fortunately rare. I do remember forty eight of us marching in uniform on campus at the opening Adelphi-Hofstra football game that fall. An exception had been made to the rule against wearing the uniform in public. "The Canaries are coming, tweet, tweet, tweet, " the crowd roared. It was so embarrassing!

We learned traditional nursing skills like taking blood pressures and pulses, giving back rubs and bed baths, and making beds with patients in them. Most hospital patients were on bed rest for weeks at a time in those years, often with side rails up. In the beginning we practiced what we could in the campus Nursing Arts Laboratory, but soon we were taken by bus to Meadowbrook Hospital, the country hospital with which Adelphi contracted. We made beautiful beds. Since there were no fitted sheets in those days the bottom sheet was tightly tucked under the mattress, tight enough as in the military, so a coin dropped on the sheet would bounce. If there were no creases in the bottom sheet and the patient was turned often enough, a decubitus ulcer or pressure sore would not happen, although we really had no concept of decubitus ulcers until we actually saw one in the hospitalized patient. It happened to me not too long after. Even though I had been warned, I was shocked when I pulled the covers back on a newly assigned patient and saw the hip bone looking back at me. In addition we learned to place a special fold for the toes at the base of the top sheet to give space for the toes in order to prevent toe sores for patients who stayed in bed on their backs for days and weeks at a time. I never actually saw toe sores as a student, or when I was working as a staff nurse, but was surprised to hear recently about a family member who had had such a complication just a few days following a hip replacement. Maybe it was also from my summer camp experiences over the years, but my mitered corners on the top sheets and spread are perfect to this day.

Those first baths for bedridden senile, incontinent bony old folks in the hospital seemed to take forever, for most of the time there was no patient communication or cooperation, and there was never enough clean linen. We folded relatively clean top sheets into draw sheets for extra protection under the buttocks when we ran out of single layer cotton draw sheets. Occasionally there were paper mats for draw sheets to protect the bottom sheets, but never enough. There were very few disposable supplies then so we washed and reused glass syringes and needles, rubber tubes, etc., and placed them in a small table-top steam sterilizer for 20 minutes for reuse. Sometimes it was a pot on a two-burner stove. (In the early 1980s, while on a professional visit with a medical group to China, I saw the very same primitive equipment and techniques in a Shanghai hospital.) Today almost all syringes, needles, catheters, tubes, drapes, etc., are disposable and there is a great deal of waste, which is one of the reasons hospital costs keep increasing.

While studying microbiology we learned medical and surgical aseptic techniques to prevent transmission of infection on the wards and in the operating room, specifically the difference between "clean" and "sterile." This included learning first and foremost the proper techniques of hand washing when caring for patients on hospital units and "scrubbing" the hands before applying sterile gloves before surgery; to use the sterile transfer forceps; to open sterile packages to change dressings, and the sequence of putting on masks, gowns, and gloves at the bedside and when preparing for surgery. ("Clean" refers to the absence of pathogenic [disease-causing] bacteria, while "sterile" refers to the absence of all bacteria.) If a glove was torn during surgery and the skin underneath was not free of pathogenic bacteria, contamination through transfer could occur.)

Actually the very first skill we learned did not seem much like a professional exercise. It was how to make a small collection bag from newspaper for soiled tissues and other refuse to keep at the patient's bedside. In the hospital there were no small brown paper bags so our newspaper bags could be helpful, if only we could find newspapers! But it was a beginning focus on an important theme in nursing, how to apply scientific theories to the need for patient and nurse safety: body discharges spread disease.

During that year, since most patients were on bed rest in the hospital, we did total care for only one patient at a time. Before we could start our care we had to research the pathology, visit to interview and observe the patient, assess the nursing needs, and write a plan of care that was reviewed by our instructor or the head nurse on the unit. We learned early on that no two patients were the same, and that even when there were guidelines according to the illness, the individual needs might be varied. Assigned patients had been selected by our instructor to represent specific needs. Over time as we took care of more than one patient we learned to organize our assignment, making judgments based on the severity and timeliness of needs; that there is often more than one way to solve a problem and sometimes you have to "think outside the box."

In the pharmacology class we also learned how to solve math problems and figure out how to fill prescriptions from large quantities in stock bottles, or to prepare special solutions; there were no prepackaged medications in those days. Medication errors have always been the most frequent accidents in the hospital, so there were principles you had to follow when preparing the drugs for administration. "The right medication, in the right dose, in the right form, at the right time, to the right patient" was the theme.

Columbia University Community Survey Course

During that second semester we had an advanced psychology course and seminars on socioeconomic aspects of public health while we made community visits on weekends throughout the culturally diverse neighborhoods of New York City. We attended religious services of all the major faiths – Protestant, Catholic, Jewish, and I think Hindu, or was it Buddhist in Chinatown, and maybe Islam? I am not sure but we met with religious leaders, physicians, and social workers to learn about some of the health-related beliefs and rituals around death and dying in each ethnic or cultural group. Every experience was new for me and most of the students, but one day stood out in the minds of most of my classmates, even years later. We often talked about this experience weeks later, and it is always cited at alumni meetings.

One Sunday morning we made a life-changing trip into Manhattan to attend church services. The Cadillacs drove up and handsome dark-skinned women with fur stoles and large hats beautifully decorated with feathers or flowers stepped out as the society women of Harlem entered the Abyssinian Baptist Church on 136th Street near 7th Avenue in Manhattan. I will never forget that Sunday sitting upstairs in the balcony and listening to the magnificent choir with the congregation joining in while the Reverend Adam Clayton Powell Jr. (later Congressman Powell) led the service. Tall, handsome, and royal in his flowing ministerial robes, he possessed a magnificent voice that was more than seductive; we were hypnotized. Every church member participated in that service. It was like a grand Hollywood movie musical. (Remember Whoopi Goldberg in *Sister Act*?) And afterwards in the basement of the church, those beautiful ladies in their magnificent hats served us a Southern fried chicken dinner, with mashed candied sweet potatoes, black-eyed peas, corn-on-the-cob, homemade biscuits with butter and gravy, sweet tea, and a choice of peach cobbler or pecan pie you could die for. I remember that meal to this day because even after living in the South for twenty years it was the best fried chicken I have ever eaten. (Paula Deen would be put to shame.)

Later in the afternoon we sat on the couches and floor of Reverend Powell's magnificent Harlem brownstone filled with art and antiques. He was married to beautiful Hazel Scott, a Julliard-trained internationally known classical and jazz pianist and vocalist. Her huge grand piano covered with photos and awards was in the room, and although she was not there, we could almost hear her soft gentle voice singing songs she made famous. Hazel was quite controversial because she became politically active and refused to perform for segregated audiences in this country.

We were there to hear an impressive young Columbia University–trained Harlem Hospital physician speak to us about the major health problems in the local population including alcoholism, drug addiction, sexually transmitted diseases, high blood pressure, sickle cell anemia, diabetes, and kidney disease. Maternal, fetal, and neonatal mortality rates were sky high, often due to illegal abortion. No one in our group of forty white female classmates, some from rural Long Island farms who had never even been to New York City before or known any African-Americans, had ever experienced anything like that day, and I would bet that most of us have never experienced anything like it again.

We also ate the common foods of the other groups we were studying each week, and most of it was pretty good, e.g., Spanish rice in East Harlem's Puerto Rican neighborhood (where we visited a public housing project and an awful tenement where a rat ran through the hall), and Chinese food in Chinatown, which was familiar for most of the students, although none was as good as the Southern soul food described above. Sushi was really unknown in those days, but we were taken to the only Japanese restaurant in the city. I couldn't swallow the raw fish wrapped in seaweed then; perhaps if it had been smoked salmon with cream cheese or the canned tuna fish with mayonnaise I knew, I might have appreciated the experience more.

Another week that stood out had special meaning for me. We attended Sabbath services at the Jewish Center Synagogue on the West Side of Manhattan one Saturday morning. Although the music by the cantor and choir was beautiful to me, I knew the service was difficult for most of my classmates, since it was largely in Hebrew, even for the five other Jewish girls in our class; none of whom had any Hebrew education or followed traditional rules of observance. But afterwards we listened to Rabbi Leo Jung in his British accent speak to us eloquently about Maimonides (the famous Jewish physician of ancient history), about Jewish beliefs on birth and death, about Jewish law, and how this law relates to health issues. I was hypnotized by this rabbi's explanation of some tenets of my own religion. I was really proud to be Jewish among my classmates and to understand my culture, but also as a result of this entire course to be able to understand and relate to other cultures as well.

My career has demanded my presence in multicultural settings, and I have excelled in this work because of this course. In fact, if one can understand why I enjoyed this course so much, one can understand why I am passionate about nursing. Above all, nurses provide comfort, and one cannot comfort if one does not understand what is comforting to each individual person. Comfort is not universal, it is specific. The best nurses I know understand this. I had never understood as well as I did that day all I thought I had learned in Hebrew School. Even my Christian classmates remarked how they enjoyed learning a little bit about Judaism.

That same semester of the second year we took a specially arranged course in Child Development at the Ann Reno Institute in Manhattan and worked in various low-income nursery schools. I was assigned to a public facility for child care experience on 68th Street between York and East River Drive. Working with groups of toddlers is much more complex than taking care of one or two at a time, which I had done extensively to earn extra money, (when I could hold a child on my lap and dramatically read an age-appropriate book.) This experience was to prepare us for the pediatric nursing course we would take at Meadowbrook Hospital in the third year of the Adelphi program. I appreciated this course later on when I had to teach a child health and family course years later at SUNY Farmingdale, and when I had my own children as well.

Clinical Training: Finally, a Room of My Own

"Nurses must get 'into the skin' of each patient to know what help he or she needs from them."

Virginia Henderson, Nurse Theorist [9]

The big reward came in July of the second year when we moved into the nursing residence at Nassau County's Meadowbrook Hospital for more classes and clinical experiences. I remember that first morning to this day. At dawn the birds woke me; I looked out and saw the trees, the

[9] Henderson, Virginia & Nite, Gladys; Principles and Practice of Nursing,6th edition, 1978.

flowers, the sun, and some squirrels scurrying about, and said out loud to myself, "Thank you, God, thank you." I thought how lucky I was. I used to look out the windows of our apartment in Brooklyn to see the brick wall and windows of the building behind. As far as I was concerned, we did not have birds in my Brooklyn; there was no place for birds. Now, there was no need for an alarm clock; I had my own menagerie to sing me awake each morning.

Living in the nurses' residence and eating in the dining room was a new experience for me. The food was not as good as the New York City automat, and it seemed as though they served roast pork whenever they ran out of the evening meal. Pork was not kosher and I had never eaten it before. Everything on my plate was soaking in gravy I was not used to; it did not take long for me to find my uniform getting tight. We had a lounge in the residence with a small kitchen supplied with white Wonder bread, peanut butter, grape jelly, and quarts of whole milk. After classes and clinical days we would gather together and review the day's experiences, laughing and joking and getting to know each other better. I thought it was wonderful, although some of the girls smoked, which bothered me. Of course I heard about all the girls' love lives, and I realized how lonely and jealous I really was.

On Tuesdays and Thursdays, we had classes taught by physicians, surgeons and nurses while we were rotating through various medical and surgical nursing units, the diet kitchen, and the operating room. Additional sciences such as epidemiology, pathology, and genetics were introduced briefly, and medical and surgical management with pharmacology were provided first by physicians and surgeons, followed by nursing faculty discussing related nursing care. Reading assignments were huge, and we were supposed to see a certain number of autopsies in the morgue, where we were questioned by the pathologist. Whenever an "O" was flashed on the Resident Call Board it meant an autopsy was being performed by the chief pathologist. He was a wonderful teacher who made the pathology course so much easier to understand. We also spent one month in the diet kitchen preparing special meals, many unheard of today, such as the Sippy diet of milk and cream for gastric ulcer patients, and the Kempner diet of rice and fruit for hypertension. We weighed out foods for diabetics' trays to be served individually, returning to the patient after the meal was eaten to subtract grams and milliliters for food uneaten and therefore be able to adjust insulin administration.

My initial clinical assignment in July was to the operating room and I was enthralled as our clinical instructor introduced us to all the routines and procedures. The first operation I scrubbed in on (gowned and gloved) was a craniotomy (brain surgery) performed by Dr. Shepherd, Chief of Neurosurgery. I was nervous, but I was reassured by my instructor who, functioning as scrub nurse stood by passing me the instrument she anticipated the surgeon needed or requested. I then passed or (slapped) it to his hand in the same precise manner as she did. Watching his moves and discovering quickly what he would probably need next, I learned the routine: cut, clamp, suture; cut, clamp, and suture. It was so dramatic, I was in heaven. Dr. Shepherd complimented me at the end of the surgery, saying he couldn't believe this was my first "scrub." I was floating, and every day was just as exciting. Funny, after that first experience I did not have a problem with major surgeries, such as open chest or complex abdominal procedures or amputations, but the day I was assigned to help in the Emergency Room with a toenail removal, I almost passed out. I still thought I would become an OR nurse. It was certainly more interesting than giving bed baths to senile old ladies. However, I soon learned the challenge of standing on my feet for four or five or more hours in a row in the OR was not easy. It did not help that I had a family history of varicose veins.

That month, standing in the operating room, I had an additional experience that was not in the curricular plan. I hesitated including the reality of this story in my memoir at first, and a few reviewers thought it was much too personal. It is very personal, but although my friends and I laughed later whenever we thought about the event, at the time I was crying, not laughing. I decided to tell the story now because I believe there is a lesson here for all young women to understand about their anatomy and sexual intercourse. *I want to communicate the importance of premarital (or pre–sexual activity) physical assessment by a qualified nurse or physician.* There are also many myths and superstitions among diverse cultures passed through generations that may need further explaining, but I cannot tell the "whole story here. *Any form of forced intercourse, or rape, is an offensive and dangerous act with much more serious effects possible than most boys or men can possibly understand.*

It was the third week of my OR experience and the second day of my menstrual period. I was bleeding heavily, and so fearful of leaking through I had managed to put on two pads. For over three hours I stood next to the surgeon passing instruments, lap pads, and sutures during exploratory GI surgery. My instructor was in the other room with another student when I realized I might be soaking through the pads, but there was no way to leave in order to change them. When we finished the surgery I rushed to the bathroom to "clean up." I couldn't understand how the OR staff managed to stand through four- and five-hour surgeries. When, back in the OR lounge, I asked my instructor what she did in that situation, she told me she wore a tampon, (which absorbed much internally) together with a sanitary napkin for the overflow during anticipated long surgeries. But I had never worn a tampon. When years before I brought up the subject with my mother (remember European born), she said "no, you cannot use a tampon; it is against Jewish law for an unmarried woman. You must remain a virgin or no one will marry you." That is what she was probably taught and I was not prepared to challenge her then.

I had never felt the need to question her until that day after the operating room experiences so, back in the residence lounge I brought up the subject and learned that all the girls wore tampons. One of my friends handed me a half-empty box she did not need just then and I went to the bathroom and tried to insert it. I seemed to have trouble so I went to my room and lay down on the bed and after a struggle inserted the tampon. I was so proud of myself and so much more comfortable. But a few hours later when I went to the bathroom and tried to remove it in order to insert another tampon, I could not without pain. To my horror, I could not get it out! It was stuck and the more I pulled, the more painful it became. I called on one of my classmates and before I knew it, there they were, three fellow nursing students dressed in OR scrub dresses, with masks and gloves, trying to remove the tampon. It was hooked onto a thick piece of internal tissue across the vaginal opening and there was nothing they could do. I would have to go the Emergency Room.

One of the girls walked with me across the back yard of the residence to the ER, where about five young interns were waiting for the ambulance to arrive. We walked in and I explained the situation to the ER nurse, saying, "Please, I don't want one of those young guys out there touching me." "No, I will call the GYN Resident," she replied.

Well it turned out he wasn't much older, and to my embarrassment he thought he could diminish my anxiety by being funny. "Are you sure I am not doing a D&C? (dilatation and curettage.) This surgical procedure is often done after a miscarriage or an abortion. I started to cry and exclaimed, "I am a virgin." I asked if one of my friends could come in during the exam, but the nurse said there wasn't enough space in the room. (If I was the RN in charge then you could be certain I would have invited the friend in the room, it wasn't that small!). Meanwhile, the resident, now dressed in gown and gloves, proceeded to examine me. He told me I had a "septate hymen" and explained the significance. "This is when the hymeneal membrane across the vaginal opening has a band of extra tissue in the middle that causes two small vaginal openings instead of one. Forceful entry causes tearing that can be very painful and lead to infections. We really do not know how common it is." He warned me the tampon removal might be painful, (which it was), while he struggled to remove the tampon. He told me my tissue would need to be surgically cut if I wanted to wear tampons from now on or, he added "have sexual intercourse." He said it could be terribly painful if I attempted sexual relations without prior surgical cutting. I asked him if he could do the procedure. He asked me my age? When I told him I was eighteen, he said he would need my parents' permission until I was twenty one or about to be married.

When I went home and asked my mother for permission, she went 'bananas.' No way, she would not give permission. She did not care about what the other girls were using. I was disappointed, but I did not bring the issue up again with my mother. However, I am a stubborn person, so when I want to do something badly, I move ahead and try to do it. I made up my mind to learn how to insert a tampon and how to manipulate it's removal without much pain, and I was successful. When my periods were heavy, I wore both a tampon and a napkin from then on, until the issue of intercourse came up during dating. When my future husband wanted to have sexual relations before the wedding, I just firmly said "NO." I remembered the pain of the tampon removal. I guess it was because I was so unsure about our relationship that I waited until a few weeks before our wedding to visit the gynecologist, this time wearing an engagement ring. Despite the local anesthesia injections the procedure was painful, physically and emotionally. When the physician showed me the thick muscular looking tissue he had removed, I was afraid the problem was not over. Unfortunately, the incision areas against the vaginal wall were not sutured, so I drained for weeks, even after the wedding. It was certainly not a good way to start a marriage.

Professionalism and Interprofessionalism

Back to the third year of my undergraduate education at Meadowbrook Hospital; after the physicians' lectures on Tuesdays and Thursdays, nursing faculty taught us about the nursing implications. We were on the patient floors all day Monday, Wednesday, and Friday. When possible we cared for patients according to the problems we were learning about in class, and of course the goals of "professional nursing." Most of our nursing teachers had been in the armed service overseas during World War II, and with GI benefits had earned bachelors and master's degrees from some of the best universities in the country. They were trying to educate us for more independent and collaborative problem solving.

Though nursing training before had been fashioned out of a military heritage, the faculty wanted to dilute that heritage; they wanted us to be more independent. "Don't stand up and salute when the physician [most of whom were males] enters the unit, **remember you're not his handmaiden**. But be sure to give him a thorough report of your assessment as a colleague," they told us. After all, we were college students, future nurse leaders and educators. I have to confess sometimes I couldn't follow that rule completely. I found myself standing up because I believed that by standing up and having direct eye contact I was demonstrating the collegial role. (There I was again asking questions no one else asks: raising questions and challenging rules.)

I learned later to play the "Doctor-Nurse Game," which is when the nurse advises the physician of what to dub, but convinces him that what he should do is really his idea, not hers (more about that later). I also learned early that the patient benefited most when there was a good relationship between the nurse and physician, when they listened to each other and respected their mutual contributions. Later the Team Concept and Interprofessional Relationships in Education and Practice became my mantra and the main theme of my doctoral dissertation, continuing research studies, program development, and publications over the years.

"Mommy, I didn't do anything wrong"

Our curriculum extended for the next two years, with more lectures and diverse clinical experiences. After the first week of classes of a three-month obstetrics rotation, with lectures and films on normal fetal development and labor and delivery, I was assigned to care for Kristina, (not her real name), a heavy-set thirteen-year-old girl who screamed and cried as she struggled with the painful labor, "Daddy, no, Daddy, no", she cried. Then crying quietly she held onto my hand and looked at me and said, "Mommy, I didn't do anything wrong." Her mother had brought her to the hospital in active labor claiming she did not know her daughter was pregnant. No father's name for the baby appeared in the record. Family members weren't allowed in labor and delivery units in those days so I never saw her mother. I held Kristina's hand, wiped her sweating face with a cool wet cloth, and washed and massaged her back in between the contractions. I whispered softly that she was doing great, and it would be over soon, which of course was a lie. Despite the "twilight sleep" (IV analgesia with Demerol and Scopolamine, (an amnesic) or because of it, she just kept on screaming and only seemed more confused between her mother and me. The labor was long and difficult; an episiotomy[10] and forceps were eventually needed to deliver an eight-pound boy. Kristina screamed and cried and cried, and finally after the baby was delivered she closed her eyes. She was exhausted and didn't want to see the baby, didn't say anything, not then or at all during the week. She was in a double room without a roommate instead of the postpartum ward where mothers would be chatting and babies would be brought out for nursing, although at that time few mothers chose to breastfeed – most were given formula. Kristina's baby was kept in the nursery and I was told later given up for adoption. Her mother never came to the hospital while I was there, but one day Kristina was discharged, I believe to a foster home. I don't know what happened to her afterwards, no one seemed to know, but my friends and I suspected it was incest, and could only hope she was given some caring guardians and mental health counseling.

As it was a county hospital for the uninsured, I saw very few happy mothers. Most middle-class patients with insurance or the money to pay directly went elsewhere to deliver their babies. At that time there was no free maternity clinic on Long Island so mothers with no prenatal care, women of all ages and backgrounds, just appeared at the emergency room in labor or in trouble. Some were very young teenagers. Most were married, often Catholic with five, six or more children at home. Some were housemaids or former staff members at the large Long Island estates, now homeless. Many women had eclampsia due to high blood pressure, or anemia and bleeding problems, and there were lots of complications from botched abortions, which, of course, were not legal at that time.

---

[10] Episiotomy is a surgical incision made to enlarge the vaginal opening to allow the fetal (newborn) head to emerge from the birth canal and prevent tearing of the perineal tissue.

There were also a lot of newborn babies with problems, particularly when the mothers had diabetes. During the obstetrics experience and later during a three-month pediatrics rotation, I saw almost every kind of human birth anomaly and childhood disease known: harelip, cleft palate, meningomyelocele, cystic fibrosis, celiac disease, and leukemia (most of who died). There was no genetic testing in those days, and most of the single white women smoked and often drank alcohol as well. The older women were often obese with diabetes and hypertension of pregnancy. We watched every new patient for signs of pre-eclampsia/toxemia of pregnancy, such as seizures.

I was only eighteen, but I learned lessons about birth and death that influenced me personally and professionally throughout my life. Kristina, the victim, haunted me. Years later, while teaching maternal child health nursing in the associate degree program, I became an active political advocate for sexual education in schools, free family planning, prenatal care, and legalization of abortion as a public health need.

Infectious and Communicable Disease

Polio was rampant in the United States in the 1940s and '50s and especially prevalent among children. At Meadowbrook there was an entire building with polio patients, mostly children, many in iron lungs. The college and hospital administration would not let Adelphi students work in those units because there was no immunization yet and we were considered especially vulnerable. Dr. Jonas Salk's polio vaccine first became available in 1954, and it was the most remarkable achievement in largely eliminating the disease in this country. Today, thousands of Post-Polio Syndrome patients with various muscular skeletal limitations still struggle with the aftermath of the disease. Thanks to Dr. Salk, and then Dr. Albert Sabin for the oral vaccine, which was more cost effective since syringes and needles weren't needed, poliomyelitis has been almost eliminated worldwide today, especially through the efforts of the World Health Organization, United States CDC, and the Rotary International Foundation. However, it still exists in India, Pakistan, Afghanistan, and

Nigeria. Recently the Bill and Melinda Gates Foundation presented a challenge of $200 million to Rotary to finish the job around the world.

We weren't able to take care of patients with polio, but actual hands-on communicable disease nursing was not entirely left out of our Adelphi curriculum. For two months in our senior year we studied about patients with tuberculosis and other pulmonary diseases at Triboro Hospital in Queens, NY. TB is not the threat today that it was in the first half of the 20th century, except for immune-suppressed patients like those with AIDS. A few antibiotic-resistant strains of the disease have been containable. Hospitalization and isolation are rarely needed in this country except when someone from abroad appears with the disease, but prior to 1950 various treatments were attempted including surgery. Triboro, an eight-floor building, was packed with patients who had been there for years and years, most with TB, but patients with other pulmonary diseases were also confined there under public funding.

Three lessons I learned through my experience stand out. We had better food served in that dining room than in any other hospital affiliation, with eggs made to order in the morning. The last thing they wanted was for a student to come down with the disease. General nutrition was very important. One student in the class before mine had developed TB and was not allowed back into the program. We all had to be tested before the rotation. Immunization with BCG was provided for students who appeared through Mantoux testing to be without antibodies and therefore vulnerable. It turned out that I tested positive on my Mantoux; evidently I had been exposed and developed resistance. My chest x-ray was clear. I wasn't given the BCG vaccine.

Most of the TB patients in the hospital received a cocktail of available antibiotics, specifically Streptomycin intramuscularly with PAS and Isoniazid orally. I remember being assigned as medication nurse for the day. Dressed in full isolation gown, mask, and gloves to protect myself from being sensitized to the drug, I administered about 150 injections of streptomycin that day. If I had ever questioned my ability to give injections before, that fear was eliminated for life on my medication day.

Another learning impact that stands out clearly in my life has to do with smoking. Many of these patients, whether it was TB or emphysema, or lung cancer, had been or were still smokers. Clearly each and every one looked much older than their chronological age. And they suffered. Breathing was not easy for anyone, oxygen was necessary for many, and still smoking persisted. I may have tried a cigarette once or twice in the shower bunk in summer camp, or with peers socially in my early teens, but after Triboro, I did not pick up a cigarette again.

But the most important lesson I learned through my Tuberculosis rotation was a lesson in ethics. It wasn't that I did not know the difference between right and wrong; but I had panicked. It started the first day I was supposed to report to Triboro in August 1953 before entering my senior year. I had four weeks of vacation and of course needed the money and wanted to get out of the city, so I accepted a job as a counselor for children four to five years of age in a Pennsylvania summer camp. I learned after I arrived that at the end of the month I was expected to take four of my young children home by bus to New York on the last day. However, I was also expected to arrive at Triboro Hospital the same day for orientation and a move into the nurses' residence there. I knew I could not make it home to get my uniforms and then to the hospital in time, so I asked my mother to call the school office and tell them I was sick and could not come until the next day. She told me she would do it.

When I came home I learned she had not made the call. The next morning, when I arrived at Triboro I was told I was late, not responsible, had not met my commitment, and could not start the program. I called the College office, but it was August and no one was there. I sat home crying, not believing what I done to myself. My brother was home on leave from the Army. He took it upon himself to ride out to Triboro and arrange an appointment with Ms. Brewer, the Director of Nursing. As I mentioned earlier, Norman just had a way of charming women, young and old. The director was able to reach my dean, Dr. Shay on the phone and they worked out an arrangement. It was the most complicated plan they could have devised. It is hard to envision unless you are actively involved. I had to stay home that month and read about TB nursing and everything I could find about ethics and responsibility.

The next month I started the rotation at Triboro with a group of students from the College of St. Rose in Albany while living at Triboro Hospital; I went home for weekends. It was very lonely. At the end of the month I continued to my psychiatric nursing three-month rotation and moved into the Creedmoor State Hospital Nursing residence. It was so complicated. In the spring we had advanced medical surgical nursing classes in the afternoon and clinical work back at Meadowbrook Hospital. I went back to living at Triboro and in the mornings took the second month of classes and clinical TB program with another group of College of St. Rose students. In this way I finished the TB course. My father took the train to work and gave me his car so I could drive from Triboro to Meadowbrook in the afternoon for classes there. At the end of the semester when all my classmates had three weeks off to prepare for state board examinations, I lived and worked alone at Meadowbrook for three weeks to make up the advanced clinical experiences I had missed, finishing the last day before the pinning ceremony which was the night before graduation.

No one appreciated that ceremony as much as I did. It was bittersweet when I received a grade of A+ in TB nursing and an A in the advanced medical surgery course. No one paid as much as I did for the mistake I had made. When I asked my mother why she had not called the school as she agreed, she said she could not lie for me, that I should have told the truth all around. I was afraid I would not get paid if I left camp before the final trip back to New York with the children and did not think the truth would have helped me. I learned a very important lesson in morality and professionalism about truth, and I paid for it.

Mental Health and Psychiatric Illness

In between the first Triboro month and the second, I took the course in Psychiatric and Mental Health Nursing at Creedmoor State Hospital. The hospital was a series of about twenty five low-lying gray government-looking buildings with bars on the windows near the Cross Island Parkway in Queens, not too far from the bridge to Manhattan. We lived and studied psychiatric nursing for three months during the senior year. Adelphi students had a special professional program at Creedmoor with a caseload of our own patients, unlike the hospital diploma nursing students from upstate New York, who were assigned general nursing tasks for large groups of patients. We also attended neurology and psychiatric lectures with the medical students and residents from Cornell University, and sat in on all the patient care team conferences.

Every case was unique, yet there were many common underlying stories and behaviors: delusions, hallucinations, and obsessions. It seemed that every patient had religious and/or sexual issues intertwined with his or her history. We did not need to read "R" or "X" rated fiction; it all seemed to be reality in the patients admitted to Creedmoor. We listened to tales of all kinds of mental and physical abuse: incest, rape, sodomy, attempted murder, and the real thing. Once we met the patients we heard the loud cursing anger at their known or unknown abusers and demons: mothers, fathers, God, saints, hospital staff, police, the government, etc. I learned more violent and sexual vocabulary in those three months than in the first three years of our entire curriculum, and ever since. Some patients seemed normal at first meeting, but their illness soon came forward in the overcrowded wards of Creedmoor. Manic and depressive behaviors and belligerence abounded. Did you see Jack Nicholson in *One Flew over the Cuckoo's Nest?* Or Olivia De Havilland in *The Snake Pit*? More recently Russell Crowe in *A Beautiful Mind* demonstrated brilliantly the bizarre behavior of the serious mentally ill, like most diagnosed with schizophrenia at Bellevue in the 1950s and sent on to the state hospitals.

All staff and students wore a rope around the waist for a long low-hanging string of many keys as we walked through the buildings. First open one door, turn and lock it behind, walk slowly down the barren hall, open another door, turn and lock it behind, down the next hall to our assigned unit, stop, take a deep breath, put in the key and open the final door, turn around and lock it behind. Again we heard those uncomfortable words, "Here come the canaries," from the male orderlies. Sometimes they were echoed by a few of the patients hanging around in the day room, although most were oblivious, just standing there looking out the barred windows with blank faces, or sleeping sitting up in an arm chair or lying down on a short bench.

Ann Miranda (not her true surname) was one of my assigned patients. She was nineteen years old, my age. She was also petite like me, with dark eyes like mine, but thinner and with a darker pale tone to her skin. Ann, who came from a religious home and lived with her mother and sister in East Harlem, had evidently been a freshman at Hunter College before she became ill and was admitted to the Bellevue Hospital. Her diagnosis when she was transferred to Creedmoor State was catatonic schizophrenia. Her behavior varied from being unresponsive or silent to explosions of violent irrational outbursts. When I first met her, Ann was dressed in a long washed-out-looking cotton house dress that slipped over her head, no buttons or zippers. She just sat in a trance-like state, her dark eyes blank. Other times she was raging, inapproachable, shouting obscene words I never thought I would hear from such a fragile-looking young woman.

In addition to Ann, I had two other patients, Ronnie, a nine-year-old autistic boy in the Outpatient Center, and Willy, a small elderly black man with a charted history of treatment for neurosyphilis and dementia. There was not much I could do for Ronnie; he never spoke, and his eyes never met mine. Sometimes he seemed agitated with weird movements of his hands. His mother talked to me during their twice-a-week visits. I mostly just listened as she talked on and on about her frustration with Ronnie and the difficulty she had taking two buses to make the trip to the hospital. He was not in school anymore; they could not manage him. I read to him from a children's picture book, but he never looked at the pictures or seemed to be listening. I tried, but I never reached Ronnie. I did not understand why he was like he was; his mother seemed loving. If I recall, Ronnie had two normal siblings. I still do not understand the root of autism, and I am not sure there have been very many advances in the understanding and treatment for autism (although some differentiation has been made among behaviors). The incidence however has apparently increased significantly through this half century, with the disease identified earlier, and a theory of causation due to childhood immunizations proposed by some researchers and parent groups, proven wrong. Recently I heard of another theory of causation linked to the age of the father. Much research is progressing forward.

Mr. "Willy," seemed almost normal to me although he looked much older than his fifty five years. I became his friend. I took him to play pool in the recreation room, and he showed me the game. It was fun; I was terrible, we teased each other and laughed at my clumsiness. He had been in and out of the hospital for almost twenty years, but had no family to care for him; he did not complain about the food, took whatever medicines they gave him, kept himself clean with supervision, and seemed content. I knew he had a complex history and was diagnosed with senile dementia, but was not considered dangerous to himself or others. I guessed he was just homeless and would have been on the street if not in the hospital.

I spent most of my patient time with Ann. I helped her in the morning to wash and dress and brushed her teeth the best I could. Then I combed her short straight dark brown hair away from her eyes, put one of my bobby pins in to keep her hair in place, and walked with her as she shuffled to the dining room. Breakfast was orange juice, oatmeal, sometimes scrambled eggs and white bread. Ann was not interested in feeding herself. I helped feed her with the spoon, the only utensil she was allowed. One day I brought her a nice barrette for her hair, but it was not there the next day. She said very little, sometimes nothing. I asked questions and tried to get her to talk to me. I asked if they had shown a movie on the previous night. They used to show cartoons and sometimes musicals. Had her mom and sister visited on Sunday, I asked? Usually there was no response or maybe a one-word response.

One Sunday afternoon I came in to meet her mother, but found Ann walking back and forth muttering under her breath – I did not understand her. I tried to talk to her. She did not look at me, just started shouting, over and over, cursing, "get that fucking bastard away from me – you bitch – get him away from me," she screamed. Her mother just sat there crying. I asked her what happened, but she just kept crying. "Ann, what's the matter?" I asked. I tried to put my arms around her, but she wouldn't let me touch her; she started hitting at me. "What has happened?" I tried to calm Ann down, but she just kept shouting and cursing at us. One of the other patients started shouting at Ann to shut up – then another – and another, the noise was terrible. It was truly "a cuckoo's nest." One of the staff nurses finally showed up. It wasn't easy, but we got Ann into a restraint, she was sedated, and things quieted down. The next day Ann was still sedated. She looked like a zombie. Remember it was the early 1950's. Those were the days of straitjackets and warm tubs to calm agitation and manic behavior.

On Tuesday, after class, I spoke to Dr. Laquer, the medical director of our program. I told him what happened on Sunday. We understood Ann had supposedly been well until her father's death several months earlier. According to her mother, Ann did not have any close friends, no boyfriend, and had never dated in high school; her father would not let her. She used to go to church, but stopped suddenly two years before. Ann had started Hunter College, and then stopped going to classes when her father died from liver disease, her mother said. Ann would not talk to anyone in her family, barely ate, and ignored her mother when pressured. She just sat home, slept most of the day, and then one day got into a fight with her younger sister. Unable to control Ann, her mother called 911 and Ann was taken to Bellevue Hospital. After two weeks they transferred her to Creedmoor.

"What will happen to Ann? She's only nineteen, my age," I asked Dr. Laquer.

"There is a lot we do not know about Ann and this family; I am afraid something has been wrong for a long time. Ann has probably been ill for years, much longer than the mother will admit. I do not see much hope for Anne since she is not responding here. She will probably end up in 'R' or 'S' building," he said, pointing out the window over the horizon to the far end of the grounds.

I was devastated. "What about your research unit, what about insulin shock?" I asked.

"I will think about it," said Dr. Laquer, "but I am afraid she has been sick too long."

I did not see Ann for a few days; we had Thanksgiving off and I went home. That weekend Mary, (not her real name) an attractive, tall, sensuous patient of about twenty five, attacked and knocked out a male attendant, grabbed his keys and managed to escape with another patient on Saturday night. The police eventually found and returned them to the hospital, where they were placed in isolation. I remembered Mary from before the escapade; she had always seemed normal looking to me, sweet, trying to be friendly. It turned out she had multiple Bellevue admissions for frequent episodes of violent behavior, had dropped out of school, fought at home with parents and siblings, couldn't keep a job, and in an alcoholic rage one night stabbed her boyfriend.

One day they started Ann on a series of electric shock treatments (ECT). It was awful! They had not warned us with a film or explanation, even though we had heard of the treatment in class. I cannot possibly describe how awful the treatment appears; the grand mal seizures *shocked me*. They did not give any anesthesia with the shock in those days in the public hospitals. I thought it was barbaric. But I got used to it. If you watch ten patients receive the shocks, one after the next, you get used to moving them off the table as a team, and changing the urine-soaked sheets on the table when the patient loses bladder control. I understand the treatment is still in use today in some settings for severe depression, but it has become more humane. There are pros and cons to the treatment. Many people claim they have been helped. Kitty Dukakis, wife of Michael Dukakis, Massachusetts Governor and presidential candidate in 1988 wrote a nationally distributed book praising the help she received from shock therapy for serious depression. There was very little press coverage when John Eagleton, long time Democratic senator from Missouri resigned as George McGovern's Vice Presidential nominee when it was revealed that he had had ECT. Supposedly the internationally known author Ernest Hemingway committed suicide a few weeks after his second series of shocks for severe depression. He had claimed the treatment destroyed his ability to write and life wasn't worth living. I could understand his depression as a result of the loss of his ability to write, but I wondered why he was so depressed leading up to the shock therapy? In any event, I got over some of my negative attitude toward the ECT treatment when during the second series Ann actually seemed to get better. She smiled after a while, and seemed to communicate more. We went to arts and crafts. Both of us started working on decorating and imprinting a copper cover with flowers for a wooden jewelry box. Ann and I were so proud our accomplishments. I still have that box stored away somewhere in a closet, it having survived many moves in my life.

Ann almost seemed normal as she came close to finishing her series of treatments. When her mother and younger sister came that Sunday afternoon, she looked good. I had fixed her hair with a new barrette and she allowed me put makeup on her face, blush, lipstick, and even mascara. Her pale olive skin and dark eyes appeared to come alive. Ann really looked pretty. I was certain she would be fine soon. But not too long after the treatments were over, Ann's illness seemed to return. She became quiet again, and the depression returned. Nothing I had wished for was happening. Ann returned to her catatonic state. I left my Creedmoor rotation heartbroken at the end of the semester.

Final Clinical Rotations

As the weeks and months of the planned senior year curriculum moved forward, various other clinical experiences presented new challenges, influencing my development personally and professionally. For eight weeks I was assigned to a county health department office in Mineola, an area close to the border between Queens and Nassau Counties, to work with a public health nurse. There were three days visiting families, at first with my nurse preceptor and later independently, as well as two days in classes studying epidemiology, complex family dynamics, public health policy, and case management. I had to live at home in Brooklyn and I needed a car. My dad, who worked in Queens then, came to the rescue. He was able to share the task with me for the first two weeks, driving me to the Mineola office on the way to work and picking me up at the end of the day. I cannot really remember how we worked out arrangements for the next six weeks when I needed to be independent, but I think he ended up giving me the car three days a week and traveling by subway for two hours each way to his Queens offices.

This clinical experience was important in many ways in helping me to understand differences in family cultures and continuity of care. I met several patients I had cared for earlier in Meadowbrook Hospital, such as a nineteen-year-old woman, Mary, with multiple sclerosis (MS). Six months before she had been newly diagnosed and her illness was still fresh. I only knew of the severity of her condition through my textbook and had no idea of the impact on her life and her long-term prognosis. There was no treatment for MS in those days. There are some newly developing treatments offered today, and some patients have longer remissions. Before she was admitted to the hospital Mary had been traveling two buses to work in an office in Queens after she graduated from high school. Now she was completely bedridden, unable to feed herself or control elimination, requiring round-the-clock care.

We also had a clinical rotation to a small private hospital the college had purchased from physician owners near where I lived in Brooklyn. It was supposed to be a culminating experience where we would have a chance to function without immediate direction of an instructor, and experience leadership of auxiliary staff members. There were only a few professional nurses in the hospital, but patients here were usually not very ill, many admitted for relatively simple surgery. Most of the physical nursing care was given by practical nurses or nursing aides, although there were a few private duty nurses with individual patients. In those days it was common for patients to have private nursing care immediately after surgery and sometimes for days following if they who could afford the expense.

One day a handsome young college student, twenty years old (my age), had been admitted preoperatively to my floor for what was considered relatively common surgery, incision and drainage of a pilonidal abscess, a cyst within the rectal cleft just above the anus; this was my first such case. His name was Robert, (not his real name) and I was smitten. My medical and surgical textbook gave some basic information; I understood the condition was fairly common in young men, although it could be very painful when infected. Evidently that was the case with Robert. During the pre-op interview there was nothing to indicate a potential problem, the patient was nervous, having never had surgery before. I was relieved there was a male orderly in the hospital to prep Robert (shave the hair from around the site) as soon as I called, which would avoid any embarrassment if I had to do the prep. I reassured Robert that the surgery would not take long according to what I had read, and he would be back in the bed he was now in. (There was no recovery room in the hospital.) After the orderly finished the prep I gave Robert the pre-op medication by injection at 11 a.m., as ordered and the orderly took him to the operating room on the stretcher. His surgery was scheduled for noon, and he returned about two hours later to my floor. I did not see the surgeon, he had left the hospital directly from the OR, but I proceeded to check the patient's vital signs – blood pressure, pulse, and respiration – every fifteen minutes and check his dressing according to routine procedures. Robert was still sedated and seemed to be resting comfortably but his dressing was soiled with some bright red blood; I reinforced it as directed on the chart.

When I examined the dressing an hour later, the blood had permeated the additional gauze. My instructor was not in the hospital that day, but I was concerned so although the vital signs appeared fairly stable, I called the supervisor and asked her to come to investigate, which she did. She told me to add more dressings with pressure since the usual procedure was not to close the wound with sutures but to pack the area to allow for drainage. There was no indication on the chart that bleeding had occurred in the OR and no abnormal pre-op lab blood test results were evident. The patient's blood pressure had lowered slightly; his pulse had increased. I was really concerned now and called the supervisor again, asking her to call the surgeon since I did not expect increasing bright red blood. The supervisor called the doctor's office and spoke to the surgeon, who told us to add more dressings with pressure, and promised to return to the hospital as soon as possible.

It was getting close to 4 p.m., time for me to report off to the private duty evening nurse the family had arranged, and who had arrived. I showed the nurse, who was an experienced LPN the saturated dressings and the vital signs record. Robert was getting restless and asked for pain medication. I did not want to leave until the surgeon arrived, but at 4:30, when he still had not returned to the hospital, I called the evening supervisor again; she was a registered nurse. She tried to call the surgeon again; she was not successful in reaching him. (Of course, there were no cell phones in those days.) She assured me he was probably on the way, and told me not to worry as she was following up, and I should leave. I walked home down Ocean Avenue, fantasizing that everything was OK. I couldn't imagine anything serious was occurring to this vibrant young man.

The next morning, when I returned to the hospital at 8 a.m., I walked past the room Robert had been in and saw that it was empty. I asked the night nurse where he was, thinking perhaps he had been discharged home. I was in shock when she told me he had been taken back to the Operating Room about 8 p.m. to repack the dressing, and that he had been given a blood transfusion, but the doctor could not stop the bleeding. To everyone's horror, Robert died during the night. I could not believe it. I was told they thought he might have had some type of blood dyscrasia. His parents had OK'd an autopsy. I do not know how I managed to work that day or the days following.

I had seen a few patients die before, but most had been much older and sicker and expected to die. I had experienced problems dealing with the dying children during my three-month pediatric experience at Meadowbrook, most of the time it made no sense to me, but I knew Meadowbrook was the county hospital for critically ill children, many with cancers, traumatic injuries, and other terminal conditions where treatments were limited. I had started to question my faith in God again then, and now it was back. How could this have happened? Robert was young and apparently healthy, in the hospital for an elective procedure. Evidently something was wrong, but I never found out the cause of death.

So many years have passed and so much has happened in my life since that awful event; I repressed the memory and didn't think about it until writing this memoir. But returning to faith has been an arduous journey; I have learned to appreciate the remarkable achievements made in medicine since those years, but I am not certain that this type of incident does not also happen today, every day. Over and over, the question of why bad things happen to good people persists for me. I have not found the answer, but I have not stopped struggling for answers. Somehow with each new life experience I made an effort to look at each day as a new learning experience and even as a blessing.

Community Mental Health

Jump ahead to July 1955. She was behind the counter, on the first floor of Bloomingdale's department store in Manhattan, selling white cotton lace gloves.

"Ann, Ann, I can't believe it's you!!" I exclaimed in my own inimitable style.

Ann looked up, "Miss Kleiman," she recognized me and said, "Miss Kleiman, I'm so glad to see you again." It was the first time she had ever said my name. All those months when she was so sick, I cared for Ann wearing my name pin on my yellow uniform pocket. But she had never said my name. Now, almost two years since she had last seen me, she remembered me and my name, and she looked so beautiful. Ann was wearing a light blue summer suit; her hair cut smartly, her face made up just like I used to do for her. She was as pretty as I remembered those few weeks when she seemed well.

"Wait for me a few minutes till I finish this sale," Ann said. I waited. She came from behind the counter, and we hugged. "This is my first job. I've been here for four months and I love it, but I'm still in rehab, I see my counselor every week" she explained. "I'm hoping to go back to school part time in the fall. You know, I don't remember very much about the hospital, but I remember you. I want to thank you so much for caring for me," she added.

The year before, about the time of my graduation in 1954, Thorazine, one of the first psychotropic drugs, came from France to the United States. With the establishment in the late 1940s of the National Institute of Mental Health in this country, research into the biology of mental illness began and eventually led to many new drugs. New communication methods were introduced over the following years. Insulin and electric shock lost favor, patients became more amenable to psychotherapy, and depression and manic behavior could often be managed better with the new drugs. Fortunately, the psychotropic drugs have enabled many patients to live independently or with their families, and to work and live productive lives. But the story isn't over.

In 1955, New York State had almost 95,000 live in-patients in its array of state hospitals. By the 1960s the Community Mental Health Movement took over, leading to the dismantling of the state hospital systems. Without adequate planning, thousands of patients were discharged from the hospitals on Long Island and across the country. Most families were not prepared, and many patients had no families to return to. Communities couldn't meet the needs. There weren't enough clinics to manage medication distribution, staff in many group homes were poorly trained, all kinds of abuses occurred, and many former patients, untrusting and homeless, took to the streets. Those are the patients who used to end up in R, S, and T buildings of state hospitals, where at least they were removed from the trauma at home they could not deal with, and were fed and clothed. Those hospitals are almost empty today. Tragically, mental health care is still in a crisis state today, and many of our city streets are home to the homeless.

My three months at Creedmoor were not in vain. No number of textbooks alone could ever have prepared me personally or professionally for what was to come. Every patient I cared for subsequently, and every student I later taught through the years benefited. I loved Ann and I believe I was one small part of her healing. Despite the long serious illness, the difficult ECT treatments she endured, and the years before our reunion, Ann remembered me, spoke my name, and said, "Thank you."

Adelphi students (1950-1954) with our nursing instructor Mrs. Agnes Clark at a Brooklyn Hospital. I am in the front on the right, Ruth Ann Weisbrod Brown stands in the back and Ann Ardelle Sickmon Raab stands in the middle on the left.

Images of classmates during Senior Prom 1954. (From personal collection of classmate Natalie Kromback Williams)

(Image of classmate Natalie Kromback Williams from her personal collection)

Here I am marching in the auditorium of Meadowbrook Hospital at the Adelphi Pinning Ceremony on the evening before graduation (Author's personal collection)

3

Beginning My Professional Career, Marriage and Family

"I SOLEMNLY PLEDGE MYSELF BEFORE GOD AND IN THE PRESENCE OF THIS ASSEMBLY TO FAITHFULLY PRACTICE MY PROFESSION OF NURSING. I WILL DO ALL IN MY POWER TO MAKE AND MAINTAIN THE HIGHEST STANDARD AND PRACTICE OF MY PROFESSION..."

THE NIGHTINGALE PLEDGE (SEE APPENDIX I)

GRADUATION

Over the last few months of school I started to think more seriously about the area of nursing I should enter after graduation. What I loved most about nursing was the care of individual patients, the opportunity to provide comfort, and the thank you when I fulfilled my role each day. But when it came time to think about actual entry into the profession I needed to make the decision and complete applications. I thought about enlisting in the Army or perhaps the Navy as one of my classmates was planning. But when I mentioned it to my brother, he threw a fit. "Are you crazy?" he objected, "You're too young, you're a religious girl, you don't belong there." I was just twenty, but I wasn't so religious, I had been eating non-kosher food since I first moved into the nurses' residence at Meadowbrook, telling my parents I did not eat the meat, only potatoes and vegetables in the cafeteria where every night, when the special was depleted, roast pork was available. (It's easy to develop a taste for the forbidden when no one is watching.)

In the meantime I had lots of questions about everything related to religion, not just food: the purpose of religion, my own Jewish faith, religious faith generally and where was God when all the awful things I had seen and heard of were dehumanizing or destroying lives. I had so many questions in my head. But now, I had an immediate decision to make.

I turned to my brother and cried, "What do you expect me to do? Work in Brooklyn, and move back here in this tiny apartment sleeping on the sofa bed? I'm not as religious as you think; I'm not even sure I believe in God anymore." (My brother said, "don't be ridiculous, and don't let mom or dad ever hear you say that. It would kill them.")

Among advertisements in the *American Journal of Nursing* I noticed a position in psychiatry at the Langley Porter clinic in San Francisco. It was a highly regarded private clinic, and they had an orientation for new graduates. I think I remember that nurses there were working with their own caseload of mentally ill patients, just as we had done as Adelphi students, which appealed to me. I knew I didn't want to work in a large state public institutional like Creedmoor. I wrote for an application, and when it arrived, completed and mailed it before graduation. Then I put the thought aside, recognizing that I would be better off thinking about first passing the state board exams scheduled for July 1st and 2nd at the Armory in New York City.

When I received an invitation to come to San Francisco for an interview, I chickened out. How could I fly across the country all by myself? I didn't know of anyone in my class who might also be interested in San Francisco. Most of my classmates were already planning their weddings and working locally. I also realized I would be better off working in general medical and surgical nursing for a year in New York before considering California. So when I saw an ad in *The New York Times* for nurses at Mt. Sinai Hospital in Manhattan mentioning the nurses' residence on Fifth Avenue near Central Park, I decided to apply for a position there.

I graduated from Adelphi in June 1954 with a bachelor's degree, a full-fledged public health nurse by virtue of the curriculum that included concepts of epidemiology, public health policy, and supervised and independent community health practice. The Pinning Ceremony was held the night before in the Meadowbrook Hospital auditorium. My education was over, I thought; I was finally out of that yellow uniform and into a long-sleeved starched white uniform. The ceremony was beautiful as the lights were dimmed while we walked down the center aisle to the music of "Pomp and Circumstance." After a few words from Dean Shay, we recited the entire Nightingale Pledge we had memorized, and then walked up individually to receive the Adelphi Nursing Pin that would be attached to our uniform over the left breast pocket by our much loved faculty class advisor, Justina Eisenhower. My parents and brother had come and I could tell how proud they were of me. I looked like a professional nurse and I smiled, but I was frightened and insecure, so aware of my limitations. I was remembering all I had gone through: the almost-failure in chemistry, the stress of deformed or dying children, the Triboro Hospital fiasco, the traveling back and forth to Meadowbrook, and the patients I had loved but couldn't save, Kristina, Ann, and Robert.

Official college graduation was scheduled the next day outdoors on the Adelphi campus, supposedly rain or shine. Unfortunately it not only rained, it poured, and the wind blew and everyone ran for shelter into Woodruff Hall, which was hot and humid and much too small to seat the crowd. I don't remember much of what was said, but somehow I walked down the aisle in my rented black academic gown and cap, shook the president's hand, and received a brown and gold baccalaureate hood representing the college colors and a hardback brown folder for the degree from Dean Shay. I was thrilled to find my family in the crowd and as the rain had stopped, we walked together to the parking lot to locate Dad's old reliable Hudson that had served me so well. I left Adelphi that day grateful to my family for supporting me through all I had experienced, and moved back home to Brooklyn with them, knowing it was only temporary. I did not return to Adelphi for almost thirty years.

The state board examination was in the Armory in Manhattan the first two days of July. I was exhausted at the end of those torturous days, traveling by subway to the hot amphitheater, certain I had failed. I couldn't anguish over the results, I was just glad it was over. In those days there were no practice exams with the Number Two pencils at school as there are today with computer-driven exams. I knew there was nothing I could do about it then. It took two months before I found out that I did in fact pass along with all my classmates. Meanwhile, I was not only exhausted, I was broke. I needed to earn money as soon as possible, but first I needed a rest.

Summer Camp Nurse

There were many ads in the nursing journal and *The New York Times* for summer camp nurses and that sounded like a good idea, so I applied for a position in a coed camp in Palmer, Massachusetts, for the rest of the summer. I had experience as a camper during the summers when I was young and then as a camp counselor for one month in between the third and fourth years of college. However, none of that was preparation for the responsibility I was to assume once I was a professional nurse. I selected the camp because they were willing to hire me without proof of my registered nurse license yet and allowed me to arrive late in order to take the State Boards. I thought this specific position would be less stressful for me than the hospital because there was a physician and another nurse in residence, Shirley, a Long Island College Hospital graduate with six months of working experience. We both learned a lot, but I had much less confidence. I was so wrong – the work was different, but in a sense just as hard.

Life that summer was a "coming of age" experience. There were about 250 campers, aged four to fourteen, and about seventy five camp counselors, spouses, and service people of varying ages, who were supposed to be "healthy." All kinds of accidents, injuries, infections, and asthma attacks occurred, and one of the camp directors had a serious coronary event on the doctor's day off, requiring an ambulance for transfer to the local hospital; fortunately he survived. Some days, the morning and evening clinics were just as action packed and challenging as a small community hospital emergency room. Kids who seemed to be able to play softball or tennis, compete in track meets in the heat, and then swim 200 yards in the lake would get into a pillow fight in the evening and end up with an asthma attack requiring epinephrine. We segregated campers and counselors with infections in the infirmary all day and night, and I don't remember ever having empty beds at night. My room was in the infirmary building, so even when I was not theoretically "on duty," I was disturbed by the activities next door. As exhausted as I might be, I never slept through the night during the summer, and I didn't get to play tennis, or to swim or paddle a canoe. (It always seemed to be raining when I might have had the opportunity.)

It was true that there was more fun to be had than in the hospital. Many of the children were really appreciative of my special attention when they were sick. One of my favorite activities was to read and tell stories and sing songs with the little ones; they all missed their families more when they were sick. On my bi-weekly half day off I went into town with a small group of counselors to have lunch at one of the local diners, sometimes see a movie, and do some window shopping; I had no extra money to buy anything. There were also many creative and talented campers and counselors who put on plays and musical shows in the evening. Most of the time we had patients sleeping in the infirmary so my partner nurse and I would take turns attending the shows; unfortunately, I missed many of the performances. Toward the end of the summer there was overall enthusiasm and excitement within the competitive atmosphere of the Color War games. To our amazement few kids got sick during this "Olympics" time; there was full participation in all the events, especially the unbelievably creative musical shows presented by both teams with a very short time for rehearsals. It was impossible to predict the winners; everyone was a winner in something.

I had fantasized meeting someone to socialize with, but to my disappointment, most of the counselors were younger or already hooked up; again no male showed interest in me. I thought the summer would never end, and when it did, I wished it hadn't. It was back to Brooklyn to my sofa bed in the living room, briefly. Fortunately my brother had moved to Texas to start a sales career for a well-established New York women's clothing company, so the apartment wasn't so crowded.

Mt. Sinai Hospital

In September 1954 I moved into the nurses' residence and started work as a staff nurse at Mt. Sinai Hospital in New York City. My beginning salary was $250 a month before taxes, and included benefits, such as free health insurance, tuition for graduate studies after six months of employment, and four weeks of vacation after a year. I paid $25 for that room in the residence; meals were extra. It didn't leave much, but with my Adelphi graduate pin on my pocket below my new Mt. Sinai name pin, I knew I was special.

In those years at Mt. Sinai direct nursing care in the main hospital wards was given primarily by students of the hospital's own training program under direction of the school's experienced graduate nurses. Most of those patients did not have health insurance; patients with insurance or able to pay privately were in the Klingenstein semi-private and Guggenheim private rooms, often cared for by private duty nurse after they had surgery or if they were critically ill. The Recovery Room closed at 11 p.m. and patients were returned to their respective rooms, and there was no critical care unit (CCU) in the hospital at that time. During the 1950s the development of mechanical ventilation led to the organization of respiratory intensive care units [ICUs] in many European and American hospitals. Care of these patients proved to be more efficient when patients were grouped in a single location. The first multidisciplinary intensive care unit in the U.S. was established at Johns Hopkins in Baltimore in 1958. It was the first ICU covered by an in-house physician [anesthesia resident] around the clock, seven days a week. By the late 1960s, most U.S. hospitals had at least one ICU.

My letter of appointment indicated I would have an orientation to the hospital during the first week, but I was told to appear on the seventh floor in the Klingenstein building at 8 a.m. on the first day. When I arrived there were many nurses and several physicians around the nurses' station; I looked for someone in authority to whom I could introduce myself. I asked a young woman in a blue uniform who appeared to be a ward clerk for the charge nurse, only to be told the charge nurse was off duty that day, and they were expecting a per diem nurse to take charge. Everyone scurried around, and I was confused. Who was in charge?

The clerk pointed to the assignment sheet on the wall bulletin board. It was clear: I was assigned as an RN staff nurse to this unit, the only staff nurse for the day with six patient names alongside mine. There was a licensed practical nurse (LPN) with the names of several other patients attached and another list of patient rooms and names on the chart with only one nurse named alongside. Obviously all the nurses listed for those patients were private duty nurses and there was no one in charge but myself for the day. The clerk said she hadn't seen the night nurse, who evidently had gone off duty without giving a report to anyone there. I asked the clerk to call the nursing director's office, and started looking at the chart of one of the patients I was supposedly assigned to care for. But where were the equipment, supplies, linens, and what about drugs?

Evidently there had been a mistake, the charge nurse had made out the assignment the day before unaware I was new to the hospital. The night nurse had been ill and left the hospital during the night after giving a report to the night supervisor, who covered for her, but had gone to the office momentarily. She was interrupted before she could come back to the floor to give a report to me, not realizing I didn't know the hospital procedures, or any of the patients. There were two aides assigned to the floor on nights, who had started morning care for patients at 6 a.m. taking vital signs, giving bedpans, and offering mouth care before the breakfast trays arrived. Doctors were making rounds. I didn't know who was who. I asked one of the aides who was about to leave for the day to please spend a few minutes with me; she showed me around until the supervisor arrived and apologized profusely. Little by little they all helped me and before long they were my friends. I survived and so did the patients on Klingenstein Seven.

It is interesting to note that during those days in 1954, the cost of care in a two-bed semi-private room, including general nursing care, was $18 a day, while a beautiful large single room in the Guggenheim Pavilion overlooking Central Park was $30 a day, including general nursing care around the clock. Medical interns earned $25 a month in those years, and about $100 when they became residents. Of course, they all received room and board and worked hundreds of hours a week.

I found myself working with some of the most famous physicians in the country at that time. Although Mt. Sinai Hospital did not have its own medical school in those days, graduate medical education was prominent there. A residency at Mt. Sinai was considered a prize, because the physicians were known all over the world for the most advanced techniques and the quality of their teaching.

The first unit I worked on was a gastrointestinal unit (GI) in Klingenstein Pavilion. Dr. B.B. Crohn had his patients all admitted to this floor. At that time Crohn's disease had not been differentiated from ulcerative colitis; most of these patients were young, primarily women, and referred from around the world for treatment by Dr. Crohn and Dr. Elster, his surgical partner. They functioned as a team. Many patients had been there for weeks for medical treatment, and finally, when remission could not be achieved, had surgical removal of the colon with resulting ileostomy, an opening from the small intestines to the abdominal wall through to the skin for removal of fecal material, the end products of digestion. This was very depressing for me, because so many patients were teenagers, or young adults like me.

My role was primarily to help the patient and the family understand the illness and to teach self-care to the patient or a family member. I would listen to their concerns and reinforce the physician's explanations. It was especially difficult to maintain the integrity of the skin around the ileostomy wound and to control the odor of the loose stools that continuously poured into a temporary plastic bag. This became a challenge for patients to deal with throughout their lives, which were often cut short due to complications in those days, and sometimes even today.

With "Dr. Nose" on his automobile license plate, Dr. Irving Goldman was a famous ear, nose, and throat (ENT) specialist, who treated the laryngitis and sinus problems of Broadway musical and Metropolitan Opera stars. Known as the "father" of rhinoplasty, Dr. Goldman (Dr. G) had developed the early techniques for correcting the deviated nasal septum that interferes with breathing and often leads to snoring and disfiguring of the profile. He was successful in improving the appearance of Broadway and Hollywood stars, such as Dean Martin and Perry Como. Patients also came to him from all over the country and the rest of the world, and I frequently found them on my Klingenstein unit. Although he himself had a nose like a "punch drunk fighter," his work was really beautiful.

Annually in July he presented a course for ENT and plastic surgeons from around the world who wanted to learn about the "Goldman Tip." Jokingly I asked him one day if he would be able to correct my septum and improve my nose. He promised to do the job as part of the international course if I helped him in his East 60th Street private office on Thursday evenings and Saturdays, when I was off duty at Mt. Sinai. Of course I accepted and actually enjoyed the office patients, and I learned how to remove nasal packing and exterior dressings painlessly, prepare patients for Dr. Goldman's postoperative examination, and reapply dressings. I was only too happy to take a week off in July for the surgery in the OR amphitheater during the course, without charge. To this day, I get compliments on my "Goldman nose" from ENT specialists I have seen for minor nose and ear problems.

In the Guggenheim private pavilion there were many interesting patients. I was working nights when Harold Rome, the composer of the Broadway musical *Fanny* (later made into a movie), spent more than a week in the hospital after surgery, taking sitz baths in his private room at night. This condition is less common today, since the importance of fiber in the diet was identified to prevent constipation, and supplements such as Metamucil were introduced. Surgery today is considered minor, an outpatient procedure, and rare. Mr. Rome was in one of those large private rooms overlooking Central Park. We had some wonderful conversations about his career whenever I responded to his request for pain medication. Before he was discharged he gave me two house seat tickets in the tenth row center for the show as a gift. It was a charming show and I appreciated the gift more when I learned I was the only nurse to receive those tickets.

Dr. Armand Hammer, president of Occidental Petroleum, later U.S. ambassador to the Soviet Union, spent weeks in one of those Central Park rooms with a view. I cannot remember his specific medical problem, but I do remember his complaints about the food, particularly about the frozen metallic-tasting orange juice the kitchen served in the morning. He had received a fruit bowl gift from a visitor so when I noticed two oranges in the bowl I called the kitchen and arranged for a small hand juicer, and squeezed and strained the juice for him myself. Later I brought in some more oranges, and every morning before I went off duty and gave a report, I made certain he had fresh squeezed orange juice while we discussed his progress and plans for follow-up care.

For weeks, I maintained continuous IVs with penicillin added for Dr. Ra-, Indian ambassador to the United Nations, who had a serious heart infection, SABE (sub-acute bacterial endocarditis). His wife, an Englishwoman, visited every day dressed in the most beautiful saris. While I was fixing the equipment for the IVs the three of us would talk about world affairs. There certainly was plenty to talk about. Even though there had been a ceasefire at the end of the Korean War, no formal peace agreement or armistice had been signed in 1953. When I became engaged, Mrs. Ra- gave me a beautiful silk jewelry case. It has been more than fifty years, and I still use that jewelry case when I travel.

I particularly enjoyed my teaching role with the aides and orderlies assigned to work with me at Mount Sinai. Since the hospital paid for advanced education after six months, I decided to go back to school part time. In the spring I continued to work nights from midnight to 8 a.m. at Mt. Sinai and enrolled in a graduate course at Teachers College, Columbia University (TC). My three-credit class, Education as Personal Development, met once a week from 7 to 10 p.m. I was able to walk down 5th Avenue to East 96th Street and take the bus cross-town to the

West Side to Broadway and then another bus to 120th Street. There were more than one hundred students in the class from the various TC educational programs; this was the first course required for all curricula. It was held in a large amphitheater in the Horace Mann Building. There was a lecture with handouts from a team of faculty, and then we were told to form small groups by rows of about 20 students and to just move around and find a way to turn to each other, select a leader and a recorder, and with guidelines discuss the questions raised during the lecture. I don't remember much about the content that semester. I was just thrilled to be in this historic hall. TC was the first school in the U.S. to develop a nursing certificate in 1899, and then a baccalaureate degree program for nurses in 1910. The goal was to develop hospital administrators and teachers. After class I had to rush to get the bus, cross Central Park at 96th Street, get to my room to shower and change into my starched white long-sleeved, high-collar uniform (almost down to my ankles), and report to my unit by 11:45 p.m.

Working nights had been an adjustment since I had never worked nights as a student, but I loved the challenge. Every night was a different adventure. I was the only staff registered nurse, assisted by a LPN and a nursing aide and, most nights, several older private duty nurses. I controlled the key to the drug closet and the narcotic box, so whenever a private duty nurse wanted pain medication she had to ask me. I got to know most of the nurses who were regulars, although many were not very friendly. They seemed to begrudge my questions about their patients.

I remember one nurse with a foreign accent who had a serious limp. She had been there for almost a week with a postsurgical patient and I tried to be friendly, but she seemed preoccupied and not interested in talking to me except when she wanted narcotic pain medication that had been ordered for every three to four hours immediately after surgery for her patient. In those days, morphine or Demerol was the most common narcotic given for pain. We had some individual 1-ml ampoules of morphine 15 mg, but Demerol was in a 30-ml multi-dose vial. One ml held 50 mg, and commonly patients were to receive 100 mg for one or two days after surgery. Usually the need for narcotics after surgery decreases by the third night, so there shouldn't be a need every three to four hours. I had to account for all the narcotics, which meant co-signing for the private duty nurses' use. One night, I noticed that the "unfriendly" nurse continued to request Demerol every three hours for her patient even though the patient had been there three nights. When I looked at the Narcotic book I noticed that the patient had only had one dose earlier on the day shift, and none on the evening shift, but had already had a dose earlier that night by this nurse. I was suspicious so I watched her more closely. She withdrew 2 ml of Demerol (100 mg) into a syringe in front of me and after signing the book, left the drug closet. I checked the book and noted that she reported giving him Demerol every three hours. I knocked on the door of her patient's room, but there was no answer, so I opened the door and saw the patient sleeping quietly, and the nurse was not in the room. I went to the utility room, pushed the door open and found the nurse giving herself the injection into her thigh. She looked up as the door opened but finished injecting herself without a word. I told her I had to report her and quickly left the room, went to the phone, and called the night supervisor. There was no further discussion when the supervisor arrived. The nurse didn't deny what she was doing. She was crying and claimed she was in a lot of pain in her hip caused by arthritis, but she never looked me straight in the eyes.

The private duty nurses registry was notified and the nurse was discharged. I think the attending physician would have been concerned if he had read the patient's chart where the nurse had noted that the patient was having continuing pain, and receiving administration of Demerol. I assumed responsibility for the patient, who was almost ready for discharge; he slept well the rest of the night. In the morning I wrote an incident report as best I could. I had no idea how long this nurse had been taking the narcotic. I did feel sorry for her; she probably lost her license as result of that incident. (Drug abuse in medical personnel is apparently more common than I suspected. It is a terrible reflection on the profession I love.)

Another night at Mt. Sinai sixty years ago stands out in my mind to this day. There was no intensive care unit in the hospital in those days, and as I mentioned the postoperative recovery room closed at 11 p.m. in the evening. It was not unusual to have fresh post-op and seriously ill patients requiring skilled nursing on my unit in Klingenstein or Guggenheim pavilions during the night early in the week, but actually most arranged for private duty nurses during the night. By the end of the week most of our patients were able to rest comfortably during the night. It was usually quiet, but one night the call light was flashing fiercely from a room with a private duty licensed practical nurse (LPN) caring for a gentleman in his late 50s who had had a prostatectomy early in the week. I ran into the room to see what the problem was. The patient, four days post-op, was just at the end of a grand mal seizure and the nurse, who had been taking care of him since the first night, was quite upset. The patient had been fine every other night under her care. He was quiet and breathing without difficulty, but his blood pressure was high. I only knew from report that he had had an uneventful elective prostatectomy on Monday and had been experiencing normal recovery. The report from the evening nurse had given no indication of any problems with the patient. I asked the nurse to show me the patient's chart. It was not unusual for private duty nurses to keep their charts in the room, so we looked through it together. The admitting medical history was extremely difficult to read; it had evidently been written by a foreign-born resident physician, although many of the American trained physicians did not write much better. With permission of the supervisor I called the resident physician on night duty and explained the incident. After he came and examined the patient, he read the chart and told us the patient had a history of epilepsy, and it was not unusual to have a seizure after surgery.

"It's here in the chart," he muttered and; pointed to the chart.

I looked, but still did not really see anything about epilepsy. I responded, "It's very hard to read this handwriting and there is no notation that the patient is receiving any anti-epileptic drug in the record. This private nurse has been with him since Monday night and no one reported to her that he has a history of epilepsy."

The resident left without writing any orders. Within the hour the patient had another seizure. I called the resident again; he fussed at me but said he would come back. While he was there the patient had another seizure, so he ordered something intramuscularly, I don't remember, but somehow I think it might have been "chloral hydrate." I prepared the injection and gave it to the patient. But it was not too long before he had another seizure.

I called the supervisor and requested permission to call the attending physician. She told me to first call the resident and tell him I was calling the attending physician. The resident was really upset, but I called the attending, since this was his private patient. I thought the patient might be having a cerebral embolism. The attending MD expressed appreciation and said he would come to the hospital as soon as he could get there. Unfortunately he did not live around the corner, and by the time he arrived, almost an hour later, the patient was dead. It might have been brain anoxia as a result of the seizure, or an embolism, but I never found out. I believed the resident physician was negligent, but I regretted not calling the attending earlier.

Many decades have passed, but I have never resolved my concerns about handwritten medical charting. The introduction in recent years of computerized data entry on electronic medical records is a very welcome advantage in facilitating communication among the health care team members, and is particularly important in preventing medical errors. That is not to say it is a perfect strategy. Patients often express frustration with the doctor or nurse giving the chart more attention than they do the patient.

Marriage

Working as a professional nurse at Mt. Sinai Hospital, at twenty one and anxious for romance I had never experienced, I was rushed into marriage to a handsome soldier, the first boy I had ever really dated. It was 1955, and all my high school friends were long married, pretty much the norm in those days. He was a son of a friend of my mother's cousin Minnie, whom I had met for the first time at a family wedding in the spring before I graduated from Adelphi. When Minnie asked if she could give a young man my phone number I agreed, but it was months before I heard from him. He had been drafted into the army after graduating from college two years before and spent the entire time in New Jersey. The Korean War was now over and while waiting for discharge he went home to the Bronx most weekends. We met for the first time just before I left for camp when he traveled by subway from the Bronx to our Brooklyn apartment. He called again in September and we went out once before I moved to Manhattan. Under Minnie's influence my parents were excited for me and joined into the welcoming conversation before we left the apartment to have dinner at Dubrow's, the local cafeteria on Kings Highway.

Gerry was trim and really good-looking in a sensual way, with dark hair and blue/grey eyes. He was quiet; he didn't have much to say except that he was looking forward to his discharge. I really didn't learn much about his interests other than sports. He had spent two years at New York University on a baseball and track scholarship, but found the training very demanding and realized his grades were affected. He had moved upstate to finish his degree majoring in history and political science. He had started graduate school at Fordham University, thinking about teaching history, but did not like it and dropped out, therefore accepting his draft notice. A few months later he came to Mt. Sinai to take me out again, but it was more of the same; he didn't know what he would do after discharge. Gerry called me frequently after that; somehow he had purchased an old car and managed to get away from Fort Dix often. I brought up the possibility of law school under the G.I. bill, and he expressed hesitant interest. I understood he had little money, so I wasn't expecting fancy dinners, flowers, dancing, or gifts, like the women received in the romance novels and Hollywood movies I loved, but I appreciated the attention. When he came to see me we often sat in the car parked on one of the side streets near the hospital and talked and "smooched." I wanted romance and thought that this was what romance was. I cannot remember anything special about Gerry except that he was a

Yankee fan; I was a Dodger fan and there was no competition between us since our teams were in different leagues. To be honest, I don't remember any interests in common; I don't think there were any except our desire for sex, although he was experienced and excited while I was petrified.

When I started working nights and attending Teachers College, Gerry began to put pressure on me. He decided to apply to law schools, but he had not taken the Law School Admission Test (LSAT). None of the New York schools would admit him without the test, so on some counselor's suggestion he applied to Boston University. He did not want to return home to the Bronx after discharge, and started talking about marriage as soon as he completed his military obligation. With hormones raging and no way to find out what it was all about without marriage, I agreed to become engaged, although I didn't know if it was love; we barely knew each other. My mother said he was a nice Jewish boy; my father was more alert and tried to get me to rethink the situation. He did not hear real interest in law school from Gerry, and told me so, "He has no goals and I don't think he wants to go back to school. I don't think he will amount to much." I was torn. I tried to back out but Gerry was insistent and wouldn't hear of a delay. He was adamant, he wanted marriage.

When my father took a short consulting position in Montreal, he called me to fly up there for a weekend to be able to discuss the situation and he sent me the airfare. Gerry was supposed to be on duty at Fort Dix that weekend, so I made the flight arrangement. When I got to the airport, Gerry was standing there; he had obtained a pass and bought a ticket to travel with me. I was in shock when I saw him but could not stop him from getting on the flight. He was adamant and I could not warn my father. Needless to say, Gerry managed to get a separate room, and I slept in my father's room on the second single bed. But there was nothing else my father could say. "Maybe if Gerry is so determined to get married he might be as determined to go to law school and become an attorney first, but wait a year," he advised.

Meanwhile, when we returned to New York my mother was insistent the wedding plans were set and it would be costly to cancel or postpone the lovely reception in the Manhattan hotel I wanted. "How could we return engagement gifts?" she asked. Also, she was superstitious, telling me it would be bad luck and I might not meet such a nice-looking boy so fast. She ruled and the marriage took place, but not until September after I had the necessary surgery recommended by the GYN resident two years before at Meadowbrook. And not until I had visited the mikvah, the traditional orthodox Jewish ritual of an immersion bath with blessings in Hebrew before I was married so I could have "kosher sex" as insisted upon by my mother. The obligation for satisfying sexual relations is discussed in the Talmud. I was the only one of my Jewish friends to fulfill this obligation to attend the mikvah before marriage.

Teaching at Massachusetts General Hospital

I gave up my job and we moved to Boston, where Gerry entered law school and I started teaching fundamentals of nursing and pharmacology in the diploma program at Massachusetts General Hospital (MGH). MGH has a long history of excellence; it was one of the first hospitals (1821) and one of the first training schools of nursing established in the United States (1873). With all the history in the city I found Boston and MGH in particular exciting and I loved my position on the faculty. There were 90 students in the first-year course, so lectures were in a large auditorium with clinical skills demonstrated within a model of a patient care unit at the front of the room. Then in small groups of ten, students practiced procedures with individual faculty supervising in laboratory rooms furnished with hospital beds and other necessary equipment. Everything was extremely well organized with procedure manuals and performance checklists; my role as an instructor was very clear. The environment was friendly and supportive in the school and throughout the hospital when we took students to meet patients as part of their orientation and initial nursing care opportunities. When in the second semester I was assigned to lecture to the large group, the outlines were clear and precise, giving me confidence in my ability to do a good job.

The MGH students were selected from applicants across the country: bright, enthusiastic and appreciative of their opportunity to attend the highly rated MGH program. Some had been valedictorians of their high school classes, or had earned some college credits, although college was not required to attend the three-year diploma program I was teaching in. There was an entirely separate abbreviated program leading to the R.N. certificate and a master of nursing degree for applicants who already had a college degree.

Gerry and I struggled from the beginning, emotionally, intellectually, and financially. I thought he should be studying; he watched sports on TV. His monthly $75 G.I. bill paid the rent, and my weekly $55 salary before taxes was supposed to cover everything else. We ate into our cash wedding gifts for a few pieces of furniture to fill our studio apartment. There wasn't much left for the law school tuition the second semester, and Gerry's father refused to offer assistance again for tuition, so at twenty two, I cashed in the $500 John Hancock life insurance policy my parents had been paying 50 cents a week for twenty years; I resented it fiercely, but there was no choice. I did not want to ask my parents for the money and we had no other source of savings. There were no credit cards in those days.

Pregnancy and the Birth of Melissa

Married sex wasn't what I thought it would be; I was still uncomfortable, draining a bit from the premarital surgery, and I was not comfortable with the birth control method we used. Six months later, experiencing nausea and vomiting and certain it was due to something I had eaten in the hospital cafeteria, I went to the employee clinic. To my horror the diagnosis was morning sickness caused by pregnancy. Gerry did not believe me; he expressed suspicion. "What the hell have you been doing at work?" he asked. I cried for days when he demanded the pregnancy be terminated somehow. This was the beginning of the lack of trust he had in me throughout our marriage. He told me one of his married classmates, also in school on the G.I. bill and with a three-year old child, had decided they could not afford another child and found abortion the answer. But I refused; abortion was not an option for me. It was illegal and dangerous. I had seen enough botched self-induced or "back of the drugstore" outcomes to know I could never take that chance.

Meanwhile as the weeks went by and I was busy at work while he was struggling in school, I became optimistic, thinking somehow the baby would bring new purpose to our relationship. The anticipation of the addition to our family provided the first real pleasure in our life together for me, but the stress continued. While I was enjoying my teaching role very much, my friend Georgette, who was married to one of Gerry's classmates, told me that when the small law school study group met after classes in their apartment near the University, Gerry rarely participated. She told me, "He sneaks into our bedroom and watches TV while the other boys are reviewing and discussing the questions raised during class." When the grades were posted at the end of May, Gerry had not done well enough in school to continue and was put on probation and required to repeat the whole year in the fall. I was devastated; he made excuses – it was not his fault he said. I did not know whose fault it was, but I was five months pregnant, and he had not been working part-time as some of the other boys did; he could not seem to find a part-time job.

With the summer off from school Gerry needed to work to increase our income, but when he could not find a temporary job in Boston he decided to look outside the city at the summer resort areas. He finally found a live-in temporary position as an assistant chef at the Mayflower Hotel in Rockport, Maine. He had some experience working in the restaurant/bar owned by his father's family in the Bronx. The interview was held in Boston, and when he was accepted, I drove him to Rockport and we looked for a room in a guest house nearby so I could come to Rockport on weekends. I was supervising students on the medical units in the hospital from 8 a.m. to 4 p.m. all week and was uncomfortable as the pregnancy progressed. I needed to get away from the intense summer heat of Boston. The heat was just as bad as in New York and there was no central air conditioning anyplace. I was forced to buy a window air conditioner for our studio apartment because I could not sleep and would not be able to keep working all summer without cool air. It was peaceful for me home alone, but the conflicts continued between Gerry and me.

The first weekend I arrived at the hotel tired and hungry Friday night after being on my feet all day and the long drive, only to find that he had made no arrangement for supper for me. Here he was working in the hotel kitchen, had dinner earlier with the staff, but never thought to make a sandwich or prepare a plate for me for dinner. There was nothing close by the hotel so we drove about 20 miles to a diner I had passed near the highway for a hamburger. On Saturday, when I met the head chef, I could not help but ask if I might be able to eat with the staff. "Of course," he said, and then continued, "Gerry, why didn't you tell me you had such a beautiful wife?" I had never heard those words from Gerry and I do not remember his ever telling me I was beautiful before or after that day. I thought what a fool I had been.

My friends at work hosted a lovely baby shower for us, and both sets of parents were ecstatic about becoming grandparents for the first time. They were particularly thrilled that I planned for the birth in New York at Mt. Sinai since my due date was around the time of Gerry's mid-year examinations the following semester. I continued to teach fundamentals of nursing for the new class that entered in the fall at MGH, but requested eight weeks of maternity leave after our Christmas holiday. Unfortunately I was only entitled to three weeks of paid leave. We decided it would be best for me to spend the first two weeks after delivery at my parents' apartment in Brooklyn while Gerry studied in Boston.

The labor and delivery were relatively easy with the commonly used "twilight sleep" I received for pain. The baby was really beautiful, with a head of dark hair and a rounded chubby face lit up by large dark eyes. We agreed to name her in Hebrew after my two grandmothers, Miriam, my mother's mother who had passed away the previous year, and Esther, after my father's mother who died in Europe, several years after I was born; I had never met her. Because we wanted a more modern American name, she became Melissa Ellen. I planned to return to work within a few weeks so I chose not to breastfeed, a common preference of most young women in those years. Melissa was a good baby once she adjusted to the formula feeding, and by virtue of my student nurse experiences I was prepared for the normal postpartum discomforts. Fortunately my mother and father, who were still working, were also able to take leave to stay home with us; it was easier for me having their help.

I had arranged with the director of the nursing program for a change in teaching schedule when I returned to Boston and moved to the evening shift, where I supervised second-year students in the Bullfinch and White buildings. Gerry went to school from 9 a.m. to noon, and with my help in the beginning, took care of the baby while I worked evenings, 4 to 12 p.m. Unfortunately it did not help the relationship when I came home tired from being on my feet for eight hours, only to find his supper dishes still on the table and the piled-up dirty cloth diapers he refused to rinse smelling in the bathroom. He did seem to be able to feed her and put her to sleep without problems in the evening. I fed her when I came home from work and in the middle of the night, and bathed her in the morning.

When the school asked me to develop a special four-week course in pharmacology for three mornings each week that would enable LPNs in the hospital to administer medications, I gladly accepted the offer, anxious for the extra money. It was the first of many part-time work assignments I assumed in order to pay the bills throughout my life. Fortunately, I was able to arrange with my friend Georgette, the wife of Gerry's classmate, who was on maternity leave but not working, to care for Melissa along with her own baby, Stephanie. The girls were born a week apart and Georgette never did go back to work during the years her husband was in school. It was not easy, but as Melissa's personality began to develop and she smiled and seemed to appreciate my voice, I overlooked Gerry's negative attitude toward school. He was not really interested anymore in studying law and was unhappy with our whole situation. When, after two years, his grades were still not good enough to continue, I cried and bemoaned my fate. Gerry still did not know what he wanted to do in his life, and although I had tried to be optimistic, he never, ever, really found his niche.

Return to New York – Teaching at Lutheran Medical Center

One day soon after a bitter fight, I returned to New York with Melissa, begging my parents for help. I asked them to find a larger apartment so Melissa and I could live with them and I could return to teaching. I could afford a babysitter while I worked but not the cost of rent and utilities and transportation. My parents had always worked, supported, and respected each other, communicating their love for my brother and me in many ways, and that was what I expected in marriage. I did not feel that respect and support from Gerry, and I did not respect him; I wanted out of this marriage. My father was not surprised, but my religious mother said, "*You have a child, you have responsibility, it is a shonda*" (a Yiddish word for disgrace), so when my husband arrived making promises to get a job quickly in New York and to try school again in the evenings I gave in, while knowing for sure I did not love him.

Understanding I couldn't afford to support myself and the baby on a nursing salary alone since there was no group day care for infants in those days, I gave Gerry a reprieve. We moved to a three-room garden apartment near the Shore Parkway in Brooklyn, where later we watched the construction of the Verrazano Bridge to Staten Island. With the help of the superintendent of the apartment complex I hired an experienced nanny for Melissa and searched for a teaching position nearby. I found success at the diploma school of nursing of the Norwegian Lutheran Deaconess Home and Hospital, later named the Lutheran Medical Center (LMC). Gerry found a job with an insurance company, not telling the manager he had failed out, but that he was going to continue law school at night, and we moved ahead. New York Law School admitted him provisionally, but required he take the LSAT. When I had recommended he prepare for the exam with available study guides, he insisted he had the two years of preparation in Boston. He took the exam, but his score was unacceptable for admission. That was finally the end of my dream of law school for Gerry.

The Lutheran Medical Center School was a small program with about 100 students and five faculty members. During the first year students traveled in the afternoons by subway to Long Island University for their basic science and liberal arts courses and learned fundamentals of nursing (now called Nursing Arts) in the morning in the classroom and practice laboratory. I was the medical/surgical nursing instructor in the classroom and in the hospital across the street for the second-year students. During the second year of the program, attending physicians lectured in the afternoons on diagnosis, pathology, and treatment for common medical problems of body systems followed by my nursing care lectures. In the morning, after 7 a.m. chapel in the hospital and hymns sung on the front balcony of the second floor, students were assigned to patient care in the hospital under my supervision. As much as I enjoyed my work at MGH, I think I felt more at home at Lutheran Medical Center; it was a smaller and a more intimate atmosphere. I loved the warmth and caring of the Lutheran Sisters who lived in the nurses' residence and sometimes cared for Melissa when I was teaching on days that the nanny couldn't make it to my apartment. One Sister would sit at the back of the classroom during my lectures holding Melissa. If Melissa got restless, the Sister moved to a rocking chair to feed her and then put her to nap in the demonstration crib in the nursing arts laboratory. On Friday afternoons the Sisters would come to my office and remind me to stop grading papers or working on lesson plans to go home for my Jewish Sabbath, which was usually at my parents' apartment, where Gerry would meet us for dinner. Then during Passover the cafeteria manager put a box of matzos in the dining room for me as the only Jewish staff person in the hospital. But so many others wanted to taste the matzo, a few extra boxes were needed and before long matzo was standard on the bread tray year-round; everyone loved New York–made Manishevitz matzos.

The faculty role at LMC included rotation for coverage of administration on weekends and holidays when service staff were limited in the ER, Pharmacy, OR, and the Blood Bank. For example, it meant covering in the ER when there were multiple admissions following major accidents; filling emergency prescriptions because the pharmacy closed at noon on Saturdays and Sundays; serving as circulating nurse or scrubbing in during multiple emergency surgeries, and running three blocks to St. Elizabeth Obstetrical Hospital where the Blood Bank was located to obtain required blood for transfusions. Because the hospital was close to the Brooklyn waterfront, accidents and injuries were frequent and serious. It seemed as though there was always at least one crisis on my once-a-month weekend assignment challenging every possible brain cell in my body; there was no one else to call upon for help. Some how I had the courage to do the best I could at the time, although I anguished before and after I acted.

Cultural Diversity

There were challenges in dealing with students. Coming from religious sheltered families, frequently in small rural areas, many of the students were not prepared for independence. They had their first chance at freedom and to rebel against strict codes in seeking companionship, sometimes with the foreign-born medical residents at the hospital or in the bars around the corner. A few married and left the program when they got pregnant, some were able to go home, but most chose to stay at Lutheran, married or not, where they received warm support from staff including the elderly Sisters. We arranged for a student maternity uniform and prenatal care. Knowledge about family planning was limited in those days, but it was clear that the topic needed to be integrated somehow early in the program. While the school was supported partially by a Lutheran Church Foundation, not all students were from Lutheran backgrounds, and those varied from fundamentalist to more liberal Christian philosophies, including a few Catholics. With much diversity among students and faculty in spiritual and ethnic backgrounds, I believed I needed consultation with a Lutheran pastor. Fortunately a young minister had recently joined the hospital staff for pastoral counseling. Finally the broad topic of cultural sensitivity came to a head over one incident.

It started one day when the Nursing Arts instructor was ill, and I had to cover for her in a skills lab on hair washing for patients on long bed rest, where the students were assigned to practice on each other. Shampooing in bed is a simple procedure with pitchers and bowls and a large plastic sheet and bath towels. As a student at Adelphi I learned the procedure through a demonstration in class on Mrs. Chase, a life-sized doll with a washable wig; we did not practice on each other. Practice was left to an actual patient care experience later in the hospital. At MGH students observed the procedure on a volunteer and then drew straws to decide which student would be the patient and which the nurse to practice in teams. At LMC practice on each other was a requirement for all, for all nursing procedures!

At the beginning of the class the two African American students, the first who had ever been admitted to the school, came up to me and asked to be excused. They said they spent a lot of money to straighten their hair professionally and it would all be ruined if their hair were to be washed during the class. They had a method for dry shampoo they used in between professional visits. When the class was over they had to leave and take the train to Long Island University for anatomy and physiology and chemistry classes, so they would not have time to fix their hair. I didn't hesitate to excuse them. I had never done the procedure as a student, and only half the MGH students did the procedure on a fellow student, so evidently the experience wasn't critical. I asked the students to stay and observe the lab, and mentioned that if I explained to the class the circumstances and expressed this as a learning experience about the needs of patients from diverse cultures, all the students would benefit.

Unfortunately when the Nursing Arts instructor returned the next day she was livid. "The two students will have to make up the experience as soon as I can arrange it, or fail the class," she said. It seems all nursing procedures had always been practiced on fellow students at LMC, including bed baths, intramuscular injections, and enemas, even with the bathroom being a flight of stairs up! None of these were done at Adelphi or at MGH. The Nursing Arts instructor was a graduate of the LMC School and had never worked anywhere else, which was not unusual at most diploma programs then, and, with the shortages of faculty, still common in many nursing programs today. Teachers in every field tend to teach the way they were taught unless they had advanced education and /or varying experiences.

I informed the program director, and the issue was brought to the Director of Nursing, who was also new to the hospital and the school. A special faculty meeting was called immediately where the discussion moved to the overall issue of student practice on fellow students. The vote was not close: the obstetrics, pediatrics, and psychiatry instructors joined me and the Director of Nursing in voting to eliminate almost all the practice on fellow students, leaving only the procedures for back rub and bed making with a patient on bed rest. Those procedures were a lot of fun to practice.

I had believed most of our students were Lutheran, but that was not the case; we had a few Catholic, Presbyterian, Methodist students, and a few nonbelievers, although they often confessed their parents did not know. I knew little of the fundamentalist or liberal beliefs among Protestant denominations, still less of those within the various synods of the Lutheran church. While I had some academic preparation for this general issue as an Adelphi student, I certainly needed a refresher course.

One day a few students came to me complaining of the prejudice they experienced, of having been told they wouldn't be "saved." It seems they did not want to attend the student organized "confraternity" session on Wednesday evenings. I still had much to learn about my own faith so I asked the program director for help. Since all students would be taking care of all kinds of patients during their nursing education and beyond, the students needed some specific instruction, particularly because the local neighborhood was changing. The majority population around the hospital had previously had Scandinavian backgrounds as families of the seamen who came into the port of New York. Recently a good number of residents, and therefore hospitalized patients, were Hispanic, primarily Catholic from Puerto Rico.

I was advised to contact the young Lutheran pastor who had recently arrived at the hospital; the elderly Sisters thought he was wonderful. We arranged for the pastor to come to the next faculty meeting to discuss how he might help us develop a broad cultural diversity program, as well as offer individualized counseling.

Graduate Studies

During my first year at LMC I realized I wanted to continue with graduate studies towards a master's degree, an ambition that was supported by the Director for the next year. Nursing education was changing with the introduction of the Associate Degree program in community colleges in response to the recommendations of the Brown Report in 1948 to move nursing out of the hospital training schools and into higher educational settings. In 1958, with released time from my teaching responsibilities one afternoon a week, I enrolled at Teachers College for the course *Curriculum Problems in Pre-service Nursing Education Programs in Institutions of Higher Education*, which focused on the Brown Report, and Dr. Mildred Montag's Doctoral Study of the Nursing Technician and the Associate Degree (A.D.). This was a two-year academic program proposed to replace the nine- to twelve-month practical nurse programs instituted in the emergency during World War II to meet the immediate nursing shortage, and to eliminate the three-year hospital-based diploma programs. It had been Dr. Montag's assumption that closure of the three-year hospital diploma programs would occur across the country, and a separate examination would be prepared for the new A.D. graduates who would be called Technical Nurses. Only the graduates of the four-year baccalaureate programs would be considered professional nurses. That never happened: hospital programs closed and the Associate Degree programs exploded, but a separate examination for the "Technical Nurse" was never instituted. Graduates of two-, three-, and four-year programs have been taking the same licensing examination, leading to the title Professional Nurse.

Despite the American Nurses Association calling for the baccalaureate degree as **minimal** professional education for nurses in 1965, and every year since, a majority of nurses practicing in the hospitals across the country today (more than sixty percent) are associate degree graduates with some older nurses still diploma educated. This debate has continued into the 21st century.

The goals and the objectives of the two- and the four-year programs are not the same. Primarily, the extent of general liberal arts and science content as pre-professional education is greater in the four-year program, where professional focus is on patient, family, and community assessment and management. Critical thinking, independent and collaborative problem-solving for individuals and groups in the community, and health policy are major concepts initiated in the upper division of the baccalaureate program to be expanded during graduate education. In recent years nursing care outcome studies in hospitals have shown that the costs and quality of patient care benefit from staffing with higher levels of nursing education. As a result, the jobs for new A.D. graduates have dwindled and post–A.D. programs toward the baccalaureate degree have proliferated across the country, especially with the development and expansion of online independent study.

While still teaching at the Lutheran Medical Center in the spring of 1959, I took the graduate course *Health Problems of Society and Their Implications for Nursing*. This course opened a whole new world for me of scientific advances that were impacting the practice of medicine and subsequently, the development of new roles for nursing focused on greater independent responsibilities for patients with complex health problems. During the 1950s there were many medical advances with the introduction of new antibiotics and other drugs, new surgical procedures, and especially improvement in cardiovascular health diagnostic and treatment methods. Critical care nursing evolved from the recognition that patients with acute, life-threatening illness or injury could be better treated if they were grouped into specific areas of the hospital, preferably close to the nursing station. The monitoring of mechanically ventilated patients proved to be more efficient and beneficial to patient outcomes when patients were grouped in a single location, and multiple health professions (medicine, nursing, respiratory therapy, physical therapy, pharmacy, etc.) were able to communicate and collaborate. Thus, the

Health Care Team was established where specially trained nurses assumed monitoring responsibilities previously held by physicians, and managed complex patient care 24 hours a day, seven days a week. The need for expanded responsibilities for nurses led to the establishment of the clinical specialist role as Critical Care Nursing Units soon became more specialized, particularly for Coronary Care, neurology and surgery.

I was excited by the new advances and anxious for more experiences, motivated to move ahead with my graduate studies, but I could not possibly pay for continuing courses by myself. While my father had given me the money to take the first two Columbia courses, I couldn't ask him to do more. Fortunately, in view of the need to improve the quality of faculty education in nursing at that time, the federal government had introduced the Nurse Traineeship Program. I applied and received the fellowship that included full tuition and a $250 monthly stipend for books and cost of living. I wanted to move out of Brooklyn to Long Island, and buy a small house so Melissa could have space to play outside, and I could see flowers and birds again. I was determined to work even harder to save as much money as possible.

During the 1959–60 academic years, while I worked at LMC part-time and attended graduate school, I also took on additional tutoring responsibilities for small groups of trained foreign-born nurses seeking U.S. professional nursing licensure. They were brought to this country primarily from England, Ireland, and the Philippines to work temporarily in New York City hospitals, where there were serious shortages of qualified experienced nurses. This role was quite different from my previous teaching; the nurses were very rigid in their attitudes toward patients and had difficulty with the multiple-choice question format of the testing; they were trained to think only the way they had been taught. I learned a lot about the psychology of learning in the process and was forced to be creative with teaching strategies, all of which was part of my academic program at TC.

A wonderful general education course I took that year influenced me greatly. The course, *Education and Society*, reviewed the history of higher education in the U.S. and brought attention to the political conflicts of the time, especially the negative factors related to segregation. In 1954 the Supreme Court had ruled that separation of races in schools did not provide equal opportunity for African-Americans. Dr. Martin Luther King and others began intensive efforts to promote Civil rights across the country, particularly in the South.

I attended classes two days of the week and had related clinical experiences two days a week. In the fall I traveled by subway to Columbia's Presbyterian Hospital on the Upper West Side of Manhattan, where I was on the *Cardiovascular Medical Team* making rounds with a large group of physicians and medical students, discussing patients with diverse cardiovascular conditions. In the spring it was necessary to take the car to reach Montifiore Hospital in the Bronx, where I was on the *Neurology Team*, and again making rounds with physicians and nurses. I was particularly impressed with the work of Dr. Lydia Hall, an adjunct nursing faculty member at TC, who had developed the Loeb Center at Montifiore, a step-down "Primary Care" nursing unit where professional nurses managed the care for patients, twenty four hours a day/seven days a week. (This concept is receiving new attention under the health care reform efforts.) Meanwhile all of our required references were the classic medical journals and textbooks developed by physician authors and used by medical students. It was within that atmosphere that I learned "how doctors think," which was the key to developing my ability to study and work interprofessionally with physicians.

I was able to carry fourteen credits each of the two semesters to complete my graduate degree. Melissa was enrolled in a full-time day care program at "Happy Town" Nursery School near the hospital during the year and she thrived. By the time I received the Master of Arts degree in the spring of 1960, I had changed. I knew nursing was not just a job for me; I knew it would be my career for life, even as I planned to expand our family. I realized I couldn't depend on my husband financially to provide the style of living I dreamed of, and I couldn't depend on him emotionally to make me happy. It would all be up to me.

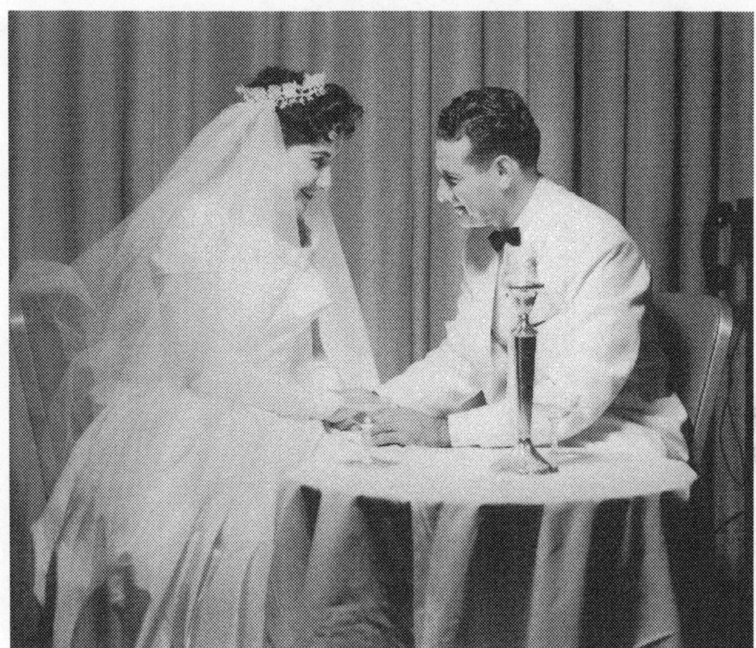

Gerald Fields and I were married September 4, 1955 in New York City. We moved to Boston and I was appointed as instructor in the basic diploma nursing program at Massachusetts General Hospital.

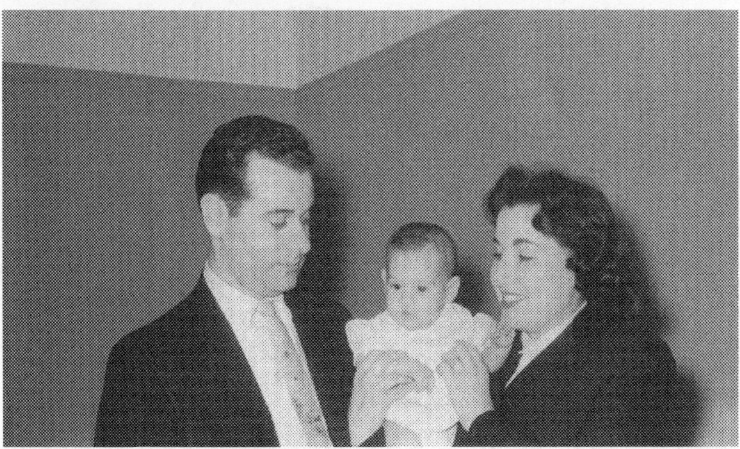

Melissa Ellen Fields was born January 17 1957; she is seen as an infant with Gerald and I in Boston, where I returned to teaching at Massachusetts General Hospital after a very brief maternity leave.

Melissa at three years of age with my mother, (Frieda Kleiman) in front of our Brooklyn apartment house on East 13th Street. Grandma made the matching coat and hat by hand for Melissa who carries a purse similar to grandma's and wears her favorite "Mary Jane" shoes to match grandma.

I receive the Master of Arts (MA) degree from Columbia University Teachers College, May 1960, majoring in Nursing Education with a focus on Curriculum & Teaching. I worked three part-time jobs and was supported by Federal Cardiovascular Nursing Advancement funds. I stand proudly with my parents.

4

Becoming a Nurse Educator in Academic Programs

"Every baby deserves to be wanted"

Our Own Home

Gerry had been working the past two years as an adjuster for an auto insurance company and I did not anticipate more graduate studies at Teachers College Columbia University at that time. Despite continuing reservations, I tried to let go of my anger over Gerry's failure in law school and arrogant attitude, hoping he would stop blaming everyone else, including me, when things did not go his way.

I felt good about myself, and adored my baby. Melissa, who seemed so mature after being in nursery school for a year, was truly a joy. So I compromised over my disappointment in Gerry and hoped he would "grow up." Now I wanted very much to save the marriage so Melissa could have stability. All our friends were moving out of apartments and into private homes and planning for more children. Gerry loved Melissa too and we decided together to give her a sibling. I was pregnant and due at the end of the year. With the family about to expand, we needed more space than our small three-room apartment and I wanted to get out of Brooklyn.

Despite Gerry's concern about the long commute to his job in Brooklyn, I was smitten with a gorgeous house we had found just off Round Swamp Road in the middle of Long Island. At $21,000, the house we selected was more beautiful and less expensive than several houses we had seen closer to New York City; I felt as if Gerry owed it to me and I could not give it up. I had worked very hard the previous two years, and managed to save more than $2,000 from my living expense stipend for extra expenses. My dream for a private home with a front porch and trees and flowers all around came true in June 1960. With financial help from our families for the down payment, we moved into a new two-story Colonial home with three bedrooms and two and a half baths in Old Bethpage.

In retrospect buying that house then was a mistake; we were naive. We should have waited until we had saved more money. Having never owned a home before, neither one of us, nor our parents, had any idea of the real cost of that move: the taxes, the utilities, insurance, furnishing, and maintenance. Together with the commuting, the expenses were more than we could really afford on Gerry's salary alone. I knew I would have to work but that was OK with me; I loved my work. I was optimistic, knowing I could always find extra part-time nursing work in the nearby hospital and hoped he would figure out how to advance in his career for the sake of our family. Unfortunately that never happened and the financial difficulties persisted throughout our marriage.

Gerry never settled successfully into something he really enjoyed, but moved from one thing to another searching for something else. He was miserable about the commute and angry when he did not get the salary increase he expected. At a friend's suggestion he took a course one evening a week to prepare for licensure as a general insurance agent, but despite the repeated fees and three attempts, he could not pass the licensure exam. I could not understand it.

All too often we just did not see things in the same way; our goals and interests were clearly different. I wanted a home with flowers, books, and music, and a spot in the world, while Gerry would have been satisfied in an apartment in the Bronx watching sports on TV. We clashed when there was so much to be done to maintain the house and yard.

As my neighbors began to move in around the new house, I learned that almost all of them were stay-at-home moms, or at least would be soon. There was only room for one car in most of the garages, including ours. The Women's Movement was just beginning to rustle and the debates about women's professional options and child-rearing conflicts had not yet taken place, except in my head. *Cosmopolitan* magazine wasn't in every suburban woman's mailbox and "the pill" had not been fully accepted, especially by the Catholic women, who represented most of my neighbors. I was conflicted; I wanted a happy family with children and yet I also knew I wanted a professional career.

In my European-born family all the women worked outside the home in some capacity to help support the family, and some of the men shared in the household responsibilities in partnerships with their wives. My father fulfilled his religious prayer responsibility early in the morning, and then made his own breakfast and cleaned up his dishes before he left for work. It was what I was brought up with; I saw it as natural. But my husband was one of three sons; his mother and aunts did not work outside the home. Before marriage Gerry had never been asked to help at home; his mother waited on her husband and smothered her boys, requiring no responsibility from them at home. For Gerry and me, our expectations of each other's contributions to the family did not match and I resented it. I fought my battles hopelessly for the next twenty years.

We were not in the Old Bethpage house but a few weeks when my mother called with a special request. It was during the Cold War, and the revolution in Cuba under Castro had turned the country into a socialist dictatorship, pushing the U.S. and the Soviet Union to the brink of nuclear war over the Cuban Missile Crisis. Thousands of Cubans, with or without family support, left the country, in most cases with little more than the clothes on their backs and what they could pack in one suitcase. Such was the situation for the children of my mother's aunt and uncle, Chana and Moshe Katz, who had left Europe in the early 1920s and immigrated to Cuba when, due to the U.S. quotas, they were unable to enter the United States like most of the extended family.

The younger family, Bella and Sol – with two teen-agers, David and Sarah – had lost their Cuban business and home and arrived in New

York with the hope of support from the family and the organized Jewish community until they could be re-established with jobs and a place to live. The elderly parents stayed in Cuba. As applications were being processed, the younger Katz family needed a place to stay right away, but just temporarily. At the prospect of parents visiting, I had bought a sofa bed instead of a couch for the family room of our new house, so I figured that we could manage to bed the entire Cuban family in our home if we could borrow two camping cots. We asked our neighbors if anyone had such beds, and the Giambalvos next door did not hesitate. The cots were delivered immediately, together with the necessary extra linens, pillows, and lightweight blankets. Our Cuban family moved in and stayed for almost three weeks. Melissa was enthralled with her older cousins, who made a big fuss over her.

It was quite a challenge; while the children spoke fairly good English, the adults spoke very little and my high school Spanish was minimal; Gerry did not know much more than me, and he wasn't happy about the intrusion. Shopping for food together with our guests was truly an intercultural experience; we all learned to expand our vocabularies and food preferences. I never was much of a cook – my specialty was broiling and I knew nothing more about seasoning than salt, pepper, and Hungarian paprika for a recipe for chicken, mushrooms and rice. Peppers in any color were not in my families' vocabulary since my father's gastric ulcer years before. Bella was a great cook, and we all enjoyed some of her meals. Unfortunately, other than bananas, many of the fruits and vegetables common to Cubans were not on the local grocery shelves. At that time there were very few Hispanics in the area. When the family was relocated to Florida by a Jewish social network, we were sorry to see them go. My mother maintained contact with them for several years, even visiting together in Florida. She reported that they were all adjusting well and had given up any thoughts of returning to Cuba.

I lost contact with them, and with my mother long gone, I have no idea where they are today, or if they are even alive. Recently, however, I visited Cuba on a People to People tour and met a leader of the Jewish community in a Havana synagogue. I was thrilled to learn he had lived next door to the Katz family, who were close friends of his parents. He knew my family well and confirmed that the elders of the Katz family had died and that Bella and Sol never returned to Cuba.

Andrew's Birth

Our son Andrew was born at Long Island Jewish Hospital on my husband's birthday early in December 1960 during a heavy snowstorm. It was a long and difficult labor and delivery due to the baby's position, and I was exhausted, and found sitting painful for months afterward. I came home from the hospital after a few days to rest and to be with Melissa alone, while the baby stayed in the hospital until after the *bris* (the ritual circumcision), traditionally done for Jewish male babies on the eighth day after birth. When we finally brought Andrew home and showed him to Melissa, who was now almost four years old, her face lit up with a big smile. She couldn't wait to hold him, and he seemed to look right up at her. It was clear theirs was going to be a special relationship (which it has been for more than fifty years.) And to make it even better for Melissa, a neighbor brought a gift for her, a tiny kitten, black with a small patch of white on his forehead and one toe. We named him Midnight, and he was amazingly smart. He lived with us for more than fifteen years.

When I tell people about Midnight, they can't believe how smart he was. For example, on sunny days I put Andrew in the carriage on the front porch and Midnight sat next to the carriage for hours. As soon as the carriage began to move, before the baby even started to cry, Midnight began to meow and scratch at the front door. As the children grew, Midnight would go down to the corner and wait for the school bus with them. Then he would parade around the neighborhood all day until the children returned, when he would wait once again at the corner. He would come in and sit with them in the family room until dinner when he would clean out his food bowl and then sneak upstairs to one of the beds until bedtime. If someone accidentally closed the basement door where his litter box was, and no one responded to his meowing to go outside, he would go upstairs to the bathroom with a tub, and do his business in there, which was much easier to clean up afterwards. "How come you didn't really potty train him better?" friends asked.

Teaching at Queens College

When Andrew was nine months old, I returned to teaching, this time in the Associate Degree Nursing (ADN) program at Queens College in Flushing, New York. I hired a lovely young French-Canadian au pair one month before to live with us and take care of the children while I worked. Ginette had already become part of our family when I started teaching adult health nursing for senior students in the two-year program. Every Sunday morning I drove her to the Catholic Church in Plainview for mass, and most time after church she went with us to visit our parents in Brooklyn or the Bronx. Ginette's English improved quickly and we all loved her. All Gerry's friends kidded him about the beautiful young girl living in our house. (I didn't particularly like the insinuations; I wanted to be considered the beautiful young woman in that house.)

I felt prepared for the new teaching responsibility by virtue of the last two semesters of my master's degree program at Columbia. The learning objectives and teaching strategies were different from those in the diploma nursing programs, with fewer lectures and more active student-centered small groups, both in the classroom and the clinical area. Most of the students were motivated and academically prepared, but the older, married students were for the most part superior. Some had started nursing programs right out of high school years before and dropped out to marry and have families. They were more serious and highly motivated. In several cases their spouses were no longer able to support the families due to the economic downturn at the time and the women needed to gain employment rapidly. In other cases the children were in school and now the mother could be out of the house with a career goal promising financial security. Through life experience as independent learners and creative problem solvers, the older women adapted quickly to the concept of the Nursing Process, the professional method for developing nursing care plans. They also knew how to express empathy for patients under their care and served as role models in independent learning for the younger students. I believe that is why so many of the ADN students were able to pass the professional licensing examinations after only two years of study.

Two days a week I was assigned to the Long Island Jewish Hospital, then a relatively new and very busy acute care facility in New Hyde Park, just over the Nassau County line. I was teaching Adult Health nursing, which focused on medical and surgical problems. It was a great learning opportunity for students since all kinds of patient experiences were available. I had to arrive early in the morning or drive to the hospital after classes at the College the day before to select patients and prepare for pre-conference. Later, after the patient care experience, we had post-conferences to review and expand the learning experience.

Advances in medicine were happening so quickly during those years; I learned procedures and new techniques that I had not seen before, along with the students. Fortunately the staff nurses and resident physicians were friendly and helpful to me, offering demonstrations of new equipment and procedures, and explaining rationale for treatment. While I loved my position, the days were long and the commuting on the Northern State Parkway was very difficult. I do not know how I would have done it without Ginette at home.

Teaching Maternal Child Health Nursing at Farmingdale

Two years later, when I learned a small new Associate Degree Nursing program had opened at the New York State Agricultural and Technological College in Farmingdale, ten minutes from my home, I changed positions. The school had not been able to recruit a master's prepared faculty member in Maternal Child Health; there were only two other faculty members at Farmingdale as the program was just beginning, and neither of them had the advanced clinical background in obstetrics or personal experience with childbearing that I had. I accepted the position and returned to graduate school one afternoon a week to become academically prepared for teaching Maternal Child Health (MCH) nursing. I quickly ordered the appropriate textbook, gathered and reviewed recommended references, and studied the important concepts and content I needed to know.

Prevention has always been an important concept integrated throughout the nursing curriculum, but it was especially important in the MCH program I was planning. I started with a quick review of anatomy and physiology, and an introduction to genetics, family planning, and prenatal care. In order to give more attention to this concept, I arranged a field trip for my students to the offices of Planned Parenthood (PP) in Mineola Inc., a private, non-profit community agency. Planned Parenthood was at that time one of the few or perhaps the sole provider of family planning and prenatal care for low-income or uninsured women in Nassau County. In those years abortion was illegal, always a secret, and dangerous. The major goal of the PP organization was to provide family planning education, prevent illegal abortions, and support healthy babies. Unfortunately at that time the high incidence of abortion was one of the major causes of maternal mortality in this country. The political battles over reform and repeal of abortion laws were just beginning across the country.

There were three young nuns (novices) in my MCH class from the Rockville Centre Diocese, dressed as was the custom in those days, in full black habits to the floor. They wore large caps that covered their hair firmly around the face, with two large wings on the sides. But on the day of the field trip to PP I looked around the room to make certain all the students had come and noticed that there were five nuns in full Christian dress. "Oh my God," I thought, "I'm going to be reprimanded, or maybe even fired."

The presentation was excellent. There was a review of anatomy and physiology of the menstrual cycle, ovulation, and implantation, and demonstration of family planning methods currently available; the students asked some very good questions. The Nurse Director also stressed the issue of prevention in regard to illegal abortion, emphasizing the legal and ethical aspects and how common and dangerous the illegal procedure was. With advances in prenatal and maternity care, most of the maternal mortality rates at that time were primarily due to illegal abortions. When the class was over and the students began to leave, the five nuns came up to me at the front of the room. One of the students introduced the Mother Superior of the convent and her assistant. I must have looked very pale; I wasn't sure what was going to be said. To my surprise, the Mother Superior smiled and said, "Mrs. Fields, I hope you don't mind my coming today. When I was a student at Mary Immaculate Hospital years ago, a faculty member took us to Margaret Sanger Clinic in Manhattan, and I was certain there is much more known today about natural and other birth control methods and I just wanted to know what was new." You can imagine how relieved I was to hear those words. But then, to top it all, several weeks later, one of the young novice students submitted, with the Mother Superior's permission, an entry into the Planned Parenthood annual essay contest for college students. The title of her essay was, "Every Baby Deserves to Be Wanted." That beautiful young woman won first prize and an award of $100. She read her essay at the Awards Dinner a few weeks later, with the Mother Superior attending.

I had the choice of taking students for clinical experiences to Nassau County Medical Center, formerly Meadowbrook Hospital, where I had had my unhappy maternity course ten years before, or to Southside Hospital, a Suffolk County non-profit community hospital in Bayshore, a drive of about thirty minutes east from Farmingdale. When I went to Southside Hospital to explore the teaching possibility ahead of the students, it was clear to me this was a much more positive learning experience than I had had as a student. The social environment in this region was conducive to establishing new families; many were Catholic. Most of the babies born at Southside were wanted, maybe not actually planned, but since there was no county prenatal clinic, the Bayshore regional physicians took most low-income mothers into their practices and provided prenatal care, delivery, and postpartum care, perhaps on credit. As a result many pregnancy complications I had seen in earlier years at Meadowbrook were prevented or identified and treated early. In the hospital new mothers chatted away happily and babies were for the most part taken home to welcoming families.

The Southside Hospital nursing staff and practicing physicians welcomed me and my students, but my schedule was very difficult. There were forty eight students admitted to our program at Farmingdale, annually. In the fall semester I had twenty four students in my class, divided into two groups of twelve for clinical days from 8 a.m. to 12:30 p.m. Students were rotated through the labor, delivery, nursery, and postpartum units; I supervised all with the help of staff nurses. On Mondays and Wednesdays I had Group A clinically and on Tuesdays and Thursdays, Group B clinically. On Tuesdays from 2 to 4 p.m., I had Lecture/Conference for group A students, and on Wednesdays from 2 to 4 p.m., I had Group B students for Lecture/Conference back at Farmingdale. I had the entire class of twenty four students together on Fridays from 9 to 11 a.m. During the spring semester I had the same routine for the other twenty four students. My fall class of twenty four students took the Child Health/Pediatrics course with Miss Horiuchi, the pediatric instructor, under the same class schedule.

Only a few months after I started at Farmingdale came the terrible tragedy of President John Kennedy's assassination. I remember hearing the news on the car radio while driving home from Southside Hospital on the afternoon of November 22, 1963, just before Thanksgiving. I ran into the house where the kids were watching TV shouting, "We have to change the channel quick because the President was shot." Andrew was not yet three years old, but Melissa was old enough to understand; she remembers that day with me. It was a terrible day. I did not know how to explain it to the children. Why would anyone want to kill this wonderful president? There was talk of a Russian or Cuban conspiracy, but nothing else came out. Two days later we watched TV again together when we heard they had arrested the president's killer. Right in front of our eyes, Jack Ruby, evidently distraught over Kennedy's murder, shot the supposed assassin, Lee Harvey Oswald. It was not a TV drama, it was the real thing. I will never forget that day.

Teaching at Farmingdale had many advantages beyond the proximity to my home; the campus had a long history as an agricultural and technical college. There was a large farm with domestic animals that created products available for purchase by faculty and staff, according to the curricula. The cows grazed the land and then provided milk, cream, and butter for minimal cost. We paid 30 cents for a half-gallon of milk that was always available, as were eggs from the dozens of free-range chickens in open pens, and when the food technology students were at the place in their program to make butter and cheeses, we could buy the "crème of the crop" very inexpensively. There were also pigs providing bacon and sausage and apple trees for apple pies during the year according to the curriculum.

The campus was also a great place to take visiting children, which I frequently did. When my brother Norman came from Texas with his four children and stayed with us, it was the first place they wanted to visit. Once when we were all gathered standing and watching at the fence around a huge sow feeding her brood of tiny piglets, we heard this terrible screeching sound. Suddenly one of the children cried out, "Look, there's a baby pig stuck under the mama." In a flash Super Daddy Norman jumped over the six-foot fence and pushed hard at the sow, grabbed hold of the piglet, and pulled until it was free. We all started to laugh and applaud, and the kids couldn't wait to tell the story to whomever they could. Later, when my mother gave three-year-old Elizabeth a picture book about the animals on a farm, she ran to me and said, "Look Mommy, a college, a college." (She couldn't understand why we started to laugh.)

In addition to my assigned Maternal Child Health course, I was asked to develop and teach a three-credit-hour interdisciplinary course for non-nursing students that I simply entitled Child, Family, and Community Health. Students in the Associate Degree Programs, *Nursery Education*, *Police Science*, and *Recreation Assistant* curricula participated on Monday afternoons. I remember that this was a mixed gender course; all the dental hygiene students were female, the police science students were male, and the recreation science students evenly divided. I made attendance required, but it was a pass/fail course with minimal written evaluation strategies. I really didn't have the time to spend marking papers and giving competitive grades. The course content was divided into units starting with health and then common illness by ages and body systems. The students selected areas of interest and formed groups to research and present to the class. They also taught each other about their individual professions, responsibilities, and requirements and discussed interests in common. It was a fun course for all of us and the beginning of my interest in teaching health concepts such as prevention and collaboration to interprofessional groups of students.

Vietnam and the 1960s

Not much later, the war in Vietnam began as a result of the Gulf of Tonkin Resolution in 1964 and escalated with bombing missions of North Vietnam and then Cambodia. Protests against the war were seen in most cities across the country, especially on college campuses where students, faced with the draft, were most vulnerable. However, there were no protests at SUNY Farmingdale, where many students were the proud children and grandchildren of Long Island's World War veterans and the American Legion had a strong base. Patriotic sentiment in favor of fighting for one's country contrasted sharply with refusals to fight, draft evasion, and flight to Canada; these passions divided families, friends, neighbors, and the military itself.

In the spring of 1968 things were not going well in Vietnam and the war seemed much closer to us at SUNY Farmingdale. The nursing and dental hygiene programs were housed in a brick building above the College Health Center, where Rose Schwarz, the nurse director of the clinic, had the radio on all day listening for news from Vietnam. Her son Laurence was a young Marine lieutenant caught in the seventy-seven--day siege of the U.S. Marine base at Khe Sanh during the Tet Offensive between January and July 1968. Every day, as we passed the clinic entering and leaving the building, students and faculty would ask Rose, "Have you heard from Laurence?" She didn't hear anything for a long time. While fortunately Rose's son, although injured, did ultimately survive, more than 700 U.S. Marines were killed, and over 2,500 were wounded during that offensive.

Many of us were questioning why we were in this war in the first place. We kept hearing about the protests all across the country, especially on the college campuses. Little by little as reports of massacres of unarmed civilians by U.S. forces came out, the moral and ethical debates in the media became wider. My son Andrew was only seven years old, but I was thinking about Rose and how I would deal with the situation if he were old enough to be drafted to fight in a war such as Vietnam. Laurence had had a deferment until, at twenty two years old, he graduated from Syracuse University. Rose told me that against her objections he had decided to enlist in the Marines, rather than wait for his draft call into the infantry, because he believed he would be safer with the Marines, who were the "best."

At home one night after watching some terrible news, I muttered, "If this damned war continues over the next ten years, when Andrew is called up, I won't let him go, I'll take him to Canada."

"No you won't," my husband shouted, "he will meet his responsibility and serve his time like I did."

I shouted back, "During the Korean War you got a deferment from the draft to finish college and then again to enroll in graduate school. Then you dropped out of graduate school and accepted the draft as soon as it looked like the War was over. You never left New Jersey. What do you know about fighting in a war?" I don't know why I didn't keep my mouth shut, but I was exhausted, fed up with his arrogance and lack of empathy.

The philosophical and political differences between Gerry and me were never resolved, but we had everyday issues to deal with managing the household and our young beautiful children, who provided us with a common bond. There were school lessons, piano lessons, the children's friends in and out, holidays, and family get-togethers. Our parents loved those children so much they wanted to see us whenever possible, so we traveled often on weekends or holidays to Brooklyn, where the kids loved my mother's chicken soup with homemade noodles, or the Bronx, where Gerry's father and his family had a restaurant/bar. It was a big treat there because the kids could have shrimp cocktails free. I kept a kosher kitchen so shrimp wasn't possible and it was considered too expensive if we ever went out to a restaurant to eat on an occasion, which was rare until McDonald's came to Plainview/Old Bethpage. Meanwhile our house was large enough for holiday dinners so as the extended family expanded, there was room for cousins to play inside and outside – there was a lot of fun to be had all around. When possible we would grill outside and everyone was happy. My mother would measure the children as they grew and made matching clothes for them. Looking from the outside in, ours was a normal family life, but of course it was not so normal for the time.

After Ginette decided to return to Canada, the stress over child care was a major problem when I was working. No one could seem to match her temperament, character, and work ethic. There was a revolving door each year for live-in nannies. Initially the young women came from overseas, which brought a unique set of problems. Then we had a few older women who came from the South. (They were the best cooks.) However, it is hard not to get involved personally with domestic help when they are living in the house. It was difficult to find local child care workers since public transportation was limited in our suburban neighborhood; there were no buses in the area. The "help" had to be driven to church on Sundays, like I did for Ginette, to the mall for shopping or the movies, or to the train station for travel to New York City.

After Ginette, Margaret came from Ireland. She had a friend who worked for one of my friends close by, which we thought would be great; we would share the transportation on Sundays to the railroad station so the girls could travel to see the sights of New York City. Unfortunately, after several months the girls were more interested in socializing and it wasn't long before they got into trouble. They were supposed to be back to Hicksville before 10 p.m. and to call to be picked up at the train station. But at 11 p.m., when neither my friend nor I had received the call, we called the Nassau County police. About 1 a.m. I received a call from the New York City police asking if Margaret Smith worked for me. After acknowledging the situation, the police agreed to send the girls home by car with one of the policemen who lived in Nassau County. Margaret arrived back home, somewhat disoriented, make-up messed, black eyes, hair unkempt, and clothes all rumpled. Margaret and her friend insisted they were frightened but all right and refused medical attention. The girls were unable to give clear descriptions of the "guys" who had taken their money and dropped them at the train station. I never got the whole story, but the police said the employment agency had to be notified. Within a few weeks both girls were sent back to Ireland. I found the next nanny through a Jewish newspaper ad seen by my mother. Bracha was a Yemenite Jewish girl from Israel. She was a live wire and the kids really liked her. They learned to speak some Hebrew and to sing and dance to traditional Hebrew songs. Bracha spent most of her free weekends in Brooklyn, where she had a close family friend who was married to a young American doctor. Things went fairly well for about a year until one Sunday morning she woke up with abdominal pain. I gave her some Mylanta, but when the pain persisted I drove her to the nearest hospital. But it was a small private hospital and Bracha had no insurance. The pain was getting worse, so suspecting it might be her appendix; I drove her to Long Island Jewish Hospital, a thirty- to forty-minute drive. The physicians in the emergency room confirmed it was appendicitis and declared she needed immediate surgery, but said they could not admit her since they were full and there was no bed for her. I could not believe my ears; I ranted and raved as they arranged for surgery at North Shore Community Hospital nearby, but I had to drive her in my car the short distance. The staff surgeon was waiting for her so she was carried quickly by stretcher from the ER to the OR. Bracha was a very sick girl by the time of surgery. I must say she was treated very well, staying more than a week under their care. Since North Shore is a non-profit hospital affiliated with Cornell University–New York Hospital, there was no charge for the surgery (probably done by a resident in training), and through social services the hospital bill was paid on an extended plan over six months. I did help with that bill. Bracha's Brooklyn friends came to take her home with them for follow-up care. Of course I had to hire someone temporarily so I could continue to work. It took weeks for Bracha to heal and then she decided she wanted to go home to Israel, so I was back to the nanny search.

When I had a third child, Elizabeth, and needed to go back to work soon after, it became even more difficult to manage the household. For a few weeks I tried a young woman from South America, but the language barrier was too much for us. Gerry was having difficulty in his latest work endeavor in the investment field and we were both tense over the finances, which probably affected the baby; she cried and cried and none of us at home could seem to comfort her. There was still no day care for infants available yet. (My mother was working again and couldn't help as she had when Melissa was a baby; Gerry's mother was much too nervous, she would have driven us all crazy.) Fortunately, one of my close friends, Fran Hourigan, a stay-at-home mother of four school-aged children, offered to take care of the baby temporarily until I found someone to help at home. I bundled Elizabeth with all her equipment and drove her to Fran's house, where she stayed all day until I came to pick her up after work. Elizabeth, who soon became Lizzie, with her big dark eyes and little round face, was really the cutest little doll you could ever imagine. All the kids loved her and Fran was magical; Lizzie became a happy baby for several months at the Hourigan house.

Some people wondered why I had had the third child; I was the maternal child health instructor who preached family planning, but I really wanted Lizzie. Although I was the experienced medical and surgical nurse and teacher, I had been teaching maternal child health nursing for two years, and I think I just got the maternal urge again. Unfortunately there were other problems associated with my unanticipated pregnancy. There was a SUNY policy at the time that required a pregnant faculty member to take *unpaid maternity leave* by the fifth month, but the school needed me to teach, so I received a temporary full-time appointment without benefits and worked until two days before giving birth. I returned to work three weeks later although still on the "no benefits" maternity leave for three months until the semester was over. Years later, when I retired I discovered that I had messed up my pension. I only received credit for fourteen years and six months instead of the fifteen years required for full pension. The SUNY policy requiring maternity leave was legally challenged in the 1980s by women faculty across the state, but I was not included in the class action; I did not have the $1,000 required for participation at the time. I was completely prepared for what turned out to be the easiest delivery I had had. Elizabeth weighed only six pounds and I received a "para-cervical block," which meant I was fully awake, with little discomfort, and watched her birth in the overhead mirror. I was so thrilled with the experience I could not wait to tell my mother what a wonderful delivery I had and how excited I was to accomplish what I called "natural childbirth." The exhilaration I had was what I had read about in the literature but had never personally experienced before. My mother, who had had two difficult deliveries, thought I was crazy.

While the salary for live-in domestic help was reasonable, there were always other expenses. We were supposed to provide some benefits such as health insurance and social security, but I confess I never could afford it. It was years later that we heard of professional women denied important government appointments because it was revealed they had not provided social security for child care or household assistance. To this day, the "nanny" issue remains a critical problem for most working mothers, especially single mothers, in this country. Fortunately we see much more involvement of fathers in child care and household responsibilities today when both parents are working than was seen in past years. Within my own family today all the young men share responsibilities; they cook, do the food shopping, change diapers, and take over bedtime bath and reading routines.

Meanwhile just after Elizabeth was born, still searching for his niche, Gerry found an opportunity as an intern with an investment brokerage firm for six months at $50 a week while training. It was very difficult; I had had to return to work too quickly. After the internship Gerry had to earn his salary completely through commissions; he bitched and complained and failed to understand when friends and family members who were potential clients refused to change their brokers. If I hadn't been working as hard as I did, we would have lost the house.

While Gerry was struggling to gain clients for his investment business, he kept looking for something else. Around this time during the mid-1960s, President Johnson introduced legislation in Congress that became known as the War on Poverty. Medicare and Medicaid funding were introduced under the Social Security Program to assist with the health care needs of senior citizens, the disabled, and families with incomes below the federal poverty level. Although there was a long history of public "alms houses" for the aged, their reputation for quality of care was very poor. Once the opportunity for federal support was made possible, the private business sector began to build skilled nursing homes and assisted living for long-term care, and the need for qualified health care administrators became very evident. When a new two-year Health Care Administration program was opened at C.W. Post College on Long Island with classes held in the evening and on weekends, Gerry applied. Fortunately there were no required objective type examinations for admission and progression (which were his weakness), and I could help him write essay papers. After he finished the program he was able to quickly get an assistant nursing home director position at a new facility on Staten Island developed by a family member of mine. It sounded like a great opportunity. Gerry was never happy with that position either; the commute was even longer than to Brooklyn and soon there were clashes over personality and ethical issues at work I did not understand. The conflicts continued as the years went by until Gerry found another position at a large hospital in Manhattan.

The stress of the household management and child care continued, so I finally gave up on the live-in au pair policy. Through a local employment agency I found Eula, a gentle soft-spoken black woman in her early thirties, who worked Monday through Friday. She was married but had no children, and lived close by in Farmingdale where her husband worked at Republic Aircraft. Eula drove her own car and was able to come in the morning when I had to leave for work or school and stayed until I came home. She prepared a simple dinner, did the laundry, maintained the housekeeping, and kept the children at peace, although she was not able to help them with school work; that remained my full responsibility. The children respected Eula and she loved them as though they were her own. Eula was with us for about ten years. She saved my life.

Despite the success of many professional women who raise children concurrently today, the child care issue in this country, especially for single mothers, remains a significant barrier to "having it all." The stories of social benefits provided to new mothers in other developed countries around the world are heartwarming, but with all due respect to Sheryl Sandberg, CEO of Facebook, who advises women "to be more ambitious, aim high, recognize the strengths they bring to the work place, have more self-confidence," the Women at Work debate continues. Most of us did not then and most women today still do not have enough support at home. We all feel guilty about "short-changing" our children when we have significant careers without family support and secure child care. Somehow my children survived and probably benefited but it is never easy. If I was in Congress you can be sure I would be fighting for humanistic social benefits for new parents, and family caregivers for dependents, children, handicapped and the elderly.

As much as I loved the house, the extra space, the greenery and enjoyed my teaching at Farmingdale, living in suburbia was definitely intellectually limiting. The world all around was shaking. In addition to the Cold War tensions, demands for racial equality, civil rights protests, assassinations, another Israeli war, among many other traumatic events such as the escalating conflict in Vietnam, the Women's Movement was coming closer to me. I realized I should consider more long-term career options for myself. In 1968 I decided to return to school to begin doctoral studies.

Gerald Fields, Melissa age 3, and I move into my dream house in Old Bethpage, Long Island, New York June 1960.

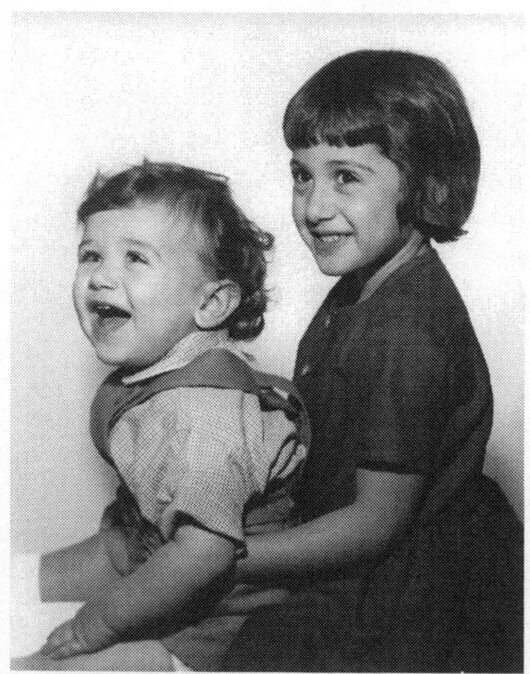

Andrew Gregory Fields was born on his father's birthday, December 7, 1960. I return to teaching Medical Surgical Nursing at Queens College, an Associate Degree Nursing Program in September 1961. Melissa (age 5) and Andrew on his first birthday.

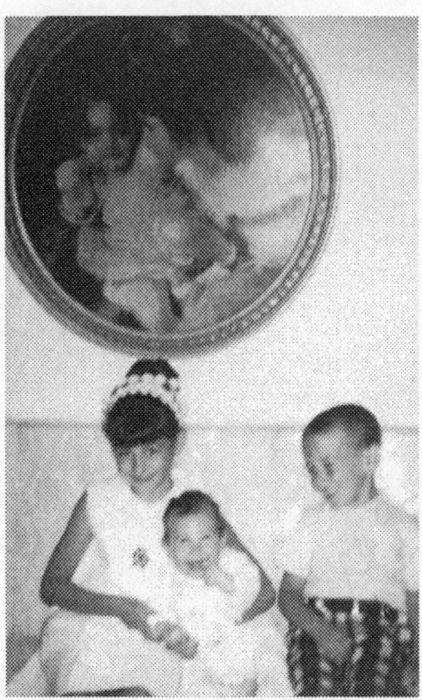

Elizabeth Carrie Fields joins the family February 7, 1965 pictured with Andrew (age 4) and Melissa (age 8). After a three week maternity leave, I return to work teaching maternal child health nursing at SUNY Farmingdale, NY 10 minutes from our house.

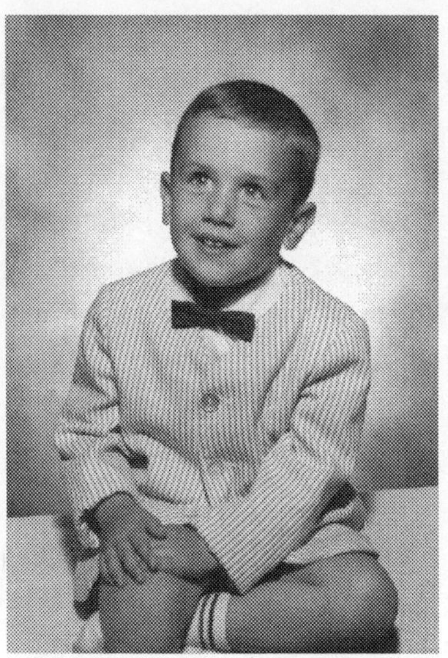

Andrew, about four years of age

5

Returning to Columbia University for Maternal Child Health Studies

"THE BASIC EDUCATION FOR A PROFESSIONAL NURSE SHOULD BE THE BACCALAUREATE DEGREE"

DOCTORAL STUDIES DURING THE VIETNAM WAR

In 1965 the American Nurses Association recommended that the baccalaureate degree become the initial entry into professional nursing. Unfortunately that recommendation went nowhere. There were still many hospital diploma programs but they were slowly closing and being replaced by the new two-year A.D. programs that offered the preferred quick entry into the profession rather than the four-year baccalaureate degree. There was much controversy about this trend, and unfortunately it continues today – in 2012, reports from the Institute of Medicine led to a fresh mandate for improved education for the nursing profession. Although some of the two-year graduates had had previous life experience or college credits prior to entry into the new shorter programs, most were admitted as new high school graduates and despite their ability to pass the required written licensing examinations at the end of their two-year programs, their liberal arts background was inadequate as preparation for expanded professional roles in primary, tertiary, and community health. Many of us in academia and nursing service administration were concerned then (and to this day) that this limited general education preparation decreased the full potential of the nursing profession.

Indeed, most professions, such as medicine, dentistry, and law, require the baccalaureate degree for admission to their education programs.

I knew advancement for me, whether at Farmingdale or elsewhere, would require further education toward the doctoral degree. When my application to Teachers College at Columbia University was accepted and the federal traineeship granting tuition and a $250 monthly stipend for living expenses was awarded, I felt energized again. I disregarded the objections at home and quickly requested an educational leave from SUNY for the academic year 1968–69.

Since I was on a ten-month contract and Gerry's income was still inadequate to cover all our expenses if I did not work, I took a position as camp nurse so my children would have a rich outdoor educational and creative experience, and we all could be away from the heat of the house, where the only room with air conditioning was the master bedroom. Despite the hard work, I was earning $1,000 for the summer including all our living expenses. My husband stayed home, worked in the city, and came to camp for the weekends and his two-week vacation, where he helped coach several sports. No matter how hard I worked during the week, without him, it was a vacation for me.

Throughout the mid to late 1960s the Columbia University campus was a hub of political activity and unrest, like a number of other large university campuses, such as the University of California at Berkeley and Michigan. There were teach-ins, rallies against the Vietnam War, demonstrations against class rank reporting (universities had been required to report grades and student rank within each class to the draft boards to determine deferments) to the Selective Service Boards, and confrontations with military recruiters. Columbia's geographic location in upper Manhattan on the edge of Harlem intensified underlying factors, including attitudes of the Columbia faculty, the administration and the trustees' prior handling of controversial student issues, especially problems involving increasingly politically active black students. At Columbia, as at other universities, students' opinions normally covered the entire spectrum of political life. However, the University had begun construction on a new gymnasium in city-owned Morningside Park, which created tension among local government officials, community groups, and students who saw the University expansion into the public park as restricting access to local community members and a form of racial segregation. The daily television and radio reports of the protests by student groups, such as Students for a Democratic Society (SDS), and the Society for African-American Students (SAS), were very disturbing. When SDS and SAS students took over University buildings despite the president's ban on indoor protests, the administration stood tough, and despite attempts for negotiation by an ad-hoc faculty group, ultimately a 1,000 police were called to intervene. With the resignation of Columbia's President, an impartial fact-finding commission was appointed to investigate the disturbances in April and May of 1968, led by Harvard law professor Archibald Cox. Faults were found all around; many students were disciplined and/or suspended; various recommendations were made for and by the student and faculty groups and by the Cox Commission. Some students never resumed their education at Columbia. When the Cox Commission Report, "Crisis at Columbia," was published soon after I arrived on the campus in the fall of 1968, the campus and the world were still not peaceful, despite peace talks taking place in Paris to conclude the Vietnam War.

While I had been thrilled about returning to school at Columbia, all the political activities on the main campus made it even more exciting and challenging. The conflicts at home continued as I was exposed to the demonstrators still active at Columbia. I could associate with the long-haired "hippies" walking barefoot across the campus, although I was sure they were not all current students. One day I had to go to the print shop on Broadway and 116th Street to pick up a box with multiple copies of a survey questionnaire I had prepared for one of my classes that day. I walked out of the shop with difficulty managing my briefcase and the large box when one of the young men with long straggly hair sitting at a card table collecting signatures for a current protest saw me struggling. He got up (barefoot), came over to me, took the box from my hands, and said, "Ma'am, I'm a Southern gentleman, I cannot stand to see you struggling; where are we taking this box?"

I said, "Main Hall on 120th Street."

"It's my pleasure, and just what is in this great box?" he asked.

"It's a questionnaire I'm distributing asking student opinions about the most important problems facing nursing education today, particularly about the role of professional nursing in health care delivery," I said.

And he responded, "That's not the problem we're having, we know what the students think, but administration doesn't want to hear student opinions on this campus."

When I told the story to my family at dinner that night, my husband's reaction was hostile: "Why were you talking to them, they're all just a bunch of drug addicts, homos, and freeloaders."

I had quite an adjustment in returning to school, but it wasn't the academic work, it was the commuting. It is amazing how easy it is to forget the difficulty in traveling from Long Island into New York City. I had arranged my classes to limit the travel days necessary, but no matter which way I went the trip was stressful and expensive, including a couple of traffic accidents that were not my fault.

I had a full program of six courses that fall, including the academic work in Maternal Child Health Nursing I had been anxiously awaiting. However, the most important course I took that semester was Dr. Eleanor Lambertsen's *Advanced Study of Professional Nursing Problems.* It was impossible with all the events around us not to see that the professional nursing role was changing within the whole world picture, particularly due to the Vietnam War protests and the rise of the civil rights movement. For sure I was changed after my 1968–69 year at Columbia.

Throughout history advances in nursing have been tied to wars and the impact of wars on the armed forces and the caretakers; the 1960s Vietnam War was no exception. In addition to the introduction of Medicare and Medicaid under President Johnson's leadership to assist seniors, the handicapped, and low-income families, other proposed but controversial changes were taking place within the health system and professions in response to the national shortages of primary care physicians and specialty trained nurses, as well as the needs of returning medical service personnel. At the same time that care in the veteran's hospitals for the large number of American casualties in Vietnam was being criticized, veterans who had served as corpsmen or medics in the fields of Vietnam were coming home with skills they were unable to use in civilian life due to legislated requirements. It was also clear that there was unequal access not only to primary care for citizens, but to educational opportunities in the health professions for African Americans, Hispanics, and Native Americans.

The first short-term Physician's Assistant (PA) program had been established at Duke University by Dr. Eugene Stead, Jr., in 1965 primarily for Navy corpsmen. Concurrently the first Pediatric Nurse Practitioner (PNP) program was started that year at the University of Colorado by Dr. Loretta Ford, a nurse, and Dr. Henry Silver, a physician. By 1967 the first graduates of the certificate programs were demonstrating their ability to expand and extend their skills. Pediatric nurse practitioners were practicing in pediatric community health settings and hospitals independently, while the physician's assistants were working closely with physicians in their offices and the hospital. Slowly both programs established increased requirements for admission and became baccalaureate and later graduate programs.

In Dr. Lambertsen's class conflicts grew over the proposed expanded nursing roles; some nurses claimed the nurse practitioners would be playing "mini doctor" and were no longer nurses. There were also concerns about competition across the disciplines and resentment over the possible higher salaries projected for the PAs as well as the potential conflict if nurses would have to follow orders given by the PA. The negative attitudes toward the nurses' expanding professional skills disturbed me.

I was excited for the potential ability of nurses to have input into health care decisions and demonstrate the value of their input. The nurse practitioner concept really stimulated me, but at that time I was not ready to think about making changes in my professional plan; I preferred to support the concepts of collaboration and cooperation. I loved teaching and under the influence of Dr. Montag, I was hoping to enter into administration, so I continued with my planned teaching/administrative/curriculum focus in Associate Degree Nursing during the spring semester.

The traineeship I received supported a full-time schedule over two semesters. It was a content-packed program and it needed my full attention. Fortunately, I was able to schedule my classes, independent clinical study projects, and library work so that travel into the city was necessary on only two or three days a week. This flexibility meant I could spend more time with my children. The dining room table was spread with books, journals, reprints, and legal-sized pages of handwritten notes, which were then translated into papers to be typed upstairs on my old Royal Portable without automatic correction; thank heaven for "white-out."

As I look back to that year, I realize how much I was also influenced by another faculty member, Dr. Maxine Greene, Professor of Philosophy of Education. Her course, *The Arts and American Education*, was a multidisciplinary examination of social, racial, and feminist issues, educational philosophy, and imaginative literature, which prompted me to take a deeper look at my own life. For Greene, the arts, specifically imaginative literature, rather than systematic philosophy and theory, were the sources of social and educational thought. It was in this course that I was exposed again to the humanities (literature, music, and art) and in-depth social sciences in relation to the role of the professional nurse. Among our many readings for discussion were *Moby Dick, The Invisible Man* by Ralph Ellison, as well as the controversial *Autobiography of Malcolm X,* and *Children of Crisis* by Robert Coles, MD, published under the heading *Conscience of the City* by the journal *Daedalus.*

Dr. Greene emphasized that the ultimate purpose of education was to help students and their teachers create meaning in their lives. That is, education ideally awakens teachers and their students to the personal and cultural possibilities and challenges that life offers. Greene stated, "My goal is to challenge the taken-for-granted, the frozen and the bound and the restricted." According to Greene, "Education is a process of teaching people to explore ideas about themselves and the world in which we live, to ask questions about this experience called living, to embrace ambiguity, to notice the unusual without fear, and to look upon the ordinary with new eyes." I swallowed everything Dr. Greene said during this class and found her writing in subsequent publications continuously challenging. Her message was that we needed to somehow include the humanities throughout professional education. "There are works of art; works deliberately created to move people to critical awareness, to a sense of moral agency, and to a conscious engagement with the world." Dr. Maxine Greene, who passed away in May of 2014 at the age of 96, helped open my mind and influenced creativity in my research and teaching throughout my career.

As I review my TC transcript I see that there were other courses that had a lifelong impact; I could write an entire text on the impact of just this academic year. Although it's hard for me to describe the specific content of the coursework in *Humanistic Psychology*, an advanced psychology course, I believe it was in that course that I was first introduced to Abraham Maslow's Hierarchy of Needs Theory and the development of humanistic psychology as a positive way to understand human behavior. Maslow focuses on human needs, beginning with the most necessary to maintain life: 1) physiological needs; air, water, food, sleep and sex and other individual fundamental needs; 2) safety and security needs; 3) love and belonging needs; 4) self-esteem needs; 5) self-actualization. This was a long distance from the Freudian psychology emphasized in earlier courses when I was an undergraduate at Adelphi and during my mental health nursing experience at Creedmoor State Hospital.

When Melissa's Girl Scout troop leader announced that she was going back to teaching and couldn't do the job alone any longer, I agreed to join her as a co-leader for that semester; it was fun for both of us. Of course, the girls would not be doing much camping with me, but the "first-aid" badge had to come first. I know they learned a lot as we expanded that badge into a baby-sitting preparation project with my little Elizabeth as a model. And then, because I wanted to include some cultural activities, we rented a bus one Saturday and took the troop (including Andrew and a few other younger siblings) to see a play on Broadway. There was no special badge associated with the experience, but it was great fun for the girls! Gerry would not let me leave three-year old Elizabeth home with him, so she had to come with us to the theatre. Unfortunately she was too young to sit through the show; I had to take her out of the theatre and we walked the streets, but when she had enough walking and wanted me to carry her, we hopped on a city bus and rode around until it was time to get back to the theatre. Then, when all the children were safely in their seats on the rented bus for the return ride, we started singing songs, and Lizzie slept all the way back home.

My parents dancing at their 40th wedding anniversary celebration.

The immediate family with author's brother Norman at the celebration.

Melissa (11), Andrew (7), and Elizabeth (3), always more like best friends than siblings.

Andrew at his Bar Mitzvah cutting cake with my brother Norman.

6

Teaching Women's Health and Supporting Abortion Law Repeal

Every Baby Deserves to be Wanted II

Advances in Maternal Child Health Nursing in the spring of 1969 focused on significant changes in philosophy from previous teachings, particularly about women's roles in society including the issues surrounding health, sexuality, and control of our bodies. Concepts in maternity and child care were undergoing dramatic changes from my experience as a student in the early 1950s, when few mothers breastfed their babies. As part of the early revolution, women were being taught to know their own bodies: to understand the menstrual cycle and timing of ovulation in order to promote fertility and/or to prevent unplanned pregnancy, to use condoms to prevent venereal disease, to get Pap smears for early identification of cervical cancer, and to do self breast examinations for cancer prevention. Women were demanding more humanistic care from their health care providers and home delivery was being promoted, as more nurse midwifery programs and birthing centers were being established. Attitudes of hospital nurses in many institutions were changing from the old authoritative models restricting visiting hours in pediatric units from one or two hours a week to less restrictive and even unlimited hours for parents. On maternity units husbands or mothers or other labor assistants were being allowed to provide support to new mothers during labor and delivery.

Women were helping other women by organizing support groups such as La Leche League to promote breastfeeding, and restrictive abortion laws were being challenged. The issue of abortion reform in the cause of public health was one I supported strongly; I had seen news reports of deaths due to complications of illegal abortions. I had also met hospitalized patients who had in desperation chosen to have illegal abortions, and were admitted with bleeding or infections, complications sometimes requiring hysterectomy. They were women of all ages, most were poor, and many were Catholic. At that time, illegal abortion was thought to be the most common cause of maternal mortality in the United States and probably around the world.

When I was given the assignment during the course *Educational and Professional Writing* to write a letter to the editor of a newspaper, I found my topic easily in the April 17, 1969, New York State legislature vote on abortion law reform. On that date supporters of abortion reform in the Assembly were confident they had enough votes and passage of the bill seemed inevitable, until Assemblyman Martin Ginsberg, the Republican representing my own district in Nassau County rose to speak. He had been considered pledged to the reform bill. Crippled by polio since infancy, and dependent on heavy braces and a cane, Ginsberg argued that a law allowing abortion for a malformed fetus could set a frightening precedent. Although the reform bill's sponsor Assemblyman Albert Blumenthal tried to explain that the bill, which allowed abortion in proven cases of fetal abnormality, had nothing to do with victims of polio or other abnormalities after birth, many of the pledged votes (including 13 Republicans) melted away and the bill was defeated. When I heard about the defeat on the news that night, I was furious.

I had been too busy in school to pay much attention to all the details of the efforts around the country and in the New York State legislature to modify or reform the law that since 1830 made abortion a criminal offense unless performed to preserve the life of the pregnant woman. The reform bills proposed permitted abortions for limited medical reasons (rape and incest) and I certainly supported those efforts, although in my experience very few women sought abortions for these reasons. I did not think outright repeal of the restrictive laws was feasible, but I was concerned with the public health issue. I wanted something done to enable women to have the freedom to choose whether or not to carry an unanticipated pregnancy to term, or the option for safe termination. My letter to the editor of Long Island's *Newsday* mentioned my experience as a nurse and educator with hospitalized patients who were for the most part poor and addressed primarily the public health issue of the outcomes of illegal abortion. While the letter started out as a school assignment, the passionate empathy I expressed for the victims of the restrictive legislation was not fiction. It was an important commentary and there was an immediate public response of support.

In his 1973 book, *Abortion II: Making the Revolution*, Lawrence Lader refers to my letter and the outcome.

> …what was more significant about Ginsberg's speech however was that it unleashed a storm of protest among Ginsberg's own constituents.
>
> Mrs. Sylvia Fields, mother of three children and a nurse teaching maternal health, criticized the speech in a letter to *Newsday*, and as a result a group of neighbors in Plainview, met at her house to organize the Nassau Committee for Abortion Law Repeal.

The most significant response to my letter to the editor of *Newsday* was a telephone call from Dr. Ruth Cusack, of the National Organization of Women (NOW), a Ph.D. in Nutrition, who was the organizer of Suffolk County's Repeal Movement and a board member of the National Association for Repeal of Abortion Laws (NARAL). She had written earlier in 1969 to New York State Assemblywoman Constance Cook asking her to sponsor a repeal bill. (Assemblywoman Constance Cook did introduce the first sweeping bill repealing all abortion laws the day the Blumenthal Reform bill was defeated.) Ruth offered to assist me in organizing the Nassau Committee. With everything else "on my plate" I could not have done it without her encouragement and experienced help. I was much too busy with my family and school to take on such a responsibility alone, and of course Gerry was not supportive, but his friends in the Democratic Club encouraged me, and Gerry agreed to have an organizing meeting in our home. We put a small ad in the county *PennySaver* newspaper inviting volunteers and asking for assistance. Among the first respondents were Anita and Alan DeLorenzo – he was the legislative director of the local United Automobile workers union. With the union's extensive mailing list we were able to put pressure on all the local legislators and to raise funds for ads and additional mailings. I invited my cousin, Fran Berg; a psychiatric social worker who I knew supported the repeal effort, to join us. She lived in Kings Point, a much more affluent area on the north shore, and was able to raise money for printing and mailing of literature explaining our organization objectives and listing the many supporting organizations in the state.

One of our first group activities was to set up a booth at Roosevelt Field Shopping Mall in East Meadow to collect signatures on petitions to our local legislators. I took the petitions around my neighborhood. Every neighbor, most of whom were Catholic, signed. Gerry was negative about the whole affair, afraid someone would burn a cross on our lawn, but that never happened. I received one negative letter out of hundreds of letters of support.

I was invited to speak to several community groups, and I was well prepared, but the most significant invitation was from a Catholic men's organization, the Knights of Columbus, a large group in Nassau County. I went to the meeting hall with the DeLorenzos wearing my full long-sleeved nurses' uniform including white shoes and stockings, cap and pin, the works! I looked like the professional I was and I was greeted warmly and respectfully. Some of the men knew Alan DeLorenzo from union activities; there was no heckling or joking – it was all very serious. (It was suspected that many of the women having abortions on Long Island were Catholic.) I always told the story of my student's essay years earlier, "Every child deserves to be wanted."

I answered as many questions as I could, but of course we did not expect endorsement from the organization. Everyone shook our hands and wished us well.

The main points emphasized during presentations and in our literature were the following:

- Women have been having abortions since the beginning of time.
- No method of birth control is 100% effective in preventing an unwanted child.
- Laws have not deterred women from having abortions; they have merely forced the vast majority of those seeking abortions to have them under unsafe and humiliating conditions.
- Abortion laws discriminate against the poor, for wealthy women can more easily obtain safe legal abortions.
- Repeal of abortion laws does not imply approval or disapproval of abortion. It does mean that decisions regarding abortion belong to a woman and her physician and are not a function of the state.

The list of supporters was very diverse, bipartisan, with all religions represented, except of course, the Catholic hierarchy. Among the 34 organizations listed on our literature in 1969 were The American Public Health Association N.Y.C., N.Y. Council of Churches, Episcopal Diocese of New York, Federation of Protestant Welfare Agencies, National Council of Jewish Women, American Jewish Congress, National Organization for Women, Parents Aid Society, The Presbytery of N.Y. City, Unitarian-Universalist Association, Women's Bar Association of N.Y., American Ethical Union, Citizens' Advisory Council on the Status of Women, Clergy Consultation Services on Abortion, Correctional Association of N.Y., and the Drug and Hospital Employees Union.

During the year following the April 1969 defeat of the reform bill in New York, a political firestorm swept the state as well as across the country. While the Catholic Church became more vocal in supporting the laws against abortion under any circumstances, the percentage of Catholic lay persons quietly supporting contraception and leaving the issue of abortion to the individual woman increased. When Republican State Senator Norman Lent, Chairman of the State Health Committee, mailed out a questionnaire in his middle-class Catholic district on Long

Island that was returned by over 7,000 of his constituents, he was startled to find that 65% favored complete repeal. He changed his thinking on the issue. Most Protestant churches supported repeal or were less vocal against repeal.

By the spring of 1970, when the repeal law co-sponsored by upstate Republican Assemblywoman Connie Cook and New York City Democrat Albert H. Blumenthal came up for vote in Albany, New York, six Nassau County State Legislators, three Republicans and three Democrats (two Catholics, three Protestants, and one Jew) had changed their votes from the previous year and supported repeal. The resulting tie was broken by an upstate Democratic legislator, George Michaels, who had been pressured by his children to change his vote, despite the pressure from his heavily Catholic district. Immediately after, Senator Duryea, the Speaker, Republican and Catholic, added his "Yes" vote for repeal to make the vote "Republican."

My active involvement was limited during this time due to family and schoolwork needs; however, the vote was a very important and dramatic event and I was there in Albany for the experience. Abortion was allowed up to 24 weeks of gestation. The end result of our activities were that in 1970 New York state repealed the old 1830 law banning abortion after "quickening," except to save a woman's life.

The following year an attempt was made in the legislature to reverse the repeal, but Republican Governor Rockefeller vetoed the bill and no attempt was made to appeal. The rest is history, and the Supreme Court ruled in 1973 to make abortion legal until 24 weeks of pregnancy across the country. Unfortunately the battle was not completely won; little by little, a woman's right to control her body, even the freedom to use contraception, has been attacked and diminished. As we know, the war continues today.

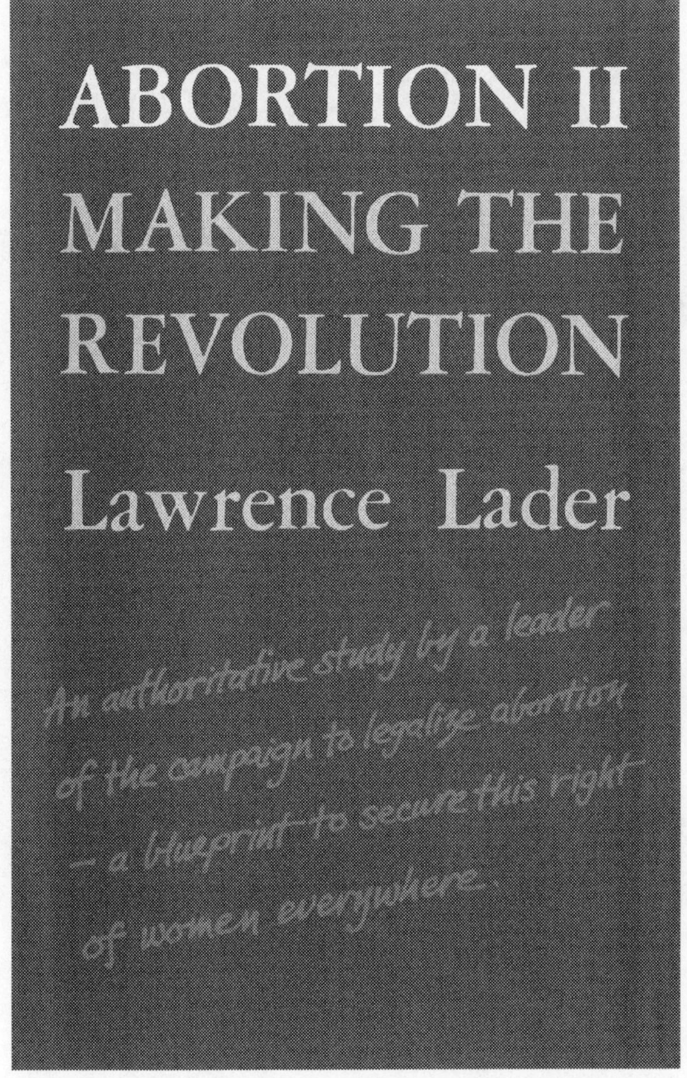

Lawrence Lader's book, *Abortion II : Making the Revolution*. 1973 Boston, Beacon Press (Page 123 in text refers to the letter I wrote to Newsday and subsequent role I played in political action)

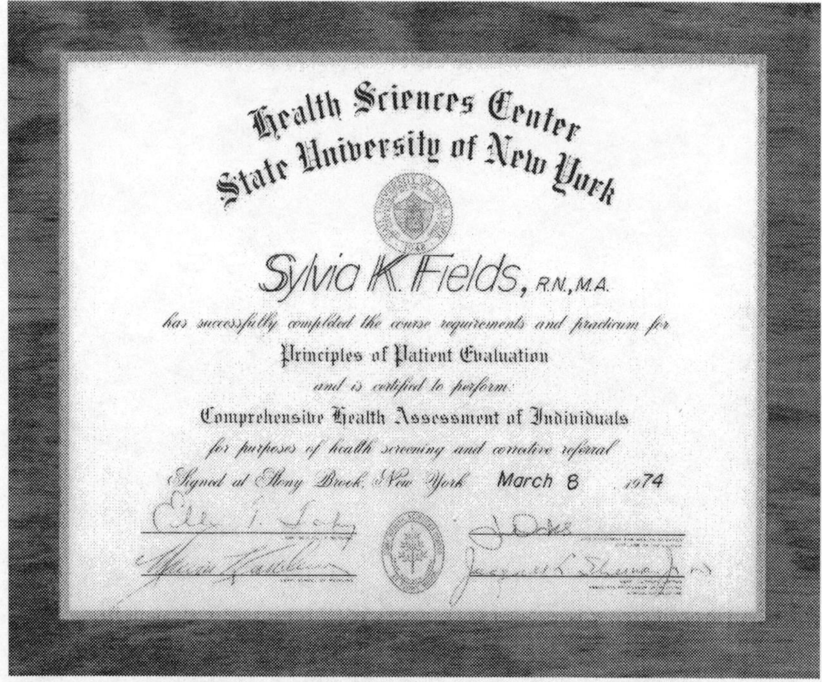

Health Sciences Center
State University of New York

Sylvia K. Fields, R.N., M.A.

has successfully completed the course requirements and practicum for

Principles of Patient Evaluation

and is certified to perform:

Comprehensive Health Assessment of Individuals

for purposes of health screening and corrective referral

Signed at Stony Brook, New York March 8 1974

I receive the *Certificate in Principles of Patient Evaluation* from SUNY Stony Brook Medical School, 1974.

7

Developing Primary Health Care Education at SUNY Stony Brook

"One of the greatest achievements in health care during the 20th century will be identified as the creation of the Health Care Team." [11]

Edmund D. Pellegrino, M.D.

Although my federal traineeship was over at the end of the spring 1969 semester, Teachers College (TC) awarded me additional tuition funds to continue part time toward the doctoral degree. Since I was scheduled to return to SUNY Farmingdale in the fall to continue teaching Maternal Child Health and Family Development, I applied for promotion to Associate Professor, which seemed quite feasible. However, I began to question my goals for the long term again; I was not certain I wanted to maintain my original curriculum plan for "Academic Administration." I fantasized becoming a nurse practitioner and teaching the new role in primary care. Although I had been a medical-surgical nurse and teacher since graduating from Adelphi, as my own family expanded during my years at Farmingdale, I became more interested in holistic

---

[11] Edmund L. Pellegrino, MD (1920-2013) Vice President for Health Sciences, SUNY Stony Brook N.Y. during my tenure there. He wrote the Forward to "Guide to Patient Evaluation, by Sherman and Fields. After Dr. Pellegrino, an internationally known medical ethicist, left SUNY he became the 11th President of Catholic University of America.

family health. I thought I could be a great family nurse practitioner, and I had some ideas about how to teach the new role. Many of the other graduate students in my TC classes that summer were also examining the potential of expanded practice roles. We began to share ideas about professional education for nursing in the health care system of the future, where undoubtedly the baccalaureate degree and graduate study would eventually be mandatory.

Then, out of the blue, I received a telephone call from Dr. Ellen Fahy, Dean of the new upper division baccalaureate nursing program under development at SUNY Stony Brook on Long Island, asking if I would consider a faculty position at the new Health Sciences Center there. I had been recommended by a dear friend and former classmate at Adelphi, Dr. Virginia Jarry Glover, who joined the Stony Brook program as Associate Dean. Dr. Fahy offered me an Associate Professorship and a position as chairperson in the department of Adult Health Nursing. She said I would be given a flexible teaching schedule in order to continue at Columbia to complete my doctoral degree and prepare for changing roles in nursing. We arranged a personal meeting the following week on the campus where all the schools of the new Health Science Center (HSC) – Medicine, Dental Medicine, Nursing, Allied Health, and Social Welfare – were temporarily located in Quonset huts. (The HSC building and the hospital were just beginning construction.) During that meeting I learned about the mission of the Health Science Center that aimed towards interprofessional education, where students of all health disciplines would have learning opportunities together.

The baccalaureate nursing degree program would be upper division, requiring for admission at least (60 credits) or two years of general education including specific course requirements in the sciences and humanities. Graduates of diploma and associate degree nursing programs, who were already licensed as Registered Professional Nurses, would be admitted to an accelerated baccalaureate degree program that focused on community health concepts, prevention, and introduction to research. A team of Stony Brook nursing faculty would also work together in the near future to define objectives and develop a graduate program focusing on advanced practice roles in primary care and hospital-based clinical specialties in the near future, as well as Health Policy. This was exactly what we had been exploring in the nursing department at Columbia.

The opportunity was exciting and although the commute from my home in Old Bethpage further east to Stony Brook would be longer than my trip from my home to Farmingdale, I was not concerned. The traffic would hardly be as difficult as my previous travel west to Queens College and Long Island Jewish Hospital. In addition, since the Stony Brook campus was a full Arts and Sciences Center, the salary was going to be higher there at $18,000 for the academic year vs. $15,000 at Farmingdale. I didn't hesitate to accept the position verbally and went home to prepare resignation letters for the Farmingdale president and the chairperson of the nursing program there.

To my disappointment, three days later I received another call from Dr. Fahy; apparently the presidents of the two SUNY campuses had consulted. Evidently there was a New York State policy against "stealing" faculty from other campuses within the state system. I was told I would have to return to Farmingdale, (where I would receive the salary increase and promotion I requested) for at least one academic year. Then, if I was still interested, I would have to apply formally to the Stony Brook campus. Dr. Fahy assured me that the program would expand, so a faculty appointment could be mine for the following year. To say I was disappointed was putting it mildly, for while I was away at Columbia the nursing department chair position at Farmingdale had become available and had been given to a colleague to whom I would have to report. I wasn't happy about the personnel arrangement, but I had no recourse.

In July I sent the children to summer camp while I was in school and now I joined them as camp nurse for August. The days were packed full and I did not think much about work in the fall; I was busy every day and exhausted. Then my husband Gerry and I received notification that our fourteen-year-old daughter Melissa had received a partial scholarship to attend the tenth grade in an international school in Israel. It sounded like a fantastic experience and Melissa was anxious to go. How could we say no? She would have to leave immediately. Melissa and I left camp to pack her things for the trip. After Gerry and I saw her off on the evening flight overseas, we went home so I could rest before returning to camp. Meanwhile I had developed a bad sore throat and laryngitis and felt awful. Unable to sleep with my heart pounding, I thought it was just anxiety about Melissa. But it was worse in the morning. I asked Gerry to call the doctor's office for an emergency appointment. I could barely stand on my feet, my head hurt, and my heart was racing. I was sure I was seriously ill.

Life sometimes works in strange ways. I was told my illness was not that serious, but it was enough to keep me from returning to camp that summer. The diagnosis was thyroiditis, a viral disorder, and the treatment with steroids seemed to work quickly over the next few days. But by the end of the week I was having terrible nightmares and my face and eyelids were swollen, apparently side effects of the steroid therapy; I felt miserable. Gerry's old college friend, Dr. Lewis Fierro, a faculty member at New York Medical College, arranged an immediate consultation with an endocrinologist at Flower Fifth Avenue Hospital in New York City. This time I was treated in supposedly the old fashioned way. I was placed on strict bed rest in the hospital and then at home with high doses of aspirin accompanied by heavy antacids for three months. With an extended medical leave I missed the fall semester and recovered slowly, optimistic that the Stony Brook position would be there for me the following year. Feeling really rested, I was well enough to return to Farmingdale for the spring semester.

Meanwhile, fourteen-year-old Melissa and I had been exchanging weekly letters. Her experience was truly remarkable. She met students from all over the world and shook hands with dignitaries such as Moshe Dayan, Israeli Minister of Defense, at services during the holy days. Later, in the spring with the help of our parents, the whole family had the opportunity to visit Israel for Passover week with Melissa as our tour guide. We were able to visit with several family members living in Israel, including the Hoffmans of Natanya who had survived the concentration camps, the Exodus and the Wars of Independence in 1948 and 1967.

When I came home I wrote an article about the letters we exchanged and the meaning of the entire experience for the whole family.[12]

A Leadership Position

In the fall of 1970 I joined the faculty of the School of Nursing at Stony Brook as Associate Professor of Adult Health Nursing and Chair of the Pathophysiology Conference Group. The professional move to Stony Brook was much more than a change in teaching assignment, or just a change in my career. I was now in a significant leadership position in the SUNY Academic Center and it changed my life.

The philosophy of Dr. Edmund Pellegrino, Vice President of the Health Science Center, on professional collaboration in health care education and practice underlined the establishment of the new institution. The enthusiastic support from the administration and staff on the Stony Brook campus, the nourishing environment provided by Drs. Fahy and Glover, and the stimulating foundation I received at Teachers College, led me to professional success I never could have dreamed for myself.

Through the next seven years at Stony Brook my clinical skills expanded tenfold; one creative accomplishment led to the next. In preparation for the new practitioner and teaching roles in community health education, I completed a course developed especially for Stony Brook nursing faculty, and received a certificate from the School of Medicine for "Comprehensive Health Assessment of Individuals." During that course given at the Northport Veterans' Hospital, we practiced primarily on discharged World War II veterans, who came to the Northport clinic for annual physical examinations from group homes in the area. It was a difficult assignment; communication was a challenge and most of the men could not completely care for themselves. Their hygiene was poor, teeth were rotten, their clothing was soiled or torn, and they often smelled. This is the tragedy of the inadequate

---

12 Fields, Sylvia K & Melissa E. Fields. *Solomon Schechter High School in Israel: Reflections of a Mother and her Daughter. United Synagogue Review. Spring 1972*

facilities and services for those with mental illness experienced by the majority of the homeless, including many veterans around the country then and even today. The veterans living in group homes were actually better off than many other mentally ill patients found on the street, who were scrounging for food and handouts with no shelter or medical care.

With a strong clinical background in medicine and surgery and much passion I was the best prepared of the faculty, and having "grown up" with medical textbooks as references, I performed at the top of the group in the assessment course. I led the class in asking questions and then incorporating holistic nursing concepts into the content. For example, in the texts used by medical students, history of the patients' health status had been traditionally referred to as the "Medical History." I insisted that we use the term "Health History." Included in the nurse's interview with the patient were questions about health habits and problems with eating, food and nutrition, sleep, anxiety, exercise, and relationships, etc.

As a result I was selected to work with the course coordinator, Dr. Jacques Sherman, Associate Dean of the School of Medicine, to develop study guides for our students that could be turned into a textbook for undergraduate nursing students across the country. I became co-author, sharing equally in royalties for the book we created, "*Guide to Patient Evaluation: History Taking, Physical Examination and the Problem-Oriented Methods,*" published by Medical Examination Publishing Company, Flushing, NY, (on my 40th birthday, January 20, 1974). It was the first book on health assessment developed specifically for nurses, and it won the *American Journal of Nursing* Book of the Year Award for 1974. As a result, nursing programs across the country began to expand their curriculums with much more assessment content.

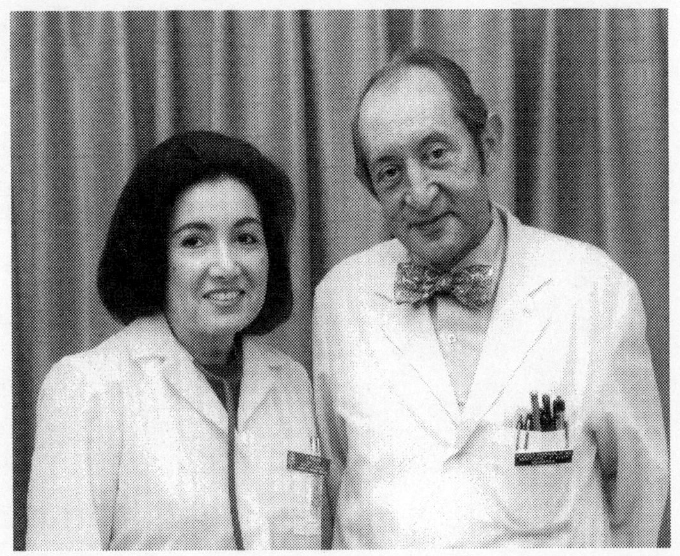

Jacques L. Sherman MD and Sylvia K. Fields, BSN, MA, MEd, RN.

Co-authors of "*Guide to Patient Evaluation,*" published by Medical Examination Publishing Company, New York on my 40th Birthday, January 20, 1974.

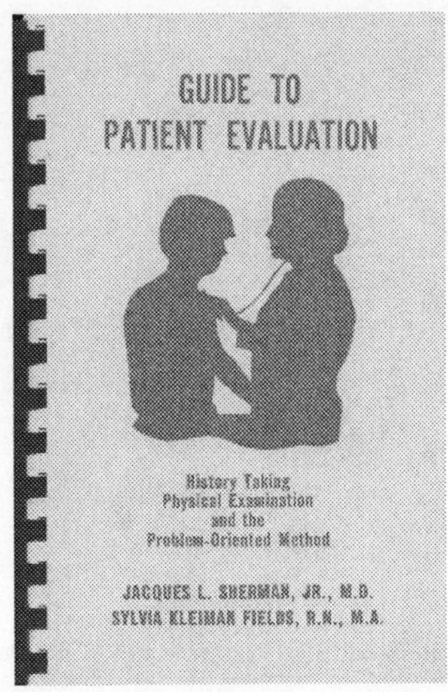

Cover of first edition of "*Guide to Patient Evaluation.*"

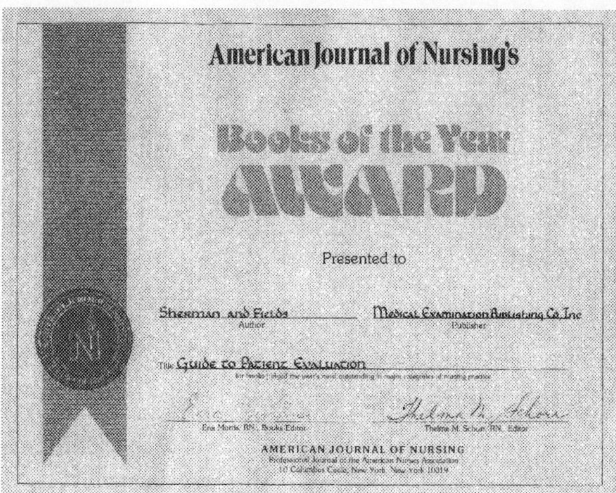

We received the American Journal of Nursing **Book of the Year Award**.

With the assistance of the other faculty members and friends as contributors, four more editions were published over the next twelve years, as we expanded the nursing content on health assessment throughout the life cycle. The first edition was also used by physician assistant and some first-year medical school programs. More than 100,000 copies were sold internationally. I never anticipated the royalties I earned; Melissa's college tuition was eventually paid through my royalties. There were several foreign translations including a Japanese edition and even an unofficial Chinese edition I found while visiting mainland China ten years later in 1984.

While the book served as a text for our undergraduate program, the need for new and creative teaching strategies became even more apparent. The Director of Media Services on the Stony Brook campus, Antol Herskovitz, suggested we write a proposal for federal funding to establish a learning laboratory specifically focusing on the physical assessment skills course. He had learned of such a project at a medical education conference at Southern Illinois University. He shared materials he had received with me and we began to write our own project objectives and outline. I could not have done it without his help since I had never written a grant proposal before, and he could not do it without me because I had the nursing content and the educational theory. We could not have done it without the help of the Stony Brook Research Development Office to identify a significant funding source, review the guidelines with us, estimate the budget, and eventually fly the final grant proposal at the last minute to Washington D.C. It was a miracle we got the proposal completed and accepted on time. I cried when we received the acceptance letter for a Special Projects Grant of $500,000 from the Division of Nursing, Department of Health, Education and Welfare for two years.

Through the project, a film production team was brought on and demonstrations of examination techniques were videotaped, performance checklists were created by nurse faculty, and available simulation practice models were purchased. A lab instructor was trained to assist as students circulated through the examining rooms independently until ready for practice on simulated/standardized patients. Two years later, a second $500,000 was received to expand the program and institute computerization of student completion records. This was one of the first physical assessment labs established at the time in this country. Today most schools of medicine and nursing have such a facility where students practice and are then evaluated before meeting actual patients.

Over the years Dr. Sherman and I also worked together on several commercial teaching/learning packages that were published and distributed by Westinghouse Learning Systems. Student study guides, teachers' manuals, and filmstrips on Hypertension, Clinical Anatomy and Physiology, and Health Assessment were marketed internationally, bringing me additional income.

These efforts also led to my being asked to participate in other program development activities. For example, soon after receiving the Medical School Health Assessment Certificate, I was invited to participate part time in a newly developing three-year project with the University of the State of New York, Regents External Degree Program. I was one of a ten-person team of nursing faculty from different New York state universities that met once a month for two-day (Friday-Saturday) sessions in Albany, New York, where we worked on development and evaluation of the SUNY BSN Program: Health Assessment Clinical Performance Examination. The exam was one of three performance and five written examinations developed to enable registered nurse graduates of two- and three-year diploma/associate degree programs to "test out" of formal nursing courses leading to the Bachelor of Science degree through guided independent study. It was not an easy program, but it made it possible for nurses to earn the BSN while maintaining their full-time nursing positions. This often led to professional advancement in hospitals and entry into community health, as well as continuation with graduate studies toward master's and doctoral degrees. The nursing program was evaluated and approved by the National League of Nursing. Several years later while teaching at Emory University, I was instrumental in bringing the Performance Assessment Program to Georgia sponsored through the Georgia Nurses Association. The program, "Excelsior College" was ultimately made available to nurses all across the country, and although still controversial among some educators and administrators, continues today as one of hundreds of online nursing programs.

A Unique RN to BSN Program "On the Job" at Stony Brook

Having spent ten years teaching in diploma and associate degree programs before I came to Stony Brook, I was very much interested in BSN completion opportunities for such graduates. Most BSN programs in the '60s and '70s were very strict about admission criteria. Sixty credits of prescribed undergraduate course work were required before admission to the junior year of the upper degree program, with specific prerequisites in the natural and behavioral sciences and humanities. At Stony Brook, registered nurses and upper division generic (or basic) students were admitted to the program from the beginning, with acceleration possible for those already licensed registered nurses who met the 60 credit requirement. I believed flexibility and creativity were necessary to encourage students to attempt to meet the requirements for matriculation on their own schedules.

One day Dean Fahy informed the faculty that the New York State University Administration claimed our original RN to BSN nursing program had enrolled insufficient students to fulfill required student-faculty ratios. "We have to admit at least ten more students immediately, or we will lose a faculty line," Dr. Fahy said. We all looked around. Who was it going to be? "Let's think everyone, put on your thinking caps… someone come up with an idea," Dr. Fahy implored us.

Previously, while exploring clinical learning sites for our Generic students we had discovered that most of the nursing service administrators, supervisors, and teachers at the Suffolk County hospitals and state mental hospital diploma schools had little education beyond their basic diploma training. Only a few held the associate or bachelor's degree. We did not have a University Hospital yet. How could we send our students into those institutions where the objectives of baccalaureate education were not addressed in patient care?

As I was driving home, I thought about the students and practicing nurses I had known over the years who had taken college courses before entering or after their nursing courses, or who voraciously read the nursing journals searching for answers to nursing problems. Some of our Massachusetts General Hospital students had taken college courses before entering the nursing program. For those applicants already holding a non-nursing college degree there was an accelerated program that later led to a master's degree. At Lutheran Medical Center, our first-year students took required sciences and some liberal arts courses with general education students at Long Island University, equivalent to at least 30 academic credits. Certainly those credits were transferable but they were not enough for full matriculation to the BSN programs anywhere. Many of these nurses needed to help support their families; they could not give up their jobs to go back to school.

That night after my children went to bed I couldn't sleep. I started fantasizing and found myself creating an outline for an independent study program for local registered nurses in leadership positions, where a guided educational experience used the students' current work setting for the clinical practicum. Why not admit these nurses to the BSN program with the commitment to complete the liberal arts requirements through "testing," or concurrent with or after the nursing courses, I thought. The next day I shared my thoughts and assumptions with Dr. Fahy. She set up an ad hoc committee of a few faculty members representing each clinical area, as well as volunteer RN students. Two community based nurses known to have the BSN degrees were invited to participate as consultants. In the meantime we announced the possible program and began to recruit potential students through networking.

A pilot program was designed and initiated in the spring of 1973. Following a philosophical and structural immersion during one week full time on campus, students took home learning packages designed for them and worked with an assigned faculty member in a mentoring relationship to meet objectives. Developing the program was not easy; it required converting the integrated nursing curriculum based on the life cycle into packaged courses for individualized instruction and independent study that could not differ from our already state-approved and NLN-accredited curriculum. The program we designed is described in depth in an article (the very first article I wrote) in the journal *Nursing Outlook*, "Nurses Earn Their B.S. Degrees – On the Job" (Vol. 24, No. 3, March 1976). Evaluation of the program was quite positive from the student's perspective, although they wanted more on campus experiences, but it also addressed the problems we encountered: increased demands on the faculty and heavy burden on the students, which raised many questions. It was clear that not all faculty members were prepared or suited for the mentoring role, which required creativity and flexibility. Some of the assumptions about nontraditional methods of higher education for adults were challenged at that time.

It is amazing to me today, forty-some odd years later, that so much of nursing education at all levels is delivered independently online, as though all students are capable of learning independently.

During my second year at Stony Brook, I returned to Teachers College and was involved with a *Seminar on Higher Education* where the issues of social stratification in the health professions were discussed. It has been well established that levels of professionalism are socially determined by the number of years of education a profession requires for entry into its ranks. Medicine, with approximately four years of graduate professional study following a foundation of approximately four years of undergraduate arts and sciences, has traditionally been at the top of that hierarchy. Since nursing has had no clear educational requirements universally for professional practice, it has always ranked below medicine, psychology, and social work on a hierarchical list. As a result, nurses usually are expected to "take orders from physicians," although sometimes this rule is set aside, especially when the nurse has more advanced clinical training or specific experience than the physician. With graduate study, nurses have been able to move up the ladder towards equal levels with medicine and the other health professions that today require the doctoral degree, such as physical therapy. In recent years emphasis on advanced education and training leading to the doctoral degree in nursing has led to more equalization of status on the health care team. However, despite attempts to mandate a minimum of a baccalaureate degree for entry into the nursing profession as preparation for graduate study, the largest proportion of nurses in this country still do not have adequate education to serve as full members of the team in practice.

In the Higher Education seminar mentioned above, fellow students Rita Wieszorek, (faculty member at Cornell University–New York Hospital), Elizabeth Pennington (faculty member at the University of Michigan), and I reviewed the challenges we had experienced in attempting to develop new interdisciplinary education programs in our unique academic positions. We prepared a paper entitled "**Interdisciplinary Education: A Model for the Resocialization of Faculty**" for the seminar. Published in 1976, it was a landmark paper, stressing the need for faculty planning interprofessional courses to have time to work together as a team before bringing students into the picture. It is still very much relevant today as schools across the country attempt to teach students together under the premise that "students who learn together will be better prepared to work together in practice." This concept became very important as I proceeded to develop my doctoral dissertation, and later provided the basis for much of my professional activities throughout my career.

It is also important here for me to mention that during this period of teaching, I was continuing my research activities on the subject of Interprofessional Education for nursing students through a survey I had developed of baccalaureate program administrators across the country. As a result of a catalogue and literature search, and a preliminary survey of 246 National League of Nursing (NLN)–accredited BSN programs, with 155 or 63% responding, I had learned of fifty two courses offered for nursing students together with students of other professions.

In my final survey of forty eight schools of nursing, the most frequently offered interprofessional course was Human Sexuality. It made sense. Although medical students are higher up on the professional hierarchy than nurses, age differences may be minimal, and male and female students of both professions are probably most often at the same level emotionally and academically, in this course. Much has been written today about the importance of sexuality throughout the life cycle, including new emphasis on patient needs and problems during chronic illness and disability. Health professionals need much continuing education in this area, but opportunities are still limited due to a shortage of qualified faculty and the impact of religious biases.

Interprofessional Education

In his foreword to the first edition of our textbook, *Guide to Patient Evaluation,* Dr. Pellegrino, [13]wrote:

> Historians of twentieth-century medicine will easily be overwhelmed by the breakthroughs and technological

[13] Dr. Pellegrino, now deceased, prepared this Forward for the first edition in 1974, it was duplicated in the next three editions published by Medical Examination Publishing Company. The fifth edition was published by Elsevier Publishing. They have been sending requests for permission to use content to me, the surviving author since Dr. Sherman is deceased.

> wonders wrought by the fruitful marriage in our era of medicine and experimental science. They may easily overlook some of our more human and equally difficult accomplishments in the organization and delivery of health care. One of these most surely is the emergence of the team concept and the sharing of clinical functions, formerly the sole province of the physician, by a variety of other health professionals.
>
> To respond adequately to the social mandate to make health care available on an equitable basis for all, we must begin to make genuine progress toward the optimal use of all health manpower. In that endeavor, medicine and all the other health professions will undergo a redefinition of their roles and functions within new models of health care teams. The social utility of team care which will emerge may well come to rival our brightest technological triumphs.
>
> If this is to happen, we much encourage the sharing of a common language among all who engage in clinical care of patients, enabling them to communicate with each other, as well as to exchange and share certain functions which the needs of patients may dictate.

As was mentioned earlier, this was the philosophical theme for the SUNY Stony Brook Health Science Center professional schools. To carry it forward in the educational programs, there was a **mandate** to the faculty of the five schools to create opportunities for students to learn together. Wednesday afternoons were set aside for interprofessional/interdisciplinary courses (interprofessional and interdisciplinary are used interchangeably here); all students were required to take at least two interdisciplinary courses during their educational program and no school could hold classes exclusively for their own students on Wednesday afternoons. Over my tenure at Stony Brook I became involved with three elective courses offered on Wednesday afternoons.

1. ***An Interprofessional Approach to Patient Evaluation;***
2. ***Health Care During Political Strife and the Arts***
3. ***Human Sexuality***

An Interprofessional Approach to Patient Evaluation

The first course related to my certification in patient evaluation. I participated with a faculty team representing the five schools within the Health Science Center: Medicine, Dental Medicine, Allied Health Professions, Social Welfare, and Nursing, in the development, implementation, and evaluation of the first interdisciplinary **clinical** course at Stony Brook. Our team, joined by twenty four students representing the schools and led by Arlene Barro, PhD, Assistant Dean for Evaluation in the Medical School, spent a full year, at first without students and then with students as we clarified the objectives, designed the learning experiences and field tested the proposed course.

In the beginning we arranged weekly sessions on campus clarifying objectives, reviewing literature and allowing introductory content from each discipline to be presented. There were demonstrations using models and films, simulated patients and discussions. We then proceeded to the various community hospitals where we had contracted for potential patient interactions, individually and in small groups. There were pre-conferences, visits to the nursing units, and then post conferences. Each week was different. Some plans worked well, some did not. As organized as we thought we were, there were many surprises.

Among the course faculty was Dr. Campbell Lamont, Chair of Family Medicine, who had come from Canada, where team development was very much valued in their health system. He was wonderful to work with. The communication was wide open and the process totally democratic as each participant, students and faculty members felt respected and appreciated; faculty and students became friends. Another great faculty person was Dr. Steve Allen, Director of the Physician Assistant Program; yes, he was Steve Allen, the comedian's son.

At the end of the year evaluations were so positive we unanimously recommended renewing and expanding the course to include more students and more faculty members with many recruited from the various community hospitals where our health science students were receiving clinical learning experiences within their disciplines.

The University administration agreed to employ a coordinator for the next semester with ten groups of twenty students anticipated, so recruitment began for twenty faculty members and 200 students. Unfortunately, the Coordinator and the new faculty from the various hospitals across the Island did not have the advantage of working together with us during the original planning semester, or even as a new group for a month together. They simply did not have the opportunity to learn from us and get to know each other. As a result, they were unable to demonstrate interprofessional teamwork to students in the classroom sessions or in the clinical area.

The program was not recommended for continuation at the end of the semester evaluation; it was clear that more faculty preparation was needed. We learned a great deal out of that experience, most of all, that leadership and faculty must be able to demonstrate respect for each other's contribution and attitudes that value the team working together to meet the needs of patients and students.

1. Health Care During Political Strife and the Arts

During one of the guided independent study courses I took at Columbia on "Instruction in Nursing," I developed a new elective course opened to all Health Science students at Stony Brook focusing on History of the Health Professions during War time. We were very much still involved in the Vietnam War at the time so there was a lot of interest. Teaching strategies involved the humanities: literature, music, dance and art. I had clearly been inspired by Dr. Maxine Greene's course. "*The Arts and American Education.*"

The students were divided into five groups and given the choice of five Wars: the Crimean War, the U.S. Civil War; World War I; World War II; and the Vietnam War. Following a brief review of literature and establishment of committees, each group worked independently to prepare individual performances for the entire class utilizing the ARTS (Music, Poetry, Literature, Drama, Dance, Art) to illustrate the specific social, political and health problems of the time, leading up to and including the special war issues. Meanwhile I worked to find appropriate guest speakers somehow related to our course objectives.

Ron Kovic, Paraplegic Vietnam Veteran had just published his book, "*Born on the Fourth of July*" about his experiences overseas and at home, before, during and after the war. It was the only required reading for all students and it made a major impression on them. Since Ron lived on Long Island, not too far from our University, I invited him to come to class after the students had all had a few preliminary lecture-seminars and two weeks to read and digest the book describing Ron's experiences. (*Born on the Fourth of July* was later made into a Hollywood movie starring Tom Cruise.) Unfortunately 150 Health Science students waited in the auditorium anxiously for Ron to appear; sadly he did not show up. I had to quickly improvise a discussion based on the readings about his experience in Vietnam and the care he experienced in the Bronx VA hospital. After class, I was devastated. I called him again, and again he promised to come the following week to class, but once again he did not appear. He did eventually send me an apology; he was really too "messed up," he said.

This in of itself became an important teaching/learning experience for students and faculty alike.

The third week class demonstration was more successful. The contemporary musical artist, folk singer and community activist Harry Chapin also lived nearby on Long Island, and was well known by our university students. What they did not all really know and understand was that his travel across the U.S. and abroad focused on identifying community problems like "Hunger" and working to raise awareness and funds through his original music and concerts to help solve such problems. I invited Harry and he agreed to come to my class to talk to our students about human and community responsibility. (It never dawned on me that due to contractual agreements, he might not be able to perform.) When he finished his talk students applauded and he started to say good- bye and to leave the auditorium. Students began to shout, "We also came to hear you perform, how about playing and singing your songs?" Harry said, "I wasn't planning to sing, I don't have my guitar." From the back of the room one young man cried out, "here, I have my guitar! Please play, just one song." "OK, but don't tell my manager," Harry said. It was thrilling, he played his most famous work, *"Cats' in the Cradle"* and another new song he had just written for his daughter's 16th birthday. It was beautiful and Harry received a standing ovation.

"Cats' in the Cradle"

"My child arrived just the other day,
He came to the world in the usual way,
But there were planes to catch and bills to pay….

……………………….

I'm gonna be like you, Dad; You know, I'm gonna be like
you Dad…"

That song and most of his other songs have significant personal, family and community messages. I learned recently that after his unfortunate sudden death, Harry's family set up a nonprofit Foundation that continues today promoting his personal community objectives.

The course was a nontraditional way of teaching and learning the history of our professions in relation to socio-political events of the time. The performances of each student group were amazingly creative. Regretfully they were not videotaped so replay was not possible. I was nominated for a State Wide SUNY Outstanding Teacher Award, but without the documentation it was hard to show the quality of the student accomplishments. I know those students were changed as a result of the experiences presented; they told me they really appreciated reading and discussing Ron Kovic's memoir and would never forget the message of folk singer Harry Chapin.

2. Human Sexuality

The third interdisciplinary course I participated in was offered by the School of Allied Health**. Wow**! The large auditorium was filled; students were knocking on the doors to get in. On the first day, after some general introduction, four movie projectors started to roll simultaneously: one to the right, one to the left, and two side by side on the front wall of the theatre. It was the shock effect of visual immersion in a variety of heterosexual and homosexual manifestations of sexual behaviors in humans and animals as well, a lot of pure pornography! As I wrote earlier, I had been introduced as a student to the variances on the subject years before in the psychiatric state hospital. And I had been married twenty years, had browsed the professional and not-so-professional literature extensively on the subject over those years, but I learned there was much I did not really know during those sessions in the sexuality course. No one walked out of the room. Much of my responsibility in the course as faculty fell to explaining over and over during and after class that:

a. sexuality is a basic human need;
b. that health professionals should understand that sexuality can affect health status in many ways;
c. that health status can negatively impact sexual functioning and personal satisfaction.

The lead faculty of the course emphasized that health professionals needed to avoid or minimize judgment of what is or isn't ***normal*** unless individuals are clearly being harmed. It was a controversial experience at a time when few homosexual individuals we knew and worked with ***had*** **come out of the closet.**

Establishing the Graduate Program: Advanced Nursing Practice

Concurrently with everything else I was doing, the graduate program was under development; a special faculty team had been assigned. Dr. Lenora McLean was recruited from Teachers' College, Columbia to lead the process and I was appointed Associate Director. Neither one of us had any prior experience with nurse practitioner education, but Lenora had experience teaching graduate students at TC. In those years educational preparation for the expanded role of nursing was limited to short-term certificate programs, but it became very clear that the baccalaureate degree and prior clinical experience were necessary before students were truly ready to enter programs preparing for full roles in primary care.

Our committee decided that prospective candidates should be screened carefully to discern their potential for graduate study and collaborative roles. It was clear all needed better basic science preparation.

With approval of Dr. Pellegrino, a decision was made that our graduate program students would take several of the basic science courses of the first-year medical school curriculum, and the second year pathophysiology course along with the medical students, and two courses with nursing faculty. Lenora developed an introductory course, including public health policy and professional role development, while I was responsible for the Advanced Health Assessment course and Problem Based Analysis. The small group of six students was remarkable. They scored so well in the medical school classes, they upset the grading curve. In July of the first year they went to Nassau County Medical Center and were assigned with the new interns to clinical teams. I went with the students the first week and helped during patient assessment. At the end of the week one of the new interns, who did not know the backgrounds of the nurses came up to me and thanked me for assigning one of the nurses to his team. He told me, "my patient was very upset, pretty hysterical crying and complaining that she didn't know what was happening to her. She did not understand what the resident physician leader of the team, had said. I didn't know how to calm her down, but your nurse Elaine put her arm around my patient and soothed her, explaining what the resident had said in simple words. I was so grateful, because I did not understand him either. It was not just that experience; I learned a lot from Elaine this week," he said.

Since there were no nurse practitioners to help serve as mentors, we recruited several local primary care physicians who expressed interest in serving as preceptors during the second year of the program. That program was the model for another year, but soon after, changes were made to take the pressure away from the students. We were able to find additional physicians to serve as preceptors until we finally had some of our own graduates nurses and a few graduates of other programs functioning collaboratively in the community to act as preceptors for the new students.

Becoming Dr. Fields

With all the course work completed, I continued to pursue my doctoral studies through independent study under the guidance of Dr. Georgie Labadie, Professor of Nursing at Columbia. I was so lucky. Originally my advisor for doctoral studies was Dr. Mildred Montag, because I had focused on Associate Degree Education Administration. She was the "guru" of associate degree nursing. When in 1973 I requested and received approval for a change of specialization for the doctorate degree to *Teaching in Higher Educational Institutions*, the well-known lead faculty member at Columbia in that major, Dr. Marie Seedor, told me she was overloaded and couldn't take me on for advisement. She recommended young Dr. Labadie, whom I had not known before. It was a coup, for Dr. Seedor's area of publication was in Programmed Instruction. (I had been there and done that.)

Dr. Labadie, not only had the time, she had interest in me and my topic of Interprofessional Education. Most of all she was interested in all I had been doing professionally and she had the temperament and patience to listen to my struggles at home. During this time my marriage was disintegrating; yet somehow with support from my co-faculty member at Stony Brook, Adele Walsh and Dr. Labadie, I stayed focused and sane while my family fell apart.

I will never forget that day I was scheduled to defend my doctoral dissertation in June 1977. I was up the entire night before reviewing the statistical analysis in order to explain the multiple regressions of outcome data collected through my survey. The next day just before the defense session, I met with Dr. Labadie to go over my understanding of the statistical procedure. I told her that I was in a panic, not certain I could describe the analysis correctly. She listened and then said "Sylvia, stop worrying, you'll be fine." Dr. Wilder was already there; he smiled and I returned his smile. At Dr. Labadie's recommendation, I had taken his three-credit course, *Methods of Empirical Research,* during the summer of 1974. I knew he supported my study but we had only a few sessions together during the years following for development and evaluation of my survey instrument.

The conversation across the room among the committee members was warm and open and the questioning during the session was straightforward, just as Dr. Labadie had told me it would be. Before I knew it, the chairperson said, "I think we have enough. Thank you, Sylvia, you can go now."

I was in shock. Could it be over already? Dr. Labadie told me to wait outside in the hall for her. I sat on the bench and waited, no more than five minutes, when Dr. Labadie came out with a big smile, and said "Congratulations, Dr. Fields, I'm proud of you."

"I can't believe it, what happened? They never asked me about the Multiple Regression, how come?"

"Maybe they didn't understand it themselves," Dr. Labadie responded. She continued, "I don't know why you were so worried, you did everything I told you to do."

Of course I had. I had probably been so afraid because a few weeks before, one of my close friends, completing her Ph.D. at New York University, had been told during her dissertation defense session that the conditions of her laboratory study were not acceptable. It took her six more months and over $3000 to redo the experiment under appropriate conditions. She admitted to me later that her advisor had warned her, but she would not listen. If that would have happened to me, it would have been the end. I have heard since of quite a few doctoral candidates who end up ABDs (all but the dissertation).

My research study would never have been completed without the never-ceasing urging, guidance, and encouragement of my advisor, sponsor, and most of all, my friend, Dr. Georgie Labadie. I wrote in acknowledgments for the dissertation, "How did she ever put up with me? Together with Dr. David Wilder, as my committee they deserve much more than acknowledgments, much more than thank you, but undoubtedly gold medals for patience and fortitude."

I completed requirements for the Doctoral Degree at Columbia University in 1977. My doctoral dissertation was *The Concept of Interprofessional Collaboration in Baccalaureate Nursing Education*

Programs: a Descriptive Survey, which was the basis of much of my future professional accomplishments.

Unfortunately, as a result of extreme stress at home, I wasn't able to rework my dissertation for publication at that time. It is thirty five years later, and my topic is once again of interest, now internationally addressed by many scholars.

Last year I was approached by the Memorial Hospital Nursing Research Council requesting a copy of my doctoral dissertation. They would like to replicate my study with a current survey of interprofessional education across the United States. I have agreed to assist with such a project and a review of literature was underway with the assistance of the hospital library director, but work on another study of *"Nurses and Physicians Attitudes Toward Collaboration at Memorial"* is taking precedence.

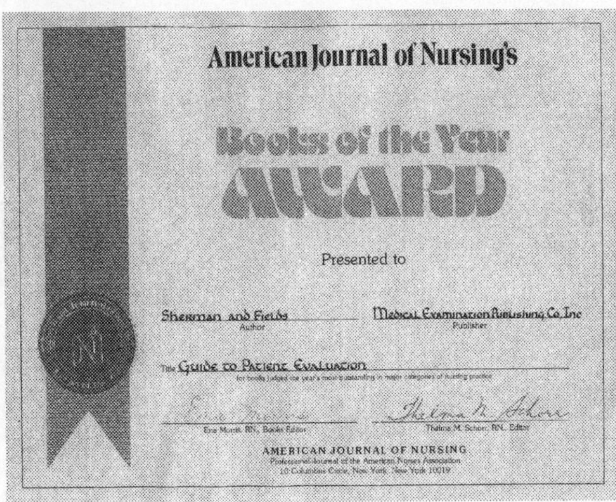

American Journal of Nursing's

Books of the Year

AWARD

Presented to

Sherman and Fields — Author

Medical Examination Publishing Co. Inc — Publisher

Title Guide to Patient Evaluation

for books judged the year's most outstanding in major categories of nursing practice

[illegible], RN, Books Editor

Thelma M. Schorr, RN, Editor

AMERICAN JOURNAL OF NURSING

Professional Journal of the American Nurses Association

10 Columbus Circle, New York, New York 10019

We received the American Journal of Nursing **Book of the Year Award**.

4861 - 3
4862 - 3
4863 - 3

INSTRUCTORS GUIDE

HEALTH
INSTRUCTIONAL
PROGRAMS for
PROFESSIONALS

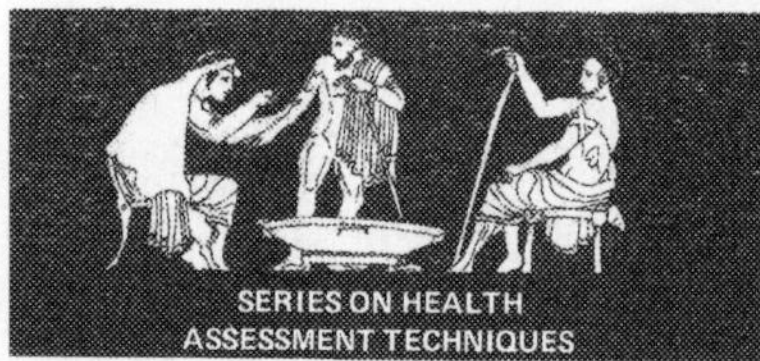

Jacques L. Sherman, Jr., M.D.
Health Sciences Center
Stony Brook, N. Y.

Sylvia K. Fields, R.N., M.A., M.Ed.
Department of Adult Health School of Nursing
Stony Brook, N. Y.

4853 5

STUDENT WORKBOOK

HEALTH
INSTRUCTIONAL
PROGRAMS for
PROFESSIONALS

**SERIES ON CLINICALLY ORIENTED
BASIC ANATOMY AND PHYSIOLOGY**

Filmstrip III

RESPIRATORY ANATOMY AND PHYSIOLOGY

Sylvia K. Fields, R.N., M.A., M.Ed.
School of Nursing
State University of New York at Stonybrook

Rebecca Fierro, R.N., B.S.
School of Nursing
State University of New York, at Stonybrook

Jacques L. Sherman, Jr., M.D.
Health Science Center
State University of New York at Stonybrook

Development of various other educational materials to support our Stony Brook Nursing Program.

Dr. Ellen Fahy, founding Dean of Nursing SUNY Stony Brook who recruited and supported me enabling me to continue my academic studies, write grants, work with Dr. Sherman to develop the "Guide to Patient Evaluation" other media and journal articles.

8

The End of the Marriage: Becoming Dr. Fields and Moving on

You are beautiful, you are smart, and you deserve more"

Dr. Jacques L. Sherman

For months I had warned him, "You're going to get fired." I begged him to cooperate, "Gerry, the hospital is spending thousands of dollars to evaluate their programs, don't be a fool; cooperate in every way possible. Show them you are part of the soul of the administration, a team member, committed to the institution." The hospital had hired a national consulting organization to critically examine each division/department and make recommendations. Too many departments were losing money including the one where Gerry was the assistant administrator. He didn't think much of the department administrator and kept telling that to Bill, the physician who was chairman of the department, as they carpooled to work several days a week. Gerry had other complaints, as he always did. "I don't need to tell them anything, they're getting paid plenty, let them find it out for themselves," Gerry responded with his typical arrogance.

Melissa was home for a month-long winter holiday from American University in Washington DC, where she was a junior in the nursing program, while Andrew, a high school junior, was in Texas at a Jewish Youth convention. Elizabeth was also home for holiday break from the Hebrew junior high school she attended. I didn't realize Gerry was in the house when I came home from my Stony Brook office on the last day before our two-week holiday; I parked the Oldsmobile with 90,000 miles in the driveway. Since we only had a one-car garage and did not have an automatic garage opener I usually pulled into the driveway, left the engine running, opened the garage with the key, and then drove the car inside. But when I opened the garage I was surprised to see that the newer car, a beautiful Mercury Cougar Gerry had leased a few months before, was inside. After closing the engine, I walked inside the house.

Melissa signaled to me, "Daddy isn't in a good mood, don't go upstairs."

"Is he sick?" I asked.

"I don't think so, but I'm supposed to call him when you get home."

But with that he came downstairs. "Where have you been? I tried to call you," he demanded curtly.

"I was in the conference room, we had a little holiday party and we were cleaning up. I didn't expect you home so early. What's the matter? Why are you home so early? You look like something's wrong," I said.

"I tried to call you, and then I called the Dean's office for you when no one answered," he complained.

"It's a holiday and we were celebrating," I replied.

Gerry's face told it all. He said, "Well, it's over. They gave us a copy of the damn evaluation report; they cut out my job. Bill said there was nothing he could do."

"Did they give you any severance pay? I asked.

"Only two weeks, I wasn't there long enough for more, he said.

"You damn idiot, what are you going to do now?" I screamed. "I warned you, over and over again, but you're always smarter than everyone else; you did it to yourself, and I warned you."

He walked upstairs. I began to cry.

Just then the phone rang, I picked up the phone, it was for me, but I didn't know who it was. I said, "Who is this? Who?" I didn't recognize the name.

"It's Miss Bello, the real estate agent. Ms. Wright, the Nursing Department secretary, gave me your number and suggested I call you."

I heard the phone click; Gerry was on the other line. "I'm sorry, I can't talk now," I said and hung up quickly.

But it was too late; Gerry came down and demanded, "Why was a real estate agent calling you?"

"I don't know, I don't know," I cried out, but I couldn't talk any more. "I don't know, I don't have anything else to say, I just have to get out of here." I grabbed my purse and ran out of the house. I got into the car and backed out of the driveway with him screaming at me to stop and get back in the house. The girls stood there, dumbfounded.

I made a right turn to Round Swamp Road past the Expressway to the Northern State Parkway and started driving east. I didn't know where I was when I saw a telephone booth on the side of the Parkway. I pulled over and stopped the car; I just sat there crying and trying to think what to do next. I talked to myself out loud, "I'm not going back, I can't explain, I've had enough."

The Dean's secretary had told us she was able to rent a really nice furnished house in the Stratford Development in Stony Brook for $500 a month plus utilities. I had asked her for the number of the real estate broker, which she gave me, but I never looked at it. I was just curious, I wasn't thinking of moving out. I just thought one day I might need it, but I wasn't ready to do anything now, not until I finished writing my dissertation. I never thought the secretary would tell the broker to call me now.

Unfortunately I could not seem to write my dissertation. I had finished the research, hand punched all the cards with the responses to the survey and taken them to the computer office at Columbia in October. The analysis was done on the mainframe computer and I now had all the data on a large reel. I had completed writing all the introductory content and Dr. Labadie had reviewed what I had written and made suggestions, which I responded to. (As always she was right on target.) Now all the data was in charts and graphs on the reel in the dining room which I used as an office, but I never told Gerry it was there. I was afraid he would open it and tear it up; he was so jealous, all he kept saying was, "This is a waste of time, you'll never finish it." But I had finished it; I just needed to start writing again.

How could I go back to that house? How would I explain about the real estate agent? I did not know where to go or what to do. I wanted to call Dr. Sherman but what could he do? I had to leave him out of this. Ever since the article about our book with a photo of us together appeared on the front page of the Stony Brook newspaper, innuendoes had been expressed around the campus. Dr. Sherman had told me that I was smart and beautiful and that I deserved more love and respect at home. Despite the eighteen-year difference in our ages, I was in love with him. But he always told me how much he loved his wife of thirty years who had survived breast cancer, and he could not leave her, so what advice could he offer to help me now? I knew if he did anything to help me now his wife would be suspicious; she probably was already. But there had been nothing physically significant between Dr. Sherman and me, just a few kisses in the car after we delivered the *Guide to Patient Evaluation* manuscript to the publisher. Later, a few more when he gave me a silver pendant he brought back from a conference he attended in New Mexico. It was then that he told me he had fallen in love with me. It was the first time in my life I heard those words. I had never heard them from my husband. That was months earlier. I never wore the pendant. I was sure it would raise suspicions.

I did not know what to do. I couldn't call my parents or drive to Brooklyn to see them. When I had done that almost twenty years earlier when Melissa was only nine months old, my mother had refused to help me. I was forced to go back to Gerry then, but now I had more confidence in myself and my ability to support my children. I kept telling myself over and over, I've had enough and I'm not going back to him. I was married twenty one years, it was half my life. Melissa was almost twenty years old now. I felt like I was losing my mind and I was sure I was having a nervous breakdown.

Sitting on the side of the Northern State Parkway, my nose running and my eyes blurred, I knew I had to do something. I got out of the car, went to the phone and called my friend, the psychiatric nursing faculty member at Stony Brook. She lived not too far from me, and already knew the whole story before this event since we carpooled together when possible and she listened to me complaining. With several children, she had survived a bitter divorce from her wealthy attorney husband who had pushed her down the stairs during a argument. Gerry never hit me; he wouldn't dare. He wasn't an alcoholic, did not take drugs and as far as I knew he did not run around with other women. It was his arrogance that always bothered me, and his inability to hold a job, but most of all, it was his possessive and demeaning attitude toward me. No matter how hard I worked and whatever I accomplished, he never told me he loved me, never acknowledged my value to his life. He clearly did not appreciate me.

I told my friend what happened. "I'm having a nervous breakdown. I must be crazy, I've been chewing Valium like candy. Now I am dizzy and I am not going back to my house. Can you get me admitted to the psych unit, I must be crazy," I cried.

"Sylvia, you're not crazy, he's crazy. You've been managing your children and the household while teaching, going to Columbia, doing your research for your doctorate, all successfully. You're not crazy, you're exhausted. I will call my friend the director of nursing at the Community Hospital. Where are you? What's the phone number? Stay there; I will call you back," she said. Ten minutes later she called back. "She also does not think the psych unit is a good idea for you professionally; you do not want it in your medical record. Do you have any other symptoms?" she asked.

I caught my breath, "OK," I said, "yes, tell her I have chest pains, tell her I have chest pains, palpitations, and I'm short of breath."

I hung up and waited for the call back. The chief of medicine agreed I needed to be evaluated and perhaps admitted. It did not take long but somehow I drove to the hospital emergency room, crying all the way. I was admitted with chest pain, elevated blood pressure, and abnormal blood enzymes. I asked the internist examining me if I could to see a psychiatrist and a rabbi, and he agreed. I am certain that any of this could not happen today. But it was 1976, and just before Christmas so many patients had been released and only emergencies were being admitted.

I was put into a private room. There was a phone on the bedside table so once I was alone I called my next-door neighbor, Gloria. I didn't tell her where I was but I gave her the direct number where I could be reached. I asked her to quietly go to my house and without letting my husband know, tell Melissa to come to her house to call me. Once Melissa was on the phone, I told her where I was and that I did not want to go back home while Gerry was there.

I had left before after a fight with Gerry, but never stayed away overnight. At that time I had demanded a lawyer and marriage counseling and Gerry had refused, but he had finally agreed when our lawyer, a personal friend, pressured him. Gerry had sat in the therapist's office with a stoic and sour face; his arms folded across his chest, and refused to say a word after I explained my complaints to the psychologist. When the fifty-minute session was over, Gerry still refused to speak, making it clear that he had nothing to say and would not agree to a further meeting. I wrote the check for $50 and we walked out of the office. Gerry finally opened his mouth, "I don't believe in any of this bullshit," he said. "I'll give you the $50 and you go buy yourself a new dress." He was in complete denial.

A few months before that episode, after a bitter fight with Gerry about his negativity toward everyone and everything at work, and his destructive attitudes and constant complaints about me, I found myself venting to Melissa about her father's attitudes and behavior, and how I couldn't stand living with him. I had moved out of our bedroom. Melissa, who had heard much of the dissension for years, said, "Mom, for God's sake, "shit or get off the pot."

Now, I told Melissa, I am determined to "get off the pot." But I knew it would be bitter and probably meant I would have to leave the home I loved so much and worked so hard to maintain. Gerry had no job now, no money, and no record of success at anything he had ever done. How would he get a new job? I didn't see any future for him or for me with him. I would have to meet with our lawyer. I asked Melissa to quietly take the computer reel holding my doctoral research data out of the house. I was afraid Gerry would destroy it. I believed he saw my doctoral study as his competitor.

I also told Melissa to secretly take my black broadtail fur jacket, (made for me by his uncle, the furrier in Niagara Falls, when Melissa was born.) I asked to include my box of twelve-place settings of sterling silver my mother had bought for me, (one place setting a year for twelve years.) These were the only things of value I thought I might be able to sell. Despite how hard I had worked all these years, I had no cash, no savings account, no extra money in my checking account, and some debt on our charge accounts. I did not have anything put away for emergencies. How could I have prepared myself to leave before? I never had extra money in my account. We had always lived from month to month on our salaries and the extra income I earned through all kinds of temporary and part-time work. I asked Melissa to pack a bag with a couple of changes of clothing for a few days including pajamas, a robe, and underwear. I gave her the hospital room number and telephone number with clear directions not to let her father know anything.

When the psychiatrist came to see me, I told him the whole story of my life with Gerry, how much I hated him, how hard I worked to keep us in the house, how much I loved my work and what I had accomplished. I told him about leaving Gerry twenty years before when Melissa was a baby, and about running out of the house the previous year, only to come back demanding a lawyer and marriage counselor. I told him about Gerry sitting next to me with his arms crossed and refusing to say anything during the marriage counseling session and what he finally said when we left the counselor's office. I told the psychiatrist how much I loved my beautiful home and children and how I was worried about leaving them in the house with Gerry.

The doctor listened to the whole story. He told me I was not mentally ill; it was anxiety and he was surprised I was able to function so well given the amount of anger I was carrying. "With some medication, and time apart, you will recover," he said. "You have been solving problems all these years, you will figure it out."

Of course I knew I wasn't psychotic; I wasn't hallucinating and didn't have any delusions – everything I was experiencing was "real." I just didn't want to return to my husband. I did no t love him, and as much as I did not want to leave my beautiful home, I understood I would probably have to give it up. I did not know then how I could manage; I knew I needed time alone to think about possible options.

I also asked to see a rabbi. I felt guilty. My mother had said it years before. I had made a commitment to marriage. How could I leave Gerry now? Elizabeth was almost twelve and she was supposed to start studying to prepare for her Bat Mitzvah the following year. Melissa was a junior at American University. How could I afford the tuition and all her expenses in that private school? I was receiving royalties on our book and the extra projects, but my salary was too low to support us all. My car had almost 100,000 miles on it and I still had tuition at Columbia for the dissertation advisement with Dr. Labadie until I finished writing up the study. I don't know what I expected from the rabbi. Maybe some advance forgiveness for leaving my husband; after all, he didn't hit me. He just didn't value me, and I didn't value him. I probably never did. I had stayed twenty one years, and it was half my life. I needed to see something different for the next twenty one years or life just was not worth living. I can do it I told myself, I will survive, we will all survive. I made up my mind I was not going back to Gerry no matter how he begged.

I called my parents and told them about Gerry losing his job after my warnings, and what I had done and where I was. I told them firmly I wasn't going back to him and I needed their help temporarily. I asked them for $1,000 to pay the first and the last month's rent on a furnished house. This time they consented and came to the hospital, expressed support, and gave me a check for $1,000. The next morning the internist came in and told me the latest EKG and other tests were now normal and that he would have to discharge me.

For five days I had lain in that bed thinking about the decision I was making. I did not know how I was going to manage and what the effect would be on my children; I just knew I could not go back to that house with him there, and I did not see how I would get him out. I started making a list.

1. Call a lawyer. Start the separation and divorce proceedings.

2. Where could I stay until I was able to find a house to rent? I thought about Dr. Arlene Barro, Assistant Dean in the medical school, who lived alone in a rented house near the university. We had worked together at the Health Sciences Center on the interprofessional course for more than two years. I called Arlene, told her my story, and asked if I could stay with her for a few days while I worked with a real estate agent. She graciously agreed to let me stay rent free. (Ten years later I returned the favor.)

#3. Call Gloria and ask her to contact Melissa for me again. She agreed but she told me Gerry was furious and not easy to deal with. I learned later that she had told Gerry I had someone else in my life. I had made the mistake of confiding in her months earlier that I thought I was in love with Dr. Sherman. I told her he was married and nothing could come of it. We had commiserated about our unhappy marriages, but Gloria was a stay-at-home wife and mother who had married late in life after a ten-year career. I knew she was bored, but I never got the sense that she criticized me. I guess she might have been envious, but I didn't think she had loved the job she gave up when she married and became pregnant. Hers was not an economic issue; Joe had a very good position and Gloria did not have to work. I never understood why she was so unhappy. Her husband Joe was always so pleasant, and great with the kids, who were the same age as my two oldest. Joe took care of the lawn and garden on weekends, fixed everything around the house (and sometimes ours), and had had an in-ground pool installed in the back yard where we were always welcome. Gerry was completely uninterested in the lawn or gardening; we had to hire outside help. Of course we never know what goes on in someone else's bedroom. I found out later that Gloria was an alcoholic; I believe she died of liver disease before she reached 60.

4. Contact Dean Fahy to determine whether Melissa could transfer to SUNY at Stony Brook immediately. The curriculum at American

University was very similar to the Stony Brook program. I should meet with my girls at the hospital to ask them what they wanted to do, since I was determined not to go back to the house. Let Melissa know I wouldn't be able to continue supporting her at American University in Washington DC. Both girls declared they wanted to go wherever with me. Dr. Fahy said she would work the transfer out, and by the time the new semester started in February, Melissa was enrolled as a junior in our nursing program. She received credit for everything she had taken before since the two programs were similar (Melissa graduated with a BSN from Stony Brook in June 1978.)

5. Notify our joint bank and credit card accounts that I would not be responsible for any checks and charges made by Gerry. Open a new checking account with the check from my parents.

6. Contact the real estate broker and look at a furnished house in Stony Brook offered for rent for six months by a University faculty member away on sabbatical leave.

7. Call Jerry Newman, executive manager at Medical Examination Publishing Company, to tell him I would have to be paid for the reviews of prospective manuscripts I had been doing gratis. He agreed to give me an advance on my book royalties for moving expenses, and $400 a month as a consultant to review prospective manuscripts for publication.

8. Contact Andrew, who was participating in a Youth Retreat in Texas and about to come home, and tell him what was happening. He wanted to come to live with me and the girls in Stony Brook, but agreed to stay with Gerry for a few months until the summer. But after three weeks alone with Gerry eating take-out Chinese food every night, Andrew pleaded to come to us. Despite Gerry's objection, our lawyers agreed that all the children were old enough to choose. Melissa picked Andrew up and he moved in with us.

9. Arrange for school transfers for Andrew and Elizabeth for the January semester.

Gerry stayed in the Old Bethpage house by himself, and the children visited him once a week. He refused to apply for unemployment or look for a position. My attorney had advised me not to pay any bills or credit card debt. Of course, Gerry had no money to give to the children, so every expense fell on me. The entire divorce process was hostile and that is the way it stayed. Gerry was sure I would give in and give up and move back to the house. Maybe if he had ever shown any understanding and made an effort to search for a new job and shown some change in his attitude toward me, I might have reconsidered. But Gerry was convinced I had been having an affair and blamed me and my relationship with Dr. Sherman for all his problems. He couldn't recognize that our problems had started years before, and that he was also responsible.

The winter was miserable; it was cold with lots of ice and snow. I was still driving back and forth to Columbia for dissertation advisement, but somehow, late at night I was energized to write up my research results. The children were completely supportive and had adjusted to the new schools and were making new friends. The Health Science Building was under construction, with ice and mud everywhere. One freezing Friday evening in the dark after work, I tried to start my car in the parking lot, but it wouldn't budge. I sat there in the car thinking about my options. I was exhausted. I managed to trudge back to the building and found a security person, but I was told there was nothing they could do. "You will have to call AAA for help," I was told. When I learned the garage service people could not come out to the university until morning, I called Melissa to return to school to pick me up. As I sat there waiting, I made up my mind that after I finished my dissertation and Melissa and Andrew graduated from their respective programs, I would search for another position, hopefully in the South where I wouldn't have to deal with the ice and snow and the high taxes on Long Island.

At the end of six months, we had to move again. By this time, the separation was legal and I was able to get the children's furniture out of the house. We looked for an unfurnished house to rent for a year. This was not as easy as it had been in December. Melissa and Andrew fell in love with one of the houses offered, a three-bedroom caretakers' cottage in Old Field on an estate overlooking Long Island Sound. They convinced me to rent it. Nothing else we looked at could match the charm of the place. However, it didn't take long to realize it was a mistake, one I probably regret to this day. While Andrew could remain in the same Stony Brook high school after the move to Old Field, Elizabeth had to change junior high schools again, and start over making new friends. We also fought over choice of bedroom; I should have given her the large front room upstairs. I was stupid.

As beautiful as the house and the view were, it was on a rural road and we couldn't meet any neighbors or walk anywhere, except onto the marsh, which could have been dangerous. Andrew loved the marsh and kept bringing home natural souvenirs. When the snow started we were isolated as the wind from Long Island Sound forced the snow to pile over the doors. One week with phone lines down, we were snowbound for four days and ran out of food and fuel.

There was a clause in the lease against pets. It meant we had to hide our cat Midnight when the owner came. Sometimes we had no warning that he was coming, so there was a mad rush to put the cat into a straw hamper in Melissa's bedroom, which was actually the dining room. Midnight knew the basket was serious business; he never made a sound when we threw him inside, despite all the dirty clothes. But later we learned the owner knew about the cat all the time; he refused to give me a short extension I needed at the end of the lease. By this time Midnight was sick. He kept throwing up in the house. I took him to the vet, who diagnosed him with cancer of the liver and advised against any treatment. Tragically we had to have Midnight put to sleep. Although I had complained constantly about the stress Midnight caused over the years, we all cried afterwards; I don't know who cried the most, probably me. All this time my children never complained.

I started the search for a new position. My main goal was a school where Andrew and then Elizabeth could receive a quality education, and of course the hope for a warmer climate. Over several months I explored different opportunities. First I visited Richmond and Charlottesville, Virginia, where there was an exciting new opportunity for a director to develop a collaborative nurse practitioner program between the Virginia Commonwealth University and the University of Virginia. I wasn't exactly sure where Andrew might fit best, but it turned out the position was a funded two-year federal project, with only one year guaranteed. Unfortunately the same situation occurred at the University of Pennsylvania, one of the finest nursing schools in the country. Although it wasn't in the south, I had such fond memories of my early years growing up in Philadelphia I was inclined to move back there. I looked forward to experiencing the Wanamaker's Department Store organ music during Christmas time and being able to walk all over the historical downtown city. But I couldn't take the chance of a short-term contract.

Suddenly I became brave and flew out to San Diego California where my friend Delores Wozniak, with whom I had worked well with at Farmingdale, was nursing department chair but moving up to the dean's position for health professions at San Diego State. She recommended me for nursing chair, but I "chickened out" from that position, and a few others in California. My aged parents, who were living in Augusta, Georgia, at that time, asked me not to move so far, and I realized it wasn't such a good idea. I liked the position as nursing chairperson offered at the Medical University of South Carolina in Charleston, but there was no liberal arts spot for Andrew there.

Emory University in Atlanta finally made me an offer that seemed perfect. In view of my background I was offered a position as full professor with tenure as Director of the Undergraduate Nursing Program, known as the Nell Hodgson Woodruff School of Nursing. The salary promised was $30,000, which was $10,000 more than my salary in New York. I learned that the cost of living, especially housing, in Atlanta was also much less than the cost on Long Island and among the benefits was a full-tuition scholarship for my children at the highly rated university. And on top of that, the winters would be warmer; no more snow. (Later I learned that Atlanta has hills and ice storms, and very few people know how to drive in the ice in the South.)

Meanwhile the awful divorce proceedings continued, with no possibility of child support, so I depended on extra income through professional activities reviewing manuscripts for publication, on top of my full-time responsibilities which were now primarily teaching graduate nursing courses in the Nurse Practitioner Program: Health Appraisal, Advanced Pathophysiology, and Adult Patient Health Management. I had to take out a loan to pay for the typing of my dissertation and final semester of advisement at Columbia.

Somehow, I was managing to do it all, but the relationship with Gerry regarding the children was horrendous. Depressed and demoralized, he refused to look for work and stayed in our home alone with some financial help from his parents, while the house was put up for sale to pay debts. When it was finally sold and bills were paid, there was only $5,000 remaining that was put into a trust fund for the two younger children. Both attorneys had to agree before any funds could be taken from that bank account, and it couldn't go to me, it had to go directly to the children. It took almost two more years before we could prove Gerry had a job, and child support of $50 a month was awarded to Andrew for his senior year and to Elizabeth, unfortunately not retroactively. Melissa never received any money from Gerry. She had chosen to move into New York City after graduation from Stony Brook and took a position as a registered nurse at Lenox Hill Hospital.

I went to Atlanta to look for a place to live within an easy commute to Emory, hoping I could find a three-bedroom house or condominium I could lease with an option to buy, rather than renting an apartment, although I didn't have money yet for a down payment. The one person I knew who lived in Atlanta was a former sister-in-law who had remarried and moved to Dunwoody, a close-in suburb of Atlanta. Kayla was thrilled that we might move close by and enthusiastically showed me a beautiful three-bedroom townhouse in the hills near her home, in a development called D'Youville Estates. It was just inside the perimeter road that circled the city and overlooked a creek; there were tennis courts, a pool, and a social clubhouse. The selling price was $60,000 and it only required a 10% down payment, but I didn't think I would be able borrow that much. I left disappointed that I couldn't afford it and kept looking, but nothing else was as attractive and convenient. I went back to the sales office to see if I could negotiate something and this time the wife of the developer was there. It was amazing; it turned out she was a nurse, an Emory graduate no less, now retired. I told her my plight, showed her my letter of appointment to the Emory faculty and she consulted with her husband. They wanted me there; I would be a good tenant, so they cut the down payment in half to three thousand dollars and agreed to pay all the closing costs for me.

I went back to Kayla's house where I was staying, and I got on the telephone to look for a lender. I didn't want to ask my parents for any more money. The first person I thought of was my friend Dr. Delores Saxton, a long-time faculty member at Nassau Community College, who was single with no children and still living in her family home in Mineola. We had commuted together flying from the Suffolk County airport laughing all the way to Albany NY for three years every month as we worked on the New York State BSN external degree program performance exam. For many years Delores was also the executive editor of Mosby's Comprehensive Review Book. She did not hesitate a minute, offered me the $3,000 and when I offered to pay her interest, scolded me, "Don't be ridiculous, Sylvia. I am only too glad to help you out." (I was able to pay her back within the year.) I am a very lucky person; friends always seem to come to my aid.

The condominium was beautiful, with three bedrooms, two and a half baths, a living room with fireplace and sliding doors to a deck, and a great family room downstairs with access to the gardens and creek outside. This time Elizabeth got her choice, the entire downstairs with her own bedroom, a private bathroom, and the family room large enough to have friends sleep over privately. My parents were thrilled that I would be closer to them in Augusta, so we could visit together. I was excited about the new life I would be starting, thinking that perhaps I would meet someone and have a new love as well.

In July 1978, two weeks before I moved to Atlanta and Melissa started work, we were able to have a vacation in Hawaii together. There was a national meeting of the American Nurses Association celebrating the organization's 75th anniversary. All the companies that publish books, manufacture uniforms and equipment, or distribute supplies used by nurses traditionally have demonstrations and receptions at professional organization meetings. This was to be the biggest and best meeting in history according to the announcements. Medical Examination Publishing Company had prepared a new edition of *Guide to Patient Evaluation*, and offered to pay all my expenses to attend the meeting. It was a perfect opportunity for me to give Melissa a significant graduation gift that we could enjoy together after the stressful years just completed on Long Island. The room was paid for, food was offered everywhere from breakfast to dinner, and there were educational and social opportunities for both of us through lectures, meetings, and cocktail parties galore. We met several professional contacts that eventually led to additional opportunities. Melissa and I were able to tour Pearl Harbor, experience Waikiki Beach, and take a small plane for a day trip to the island of Maui. It was a marvelous time together we will never forget.

Through the many years that followed, with all the family events that should be happy, including birthdays, weddings of each child, the births of grandchildren, and some sad happenings, such as the death of Elizabeth's first husband, Mark, from lung cancer, Gerry and I were never able to have a civil conversation. Not once. Although I remarried almost ten years later, Gerry never did. After living in Manhattan and traveling for more than twenty years with a lady friend who owned a travel agency, he worked only intermittently for a hospital employees union. Gerry died of lymphoma soon after Hurricane Katrina hit New Orleans, where he had moved to be closer to two of our children.

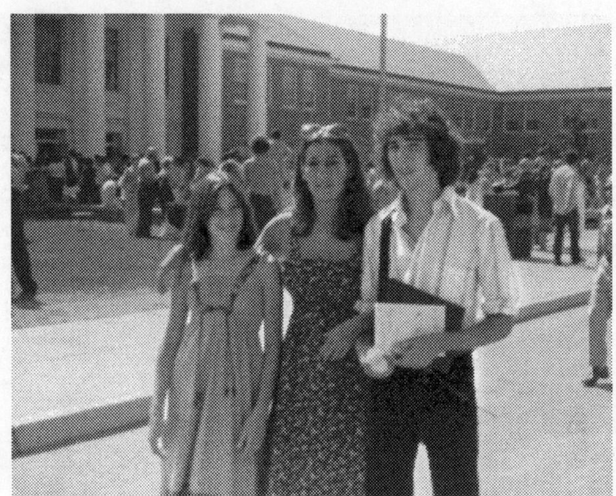

Andrew graduated Ward Melville High School, Setauket, New York 1978 (with Melissa and Elizabeth).

Melissa graduated SUNY Stony Brook Nursing Program 1978. As faculty I marched in the procession.

I complete my dissertation and received the Doctor of Education Degree, 1977 at Columbia University.

Melissa and I at the American Nurses Association 100th Anniversary Meeting in Honolulu and Maui, Hawaii, courtesy of Medical Examination Publishing Company who paid all expenses.

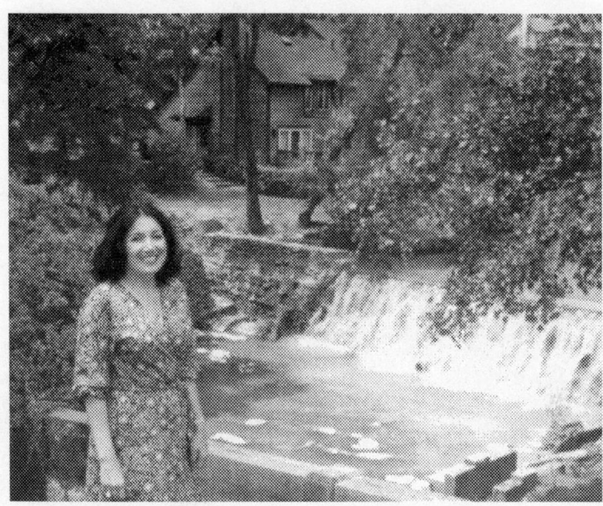

I am appointed Professor and Director Undergraduate Program, Nell Hodgson Woodruff School of Nursing. At the rear of my beautiful condo at D'youville Trace, Chamblee-Dunwoody Rd, Atlanta, Georgia.

A Sketch of the Nursing School Building, (Artist Unknown) 1978.

9

Emory University: The Harvard of the South

("Change Takes Place Slowly in the South")
This section is based upon an interview conducted in preparation for an alumni newsletter about my professional life after graduation.

Interviewer: Sylvia, I understand that you left the State University of New York, Stony Brook in 1978 and took the position of professor and director of the undergraduate nursing program at Emory University. What attracted you to the Nell Hodgson Woodruff School of Nursing at Emory?

Sylvia: I had been very productive at SUNY Stony Brook, including earning tenure and completing my doctorate while going through a hostile and painful divorce. But living expenses were very high, and I thought I needed a change of environment; I hoped for a warmer and less expensive climate than New York. I was still fully responsible for supporting two children and was looking for a first class educational opportunity for them. I understood Emory was a highly regarded small private university, but I knew very little about the Nell Hodgson Woodruff School of Nursing. I did not know the nursing dean or faculty through professional organizations and had not noticed any publications in the nursing literature by Emory nursing faculty members, but I was confident in my ability to bring something positive from my education and experiences. To be honest, I was optimistic that I might meet some new people and find a new personal relationship.

I had answered an advertisement in the *American Journal of Nursing* for the position of undergraduate director. In response I was sent an

Emory catalogue and brochures which described the undergraduate and graduate programs offered with an application for the position within the nursing school. It was not until I came for an interview that I really learned more about the history of the school's beginning as a hospital diploma program and the change to a generic baccalaureate program after World War II, with collaboration of the medical school for the teaching of science courses. The high qualifications required of students and the specific components of the curriculum seemed similar to the best established baccalaureate programs I knew. I was also impressed by the graduate programs in nurse midwifery, nurse anesthesia, and community mental health that included collaboration with the medical school faculty and cooperating Atlanta health care providers, such as Grady Memorial and Crawford Long Hospitals.

It was warm and pleasant the day I arrived for my interview, and as the taxi carried me to the campus from the airport I was impressed by the beautiful surrounding neighborhood, lovely flowers within the compact campus, and then the handsome contemporary architecture of the nursing school building, named after the wife of the president of the Coca Cola Corporation, Robert Woodruff. The Southern hospitality offered by the members of the search committee who greeted me made me feel at ease immediately. I thought my son could be happy on the campus as well. And then there was the subject of the salary; underneath it all, I was fairly confident I could afford to live in Atlanta quite comfortably on that salary.

Interviewer: Within a year you were approved by the Emory Board of Trustees for tenure. Why do you think your appointment met with such rapid acceptance?

Sylvia: I clearly had all the requirements. My twenty-year academic and clinical background offered the full range of potential for nursing education and practice in the future. I thought my recent involvement with innovative curricular strategies related to the development of expanded roles for nursing had been the main attraction; some of the faculty members were using my award-winning book *Guide to Patient*

Evaluation in the program. I had several other professional publications and a history of successful grant writing. All of this writing and publication was deemed helpful to the re-accreditation process that was on the horizon.

I also assumed my advocacy for diploma and associate degree graduates earning the baccalaureate degree was important to the nursing community and the university administration. I made strong pleas for such opportunities and early in 1981, as an experienced program director, I was asked to provide a statement to the National Commission on Nursing, corresponding with public hearings held nationally, in relation to the significant drop in enrollment in professional nursing programs across the country at that time. My paper entitled "Nursing Education and Entry into Practice," which focused on the need to develop creative strategies for registered nurses to be able to earn the baccalaureate degree, was approved by the dean and was well received that day of presentation.

Interviewer: Did you have any problems coming from the north to this southern school? For example, as a leader of the faculty, how did your style fit the institution?

Sylvia: There were some adjustment issues for me as I assumed more administrative responsibilities for an established curriculum and a larger group of faculty than I was accustomed to working with. I was an activist used to problem solving and much freedom in developing new programs. What I thought was important for the undergraduate program was not universally perceived that way by some of the faculty members. I recognized over time that my strong personality may have created some problems. I probably did not listen to diverse faculty often enough and I wasn't patient.

After meeting with many practicing nurses in the hospital that adjoined the nursing school building, I believed there was a need for an accelerated program to enable diploma and associate degree graduate nurses to matriculate in the Emory baccalaureate degree program. Many of these nurses were Emory diploma graduates who were limited in seeking role advancement in the hospital without the BSN degree, but could not afford to give up their positions to study for two to four years more. Some of the Emory nursing faculty members were rigidly opposed to what they believed would be "diluting" the program requirements in any way and were reluctant to develop a part-time offering that would permit the nurses to maintain their clinical positions. In my previous positions in diploma and associate degree programs I had known many wonderful bright nurses who were assisted in earning the baccalaureate through innovative programs that enabled them to obtain graduate degrees later, all the while making significant contributions to the profession and the public.

The Dean of Nursing was not enthusiastic about developing an accelerated program because she wanted to seek external funding to expand the graduate program and offer the Doctorate in Nursing Science under the control of the nursing school. At that time some nursing faculty had completed doctoral study through an Emory University graduate program where they designed research studies leading to the PhD in collaboration with other disciplines, such as psychology or sociology. Several other nursing faculty members were currently actively enrolled in such programs. Establishing an experimental accelerated program towards the BSN would probably not provide the professional status and reputation of the Doctorate in Nursing Science degree the Dean was anxious to achieve. Apparently, however, the University President was not willing to support the latter project. I believed he might support an accelerated program first.

Without the support of the Dean and the majority of faculty, I could not challenge the curriculum committee to develop an accelerated BSN track for experienced graduates of diploma or associate degree nursing programs. So, with the encouragement of a few faculty members eager for an alternative approach, I brought information about the New York State Regents External Degree Programs (REX) and the Clinical Performance Testing methods I had helped to develop to the attention of the Georgia Nurses Association (GNA). GNA moved ahead to offer the option for Georgia nurses and established a clinical performance testing center through the Southern Regional Nursing Board. With my encouragement a few Emory nursing faculty members participated as clinical evaluators, but the Dean was not happy with this development in general and with me in particular. She may have felt the external degree program would discourage potential RN students from coming to Emory, creating a financial deficit for current Emory programs. However, the individualized REX nursing programs were NLN accredited and always required at least two years of previous experience in the health care field prior to admission, as well as general education prerequisites comparable to on site academic nursing programs.

Interviewer: I understand that the University President was impressed with your interprofessional activities on the campus. Can you describe what they were?

Sylvia: In view of my past interprofessional experiences at Stony Brook, when the dean was asked to recommend someone from the nursing faculty to participate in a new collaborative curriculum project at Emory, I was given the assignment. The Department of Community Health of the School of Medicine at Emory, which sponsored a Dietetics Internship program, had received a federal grant from the Health Resources Administration, Public Health Service, and Department of Health and Human Services, to increase the nutrition content in the medical school curriculum. Emory became one of 13 health professional schools funded for curriculum development projects in applied nutrition, with the requirement that an interprofessional approach be utilized and that medical students and students of at least two other health professions be included. I was thrilled to serve as an expert in interprofessional learning and have the opportunity for our nursing students to be actively involved.

The Emory project had proposed a national conference be held to allow for sharing of activities and discussion of problems encountered by the thirteen schools. We held the first conference at the Woodruff Medical Center in September 1980, followed a year later by a two-day national workshop on nutrition education in health professions schools held in Washington, DC September 30–October 1, 1981. We were responsible for conducting the conference and workshop, clarifying objectives, selecting the panel of expert consultants, and publishing the papers presented in Washington. I was proud to have the paper I prepared on "Interprofessional Education and Collaboration," describing the advantages and the barriers, included in the final publication.

The topic and extent of nutrition content in the medical school and other health professions curriculum is unfortunately as varied and vague today due to those barriers as it was in 1981, although as predicted then, the impact of the computer has made a significant difference. One of my recommendations was that students learning together needed to be at the same academic level, preferably at the graduate level. The following is quoted from my published commentary and conclusions. [14]

> In view of the many common barriers to interprofessional learning, it is perhaps more important that we focus in our programs on preparing each health professional with the skills necessary for beginning independent practice and plan to prepare him (or her) for collaboration when professionally ready, through graduate or continuing education and on-site team training.
>
> Computer programs for assessment and management of problems in nutrition such as the ones recently developed by certain interdisciplinary projects within this collaborative enterprise could be tested and made available to practitioners across the country. We would have the benefit of the knowledge of the most expert health care team available with much greater opportunity for quality health care practice. Imagine the cost effectiveness if we don't need the "traditional "team" in every center, yet have access to the knowledge of a team of experts!

[14] National Workshop on Nutrition Education in Health Professions Schools: Interprofessional Collaboration and Education; September 30-October 1, 1981 Washington, D.C. Sylvia K. Fields EdD, RN

Reading these papers now more than 30 years later, I am amazed how the problems identified then are still pertinent. There are very few words I would have to change if I had to present such a paper today.

Interviewer: Were you involved in any other significant university-wide activities during your four-year tenure?

Sylvia: In 1979 the University received a gift of $105 million dollars in Coca Cola stock from Robert and George Woodruff. At that time this was the largest gift ever to an American University, exceeding the endowment of Harvard University. I was pleased to be appointed to represent the Nursing School on the University Faculty Committee that was given responsibility to recommend how funds were to be dispensed.

This was an intimidating assignment for me; I did not know any of the other committee members and I was the only woman in the group of about twenty faculty members representing all the Emory schools: Medicine, Dentistry, Theology, Graduate School, and departments at varying levels. At that time there were few women leaders on the campus. The chairperson was an Emory alumnus and long-time non-clinical Emory Professor of Medicine. He started our initial meeting setting the tone of his leadership, determined to push first and foremost for faculty salary increases, exclusively. He did not want anything else proposed that might dilute the major need he saw to be fulfilled by the grant. He presented much data in posters and charts showing the Emory faculty salary scales in comparison to those of other private and public universities across the country. There was no denying the discrepancies, and we all understood how important this objective was to all of us. (I had been recruited with the promise of $30,000 annually and learned after I had moved to Georgia that they had to start me at $28,000, which I never fully understood. How could I complain, when my final salary at Stony Brook had been only $18,000, a salary that was not a living wage for a family?)

Several faculty members tried to suggest other needs such as laboratory facilities, library expansion, and an improved faculty club. I was sitting next to the representative from the Yerkes Primate Center on the campus, where much animal research was being done. I quietly mentioned to him the concept of a Central Research Development office, like the one at Stony Brook that helped identify funding sources, advised on proposal preparation, and assisted with budget determinations. It played an important role for young faculty members like me in helping to obtain funding and conduct research. My new Yerkes friend agreed with me. He thought it was a great idea, and pushed me to make the suggestion, so I did. I was shaking, my heart was pounding, knowing the reaction would not be good, but I managed to get it out. The Chair bluntly said, "Forget it, we need faculty salary increases first." No one else supported my suggestion.

The next meeting of the faculty committee a month later was in the Presidential Suite, a beautiful wood-paneled boardroom with the president, Dr. Laney, and three members of the Emory University Board of Trustees present. I found a seat next to my new young friend from Yerkes. I was still the newest faculty member on the campus and the only woman in the room as we were asked to introduce ourselves and explain our role on the faculty to the Board members. The Chairperson handed Dr. Laney his written report with all the financial data inside and then brought out his posters for demonstration and interpretation, reporting verbally for more than 20 minutes as though it was a demand. A few Board members raised some questions, which were addressed as Dr. Laney listened. And then he said. "Thank you, Dr., is this it? Is this all?" No one else responded. My Yerkes friend shoved me, whispering, "Go ahead." So here I was, my heart pounding again. I raised my hand and avoiding eye contact with the Chair looked straight at the President. I said, "Dr. Laney, there was an addition, a minority report by my partner from Yerkes, Dr. "Y" and me, but it is not written, and we don't have any support data to present. We believe it would be helpful to establish a Central Office of Research Development to help faculty, especially young faculty to identify funding sources for their research interests and assist with preparation of grant proposals. This could enable the faculty to expand the benefits of the Woodruff funding."

I didn't dare look around. I knew the Chair was furious with me. Dr. Laney smiled and thanked us profusely, clearly grateful for my recommendation. I don't remember exactly how long it took, but I think in addition to faculty salary increases, eventually the Office of Research Development was established. In subsequent years, the Woodruff family has added significantly to that endowment and Emory has achieved recognition as the most endowed research institution in the south.

Interviewer: Is there anything else you would like to say that reflects your contribution to the faculty and or the nursing program?

Sylvia: I had brought my extracurricular interests in writing and publishing to the nursing faculty. There was much talent among the faculty at Emory that needed encouragement and mentoring in terms of professional publication development. While at Emory I worked on a new edition of *Guide to Patient Evaluation*, offering nursing faculty the opportunity to serve as writers and reviewers to supplement their salaries and receive publishing credit on their Curriculum Vitae. Recently, I had the opportunity to communicate with one of my former Emory faculty members, Dr. Rose Cannon, who frequently writes articles of historical significance for *Georgia Nursing,* the GNA newsletter. Rose reminded me of this contribution, "I love that you are writing your memoirs. You were a bright light at Emory, and were so good to get so many of us involved in editing and updating your physical assessment books." [15]

Earlier, I mentioned that some of the Emory faculty participated as mentors and evaluators in the Southern Region clinical performance testing center, receiving acknowledgement for promoting professionalism within the nursing community.

Later I worked with Dr. Ruth Yurchuck on the development of four nursing course review books to prepare undergraduate nursing students for successful completion of the National Council on Nursing Education Licensing Examination (NCLEX-RN). Emory faculty helped develop

---

[15] Personal Communication

content outlines and wrote some of the test questions, again earning supplemental income and academic credit.

Even after I left Emory in 1982 I was invited back for several years to speak about writing and publishing to students and faculty, and I continued to recruit Emory nurses for innovative interprofessional books I was promoting at F.A. Davis Publishing Company. For example, Julia Ann Purcell, MN, RN, CCRN, a clinical specialist in cardiovascular nursing at Emory Hospital and faculty member in the School of Nursing, was a lead author of *Dreifus ' Pacemaker Therapy: an Interprofessional Approach*, published in 1986, which was developed on request by nurses and technicians attending the various cardiology meetings where we displayed our medical books. And years later when one of my former Emory faculty members, Jacqueline Zalumas, called to ask if I would review her Ph.D. dissertation, an oral history of critical care nursing, I gladly accepted. We had had several conversations earlier about her research activities related to Post-Traumatic Stress Syndrome and the Holocaust survivors after World War II. I was glad to hear of her study completion, recognized the high quality of her writing, and believed it was certainly worthy of publication, but not appropriate for F.A. Davis Company. I referred Jackie to other publishers I thought would be interested such as the University of Pennsylvania Press. Apparently Joan Lynaugh, General Editor of the U.P. Press, was very enthusiastic about the significance of the work and subsequently *Caring in Crises* was published as a volume in the University's series *Studies in Health, Illness, and Caregiving* in 1995.

Interviewer: It seems as though you made many friends while at Emory, why did you leave?

Sylvia: I did make many friends at Emory and with several neighbors at D'Youville, especially with Kathy, a younger nurse administrator, also divorced and with a young daughter, named Heather. We had fun socializing with neighbors at the Condominium, various events downtown and outside Atlanta. We visited a few beach areas along the Georgia Coast and made my parents happy in Augusta when we brought Heather. From a personal perspective, I was disappointed. I found compatibility with one gentleman, and we had a few good times together over the years, but I realized there was no future there for me. I was still young and my children were growing "away." I was anxious for a serious relationship but I did not find the love I was looking for in Atlanta.

Meanwhile, as you can tell I had many interests. I was always a nurse and faculty member who multi-tasked. If I wasn't taking advanced courses while nursing or teaching, I was creating innovative teaching strategies or functioning as a consultant, particularly in curriculum development and I was writing study guides for students. While at Emory I was invited as a consultant by several other university programs. Dr. Georgie Labadie, my Teachers College doctoral advisor, who had recently accepted the position of Dean of Nursing at Florida A & M University in Tallahassee, asked me to provide consultation to the curriculum committee and faculty as they prepared for an NLN visit for continuing accreditation. I most likely focused on the importance of harmony among philosophy, objectives, and conceptual framework and stressed the need for creative thinking about curriculum implementation and evaluation. I assume I stimulated thinking just by telling of my own diverse curriculum challenges. It seems wherever I go, my passion and creativity are appreciated.

When my son Andrew was getting ready to graduate from Emory in June 1982, my daughter Elizabeth announced that she did not want to go to Emory; she wanted to study business at Georgia Southern University with a close friend. There was no way I could change her thinking. I began to look for something else. I had loved working with Dr. Sherman to develop "our book." So when I had the chance then to pursue something different, a challenge outside the academic world, I chose to immerse myself in my favorite hobby – reading books. I accepted the challenge of an adventure in private industry with a publishing company in Philadelphia, where I led a program developing books for medical students and clinicians. As the opportunity became a reality, and included another increase in salary, it was too good to turn down.

Andrew Fields graduated Oxford College of Emory University 1980. (Andrew continued on the Atlanta Campus to graduate with a Bachelor of Arts, 1982 with a major in English Literature. Subsequently, he studied Business/Accounting at Georgia State University and became a CPA.

NATIONAL WORKSHOP

ON

NUTRITION EDUCATION

IN

HEALTH PROFESSIONS SCHOOLS

SEPTEMBER 30 — OCTOBER 1

1981

DIVISION OF NUTRITION
DEPARTMENT OF COMMUNITY HEALTH
EMORY UNIVERSITY SCHOOL OF MEDICINE
ATLANTA, GEORGIA

National Interdisciplinary Nutrition Conference Program includes the presentation of my paper, "*Interprofessional Collaboration*," Washington D.C. 1981.

Melissa married Ami Steinfeld and later I am presented with my first grandchild, Alix Sara Steinfeld in July 1981.

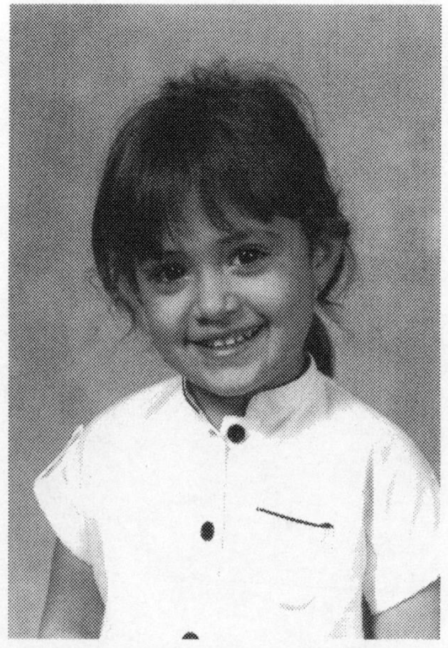

Alix at three years old.

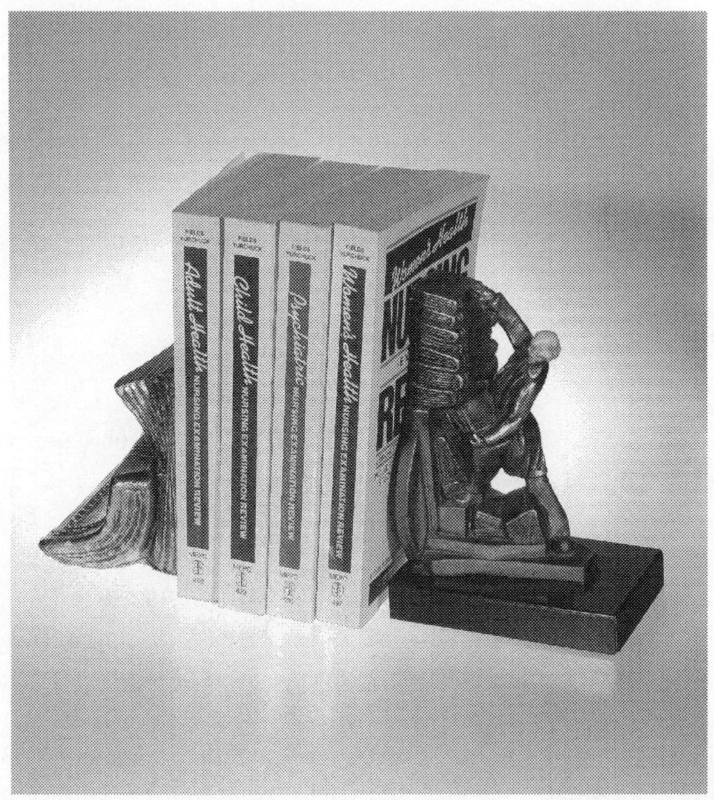

Nursing Examination Review books I developed with Emory Colleague Ruth Yurchuck and participation of many Emory faculty members: *Adult Health, Child Health, Psychiatric Health, Womens' Health, published by Medical Examination Pub. Co. 1985.*

10

For the Love of Books: The World of Medical Publishing

"The World was hers for the reading."

Betty Smith, A Tree Grows in Brooklyn

I love books; I have loved books since I first learned to read. It began with *Dick and Jane,* the first reader I brought home from school so proudly. It didn't take me long to devour the words and memorize the lines. Once I was introduced to the library, where I could take books out overnight, I found a second home. I think I had read almost every book in the small children's section upstairs at the library around the corner in Brooklyn until it moved to a freestanding building on Ocean Avenue a few years later. But I really loved owning my own books. During those years I was hooked on the *Nancy Drew* series of individual mystery stories. For 60 cents I bought and read an entire book in a few hours, put it on the shelf in the hallway at home, and read it over and over until I could afford the next purchase in the series. Unfortunately I didn't know of the *Cherry Ames* nursing series then; that came later. But I did progress to the children's classics recommended by teachers or librarians such as *Little Women, Anne of Green Gables,* and then the wonderful English novels, such as Jane Austen's *Pride and Prejudice,* and the Bronte' sisters, Charlotte and Emily, primarily love stories for young women.

I wanted happy endings, but *Marjorie Morningstar* taught me that endings were not always happy. Life in books did not always work out the way I thought it should; there were many surprises that left me wondering, "Why?" So, I kept reading and asking questions, although it was difficult to include fiction once I started college and then graduate school. Not impossible, just more difficult to include love stories as I branched out into a wider world of literature over time and then history and current events. For years I belonged to the Book of the Month Club, so I was reading a very diverse collection that many others were reading. Meanwhile children's literature became my thing as my family expanded; I loved reading to or with my children. Anna Quindlen said it all for me in her national bestseller *How Reading Changed My Life.*

I love the feel of a hardcover book. Somehow the pleasure of reading is not the same for me in soft-cover. A soft-cover seems to imply to me that the book is abbreviated; I don't think I have the whole story. I don't enjoy reading a book on a Kindle as much either. Recently I bought Supreme Court Justice Sonia Sotomayor's memoir, *My Beloved World*, for my Kindle while traveling, but I was not satisfied with the read. When I came home I bought the hardcover edition; I needed to hold the story with all the photos in my hands. (I am sure it is a generational issue.)

I also love the extra-large hardcover books often referred to as coffee table books. I have several such books, including interesting museum volumes on art, antiques, history, travel and flowers, often received as gifts. My daughter Melissa shares the love of books with me; I think she has given me more than I have bought for myself. For Mother's Day several years ago, Melissa gave me a large, magnificently illustrated hardcover book demonstrating the beauty of personal book collections in various homes, *At Home with Books: How Booklovers Live with and Care for Their Libraries.* With its place secure on my coffee table, I get pleasure every time I sit nearby and peer, I have seen many times before.

All my adult life I have loved to roam bookstores. When I was alone after my divorce, more than anything else I enjoyed spending time in bookstores; it made no difference whether at the mall in superstore showrooms like Barnes and Noble, or in small independents and boutique shops where rare or used books are available for perusal. I am never lonely when I am in a bookstore and I rarely leave empty-handed. I may not find something I must have right then for myself, but I always find a new wonderfully creative book for one or more of my grandchildren.

Several years ago I visited the gallery of sculptor Patrick Farrow (brother of well-known actress Mia Farrow) in Castleton, Vermont, where I found a few shelves of very interesting contemporary jewelry. I was immediately drawn to a sterling silver pendant of a young girl sitting on a swing reading a book. It was simply entitled, "The Reader." There was no way I could resist; I had to have that pendant. I wear it everywhere and it has brought me continuous pleasure in the compliments I have received through these years. Is it any wonder then that in 1982 I jumped at the chance to make books my new career?

The Move to Philadelphia and the F. A. Davis Company

In the past when I had attended professional nursing meetings I loved to hang out at the book publishers' booths, scouring new publications and making friends with the editors, hoping for complimentary review copies for courses I was teaching; many times I was successful. During a conversation with the F. A. Davis Company president, Robert H. Craven, Sr. (known as "Bobby" since childhood), at one such nursing meeting in California in the spring of 1982, I learned about the position he had open for an acquisitions editor for medical books; I was intrigued.

The family-owned publishing company in Philadelphia had been founded in 1879 by Frank Allison Davis, a widower who in 1895 at the age of fifty married Mr. Craven's aunt, Irene Craven. She was not yet twenty one years of age, a year younger than her husband's son at the time. According to Mr. Craven's "very personal history" published in 1979 in honor of the company's Centennial (*F. A. Davis Company 1879-1979: A Very Personal Account*). When Bobby was five years old Aunt Irene had adopted him following his father's premature death. This was ten years after the untimely death of Mr. Davis. Aunt Irene, who had taken over the company, had plans to groom Bobby to become her successor, Mr. Davis's son having completed medical school and having no interest in the publishing business.

The whole history is much too complicated to repeat here, but it was clear F. A. Davis was a dynamic gentleman and entrepreneur who had real estate and other business interests in addition to the highly competitive international medical publishing industry. There were financial ups and downs during the early years and following his death, but with the help of many associates and friends, Aunt Irene kept it all together. The personal story of Clarence Taber and the development of *Taber's Cyclopedic Dictionary,* also described in Mr. Craven's centennial publication, read like a good novel and could create another chapter here on its own.

Through much of the 20th century almost every nursing student in this country was required to purchase a copy of Taber's dictionary upon admission to a nursing program, and it was usually found on a shelf at the nurses' station of most hospital units in the United States. It has undoubtedly been the foundation for the company's evolving financial success. *Taber's,* (which was in the 14th edition when I arrived at the company), is in its 22nd edition today and I believe it is still the largest selling dictionary for nurses in the world, now available in various formats. Gratefully, I had very little to do with the dictionary, other than to accept with appreciation a copy of the latest edition with my name engraved on the cover.

In 1960, after years in preparation fulfilling many roles necessary from the ground up, and serving as an officer in the U.S. Navy, Robert Craven, Sr., assumed the presidency of the Davis Company and led it towards publishing the emerging disciplines of allied health. Under his leadership, some of the great nurse theorists I knew published their most important work with the company, including Dr. Martha Rogers of New York University, whose graduate-level text *An Introduction to the Theoretical Basis of Nursing* was a landmark publication in the field of nursing theory. It offered a framework for nursing practice based on assessing and maintaining homeostasis within the internal and external environments of individuals. Dr. Madeleine Leininger, a nurse anthropologist whose model on Transcultural Nursing Care, a "learned" subfield or branch of nursing that focuses on health-illness values, beliefs, and caring practices of comparative cultures, was also published with the Davis Company (*Transcultural Health Care: Issues and Conditions,* 1976). I believe *Transcultural Health Care* remains the most practical and understandable theory for nursing developed beyond that of Florence Nightingale.

The thought of returning to Philadelphia, living in Center City, and working with physician editors and authors to develop new books sounded like a very exciting opportunity for me in 1982. There was a large list of books the company had published for physicians under the forty-year leadership of Robert H. Craven, Sr., but during that time the number of medical publishing houses for books and journals had increased significantly so that the competition for new titles and authors was serious. It was not to be an easy task, but Mr. Craven, who was interested in retiring, stayed on for a time to help mentor me. I had always worked well with physicians, certainly evidenced by the success of *Guide to Patient Evaluation* and other teaching products with Dr. Sherman at SUNY Stony Brook. A friend recently asked me, "How is it you have been so successful earning respect from physicians you have worked with?" I thought about that question.

Physician faculty often played an important teaching role in the hospital diploma programs during the early years of the nursing profession, and the custom continued beyond the first half of the 20th century into many developing baccalaureate programs. It was considered important for nurses to understand the characteristics of common disease processes including subjective (symptoms), and objective (signs), as well as the pathophysiology of underlying disease conditions and the rationale for medical and surgical treatments. After the doctors' lectures, graduate nurses presented their interpretation of appropriate nursing care based upon the problem solving or nursing process. Such was the case in my own baccalaureate nursing education at Adelphi in the affiliated hospitals during selected components of the third and fourth years of the curriculum. This was extended into the psychiatric hospital, where we lived in the nurses' residence and attended the physician lectures for medical students and psychiatric residents as well as interdisciplinary clinical case conferences. We learned a certain degree of respect for physicians in those classrooms where we were introduced to how physicians think: how they collected, analyzed, and integrated information from various resources, including patients, families, specific references, and past experiences to determine diagnoses and develop management plans addressing individual patient problems.

In the late 1950s, when I was a Columbia University graduate student on the cardiovascular clinical team at Presbyterian Hospital, there were very few graduate-level nursing texts or journals, so introduction to the classic medical textbooks and journals was necessary. Using medical resources I learned what physicians had learned, and read detailed descriptions of their "thinking process." But at the same time I was also learning how nurses should think when addressing patient problems. Since Florence Nightingale published her Notes on *Nursing, What it is, and What it is not* in 1859, nurses have been taught to think holistically, about the patient's total environment. I always believed that when we put the two forms of thinking, doctors and nurses, together, we are more successful in meeting patient needs.

As mentioned earlier, when I was developing new programs at the Health Science Center at SUNY Stony Brook, the major philosophy supporting the new institution included the concepts of collaboration and the "health care team." We utilized the problem oriented medical record (POMR), where clinicians of multiple disciplines contributed their own professional insight and communicated in discussions on the patient's medical record. Confident in my own professional nursing role, I was able to share my knowledge and skills with the other faculty of the teaching team, particularly the physicians, and listened to them share their perspective. Collaborative relationships among the faculty were established as we developed the first interdisciplinary clinical course in the Center where each professional earned the respect of colleagues for their unique contribution. All students benefited from the team approach, but in a paper written with classmates during my graduate studies (Wieszorek R., Pennington, E., Fields, SK, and "*Interdisciplinary Education: A Model for the Resocialization of Faculty.*" *Nursing Forum* 1976; XV: 52–60) we reported that it was necessary for faculty to demonstrate collaborative efforts if students were to learn the value of the health care team. Over the years since, I have been able to carry that interprofessional training experience over into practice and development of new innovative programs, gaining recognition from collaborating physicians.

I hope I have answered my friend's question, but I know that understanding how physicians think is much more complicated than my few lines in this memoir. There is no simple recipe for learning to solve problems in health care, only more channels. Much has been spoken and written throughout the history of medicine in journal articles, monographs, and textbooks (and today on-line) about the decision challenges professionals face every day in health care. The medical publishing industry has certainly thrived as a result. For those wanting more specific examples I can recommend Dr. Jerome Groopman's 2007 New York Times bestseller, *How Doctors Think.*

In any event, back to the decision I made to accept the role of medical acquisitions editor for the F. A. Davis Company. I repressed the issue of cold winds, rain, snow, and ice if I went north again, thinking about how much easier life might be without commuting in heavy traffic to work every day, as I had done for years in New York and Atlanta. I also thought about the cultural advantages of Philadelphia: history, art and science museums, theatre, and music. In addition, it would be great to be closer to my daughter Melissa and granddaughter Alix, just a bus or train ride to New York City. Putting thoughts of my elderly parents (in Augusta, Georgia) to the back of my mind, I listed the D'Youville townhouse in Atlanta with a rental agent and moved to Philadelphia to begin a new adventure in my life. And what an adventure it quickly became.

I soon moved into a furnished studio apartment on Rittenhouse Square with an easy walk to the Arch Street office, although the route north was a wind tunnel. I loved living on the Square, and joined the hundreds of local residents who jogged around it starting at dawn.

Together with the walk to and from the office I kept in shape with lots of exercise, an important habit I had learned in Atlanta, where I jogged each morning around the Condo parking lot and had joined a Women's Spa.

At the end of the rental lease I moved into a two-bedroom apartment in a lovely new building around the corner at 2020 Walnut Street and had some of my furniture shipped from Atlanta. My floor-to-ceiling windows looked out west across the Schuylkill River towards the University of Pennsylvania. A few years later, I sat and watched through those windows as a major fire consumed a whole street of row houses after the 1985 bombing by police of homes owned by the radical MOVE cult.

I didn't realize it at first but the apartment building on Walnut Street became an attraction for young professional gay and lesbian residents, with frequent parties held upstairs, often with dancing. I made friends with Tom, my next-door neighbor, a young physics professor at the Philadelphia Community College who liked to dance and to cook. He often invited me to dinner when I returned from traveling, a major responsibility of my new position. Over the next year Tom, his friend Bob, and another woman (whose name I can't remember) and I frequently went out together to foreign films in Society Hill and to special Center City events. Recently I was reminded of one event we attended at the Old Swedes' Church around Christmas time. I think it was December 13, St. Lucia's Day, a holiday celebrated in Sweden and by Swedes around the world, where a young girl in a long white dress with a red ribbon around her waist and a crown of lighted candles leads a procession of attendants in white gowns carrying lighted candles and singing traditional Swedish songs. This historic "Festival of Lights," I am told, is celebrated in honor of a young Italian girl who devoted her life to helping the poor and was martyred for her faith. While I was sure those candles would start a fire any minute, I really enjoyed the lovely ceremony, the delicious Swedish foods, and especially the sweet treats served after the service. I remembered some of them from when I worked at the Lutheran Medical Center in Brooklyn, but had never been to a similar church service. I have always been interested in learning about the religious rituals and celebrations of those other than my own Jewish background.

Bob, a Harvard-educated professor at the University of Pennsylvania Medical School, came from a prominent "Main Line" Philadelphia family and lived in a beautiful historic three- or four-story brownstone house on Washington Square. His home was another gathering place for our expanding group of friends. They were all interesting, well-educated professionals, younger than I, as I approached 50, and like no other groups I had ever socialized with before, not when I was single and certainly not when I was married. I had several friends and colleagues at work who were single, but I gave little thought before to their sexual activity. Those were days of silence; I assumed they were gay, but we never actually talked about it. Twenty-Twenty Walnut Street was evidently not going to be the place for me to find a significant long-term personal relationship, as I am most definitely heterosexual.

Becoming an Acquisitions Editor

While I loved the concept of developing books as educational tools when I arrived in Philadelphia, I had only a general idea of the role of the acquisitions editor. My understanding of the medical publishing industry was limited, and I was for the most part unaware of how many publishing houses were out there developing and marketing medical books internationally. I didn't know how complex the design, manufacturing, and marketing of medical books was. Although there was a book designer, graphic artist, and publicist to consult with and copy editors to correct spelling and grammar at the company, I needed to understand much more, including basic options for design, paper, typeface, and production to determine projected publishing costs, etc. I had functioned before as a *content* consultant for medical publishers, but there was much I needed to learn about manufacturing and marketing books as I worked with authors in the development of their work. So not long after I arrived in Philadelphia I was sent to attend a short publishing course for editors at the Rochester Institute of Technology to help introduce me to the technical processes of publishing; it was a very interesting new challenge for I was really green.

To become an effective acquisitions editor it was also very important that I know the background of the clinical field, the issues and problems, the author's objectives, the market for the work, and the competition. It was necessary for me to read an unbelievable amount of highly technical literature and to attend appropriate professional conferences where our publications were exhibited, such as the American College of Cardiology, the American Academy of Neurology, the American Society for Anesthesiology, and conferences related to other clinical disciplines we were exploring for potential publication, such as the American College of Sports Medicine. I reviewed the programs for topics under discussion, attended presentations of latest research and controversies, reviewed and evaluated competing publications, and often hosted social events to make friends with potential authors for possible new editions when appropriate.

Meeting with existing or potential new authors often required travel to University campuses and well-known medical centers outside of Philadelphia. I loved making my way around the campuses, visiting bookstores and looking at competitive titles, and meeting managers to learn their perspective on why certain books seemed to fly off the shelves while others gathered dust. It was as though I was back in school studying a multitude of new topics every day. Mr. Craven had asked me to work at developing a new series of small soft-cover textbooks for students similar to a very successful one already on the Davis publication list, *Manter and Gatz's Essentials of Clinical Neuroanatomy and Neurophysiology,* last updated by Dr. Sid Gilman, chair of neurology at the University of Michigan, who had become one of our clinical neurology editors. With a view toward the first two years of the medical school curriculum, when students tend to buy books recommended by faculty and upper classmates, I scoured the bookshelves for curricular topics where small volumes might fill a void, especially if there could be interest among student audiences in addition to medicine, such as nursing, physical therapy, and respiratory therapy. I became successful in recruiting authors I knew from SUNY Stony Brook and the Medical College of Georgia, and eventually we published the following books: *The Medical*

Interview: A Primer for Students of the Art, *Essentials of Gross Anatomy*, *Airway Management*, and *Essentials of Clinical Nutrition*.

In Philadelphia I worked closely with Dr. Albert Brest, Chair of Cardiology at Jefferson Medical College, in development of three monographs a year in the Cardiovascular Clinics series. This was a very successful twenty-year series, offered through subscription, that also supported the publication of several exceptional free-standing textbooks for the cardiology audience, such as one on stress testing (Ellestad, M. (1985) *Stress Testing: Principles and Practice,* ed. 3. Philadelphia: F. A. Davis, 1985). While these technical volumes were strong sellers, I was particularly proud of my influence and efforts to address socio-cultural and humanistic areas of health care. To that end, I pushed for development of two monographs within the Cardiovascular Clinics where there were unique cardiac characteristics in specific populations not addressed well in the general cardiac literature: African Americans and Women.

At a conference I attended during the American College of Cardiology meeting Dr. Elijah Saunders, professor at the University of Maryland medical school and president of the Black Cardiology Association, spoke. *"Although amazing advances have been made in cardiovascular disease resulting in reduced morbidity and mortality generally, there were significant controversies and discrepancies reported in the medical literature regarding health disparities between the (ethnic) minority and majority populations. He continued:*

"Minorities clearly do not have access to the higher quality of medical and surgical treatments available to majority populations in this country and around the world, however we know that hypertension remains more life-threatening in black persons than in Caucasians, regardless of socioeconomic aspects related to health status and medical care."

After attending the conference I asked Dr. Brest to invite Dr. Saunders to put together a volume for the Cardiovascular Clinics that would include basic science and clinical findings related to the inequality in care and differences in outcomes, among blacks and whites internationally. Dr. Brest agreed there was enough unique content for such a volume, particularly on hypertension, but Mr. Craven was concerned about the marketability to the general audience of cardiologists and internists, particularly outside the South. I was naive, never imagining that this professional group could be biased against a large segment of the population whom they might be treating, but it was brought to my attention that access to specialty care for large inner-city primarily minority populations might not exist, except in university medical centers. I was advised that if I wanted to publish this title we would need to find a sponsor who could contribute publication expenses for at least the first 1,500 volumes.

I prepared a formal proposal and began to seriously pursue potential contributors, particularly among the pharmaceutical manufacturers of antihypertensive drugs. Meanwhile, Dr. Saunders worked with Dr. Brest to prepare the outline and identify appropriate contributors for the volume. At this time most of the volumes in this hardcover series were listed at between $50 and $75, based on size and 2,500 subscribers, mostly cardiologists and internists as well as hospital and university libraries. We were all extremely grateful to the Smith, Klein, Beecham Company, that purchased 1,500 soft-cover editions of *Cardiovascular Disease in Blacks* for distribution free to the members of the Hypertension Society and the Association of Black Cardiologists. We all appreciated as well the Honorable Louis W. Sullivan, Secretary of Health and Human Services, for his foreword to the volume.

At the first meeting of a new Professional Women's Health Consortium I had joined in Philadelphia, I became friends with a young physician, Dr. Pamela Douglas, who was completing her cardiology fellowship at the University of Pennsylvania. At dinner together a few weeks afterwards, I brought Dr. Douglas a complimentary copy of the latest volume in the Cardiovascular Clinics. She mentioned to me that she had looked at library copies of other volumes in the Davis series as well as publications by other publishers and was disappointed that the unique characteristics of women with coronary disease were not being addressed. I took Pam's suggestion for a volume in the series on heart disease and women to Dr. Brest. Upon review, Dr. Brest proposed that she outline such a volume.

A few weeks later Pam brought me an outline of topics she proposed with possible authors. Dr. Brest reviewed the outline and made a few editorial changes, but nothing significant. Pam was very anxious to be listed as the Clinical Editor on the cover of this volume. Most of the other volumes were coordinated by well-known cardiologists in leadership positions at universities or highly regarded researchers such as her own division chair, Dr. Mark Josephson of Penn. Although Pam's name was not yet known within the cardiology community, she had identified most of the necessary topics and appropriate chapter authors. She wanted to assume responsibility for contacting each of the proposed contributors, and maintain communication with them. I convinced Dr. Brest to let her name stand alone on the cover as Editor, since his name appeared at the bottom of the cover as Editor -in-Chief of the Cardiovascular Clinics Series. The book was finally published in 1988, and it was very well received as the first scholarly book on women and heart disease. The following year when Dr. Douglas moved to Harvard Medical School and was promoted to Associate Professor, I was certain that my efforts to publish the book *Heart Disease and Women* played a significant role in advancing her career.

A few years later, after I had left the Davis Company, Dr. Douglas was asked by a W.B. Saunders Company editor to produce a new volume on the topic of cardiovascular disease in women. Pam called me requesting my assistance, and when I consented, she sent me her new outline to review. I responded with my concerns, "Pam, I know the content will be updated with any new research findings, but this outline is just the same as the first volume. Something is missing. Nowhere is there discussion of the need for the physician to think differently when approaching the female patient versus the male; signs and symptoms may present differently and they may be repressed. Why does the female patient ignore symptoms and come late to the physician when she should be in the emergency room? Studies have shown that while most women die of heart disease, they are more concerned with breast cancer and think heart disease is a man's disease."

Pam's response was, "OK, Sylvia, you're right, please write the chapter and we'll start the book with it." Needless to say, I thought, why did I open my mouth? I was in a new position and didn't have time to work on such a chapter. But I could not refuse to try.

I put some ideas to paper and then I decided to seek help from two young clinical internists working on research studies part time in the Center for Research in Medical Education and Health Care at Jefferson Medical College, where I was by that time a Senior Research Associate. They were thrilled to be invited, which would give them academic publication credit. We all started to explore the literature outside of the cardiology specialty, such as psychology and general communication in medicine. It was much more difficult to access the literature in those days: no "Web MD", or "Google" and few other search resources. The new book, *Cardiovascular Health and Disease in Women,* was expanded from the original cardiology volume and published in 1993. When *The New England Journal of Medicine* reviewed the volume, the reviewer claimed that the first chapter, "The Female Patient," was the best chapter in the book. Several years later I was thrilled to hear the news that Dr. Pamela Douglas had been elected as President of the American College of Cardiology. Recently I noted an update to her biography:

> Dr. Douglas is the Ursula Geller Professor for Research in Cardiovascular Diseases at Duke University. She is internationally known for her scientific work in noninvasive imaging, exercise physiology, and heart disease in women. Her contributions in imaging span an enormous range from technological innovation to health care delivery, including shaping a national program for quality improvement in imaging. Dr. Douglas also had a significant role in creating the field of heart disease in women as an early and pervasive champion of its distinctive importance and relevance.

F. A. Davis Publishing Company was also known for publishing in the areas of Neurology and Anesthesiology. Dr. Burnell Brown, chair of the department of anesthesiology at the University of Arizona, was the editor-in-chief of the Anesthesia series; he helped produce two volumes a year for physicians in that discipline. Although outside the Anesthesia series, the most important individual volume published by Davis in anesthesiology was a large hardcover "tome" by Dr. John Bonica on "Pain" published many years before. Mr. Craven had said it was time for a new edition, and I was asked to contact Dr. Bonica at the University of Washington in Seattle where he was department chairman. Several months later I was finally able to meet with him.

Meanwhile, at various professional meetings I had already met with the neurology editors, who were all highly regarded research leaders in the neurosciences: Drs. Fred Plum (Cornell), Joseph Martin (Harvard), and Sid Gilman (Michigan), who were proposing development of several new neurology books on topics as varied as Neuroimaging, Epilepsy, Aging, and new editions of our books on Stupor and Coma, Head Injury, and Neuro-endocrinology. The months flew by and one by one new contracts were being negotiated and previously contracted typed manuscripts were arriving by mail; those were exhilarating months for me.

One manuscript proposed to me at a meeting was already under development, and actually led to creation of a whole new series. Such was the case with the Contemporary Exercise and Sports Medicine Series. At a meeting of the American College of Physicians (the professional society for physicians board certified in General Internal Medicine), Dr. Gary Wadler came up to the F. A. Davis Book display looking for a copy of the latest edition of the well-known *Stupor and Coma* by Drs. Fred Plum and Gerald Posner. Dr. Wadler, a Cornell Medical School graduate who had studied under the authors, was an Associate Professor of Medicine at Cornell familiar with an earlier edition. As a Tournament physician for the U.S. Open Tennis Championships, he and Dr. Brian Hainline, Assistant Professor of Neurology at Cornell, were interested in the hot topic of drug abuse by athletes, which were just being exposed. It didn't take long to negotiate a contract and before we knew it we had the manuscript, which Fred Plum reviewed for us and for which he then agreed to write a foreword. The book was finally published in hard- and soft-cover in

1989. Dr. Plum's Foreword addresses the significant contribution this first book made to the education of all sports medicine activists as well as a much wider audience of generalist physicians, orthopedic surgeons, physical therapists, athletic trainers, and physical education teachers. Sadly, although many regulatory changes have taken place since the book was first published, given the recent confession of doping despite denials for years by Lance Armstrong, the topic is as timely today as it was twenty five years ago. As the overview states:

> In *Drugs and the Athlete*, Wadler and Hainline have produced a trailblazing book that for the first time addresses in a comprehensive, balanced, well-researched, yet candid way, one of the saddest and most unsavory topics of our time. Sad is the tale, because it sets out the enormity of a blight that is damaging or destroying the lives of increasing numbers of young persons. Unsavory it has become, because it necessarily implicates either the neglect or willful greed of trainers, managers, owners, university powers, and media purveyors who have exploited sports for their own small gains with little or no regard for the well-being or fulfillment of the athletes. Further, just imagine what all of this says to the inner-city and suburban youths who idolize those athletes. Facing these issues squarely, *Drugs and the Athlete* describes in detail the size, the affected numbers, the many substances, and the difficulties in treating, what has become an international scandal.

Somehow it was amazing how I managed to maneuver the networking system, making contacts with potential authors through many various channels, and keeping my mind open to so many different titles. For example, While *Drugs and the Athlete* was being developed, I attended a meeting of the American College of Sports Medicine (ACSM) at the suggestion of Dr. Pam Douglas, in order to meet Dr. Mona Shangold, an obstetrician/gynecologist who specialized in sports gynecology and endocrinology, and who became interested in preparing a manuscript on *Women and Exercise* with her husband, a well-known radio and TV commentator on health topics, Dr. Gabe Mirkin. Dr. Douglas was to provide a chapter on women, heart disease and exercise. Both women were friends and ACSM members who participated as researchers in the Ironman Triathlon Competition in Hawaii in 1982. Exercise and sports for women were exciting new topics receiving much attention by basic scientists, especially physiologists, and other academics in the athletic arena as well as the public across the country, from elementary school to higher education. Eventually this book became the first in the new series we were contemplating, *Contemporary Exercise and Sports Medicine.* Dr. Alan J. Ryan, the chairman of the Minnesota Governor's Council on Physical Fitness and Sports and member of the Editorial Board for the *Journal of Kinesiology and Medicine for Dance,* was recruited to lead development of other volumes for the Series. I thought the topic of Prevention was important to physical education and sports medicine professionals and graduate students as well as physicians; it didn't take long before such a volume was created. *Winter Sports Medicine* came next and then several years later, well after I left the Davis Company, a book about golf medicine, *Feeling up to Par: from Tee to Green,* was finally published. It was a volume I had been anxious to produce in honor of my future new husband, a very serious golfer.

At the Davis Company, my responsibility focused primarily on books for physicians, but I was often consulted on nursing books and stayed active with my own publications for nurses, preparing the fourth and fifth editions of *Guide to Patient Evaluation*. In the last edition I was called upon to expand the concept of Nursing Diagnosis. Dr. Sherman was not interested in participating in this volume, but I recruited many of my old colleagues to review and add to the text. Meanwhile I recognized that many of the medical books on our Davis list were of interest to other professionals on the health care team, especially nurses. So when I examined some of the manuscripts submitted for medicine I always thought of the broader markets. Nurses actually spend much more time with hospitalized patients than physicians, so I tried to bring appropriate medical content to the potential nursing audience by recruiting my highly qualified nurse friends to join the authoring teams when possible. I was most successful with two cardiology texts, reinterpreted as interprofessional approaches: *An Interprofessional Approach to Cardiac Surgery* and *An Interprofessional Approach to Pacemaker Therapy.*

In the eight years I was associated with the Davis Company, I met many interesting and important people, making new professional friends in Philadelphia in a variety of ways. When I learned that the Company offered a $10,000 fellowship for doctoral studies in nursing, awarded every two years, I suggested we consider a similar type of award for medical students. Dr. Claire Fagin, the nursing dean at the University of Pennsylvania at the time, whom I knew from previous professional encounters, suggested I contact Dr. Fred Burg, Associate Dean for Academic Programs in the medical school. I told Dr. Burg about my efforts years earlier to promote creative humanistic activities for interprofessional students at SUNY Stony Brook, based on the ideas I had experienced under Dr. Maxine Greene at Columbia University. Dr. Burg and I came up with the idea for an annual award of $1,000 for student achievement in the creative arts at the School of Medicine.

In an article in the University of Pennsylvania student newspaper we wrote:

> Health professionals who are "tuned in" to music, art, and literature may be more sensitive to physical signs in the eyes, face and skin, as well as the voice and posture. They may see and hear more and perhaps better understand human behavior and consider the uniqueness of each individual patient in relation to his health and illness. We hope that this new award will help to foster humanism in health care by encouraging students to express personal concerns and experiences through the arts.[16]

16

Student entries into the competition for the first award included creative writing, journalism, photography, drawing, and sculpture. Unfortunately, managing the competition, selecting judges, and arranging the awards reception became more time-consuming for me than anticipated. Although we had hoped we might publish an anthology of written work produced by the students, when we weighed the potential benefits against the costs in time and effort, a pragmatic decision was made *not* to continue the program after the first year.

At a meeting of the Association of American Medical Colleges (AAMC) in Washington D.C., I ran into an old friend, Dr. Arlene Barro, SUNY Stony Brook Medical School Dean for Evaluation, with whom I had worked during the course, *An Interdisciplinary Approach to Patient Evaluation*. Arlene invited me to dinner in Washington that night with several other members of the AAMC she knew including Dr. Joseph Gonnella, Associate Dean of Jefferson Medical College in Philadelphia. I did not realize at the time how important this introduction would become later. I told Dr. Gonnella about some of the projects I was working on, such as the medical student study guides and the computer-assisted learning program on ECG interpretation being prepared by Dr. Abdullah Abdullah of the Medical College of Georgia (MCG) in Augusta. When I mentioned that the ECG program needed review by medical students, Dr. Gonnella suggested I contact Jon Veloski, Associate Director for Medical Education Research in the Center for Research in Medical Education and Health Care (CRMEHC). After the meeting, I made the contact Dr. Gonnella had recommended, and that was the beginning of a tremendously satisfying and productive association with Jefferson Medical College.

I did not always know how important some of my contacts were at the time: only years later, well after I left the Davis Company, did I realize whom I had met, and how significant their contributions to society were. Two stand out in my mind today. Rebecca W. Rimel was an Emergency Room nurse and faculty member at the University of Virginia Hospital who participated in an international research study on the aftermath of head injury that included two well-known neurosurgeons,

Drs. Bryan Jennett and Graham Teasdale, professors at the University of Glasgow, Scotland. Through their contacts with Dr. Fred Plum, F. A. Davis had published a volume in the Neurology Series on *Management of Head Injuries* in 1981. I met Ms. Rimel in 1983 upon the request of Dr. Jennett, who was coming to Philadelphia to meet with her. He told me she had just moved from Virginia to Philadelphia to work for the Pew Trust Foundation and asked me to set up a meeting to discuss a new edition of the head injury book. Later Rebecca told me her story, which I found fascinating. If I remember correctly, she had completed a master's degree at the University of Virginia and had presented her research outcomes report at a conference at the University the year before. A Pew family member was attending the meeting, and came up after the meeting to compliment her on her presentation. He was very impressed with Ms. Rimel's professional contribution to the study and her general knowledge of health care policies and management. Later she was invited to a new professional position at the Pew Foundation. Although Rebecca and I had little further communication that I recall, I remember reading in the public press that just five years after her arrival to Philadelphia, many changes in the structure and the philosophy of the Pew Trusts had been made and Rebecca Rimel was appointed President of the Foundation. I was flabbergasted and have been following her accomplishments ever since. I mention this here because I am so proud to write that Rebecca Rimel started out as a professional nurse graduate of a the University of Virginia program. Today she sits on the boards of dozens of distinguished public and private organizations, and her leadership of the Pew Charitable Trusts has been making a difference in communities throughout the world. Interestingly, her important editorial in a recent quarterly report, "Trust," is entitled, "The Art and Beauty of Compromise." The overall theme is "Pew brings people of varying interests together to find shared purpose and common ground."

I believe I first met Dr. Francis Collins at the University Of Michigan School Of Medicine in 1988 or 1989. Dr. Sid Gilman, chair of the neuroscience department/division, had set up the appointment for me and I had flown to Ann Arbor. The Neurology Series editors recognized that genetics was becoming a new important factor in medical research affecting understanding of pathology, treatment and outcomes; they wanted a basic book on genetics for our F. A. Davis medical book readers. I remember our meeting and the promise from Dr. Collins that he would contact me and Dr. Gilman as soon as he completed a report of his current study. Afterwards I had a marvelous experience roaming around the bookstore looking for a basic book on genetics to review.

I left the Davis Company in 1990, and didn't think much about it until I read that Dr. Francis Collins, one of the world's leading scientists, was leading the Human Genome Project in Washington. Isn't that a coincidence, I thought. Well time surely passed; I retired a few times. I guess it was about four years ago, when I was still searching not just for a soul mate but for more understanding of the controversies, particularly here in the South, surrounding science and religion, specifically the teaching of evolution and what was being identified as "intelligent design." One of the local physicians was presenting a discussion of the topic at a senior citizen center locally. It was free so I decided to go. Some of the suggested references were being passed around the room after the presentation; I quickly scanned them to jot down the titles and publication information. All of a sudden it dawned on me; one of the books was *The Language of God*, published in 2006 by Francis S. Collins, M.D., the very same Dr. Collins I had met in Ann Arbor. There was his photo inside the back cover. I could hardly believe it. And then to make it even more interesting, in 2009 Dr. Collins was appointed Director of the National Institutes of Health in Bethesda, Maryland.

As I look back and reflect on my years at F. A. Davis, I realize how lucky I was to have had the opportunity Mr. Craven gave me to expand my horizons to private industry supporting medical education at all levels. I was able to continue the work I loved in development of educational learning materials that had originated with my studies at Columbia University for my master's and doctoral degrees in education. I truly appreciated the mentoring Mr. Craven provided, but I don't think I realized then how many important individuals I had met in addition to the authors and editors with whom I worked. ***I certainly did not***

know how much confidence I had gained in my ability to learn what I needed to know when I needed it and how much that confidence would support my continuing career after I left the company.

I loved every book we published. Of course, with the introduction of computers, the internet, e-books, iPads, iPods, iPhones and Kindles, Nooks, etc., students and practitioners of the health professions today experience medical literature much differently in the 21st century from the medical publishing experience I encountered in the 1980s. There is no question that individual hard- or soft-cover medical books are no longer the primary source of information support.

I am very proud to describe our diverse publications in this personal memoir, for I worked intimately with highly skilled and passionate F. A. Davis staff, leading physician clinical editors and authors, and sometimes nurse authors as well. I was fortunate to have had supportive and enthusiastic assistants, Mary Ellen D'Orazio as secretary, and Linda Weinerman, my very special friend and editorial assistant. It was always a team process focused on caring human interaction, and as a result extremely fulfilling. I must say it again, I loved every single book I helped create; they were like my babies.

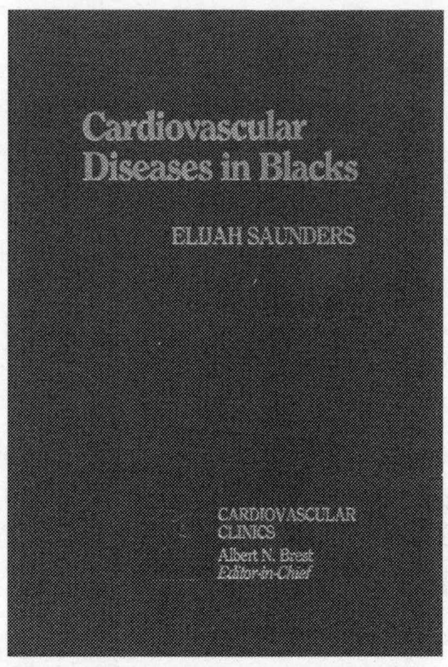

F. A. Davis Company: Contemporary Cardiovascular Clinics and varied monographs on heart disease (Cardiovascular Disease in Blacks- Elijah Saunders, MD).

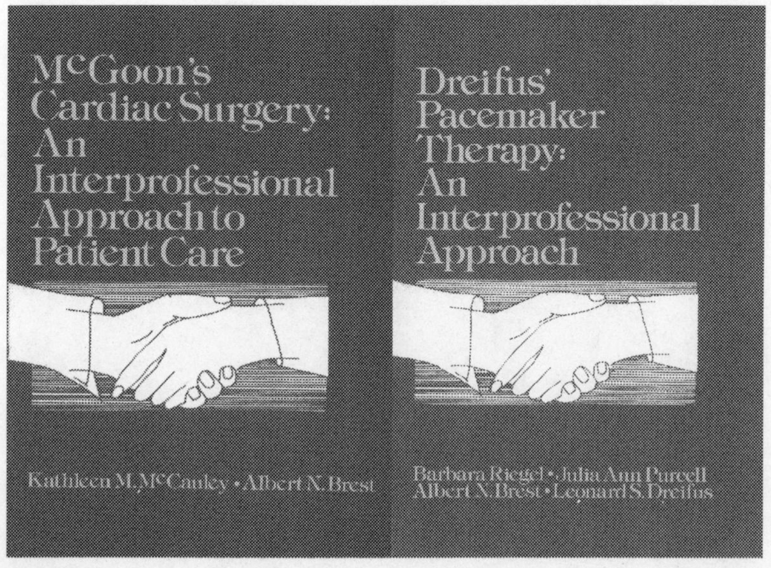

Interprofessional Books for Physicians and Nurses (Cardiac Surgery & Pacemaker Therapy).

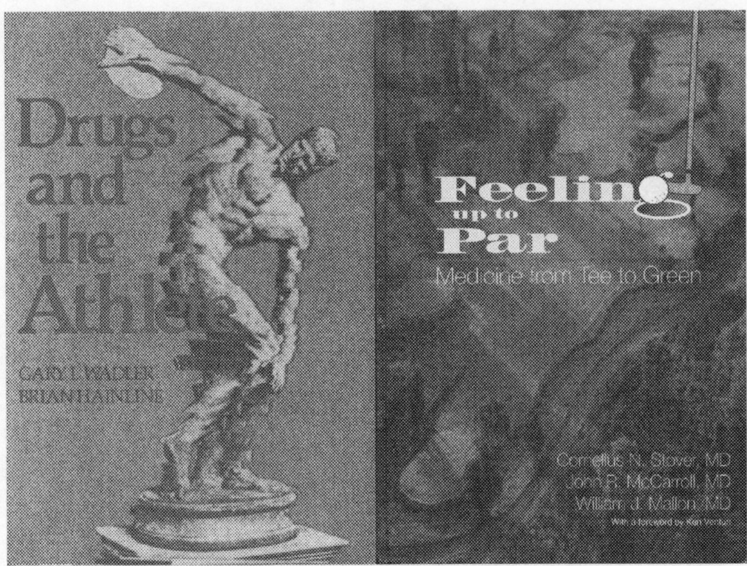

Sports Medicine: Drugs and the Athlete/ Golf Medicine (Feeling Up to Par).

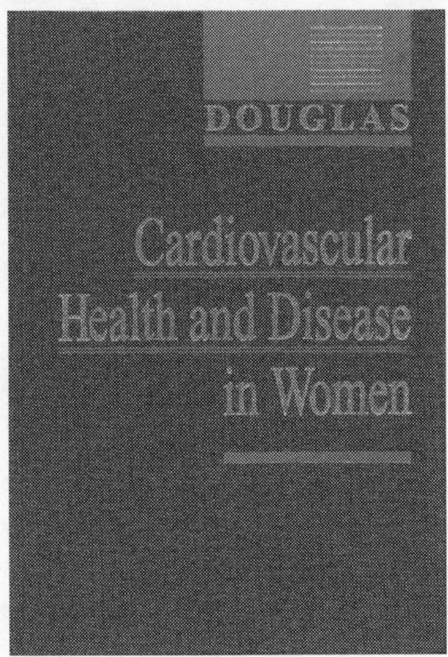

Pamela Douglas: Cardiovascular Medicine (Saunders) I co-author Chapter One, "The Female Patient." With Marie A. Savard, MD and Kenneth R. Epstein, MD

Alix with darling white puppy. When visiting Philadelphia she came to the Davis Company where she loved acting as a junior office assistant, mastering the Xerox machine.

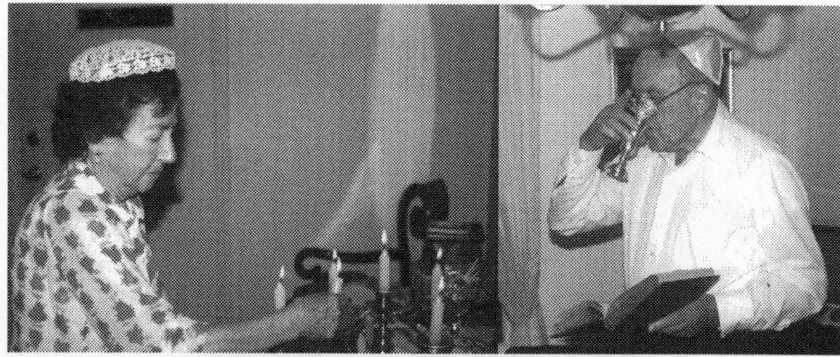

My parents retired and left Brooklyn to move to Augusta, Georgia, to be closer to me and my brother who was living in Columbia, South Carolina. My mother is lighting the Sabbath candles while my father is reading the Sabbath prayers and sipping sacred red wine.

11

An International Adventure: the Philippines, China and Japan

"LIFE IS EITHER A DARING ADVENTURE OR NOTHING AT ALL."

SOMETIMES ATTRIBUTED TO HELEN KELLER

In May 1983, I was in Las Vegas to attend the annual American Society of Anesthesiology (ASA) meeting, for the first time, waiting in line at the Convention Center to register for the meeting. I suddenly became aware of a poster at the right side of the registration table announcing in big black letters,

Dr. John Bonica, President 8th World Congress of Anesthesiology
Welcomes you to join me in Manila, the Philippines
January 19th to 27th 1984
"Post Conference Trip to China"

I picked up the brochure and tried to read it as the line moved up. "President Marcos and his wife Imelda welcome you to the opening of the new multi-million dollar Convention Center in Manila," but all I could see was, ***"trip to China – January 28th – February 05, 1984," and "John Bonica, President."***

I read the itinerary: "Jan 19: New York to Tokyo; Jan 21: Tokyo to Manila." All I could think about was my birthday, a very significant birthday, January 20, 1984. If I went on this trip, I would never have that dreaded birthday – my fiftieth… Of course I would still have it, but in my mind I would miss it as we flew over the International Date Line. And, even though it was under Communist rule, I could actually visit China. It was very high on my travel wish list.

Pearl Buck's Pulitzer prize-winning novel, *The Good Earth,* came to my mind immediately. I had read the book in the library when I was about eleven or twelve and years later saw the 1937 movie on television. Then I was abruptly reminded of why I was so attracted to that movie and had put China on my travel wish list so many years ago. It was the Chinese laundry shop near the corner on my street in Brooklyn, where for years since our move there in 1943, I took my father's white business shirts to be washed and ironed every week. Although I had seen Chinese soldiers in the news reels at the movies, I had never known any real Chinese people. So, friendly and curious as I was, I always tried to start a conversation, but the laundry man was quiet and spoke very little. If he had a name I never learned it. "No starch, I know," he always said, barely smiling when I came in. His wife just stood there ironing; she never said a word. "Where's the baby," I would ask? "Sleep" he would answer. I wondered where they came from and how they got to Brooklyn, if they were related to the people in the Chinese restaurant on Kings Highway and whether they had family back in China. "Someday I will get there," I thought.

Through the years after World War II, with the Cold War when in 1949 China became Red, followed by the Korean and Vietnam Wars with the U.S. on the opposing side, I was sure I would never actually have the opportunity to see China. Then to our surprise (probably hoping to finally end the Vietnam War), President Nixon and his wife Pat made the strategic visit to China in 1972. At that time, living on Long Island, even though I was overly committed to doctoral studies, my faculty role at SUNY Stony Brook, and my family, I fantasized again and China returned to the top of my travel wish list.

Now, ten plus years later, back to the Las Vegas Convention Center, out loud, I said "Oh, my God." I could turn this dreaded birthday into a very exciting adventure! Could I possibly go? The receptionist looked at me. "Is there anything wrong?" she asked. "No, no, nothing wrong," I said, smiling. "I just had an epiphany." I told her my name and she handed me my registration packet. I opened it, found my registration tag, the program and the exhibit list, and located the Davis booth. Wondering if Mary Ellen was there already, I couldn't wait to show her the brochure about the World Congress.

I had been at F. A. Davis in Philadelphia less than a year, and I was still "broke." Regardless of the increased salary, with the cost of moving my things from Atlanta, "fixing up" the apartment and flying back and forth to my aging parents in Augusta, Georgia, I had no savings I could withdraw without penalty. Although Melissa and Andrew were both independent now, Elizabeth was a sophomore at Georgia Southern, and I was responsible for all her expenses: tuition, housing, food, clothing, transportation, gasoline and automobile maintenance, medical and dental care and insurance, contact lenses, even lost orthodontic retainers. I had never been able to save, not before or after the divorce, despite all my supplemental earnings. I lived by borrowing from the bank and paying back, borrowing and paying back; fortunately, as a result, my credit was impeccable.

I checked to see if Dr. Bonica was attending the meeting and learned he couldn't make the trip to Las Vegas. I arranged to meet with Dr. Burnell Brown the next day at the Davis booth in order for him to look at all our publications and talk about possible new topics for his Contemporary Anesthesia series. He said he was thinking about doing a book on the liver, independently, without contributors. I asked if he was going to the World Congress in Manila; he said he had been invited to speak and was probably going to accept. Meanwhile I had shared my dream with my companion and we couldn't stop talking about it. Encouraged by her support I figured out a plan of how I might be able to pay for the trip. I couldn't sleep for two nights; China was all I could think about. The ASA meeting could not be over soon enough.

When I returned to Philadelphia I called the bank where I had opened a checking account with the assistant manager, requesting an urgent appointment. She had told me to call her personally if I needed anything else, so when she said she was available then, I rushed to her office immediately. She smiled warmly and called me in. I told her about the China trip and the significance of my upcoming miserable, lonely 50th birthday. I kept telling her how important it was for my psyche to have something positive to look forward to, possibly an adventure. She knew my credit history and that I had no savings. I needed $1,800 for the basic travel agency expenses, but I wanted to borrow $3,000, to cover unanticipated extra costs. I didn't really need to go to this meeting since we had an Asian distributor from Singapore who would be there to exhibit our anesthesiology books. However, I explained I might meet some new potential authors for our publishing program. Certainly that could justify the F. A. Davis Company paying the $450 registration fee for me to attend the meeting. I was confident I could claim all the unreimbursed travel expenses on my income taxes. It was the clincher; my banker friend agreed to a $3,000 unsecured loan if the company supported my registration. And fortunately Mr. Craven agreed to support me when I showed him the brochure listing Dr. John Bonica as the President of the World Congress. With much confidence, I was hoping to convince Dr. Bonica to start work on a new edition of his *Pain Management* text.

I had more than six months to dream about the trip. Meanwhile my family and friends were excited for me and volunteered extra cash as my birthday gift, asking only that I bring them back some Chinese trinkets. Once all the arrangements were made with the travel agency and I received the visa, I told Dr. Gonnella at Jefferson. He told me of two important physicians in China he knew who had come to Philadelphia to study medical education research several years before, and he was certain they would want to meet me. He offered to write to them with my itinerary, and at his suggestion I sent each of them copies of my new third edition of Sherman and Fields' *Guide to Patient Evaluation* book and copies of one of the Davis small soft-cover student textbooks. He expected they would respond by visiting with me and my anesthesiologist group, and he was right; they did come.

Coincidentally, at that time two young Japanese physicians, the Doctors Kaga (Kimi, an academic neurologist, and Machico, a pediatric neurologist), were studying in the Jefferson Research Center, and I was invited to have dinner with them and Jon Veloski, the director of medical education research, who was now involved in reviewing Dr. Abdullah's EKG computer program we were hoping to publish. The dinner was a magnificent eight-course banquet specially prepared for us by Dr. Gonnella's friend, the head chef at the top Chinese restaurant in the city, at 12th and Walnut Streets. Kimi was already a subscriber to the Davis neurology series and was thrilled to meet me. When the Kagas heard I was going to China in January, they made the case for me to visit with them for a few days at the end of my official Asian trip. I thought, why not? I might never get to Asia again. [17]I learned that some of the F. A. Davis medical books were translated into Japanese with publication rights paid, such as Plum and Posner's *Stupor and Coma*. That was not the case with several other publishers at that time; they just pirated the content, translated the work and printed, retaining our original graphs and ethnic photos.

As the months flew by and I was traveling for the Davis Company to and from other meetings with authors and editors, I knew I wanted to learn more about China than the fiction of *The Good Earth*. From my early school lessons, I knew the country was probably around five thousand years old, and that it was vast, with millions of people, mostly poor, and had long family dynasties with emperors or empresses who ruled and then were overthrown by warlords or others like the Mongols. Of course I knew the Japanese had invaded the country more than once and that General Chiang Kai-Shek had set up a republic in Taiwan, but the main People's Republic was established with Russian help as a Communist government by 1950, the year I graduated from college.

I needed a refresher course for I was vague on how it had all come about. I understood there had been efforts since Nixon's visit toward

---

[17] Little did I know then that I would have another opportunity to visit China in 2015 with a high-speed train to seven world heritage sites. A topic for another day.

economic reform, and some of the leaders were pressuring for opening up the country for investment and tourism. We didn't have the internet and Google then, so I needed to do some research. I needed a book I could hold for a while to review the history of China and the easiest way for me to find it was to visit the closest Barnes and Noble bookstore on the way home from the office. Luckily, I found a recently published authoritative, yet easy to read overview, *Inside China* by Malcolm MacDonald, with wonderful photos (MacDonald, Malcolm, MacQuitty, William, *Inside China.* Boston/Toronto: Little, Brown and Company, 1980). I was able to carry it with me when traveling. The book was a brief narrative of the events that led to the creation of the People's Republic of China in 1949, and what had developed there since. It was not a research-based analysis of official papers, but mostly a report by MacDonald, the son of a former British Prime Minister and distinguished traveler in China, on what he observed there during periodic intense visits across the country, beginning in 1929 and then after World War II in 1948, and each decade until 1979. He provided glimpses of the remarkable changes that took place during those 50 years and especially since Mao Zedong (Mao Tse-tung) and his comrades gained power throughout mainland China.

The book was a wonderful introduction to the Chinese society at the time and its government's outlook on international affairs I would soon hear about and see during my China visit in a few months. The months flew by in 1983, and before I knew it the adventure began. I was on the commuter plane from Philadelphia to New York, but that was as far as I got on January 19th. When I arrived at JFK I learned that Japan Air Lines Flight 5 to Tokyo was cancelled due to a snowstorm in Tokyo. In fact there was snow everywhere, all across the northern part of the U.S. as well. There we were at the gate, our group wearing the ID tags the travel agency had sent, with our luggage already checked in, when the announcement was made. We all started introducing ourselves, sharing our disappointment. We were told to pick up our checked luggage, and that the flight would be rescheduled for the next night. Room reservations were arranged at the airport Hilton and we were soon on a bus, talking about dinner. I met several couples, and one single gentleman, Dr. S from Fairfax, Virginia, invited me to have dinner with him; I think he was disappointed when I insisted on Dutch treat.

While I had expected to be on the way to Japan, I spent the night in an airport hotel at a charge of $115 with a room service breakfast. My birthday did happen on January 20th, but in the JFK airport lounge and on the plane. I loved the little wet hand towels we were given before dinner, and ordered a small bottle of wine, but I was surprised the meal was definitely American steak. At 2 a.m. in the middle of the night we stopped in Anchorage, where all we could see outside was snow and the temperature was 6 degrees Fahrenheit; it was not what I had so long planned for my birthday. (I never told anyone it was my 50th.) After browsing in the gift shop and talking to a few others, we were back on the plane, for more drinks and another dinner, this time Japanese sushi and a nice white fish meal with green noodles accompanied with sweet sauce, and ice cream for dessert. Sitting next to me on the plane was Dr. Kimura of the Asian Study group at the Kennedy Bioethics Center. He worked with Dr. Pellegrino, whom I had known so well at SUNY Stony Brook when he was Vice President for Health Sciences. Dr. Kimura, who was not related to the Dr. Jun K, whose book on *Electrodiagnosis* was published by the Davis Company, wanted me to help him write an article for the Japanese nursing journal. We exchanged business cards, but somehow the idea never came to fruition. Our conversation was very interesting about the differences between nursing education in Japan and the United States.

There were more introductions on the line to the restroom; I met Dr. J, an anesthesiologist of Philippine origin was married to a Brooklyn dermatologist who was not on the trip. She was staying with family during the meeting in Manila, but was my assigned hotel roommate for Hong Kong and China, where single accommodations were not possible. We all watched a couple of videos shown on the screen, one about economics in Japan and then one on Kabuki, the ancient form of Japanese theatre. But then the lights went out and I tried to sleep. I dozed on and off, but never could become comfortable enough.

It was January 21st when we arrived at Narita Airport in Japan and there was snow everywhere. It was freezing cold as we all gathered our luggage and went through security and customs and took the bus to the Nikko Narita Airport Hotel. We were given dinner and breakfast coupons. Once in the hotel bedroom I started writing notes in a little travel log, but I could not keep my eyes open, I slept well.

The next morning I had a 6 a.m. wakeup call since we were scheduled to have breakfast together and take the bus to the airport at 8 a.m. I couldn't quite eat the Japanese raw eggs; fortunately they had some delicious scrambled eggs, and since the coffee was too strong for me, I was introduced to tea for breakfast. Soon after, I was on the plane to Manila, packed in the middle seat between two big Navy captains on their way to Manila to inspect ships. I wanted to sit by the window but they wouldn't let me. There was a group of ten Navy inspectors on the plane, and they were drinking already. The jokes went back and forth across the aisles; it was like a Hollywood comedy. What a treat, these guys had me laughing all the way, and I felt very special.

But the atmosphere changed once we disembarked in Manila. We arrived under heavy security and were surrounded by very serious looking armed police. We passed through metal detectors and encountered more armed guards everywhere. The country had been expecting a revolution against President Marcos for months, no, years. On the ride to our hotels, after seeing the extreme poverty of dilapidated shacks and dogs and chickens running around loose, as well as adult men urinating on the city streets, I was surprised it took so long for the revolution to happen. (It eventually occurred two years later.)

There had been years of opposition to Marcos with reports of embezzlement of funds, torture and disappearance of opposition members, and charges of fraud during a sudden election that effectively gave Marcos an illegal third term. More reports continued of crimes and political disruptions by rebels pushing for a shift to Communism, and then, six months before the World Congress Meeting, the assassination of the exiled main opposition leader, Benigno Aquino Jr., as he got off the plane from the U.S. attempting to return home. As part of the Cold

War, the United States continued to support Marcos because he claimed he was keeping the country from going Communist. Meanwhile he kept changing existing laws, called for martial law, and rewrote the constitution. Despite the economic disaster and continued extreme poverty, there were reports of Imelda Marcos shopping for luxuries in Paris and Fifth Avenue as millions of dollars were secretly embezzled and deposited in foreign banks. I don't understand how the decision was made to have the 8th World Congress of Anesthesiology in the Philippines.

But I was on an adventure that first day, arriving in Manila on the 22nd of January. Despite the well-armed guards everywhere I was oblivious to any dangers and followed the tour director who met the plane to the bus for the ride to the magnificent "Manila Hotel," where a bellman in all white greeted us at the door. The reception lobby with palms and flowers was elegant and my dark bamboo-walled bedroom covered with several art prints was just beautiful. This hotel was where General MacArthur had had his penthouse headquarters when Pearl Harbor was attacked initiating World War II, and from where he abandoned the city for Corregidor when the Japanese troops overpowered the Americans. I knew this history well. But I had to rush to unpack, shower, and dress for the opening reception and dinner at the Convention Center.

It is impossible to describe that week of the convention. President Marcos never appeared publicly for he was supposedly ill, so Mrs. Marcos welcomed us and spoke of the significance of the new convention center to the economic development of the nation. Together with my notes, I kept a copy of her keynote address entitled, "***The Pain of a New Idea***," where she referred to the political and social problems of the country, directed specifically to the audience of anesthesiologists. I include here a few lines.

> There is a great deal of moral, physical and spiritual pain in the world today. It has been said that man, for all his science and sophisticated technology, has not yet discovered a panacea for that agony which leads to conflict and war – the agony of alienation, the pain of misunderstanding.

> This is especially true in relations among peoples of nations, large and small, weak and powerful.
>
> This Congress of Anaesthesiologists being held here in Metro Manila with an enlightened theme, "Anaesthesia for Safety," reflects on your compassion as physicians, for you have decided to hold your annual congress in a developing country like the Philippines.

The entire speech is much too long to repeat here, but it clearly expressed recognition of the extreme poverty, limited resources, education, and poor health care for the general population as very serious problems. In further discussions with locals and the few Philippine physicians from the U.S. and other countries who were part of our group, there were no easy answers, but surely political changes were absolutely necessary. We learned that there were few industries operating in the country that could bring jobs for the masses. There was hope that general tourism, education, and medical education could be increased if there was foreign investment. Many Philippine physicians went abroad for advanced training, and while they generally sent funds home to support their extended families, they tended not to return home permanently to invest in their own nation. I had known several when I worked in New York City hospitals in the 1950s. There was a shortage of American-trained medical interns, particularly in the smaller hospitals, and anesthesia was not a first choice for the Americans. The foreign-trained interns seemed to select anesthesia because in many cases when English was not their first language, they had difficulty communicating with patients and other professionals.

Obviously President Marcos wanted to put on a great show for the audience. That first night and every night after were unbelievable dining experiences. The huge pigs were turning as they roasted in open pits, the bars were open for alcohol of your choice, French and Italian wines were served with every course, music playing, dancers dressed in their cultural garb performing native dances. No one seemed anxious about revolution that night, or any other night that week. All week long we were wined and dined and entertained each evening with music and dancing for hours. There was no way to return to the hotels before the closing; we were restricted to our group because of the safety concerns.

There were about 400 anesthesiologists from around the world attending the meeting. Our ASA China group included about thirty five, mostly American physicians with spouses, and a few young single anesthesiologists. It was a wonderfully friendly group, and I felt accepted and comfortable.

I introduced myself to Dr. Bonica at the end of the reception and he hugged me to express his appreciation for my attending. I was absolutely thrilled when he arranged a special invitation a few days later for me to visit the Palace for tea with him and his wife and a few officers of the "Congress" to meet the President and Mrs. Marcos personally. I really felt honored, for only a handful of meeting dignitaries were invited. Imelda, always dressed in the beautiful traditional Philippine dress with large puffed-up shoulders, was filled with smiles and was unbelievably gracious. I couldn't believe it when she gave me and the two other women participating, a lovely personal fan engraved with her name; I have it on display in a glass cabinet in my living room to this day. We had a brief tour of the main floor of the palace, which was elegant, but minimally filled with magnificent European furnishings. However, we did not see Imelda's famous shoes other than those she wore. There were individual photos taken with Imelda for everyone, and we were supposed to get them the next day. Unfortunately, I don't know what happened to my photo, but it was not with the rest of them on the board when I looked. I was terribly disappointed.

On the first official day of the meeting, Dr. Burnell Brown lectured on "Anesthesia Toxicity" to a very large audience. There were other lecturers each day, but I did not note all the topics. I had lunch with him and his wife and again he talked about a book on "the liver." The next morning I had breakfast with K.C. Ang, of P.G. Publishing, who was exhibiting books for F. A. Davis and Wright Publishing, a British company I did not know. Then we went to the P.G. exhibit booth and I met the salesmen. On the last day of the exhibits I returned to the P.G.

booth to find out how sales had gone. The salesmen were very excited about their sales and Manila as a center for conventions. While I was there the Vietnamese physician from Hanoi I had met earlier came to look at the books. He had listened to Burnell speak and he wanted a copy of his latest book. I had told him to come back the last day and I would see what I could do. Now it was the last day of the exhibit and I couldn't help but give him the last copy of Burnell's book on newer drugs. He was so happy; it made me feel good to think I was helping the people of Vietnam in some small way.

Shopping and Touring in the Philippines

One afternoon, some of our group went shopping. Our first stop was a factory where women were working at sewing machines to see the characteristic Philippine clothing made as well as some work being done for American companies and then to Tsorias, a department store. I couldn't help myself from buying a black embroidered lightweight cotton jacket with a mandarin style collar. I had that jacket for years, wearing it with black pants and receiving compliments everywhere. I also bought three lovely beige crocheted dresses for my daughters and daughter-in-law, and "Panama" style embroidered shirts for my father, son, and son-in-law, as well as a doll for Alix, my only grandchild at that time. We were being encouraged to spend money by the tour director, and our group was very happy to contribute. By shopping, I felt like I was helping to fight the poverty everywhere.

One afternoon I decided to join the spouses who were invited to tour the Villa Escuadero, a plantation in the countryside. During the drive we saw more of the disturbing signs of why a revolution might be expected. As the bus rode along the dusty roads cluttered with falling down shacks and wandering animals we saw many bare-bottomed toddlers with distended bellies of malnutrition watching us travel, including several within the entrance to the plantation.

There were a few interesting experiences at the plantation such as a water buffalo ride, and a demonstration of how to get juice from a coconut, although I didn't particularly enjoy the taste. In the plantation museum, the exhibitions of natural flora, insects, and primitive collectables, including a shrunken head, where stunning. The museum was also filled with elegant manikins dressed in elaborate gowns covered with jewels. There were Christian religious statues and icons practically wall to wall, again covered with magnificent precious or maybe semi-precious jewels. One could not help to wonder why they were showing all this excess glitter and extravagance to us while extreme poverty was so evident everywhere. It reminded me of similar scenes I had experienced in Puerto Rico walking just outside a lavish resort we once visited during a short holiday weekend cruise to the Caribbean. It too left a bad taste in my mouth. (To be honest for years I felt no interest, until recently, in visiting any South American countries where the Spanish had conquered and decimated the native cultures.)

Traveling and Learning in China

At the end of the week we left Manila and flew to Hong Kong for a continuation of my adventure. Gathering up our luggage, going through customs, was a hassle. I looked for my bags on the carousel, but did not see them. Evidently several planes had arrived at the same time, so the place was packed. I saw people taking their bags off and placing them on metal carts, but I did not see any extra carts. Suddenly I saw a tall man pushing a cart. "Where did you get that cart?" I asked, and he pointed across the room.

But then he said, "Here, take this one, I can get another." I thanked him profusely; just then I saw one of my bags, and raced to take it off before it went around and around again. I just got it off, when the second bag appeared.

"That was luck," I heard from behind. I turned around to see the tall and good-looking man with an English accent.

"My hero !" I exclaimed and smiled.

He said, "What are you doing here?"

"I am with a group of physicians; we are going to China in two days."

"What hotel are you in?" he asked.

I replied, "The Royal Garden."

He said, "That's my hotel, how are you getting there?"

"We have a bus to the hotel."

"Come with me, I have a car waiting for me. We'll go to dinner after you get settled in."

"I can't, it's a group and they are waiting for me," as I noticed Josephine waving to me.

"Here is my card, call me when you get settled, what's your name?"

I said, "Sylvia," and took the card. He was John W, from Switzerland. "Maybe, thanks so much for the cart." I said.

Josephine came up, "they're waiting for you. Come on." I waved goodbye to John W. This really could have been an adventure!

During the next two days we received an orientation to the history of Hong Kong and the economic advantages of capitalism under the agreement made with the Chinese when the colony was leased for 99 years to the British after the Opium Wars. It was scheduled to end in 1997. Many were afraid that China would not wait and just invade, but fortunately the two countries evidently wanted to maintain trade; economics won out and peace prevailed when the agreement was completed.

What an exciting, colorful, rich island, I thought. Our Royal Garden hotel was exquisite, the meals magnificent; Hong Kong is a unique world, but crowded and flashy and not particularly friendly. We had the opportunity to shop for cameras, watches, and other technological "stuff" in the narrow crowded streets one often saw in newsreels, but there was no formal tour of the island. I would like to return.

Entering China through Canton (now known as Guangzhou), was an unbelievably exciting, almost frightening experience, with young soldiers everywhere in their drab olive uniforms, the red star vividly displayed on their caps, holding rifles as though they were ready to fight. We felt the first blow of cultural difference when the China Air plane landed and we were taken to a restaurant for lunch. By this time I had to go to the bathroom, as did most others, so there was a line. Although we had been told in our printed directions to bring small rolls of toilet paper or tissues and antiseptic hand wipes with us for the trip, I was completely unaware that there would be only primitive toilet facilities in the cities; I could not believe the stench. To my shock, it was the custom to relieve oneself while standing on stone blocks, legs wide apart and squatting. I don't remember any rinse water dropping down from above into the hole in the ground, but I was certainly glad I had the tissue pack and hand wipes for there was no running water outside the stall to wash our hands before returning to the dining room. Later, in the fairly modern hotel we were assigned to, the situation was better, but in 1984 only a few of the hotels and restaurants that we visited in China offered the modern lavatory facilities most of us grew up with at home. When I showed the photos of the toilet facilities I took home for my children to see, they laughed and made faces. To my surprise years later while traveling in some rural European areas, I found similar primitive facilities.

An outstanding experience was a cruise on the Li River to Guilin and the surrounding tall narrow mountains (karst) often seen in foggy shadows in Chinese paintings. I bought a scroll with such a painted scene and had it framed when I got home; it hangs over my bed to this day. The night before the cruise, we had been given an orientation and shown a film of life along the river including how the natives caught fish with birds. We saw the real thing during the trip, other fishing techniques, women washing clothes on the banks of the river, and peasants carrying baskets on their shoulders or using rickshaws to transport people on the roads. Everywhere we went the people were wearing the drab olive Communist jackets and pants, but the babies being carried were dressed in colorful cozy warm suits. On the road as we walked along to get to the boat, peasants were trying to sell us all kinds of stuff. I still have the dark green Chinese soldier's winter hat lined with fake fur I bought for two yuan, with little pins representing the flags of various countries of the world attached to the front piece of the hat to protect the eyes and then turned down to warm the ears. It was a lifesaver. By now it was February and it was freezing cold but once we were on the boat we warmed ourselves through lunch with the "Hot Pot." That is a large community pot filled with steaming broth. Plates of vegetables, fish, and then meat were brought for us to dip into the soup and then eat with chopsticks. The taste was marvelous.

In Shanghai there were crowds of people shopping on the narrow twisting streets where there were very few automobiles, but dozens and dozens of bicycles everywhere. One day after touring the city and visiting a wonderful museum filled with ancient art works and historical artifacts, I received a message that Dr. Gonnella's friend, Dr. Xu, Dean of the 3rd Medical College in Shanghai, was calling for me. My tour guide spoke to him and arranged a meeting with our group on the bus the next morning before a scheduled hospital visit.

Dr. Xu described the status of medical education and health care at that time in China, emphasizing that there were many needs. He mentioned that all medical students were now required to learn to read English, and English was being taught in the public schools, but there were shortages in teaching personnel and of course modern equipment. When one of our physicians asked Dr. Xu what the greatest need China had to improve their care, he replied, "the CT scan." All diagnostic technology methods were very limited.

Because of questions from the group he talked about acupuncture and as he led us on a tour of the local hospital. The best description I could give of the facility was that it was "primitive." It reminded me of a small private "Doctor's Hospital," in New York I had worked in briefly, probably built in the 1920s. Walking through the hall we spotted an open door. Apparently we were looking into an operating room where we were told a patient was having abdominal surgery with only acupuncture for pain prevention, and the door was open! It was hard to believe then, but today traditional acupuncture is an accepted companion to Western medicine or independent treatment for various conditions all over the world. To avoid taking drugs, I tried it one year at a friend's suggestion for a bladder problem. My friend had had wonderful results for Crohn's disease, but I was not as lucky; the tiny needles inserted into the skin over the shin bones were painful and I did not feel any improvement. After one series of ten shots I opted out of a second series.

One of our experiences involved visiting the apartment of a middle-class family in Shanghai to see how they lived. The resident was an elderly widow of a prominent physician, who had been partially educated abroad. This was her home, but her married daughter and grandson lived with her. She was educated and spoke English very well, having worked for the British years before. The apartment was filled with books and there was a phonograph and musical records. I am not certain, but I seem to remember that there was a TV set. The living room was large enough for our group with comfortable old furniture and some extra folding chairs, although a few of the men sat on the floor. The kitchen and bathroom were small and looked as though they came from the 1920s; an old-fashioned washing machine with a wringer was also in the kitchen, and there were some clothes hanging to dry in the bathroom.

It was during the time of the Chinese New Year, and there were celebrations everywhere. After dinner in the hotel restaurant one evening we were all invited to the rooftop social hall where Chinese beer and Coca Cola were offered. There were many teenagers in jeans, sneakers and sweaters chattering and laughing just like young people in the United States would do. Some were dancing, and we suddenly realized the band was playing American music. I particularly remember "The Tennessee Waltz" and some other country music, and then we were really surprised to hear Frank Sinatra. Of course Shanghai had always been an international city, I thought. We were told not to order the Coke. The bottles were not refrigerated like the cans of beer, so the soda was placed into a glass and ice added; it was not safe to drink. I never particularly liked beer, but it was cold and safe since we could drink it from the bottle without ice; I quickly developed a taste. Chinese beer remains my beverage choice in Asian restaurants today.

Everyone in our group wanted time for shopping and the word spread that even furniture could be purchased by taking credit cards to the bank to withdraw dollars and exchange them into Chinese yuan. Several physicians from New England mentioned that although it took about three months, friends who had visited the previous year had shipped furniture to the States and Canada successfully. Once I knew I could use my credit cards, I joined the group going to the recommended Friendship Store. Time was limited, so first I looked for the jade beads and carved brooches I had admired in a shop in Guilin. I settled on a fine green jade brooch for my favorite aunt Sonia, who had given me some money for the trip. She later had it set on a gold chain. I selected a similar green brooch for myself and had it attached to a necklace of black jade beads. I decided I would rather buy something of permanent value than another trinket for my children. I selected three lovely five-feet-tall hand-painted red lacquer cabinets and had one shipped to New Orleans for Andrew, one to New York for Melissa, and one shipped to myself in Philadelphia to be held for Elizabeth until she graduated from college. Why oh why did I not buy one for myself? The cost for each cabinet including shipping was $300. As soon as that cabinet arrived and I had one of the Davis warehousemen pick it up at the port, I regretted not buying one for myself. It was more beautiful than I remembered. Unfortunately, Elizabeth, who moved to New Orleans two years after graduation, lost that cabinet in 2005 after Hurricane Katrina, when her house was inundated with eight feet of water for three weeks.

I had had enough shopping so when more free time had been set aside on the next day in Shanghai and it was sunny, I decided to walk by myself along the Bund, a wide sidewalk along the river. People smiled at me and came up to talk in limited English, asking where I had come from. I think they were trying to practice their English, and I felt really safe and welcome. All through the trip I felt comfortable with the people I had a chance to talk with.

While I was touring in Beijing a week later another friend of Dr. Gonnella came to visit with me and my group. Dr. Lee was the vice president of the entire public health system for all of the Peoples' Republic of China. He was a very charming man, who spoke in elegant English about the health care advances and the many needs in the country. He had received the books I had shipped and expressed much appreciation. After his talk Dr. Lee wanted to take me shopping. I can't possibly describe how I felt walking through the streets of Beijing to the Friendship Store with this distinguished leader. He helped me pick out silk ties for the men in my family and lovely silk scarves for the women, and insisted on paying for them.

It is impossible to fully describe the rest of this trip, visiting temples, museums, and music halls where we experienced acrobatic performances and Chinese Opera. In Beijing we spent hours at the Winter Palace (Forbidden City) entering one house after another. The whole scene would have been more meaningful if I had seen the movie, *The Last Emperor,* the story of Puyi, who at the age of two in 1908 was appointed Emperor by the dying Empress Dowager Cixi. Unfortunately the film was not made until 1987. The Academy Award–winning Best Picture was based on Puyi's autobiography and showed his remarkable life from the ascent to the throne as a small boy in the Forbidden City, his education by an Irish tutor played by Peter O'Toole, his forced compliance with the Japanese, to his imprisonment and political rehabilitation by the Chinese Communist authorities. Interestingly, *The Last Emperor* was the first feature film authorized by the Chinese Communist government to film in the Forbidden City in Beijing.

Later outside Beijing we visited the Summer Palace, where skaters were enjoying the ice. There was art everywhere, beautifully decorated porcelain tiles inside and outside, overhead and underneath.

We then visited the Great Wall, but I must confess, despite the fact that I was wearing thermal underwear and had thermal lined gloves and boots, I was freezing. I could not stay outside very long. I don't think I walked more than 1,000 feet before I ran back to warm up in the reception area, which was filled with tourists from around the world; I could no longer feel my toes or my fingers. Yet, as soon as I defrosted I had to buy a T-shirt in the gift shop. It reads, "I Climbed the Great Wall of China," and I am still proud to have that shirt, even though I didn't climb very far. I also still have the engraved chop sticks and a porcelain stamp that spells my name in Chinese, which I was given after the final farewell dinner of Peking duck at a banquet in Beijing.

Meeting My Japanese Friends in Tokyo

Before I knew it I was off to Tokyo to meet my Japanese friends from Jefferson, Drs. Kimi and Machico Kaga. I had a wonderful two days touring Tokyo with them. I loved the Tea Service and the flower arranging demonstration given by two beautiful geisha women and the visit to a wonderful Japanese garden. Again I could not resist shopping for something Japanese, so I stopped with Machico at a shop she recommended to buy some pearls. At home I had a full necklace of fine pearls I had bought with my first husband on our tenth anniversary, which I rarely wore anymore. This time I selected a delicate necklace of gold chain with small Mikimoto pearls intermittently linked in all around. I loved that necklace. Though she was not ready for college, and probably did not appreciate my effort at that time, I bought my granddaughter Alix an imprinted sweatshirt at the University of Tokyo bookstore where I found F. A. Davis books in Japanese and English, and a Japanese edition of *Guide to Patient Evaluation.* (Years later when Alix graduated from college, I gave her the pearls. I know she has appreciated the necklace more than the sweatshirt; she wore it to a family celebration a few months ago.)

I had a wonderful Japanese dinner with the doctors Kaga after a long ride in a crowded subway packed like sardines that reminded me of rush hour in the BMT trains I traveled from Brooklyn to Manhattan. The next day I boarded the high-speed bullet train to Kyoto alone to tour the ancient city and visit temples and museums. Fortunately I was able to arrange a personal tour with a guide for the day because it was hard to follow the brochure I was given, even though it was printed in English. It was cold outside, no one seemed to speak English, and I could not speak more than a word or two of Japanese no matter how hard I tried. I wished I were not so alone that day and the next as I returned to Tokyo to meet my scheduled flight home.

I am forever grateful to the entire "F. A. Davis" (Craven) family for the opportunity I was given to celebrate my 50th birthday with such style. It was a remarkable adventure I will never forget.

It is quite evident from news reports and films that China has experienced amazing changes since my visit thirty years ago. Much of the manufactured products we live with every day are made in China, travel is made easier as a result of modern construction and technology, and the advantages of middle-income living are evident in the number of Chinese students enrolled at universities around the world, especially in the United States. I was pleased to read in the latest school newsletter that at my alma mater, Adelphi (and probably many other nursing programs across the country), this advantage has been extended to nursing students through an exchange program where nurses from both countries are learning in each other's institutions.

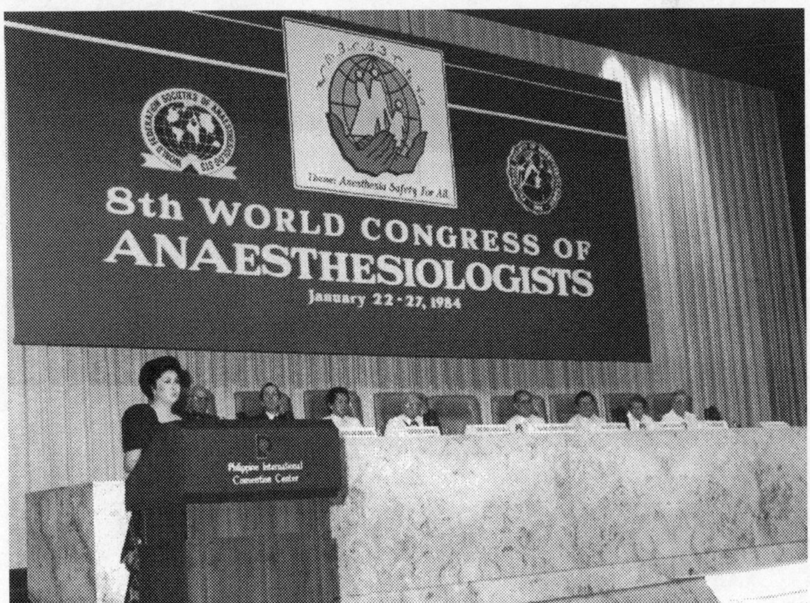

The 5th World Congress of Anesthesiology is held in the Philippines led by Dr John Bonica, author of leading F.A. Davis Textbook on "Pain."

The Pain of A New Idea

Imelda Romualdez Marcos
First Lady of the Philippines
and
Minister of Human Settlements

Keynote address delivered at the
8th World Congress of Anaesthesiologists
Philippine International Convention Center
January 22, 1984

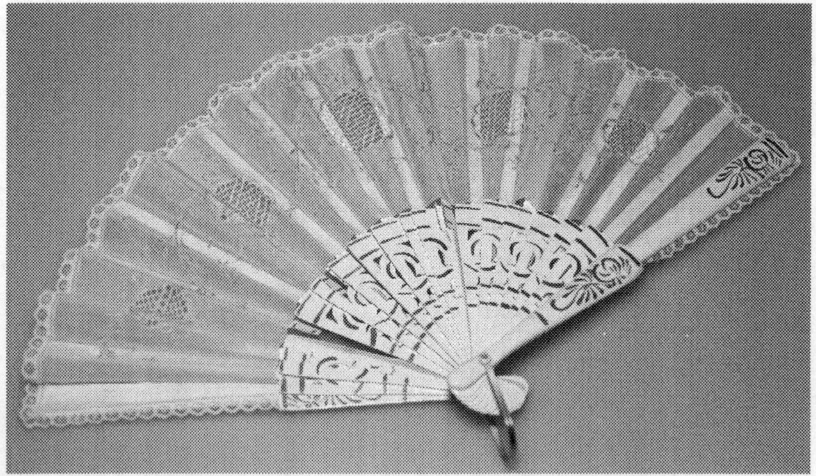

I was invited to tea in the palace and Imelda Marcos gave me a fan engraved with her name. I did not get to see any of her famous shoes.

I purchased and had shipped three Chinese Cabinets, one for each of my children; Later I regretted not purchasing one for myself. Unfortunately Elizabeth's cabinet was destroyed by hurricane Katrina in New Orleans.

中华人民共和国
The Great Wall of China
长 城
证 书
Certificate
This is to certify that
did climb the Great Wall on
Issued by LUXINGSHE
China International Travel Service
Signed
Manager of Badaling Great Wall Administration Office

Visiting Beijing, I was impressed by the amazing winter and summer palaces. I froze at the Great Wall despite my thermal garments, but I was able to obtain this certificate anyway. (It was February!)

At the Tokyo University Book Store I am holding a Davis Publication, Plum and Posner's "*Stupor & Coma*" in Japanese.

In Kyoto I visited the Shrine at Nara.

Feeding the deer at Nara Preserve.

Elizabeth graduated in 1986 from Georgia Southern University in Statesboro Georgia, with a major in business. She then moved to New York City and lived with Melissa and her family during the first year while beginning her career in banking.

12

A New Relationship for Love, Marriage and Travel

Food, Fun and Fascination after Fifty[18]

Sylvia K. Fields and Francis A. Marzolf

The flight home from Japan seemed endless. I was exhausted but couldn't fall asleep; my mind was retracing the trip beginning with the late departure on January 20th. I had tried to write daily notes in a small travel record, but I had missed several days. Some entries were packed with detailed explanations, while others were virtually empty or terribly vague. Attempting to fill in some of the details, my mind raced faster than my pen into short summaries I couldn't read; I was too tired. Maybe later I thought. I finally drifted off. Although I can remember some scenes as vividly today as when they occurred, my travel log is still incomplete.

Traveling alone might be a very exciting experience when you're young, the anticipation alive and well, but at the half century mark it's just not as much fun to be alone on an adventure. Back to work in Philadelphia, another year went by filled with new and continuing projects for the Davis Company as well as more personal disappointments

Years before in Atlanta, thinking I might meet some interesting people, I had considered joining the American Jewish Committee

---

[18] The title of the book my new friend and later husband "Frank" and I planned to write about senior romance.

(AJC), a civil rights organization I believed in. I supported the goals of the internationally recognized group to "pursue social justice, defend religious freedom, fight anti-Semitism, support the right of Israel to exist in peace and security, and provide humanitarian relief to victims around the world through research, education and innovative programs." But I knew no one else with similar interests and I did not have the extra funds to be a financial supporter. I hesitated traveling downtown to a meeting alone. As a result I never actively pursued the interest in Atlanta.

When I learned the AJC national organization was having a weekend meeting in Philadelphia, I called and signed up for the meeting. Fortunately, at dinner the first evening I found myself sitting next to Dr. Elizabeth Levy and her husband Robert Langer, known as Betty and Bob from then on. They were very friendly and I found it easy to share my background and current work in medical publishing. I learned that Bob, a social worker, had a long career in non-profit administration and was currently with the Philadelphia United Way organization, while Betty was a psychiatrist on the faculty of Hahnemann Medical School. Since I had just received a new manuscript for a 2nd edition of a neurology text for psychiatrists Davis was publishing, I asked Betty if she would be willing to review the manuscript for me. Betty was very interested.

We became friends easily and since Bob loved to cook, I was invited to dinner in their Pine Street townhouse. One evening, sharing cocktails and conversation with the Langers and another couple, we waited for a single gentleman friend Betty thought I should meet. The time moved by slowly and that single gentleman failed to arrive. Bob tried to telephone him but when there was no answer he assumed the anticipated guest was on his way. Thirty minutes later, with the dinner long overdue, we moved into the dining room for Bob's specialty, homemade crepes with varied fillings; the meal and the wine were delicious.

After dinner and more conversation the other couple said their goodbyes. I was embarrassed and disappointed that night. I asked Bob who the mysterious guest had been. When he told me, I realized I had met this man professionally several weeks before. He was a Hahnemann Dean and I had interviewed with him for the position of nursing department chairperson. I had been recommended by a nursing faculty member who knew me from Columbia University, so I went for the interview although I really did not want to go back to nursing education. Bob could not remember telling the gentleman on the phone who else was invited to dinner, but he might have. A few days later Bob called him again to find out what had happened. Evidently an apology was received with the explanation that he had mixed up the date with another invitation. I never found out if his claim was true or if he was not interested in me and had preferred not to socialize with me; I never saw him again.

Several weeks later I was invited to dinner again by Betty, but she insisted this was not supposed to be a "match." Bob had invited several other United Way colleagues and their spouses; he thought I would find the company generally interesting and he was right. Among the invitees there was one single gentleman, a highly respected United Way executive in Philadelphia who was divorced. Frank, a Notre Dame graduate with a master's degree in social work administration, had formerly been the Senior Vice President of United Way of America in Alexandria, Virginia. Unfortunately his twenty five-year marriage had fallen apart as the result of his wife's mental breakdown following the sudden death of his oldest son, who was killed in an auto accident the night before leaving for his father's alma mater. As a divorced Catholic, now s single father of two teenagers and two remaining young adults, Frank had left the United Way home base due to a disagreement with the President and had moved back to Philadelphia, where he had previously held an administrative position and maintained several friendships. The conversations were vibrant and interesting all around; I had a stimulating evening and more wine than I usually drank.

After dinner and the other couples had said their good-byes, I asked Bob to call a cab for me, but Frank offered to take me home instead. I had enjoyed his attention during the evening, but he was somewhat overweight and I was not particularly attracted to him. As we walked to his car he asked if I would consider having dinner with him one night. I had been struggling in high heels across the cobblestones when he asked and I hesitated to respond. I did not want to make him uncomfortable, so I said, "Of course," as I reached for the security of his arm. When we crossed the street I moved my hand to his hand for more security; I appreciated the warmth and the strength I felt. A week later we had a lovely dinner in the garden of a well-known Philadelphia French restaurant not too far from my apartment. We continued with dinner dates, always finding much to talk about related to our work and families. When he asked if he could kiss me good night after dinner one night I said "yes" and enjoyed the gentleness. One night we went to a spot in the suburbs where there was dancing, slow dancing appropriate to our ages. It was fun too and I looked forward to returning.

Getting to Know the Altar Boy

Meanwhile, I had learned about Frank's schooling in Ohio Catholic schools until entering Notre Dame and his life as an altar boy. His father, now deceased, had been a professional golfer and Frank had played on the Notre Dame Golf team. In the past he had been a country club member, receiving the benefit attached to his executive position; he loved the game and had won many tournament trophies, but had given the game up because he no longer had the benefit and could not afford to play. I talked about my family life growing up Jewish in Philadelphia and New York very much affected by World War II and the impact of the Holocaust. He could not address that issue. We shared stories about our children. The differences in our religions and professional backgrounds didn't seem as significant as the weeks went by; we enjoyed the companionship and had enough professional and personal interests to support a relationship. For months we had fun exploring cultural activities in and outside the city and trying some new weight loss recipes Frank had been given as he was trying successfully to pare himself down. We even toyed with writing a book together entitled *Fun, Food and Fascination after Fifty*. As the months went by I found Frank more attractive. His efforts toward weight loss were paying off and with a new short hair cut; everyone commented how much better he looked.

When a terrible tragedy occurred in 1986, the bombing by the Philadelphia police of a terrorist cult who barricaded themselves in a South Philadelphia row house threatening their neighbors on the street, we watched in horror from my 18th floor Walnut Street apartment windows while most of the homes went up in flames. As soon as we learned what had happened from the TV news Frank was out the door, joining the mayor to coordinate the various social welfare organizations in the official response with plans for temporary shelter, clothing, food and emotional support for the victims. For weeks he met with the homeless families, social workers, and other service people to facilitate continuing support and then permanent housing. I began to join Frank at other United Way events, admiring the way he worked with community members as well as the staff, volunteers, and corporate executives who raise funds to support the various community agencies.

I was proud to be Frank's friend during these unfortunate times, and began to think about the feasibility of joining him on a long-term basis. I admired Frank for his good writing skills. When I was asked to review and help prepare the manuscript developed by my gay friend Bob for publication while he was apparently fatally ill with AIDS, Frank helped me edit and develop a publishing proposal. My neighbor Tom invited Frank and me to dinner one night, and we had an enjoyable evening. When I asked Tom if he had seen or heard from Bob, he said he hadn't for several months; he thought Bob was in England. Tom was very upset when he heard about Bob's hospitalization and the manuscript. We learned later the manuscript was being considered for publication, but I never received any further information until Bob's obituary was published in the *Philadelphia Inquirer*.

My children were now independent adults living their own lives at a distance, not just in miles. I was not happy with my ten-year single life, as my fifties moved along, despite a productive and satisfying professional life. Frank was living in the suburbs commuting by train to his Benjamin Franklin Parkway office while I was jogging around Rittenhouse Square in the mornings when in Philadelphia and traveling to professional meetings across the country, where I frequently used the gym for exercise. After a year of dating we were very comfortable with each other, maybe even in love and thought we could overcome some of the demons from our former marriages, so when his lease ended, Frank moved into my apartment to consolidate expenses. We had developed a close relationship with the Langers and enjoyed attending concerts and dinner together and playing bridge with them, (although I had never been interested in playing cards or other games, and never knew what I was doing.) I wasn't particularly athletically inclined either and didn't play golf then, but I was happy to entertain myself by walking outdoors or reading on a bench outside our hotel while the trio occasionally played golf on weekends or holidays at the Seaview Country Club near Atlantic City. Learning the games of golf and bridge at that time was not on my agenda; golf and bridge came much later for me.

I knew what my own issues were and thought I understood what Frank's problems were; however, he managed to keep his bitterness, his financial anxieties, and his real goals submerged. I did not know then the dysfunctional state of his former marriage before his son was killed and the severe financial debt the divorce had imposed on him. I didn't realize the negative impact on the remaining children and could not foresee the problems they all soon encountered. I knew my own children had faced problems as a result of my unhappy marriage and eventual divorce, but they were very aware of my problems with my former husband and had supported me in my decision to leave him. I thought that my children had all adjusted pretty well and I was relieved to see my financial situation improve after Elizabeth graduated from college.

A Marriage Begins

Frank was uncomfortable with our unmarried living situation and was feeling social pressure to marry, but I was not in a rush. I was denying the many problems this relationship presented for I knew my elderly parents in Georgia would not accept any relationship with a Catholic very well, regardless of how liberal his thinking was, so I had never mentioned Frank. There were a few times in the beginning of our relationship when

I wished I had the guts to cancel it all due to my concern for my parents. I might have been imagining some of the satisfaction I thought I had with the relationship. However, I valued the companionship, appreciated his touch, and was tired of being alone and of the pursuit of married men I had to fight off.

I don't think Frank's widowed mother, who lived near his sister and her remarkable family in Sacramento, California, had any negative thoughts about me, my religion, or our living situation; they seemed happy that Frank was happy. I felt completely accepted and "at home" when we visited California and envied the beautiful relationships within Frank's sister's family with eight children, twenty-plus grandchildren, and counting. I dreamed Frank and I could have such a joyous family life too, yet I still held out about the marriage issue. Then at a week-long United Way Conference in Arizona Frank's associates urged us to be married right then and there during the week by the wife of one of the executives who had recently been ordained as a minister. It would be her first experience performing a marriage and she thought even more interesting since she would study Jewish marriage rituals and combine the Jewish and Christian spiritual rituals. These were all Frank's friends; I only knew one couple, the president of the Philadelphia organization and his wife, and I did not know them well enough to confide my hesitancy.

The United Way Hosts Our Marriage in Tucson Arizona

It all seemed exciting and there would be no expenses for a wedding since everything at the country club setting was included as part of the meeting. It seemed advantageous and even romantic; I finally agreed to a wedding. The only thing I had to do was shop for an appropriate dress. The ceremony was held outside by the beautiful gardens with the mountains in the background and a classical guitarist providing music as had been arranged for the final dinner of the United Way meeting. Andrew flew out to Tucson to "give me away" and the photos taken attested to how lovely the event was. Unfortunately the rest of our children were upset that we had left them out of the celebration. There was no way we could possibly afford to pay for seven children, five spouses, and grandchildren to participate at that time in Arizona.

After we returned to Philadelphia, as my apartment lease was coming to a close, we started searching for a house to invest in together, although we had limited funds for a down payment or significant restoration. I insisted we stay in Center City, for in my mind it made no sense for us to commute. We finally found a reasonably priced four-story glass front contemporary town house between 9th and 10th Streets on Latimer, a narrow Philadelphia alley behind Locust Street within walking distance of both of our offices. The house had a large country kitchen with a fireplace and sliding glass door to a charming deck with a few steps down to a small garden. It didn't take me long to line the deck with flowers while Frank cultivated the garden downstairs. The top floor had two extra bedrooms and a full bath. Although I preferred to jog through the streets early in the morning (often to the Delaware River), we put my treadmill in front of a TV in one of the rooms upstairs so I could exercise indoors in bad weather. I really enjoyed living there around the corner from the Wills Eye Hospital and just four blocks from the Academy of Music, two blocks from the Forrest Theatre and two blocks from the Walnut Theatre in the other direction. We were close to Independence Hall and the entire historic section, not too far from Suburban Station of the Pennsylvania Railroad and the bus terminal, surrounded by all kinds of shops and ethnic restaurants near Chinatown. In addition, we were only a short walk across Washington Square to the Langer's new apartment. They had purchased a beautiful condominium on the Square with a great view of the Delaware River. Meanwhile we quickly made new friends among our next-door neighbors on both sides; I thought I was as happy as I might ever be.

A Course in Judaism for Both of Us

Hoping it would relieve my parents' anguish over my relationship, Frank and I took a course in Judaism together with a group of young couples anticipating an interfaith marriage; we both enjoyed the stimulating questions and interesting discussions. But I kept asking questions about my religion and all religions. I learned how much I did not know before, and I understood that I was probably never going to be satisfied with the answers by the rabbi (or a priest or minister) that required my complete faith in an invisible spirit. I did not always see a "loving God" accomplish much. I never could accept the fantasy of heaven and hell as depicted in fairy tales, Hollywood movies, and other media, and I could not envision a "life after death." In my mind there was too much cruelty in the Bible stories and too many wars throughout history over minor differences of belief. Meanwhile, I found no solace in prayer, over and over again and again. I had received the ethical messages of the Ten Commandments; wasn't that enough?

Be a Good Person; Love thy neighbor as thyself; be a good friend; help those less fortunate than you; live each day so that at the end of the day you can say my day has been worthwhile; ask not what your country has done for you, ask what you can do for your country? To those who much has been given, much is expected! (I don't think that is a direct quote, but it's the right idea.) And I had taken the Nightingale Pledge. Isn't that enough?

But I felt guilty; I really did want to honor my mother and father's teachings, and I had worked very hard to pass on our heritage to my children.

I always enjoyed the music of my own religion including the Yiddish songs my father and uncles taught me. But I also enjoyed the music of other religious services where I willingly sang the Christmas carols and hymns I learned at Birney Public School in Philadelphia as a child. The music of the Jewish services Frank and I attended at the reform synagogue Rodeph Shalom in Center City, Philadelphia with the Langers were the melodies I remembered from my early childhood and young married adulthood with my children on Long Island. Those melodies (with some modifications) are evidently universal for Jews around the world.

A Jewish Wedding Helps Heal

The wife of the senior rabbi, who had recently retired at Rodeph Shalom, had been president of the United Way Board, and worked tirelessly with Frank in the community to provide needed services for the indigent of all faiths in the city. Frank respected the couple tremendously for their efforts and accomplishments. I decided I wanted to learn more, but first be married again in the Jewish temple for my parents' sake and for my children. Although transporting my parents and all the children to Philadelphia was going to be stressful and expensive for us, I convinced Frank it would be the smart thing to do. He agreed and decided to go ahead with the conversion process to Judaism. He set up a schedule of private tutoring with the new young associate rabbi, Elliot Holon, whom we really liked and who agreed to marry us in the small temple chapel on a Sunday morning. We made arrangements for my parents and some of the children to stay in the Society Hill Hotel near the Delaware River. My parents were surprised and pleased at how traditional the marriage ceremony was, with the grandchildren leading us down the aisle and Frank breaking the glass, as they all shouted "Mazel Tov," etc. I had arranged a lovely luncheon after the service in the hotel for family and friends and some professional associates. My elderly Aunt Sonia and her son and his wife came from New York City. A keyboard player and violinist provided festive Jewish music and we all danced to the traditional "Hora" and my father and I even danced a Hungarian Czardas we both loved. It turned out to be a great day I will never forget.

The next day I gave my parents a tour of Center City and took them to see our old neighborhood of Logan in North Philadelphia, where of course "I had had my own room." There were changes in the faces of the few people we saw on the street, but to us the neighborhood looked very much as it had looked when we lived there fifty years before. My parents returned to Augusta a few days after the wedding, obviously more satisfied than they had been before.

Unfortunately the following year my father suddenly became seriously ill with a good deal of pain that had been difficult to diagnose. After an unsuccessful chemotherapy regimen, he died of Multiple Myeloma; he was eighty seven years old and very much loved in the Augusta community. The director of the health center where he went to exercise regularly wrote a beautiful article as a memorial about his participation and the wonderful smile he always brought with him to the Community Center. My mother, who had the traditional health problems of women over 65, – diabetes, coronary heart disease, and a minor stroke – was devastated by his death, as we all were. Now she was alone in Augusta. I did not know what to do; she did not want to go to a nursing home there and she wasn't ready to leave Augusta, where she and my father had enjoyed the last ten years. I hired a fine senior age widow who was recommended by a neighbor as a companion for my mother and they did pretty well together for almost a year in between my mother's hospital admissions and readmissions. I flew back and forth for business always in and out of Augusta and back to Philadelphia. Finally my mother's illness became too much for the caretaker to manage and the traveling too difficult for me. Hoping I could find a local person capable of managing her care as long as she was ambulatory, I moved her to my home in Philadelphia. I tried one person after the next but no caretaker satisfied my mother. Although the physicians could not find a cause, she had difficulty swallowing solid food; everything had to be blended into a soup. Since her mental capacity was very much intact, I considered moving her to the lovely Chestnut Hill Assisted Living Home. I knew she would like the elegance of the place, but they would not accept her if she could not eat the regular diet in the dining room, where the tables were covered in white linens and I think the servers wore white gloves. It just wasn't meant to be. Mom soon returned to the hospital with another cardiac episode and I made the decision to move her to the Philadelphia Geriatric Center.

I thought she might be satisfied where there were Jewish services on Friday nights and at least the food was kosher. But she was miserable there. The side rails were put up on her bed at night so she had to use the call button when she needed the bedpan. She had had a commode at her bedside and could manage by herself during the night for several years in Augusta and in my house. When the nursing aides did not respond quickly at night with the bedpan, she cried as she wet herself, and cried to me afterwards when I visited every day after work. While I traveled, Frank visited Mom daily after work, brought her the newspaper, and walked with her to the dining room. When my Aunt Sonia came from New York to visit her, Mother told her Frank had been wonderful, "a better son to her than her own son." I know she did not really mean that, but what difference did it make by that time. Mother was so depressed she refused to eat, refused proposed tube feedings, and said, "No more" to intravenous fluids. She signed the necessary papers asking to be denied any special procedures to keep her alive. She died peacefully in her sleep, also as my father at eighty seven years of age, leaving me with terrible guilt that I did not take her back to my house from the nursing home when close to the end, she asked me to take her home.

Family members at my mother's funeral in Elmont New York. Starting on the left is my favorite cousin Saul Berg, then his mother, my dear Aunt Sonia next to me. (Saul's wife is behind us.) My cousin Fran Berg is in front of Frank with Melissa next before my brother Norman and his wife Marcia.

Frank and I Traveling Together to Alaska

Frank wanted to visit his mother and sister in Sacramento and we needed a change of scenery. We decided to arrange a cruise to Alaska, stopping along the way in Sacramento. The weeks flew by and before we knew it we were on the way to Seattle after visiting his mother. Frank was really feeling good and much more relaxed now until we learned when we arrived that there had been a problem with the ship and the Holland-American cruise was cancelled while we were in Sacramento. Unfortunately, they were unable to contact us. We were supposed to go to Vancouver and Victoria and then through the inside passageway to Sitka and then on to Juneau. We were scheduled for travel by train across Denali Park and then to Anchorage. However there was no other cruise we could join right away; everything was booked. The representative offered to reschedule us in October, but I could not take time off in October. Frank was ready to go home, but I fought and fussed and finally after staying in Seattle for three more days, we were booked into a different seven-day cruise. However all our land arrangements were messed up. From day to day we did not know where we were staying, and what we could see; all our previous reservations for admissions had been cancelled. We experienced highs and then lows, ups and downs, one night we almost slept in the hotel lobby because they could not find a room for us, until there was a "no show." As difficult as it was, I have some wonderful memories with photos of the lovely city of Vancouver, a large print from the beautiful Butchart Gardens of Victoria I later had framed, and other mementos of different scenes in Alaska. I remember seeing the whales from the ship, the fun of canoeing in Ketchikan, salmon and more salmon for lunch and dinner every day, seeing the famous pipeline, and visiting the marvelous native museum in Anchorage.

We returned to Philadelphia exhausted, went back to work and settled into our old routines.

Travels to England and California

In the spring of 1987, out of the blue I received a letter from my former childhood pen-pal in England, Joan Carter. Apparently after her mother died, among her mother's things she found one of my letters mailed from Brooklyn when I was about fourteen. She proceeded to write to me at the return address on East 13th Street. The letter had been forwarded to my parents in Augusta Georgia and then forwarded by them to me in Philadelphia. I was now well past fifty. I decided to write back and the correspondence began again. Joan, who had left school as required at fourteen during World War II, had worked in an office until she married and had one son, now about my son Andrew's age. Our backgrounds were completely different; she had gone no further in public school, and had therefore never graduated from secondary school or attended a university. At Joan's request I followed up the second letter with a phone call from my office and then began receiving calls in my office from Joan. She wanted very much to come to the United States, but could not afford the trip and was begging me to invite her to come to Philadelphia. I explained to her that there was no way I could arrange such a trip for her due to my business and travel responsibilities. I felt terribly bad turning her down, but then I got the idea to visit Joan in England, which was high on my "travel wish list" after Alaska. When British Airways advertised a two-week inclusive Bed and Breakfast "get-a-way," I raised the issue with Frank. After much debate we agreed to take advantage of the deal during our next vacation time so we could meet Joan Carter in person.

We searched through the British Airways brochures and as much other literature about England we could find to determine what we really wanted to see. We began with the first week in London and then arranged to rent a car to travel around the countryside for the second week. Joan was surprised and excited when I called to tell her we were coming to London; we set up a "tea" meeting in our hotel toward the end of the first week. Frank and I had a wonderful week traveling by "underground tube" and buses to all the places tourists are advised to see, such as the Tower of London, the Queen's Jewels, Changing of the

Guard at Buckingham Palace, St. Paul's Cathedral, and Westminster Abbey. My first choice, however, was to visit the British Museum to view the ancient manuscripts; Frank was most excited about Churchill's underground headquarters. Then I was thrilled to see the statue of Florence Nightingale, the Wax Museum, and Prince Albert Hall. We loved the fish and chips best of all the meals.

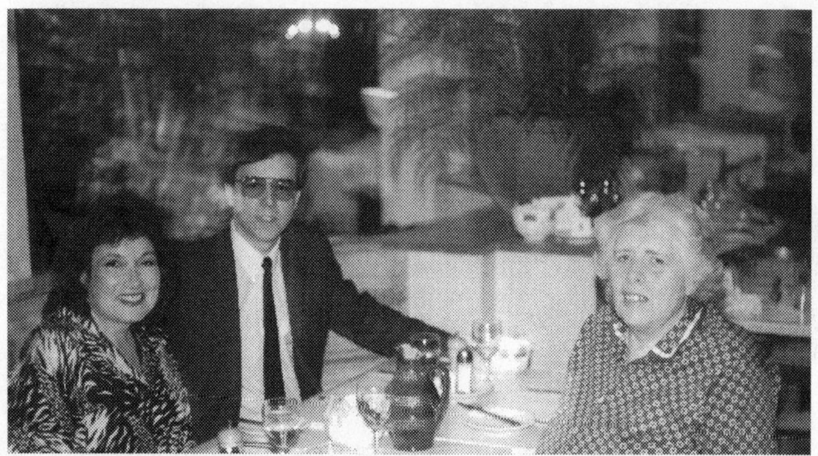

Tour of England: Visiting with my childhood pen pal Joan Carter and her son after almost fifty years.

I was surprised that Joan arrived to the Lancaster hotel for our date, not with her husband, but with her son, and I was shocked at how old she looked. She had white hair, was much overweight, and had several missing teeth. I don't know what I expected, but I had found a picture she had sent when she was about 14; she had been a pretty girl. She was only two years older than me, but I thought she looked older than my mother. It was a difficult meeting; she explained that her husband was ill and could not come, but I could tell she was uncomfortable in the elegant hotel dining room. I struggled to find something to talk about; meanwhile her son was restless. He explained that he was a chauffeur for a Saudi Arab sheik, and said it was interesting work and paid well. He asked Frank what his work was and Frank told him about the United Way and the services they offered. I told them about my work in medical publishing, although Joan already knew about my traveling. Joan asked Frank about his children and we showed photos of our grandchildren.

When I explained that we were planning to take a tour of Windsor Castle the following day, Joan's son jumped in with the offer to drive us to Windsor since he was free the next day. Joan piped up that she had never been to Windsor Castle and wanted very much to go there too. Although Frank and I were not anxious to accept the invitation, there was no way we could back out once Joan said she always wanted to go to the Castle, but never had the means to go.

In the morning after breakfast we waited outside the hotel entrance for Joan and her son to pick us up. When the car arrived we were surprised to see that Joan's son had also brought along his girlfriend, the frumpiest looking "chick" I had ever seen. She never stopped talking during the drive but I barely understood a word she said due to her cockney accent. She sounded like Audrey Hepburn in the beginning of the movie *My Fair Lady*. It was an indescribable nightmare of a trip, as we struggled to find conversation and she chatted on. The son could not quiet his girlfriend up, they argued the whole way and then he got lost. We were late for our reservation so we waited until the next group was invited in. It was a wonderful tour. I had heard about the English country homes but I had never been in anything like this before. The house and gardens were magnificent, but what I remember most was the big thrill of seeing Queen Mary's dollhouse. It was a wonderful experience all around despite the girlfriend. Joan was happy after the tour and things quieted down on the trip back to London. She wanted to set up another meeting, but we had no idea where we would be before we went to the airport for our trip home. I could not wait to get out of the car, promising to call again before returning to the U.S.

We had arrangements for a rental car the next day, which was truly a challenge for Frank. He was a great sport, but driving on the left side of the road with the driver's seat and wheel on the right side of the car was certainly not easy, especially with all the roundabouts and cars racing past us at what seemed like a hundred miles an hour or more. We started out going north, first to Oxford University and Shakespeare's

House. I loved the bookseller's shop in Oxford and found medical books primarily by English physicians published by British publishers, with a few American works. The next day we visited Blenheim Palace and Gardens. I fell even more in love with England that day; the homes, the furnishings, the gardens and the countryside all had a fairy tale feeling to me. (No wonder I became a *Downton Abbey* fan when the PBS series started a few years ago.) After staying in a lovely B&B that night we continued north towards the Lake District, with a few stops of historical relevance. The first destination was in the walled city of Chester built by the Romans in the first century A.D. The wall is still very much intact despite damages as a result of the fall of the Roman Empire between the 4th and 5th centuries A.D. We also stopped in Stoke, the original home of Spode English Bone China, where I searched for a sample pattern I might select for purchase. I could not make up my mind for an entire set, but I did buy a few pieces of one pattern, Trapnell Spray, to consider. When I learned I could buy the set in the U.S. at the same cost without shipping expenses, I decided to wait until I got home. I never did buy a whole set but I have enjoyed using the samples as serving pieces through the years.

We moved on toward Lake Windermere and stayed in a lovely spot nearby, "The Swan" at Grasmere. The next day we walked all around the lake and it was a wonderful feeling thinking about the great English novelists who wrote marvelous stories about this beautiful area. Of course *Lady Windermere's Fan* comes to mind immediately. I drove Frank nuts when I told him I wanted to drive back down south to Stonehenge, to see the prehistoric monoliths and then to Bristol by the Sea and even Bath, cities noted in so much of English history and literature. We returned for the last night in Ascot, where the famous races were held in *My Fair Lady.*

I called Joan and then promised to try to plan something for her in Philadelphia the following year. We spoke a few times after my return home; she told me again that she was happy I had had the chance to see her country. It was a wonderful trip, and I am grateful to have had the opportunity. I did not hear anything further from Joan for a few months, when she wrote that she was ill but still looked forward to visiting the U.S. one day. Unfortunately, I never was able to bring Joan to Philadelphia. It was not too long after that last letter that I received one from her husband with shocking photos of her in an open casket. Joan died of breast cancer eight months after we took her to the Castle at Windsor for the first time in her life.

An Earthquake in San Francisco

The next year moved by filled with work and family, when we learned that on October 17, 1989, there was a major earthquake in San Francisco and Oakland, the strongest in the area since 1906, supposedly caused by a "slip along the San Andreas Fault." There were sixty deaths, many when significant bridges went down; thousands were injured, and there was widespread property damage, but the impact could have been worse. The event occurred just hours before the start of the third game of the World Series between the San Francisco Giants and the Oakland Athletics. The game was suspended for ten days and general travel to San Francisco was cut off sharply. Businessmen and most tourists cancelled their trips fearful of aftershocks. However, to encourage people to return to San Francisco a national appeal was announced with offers for $200 round-trip flights from anywhere in the United States to San Francisco through the end of the year. I had a brainstorm. Frank's 60th birthday would occur late in December. I decided to throw him a party in San Francisco and invite all of our children from the east Coast – New York City; New Orleans; Greenville, South Carolina; Alexandria and Norfolk, Virginia – to celebrate for a weekend with Frank, his mother and his sister and her family in Sacramento. I called Frank's sister Ellen and she agreed it was a wonderful idea. Using the large hotel guide in our F.A. Davis office I found the famous historic Claremont Hotel in Oakland where we could have a private room and black tie dinner with an open bar at a reasonable cost on Saturday night during the weekend of December 8–10. Then I found the Marriott Marina Hotel in Berkeley that offered us a wonderful hospitality suite free and rooms for $95 a night. My travel agent was able to schedule all the flights at the $200 rate to arrive Friday before noon. Frank's sister and her husband hosted a casual dinner in the hotel dining room, where all my children had an opportunity to meet everyone from Frank's family they had not met. In the morning after breakfast, all the young adults went to San Francisco, the first visit for my children. We older adults took care of the little children, mostly Ellen's grandchildren in the hotel all day. Later we all gathered at the Claremont Hotel for the birthday/holiday celebration, the men in formal wear and the ladies in black for the cocktail party hosted by Grandma. After the dinner, the toasting and roasting began; it was much more fun than I could ever have expected. No one noticed as all the young women (Frank's daughters, daughters-in-law, and mine) slowly and quietly left the room one at a time, only to return singing at the top of their voices, doing the can-can, and wearing large red T-shirts over their black dresses which read "I'm his favorite daughter." The evening ended with a grab-bag of inexpensive fun gifts for everyone. It was a marvelous celebration, a weekend for all to remember.

Pressured by his United Way friends at the annual meeting in Tucson, Arizona in 1986, Frank and I were unexpectedly married by the wife of one of the United Way Directors who was a newly ordained minister. We wrote our own interfaith service together.

To make my parents and children happy, Frank and I arranged a very intimate traditional Jewish wedding in 1987 in the chapel of the Philadelphia Reform conducted by Rabbi Elliot Holon in Congregation Rodeph Shalom where we had attended services with our friends Bob and Betty Langer. Scene includes our grandchildren.

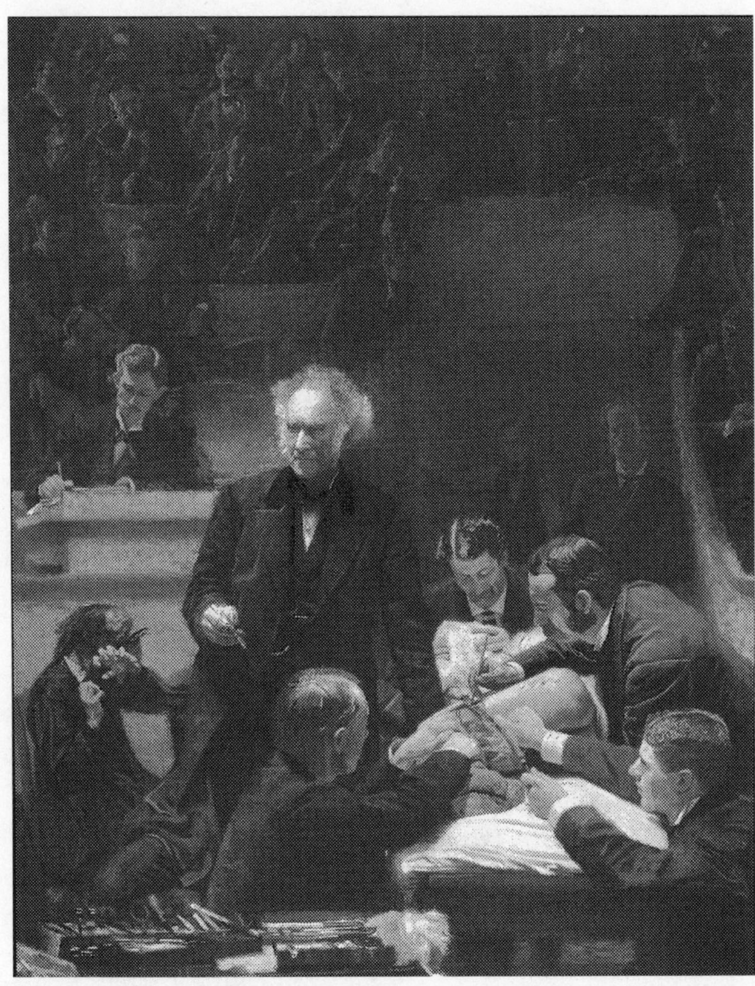

Thomas Jefferson University- Famous Painting by American Artist, Eakins "*The Gross Clinic*, was purchased originally as a gift to the Medical College by the Medical College Alumni and housed with restricted access in the College Building on Walnut Street. It was purchased by the Pennsylvania Academy of Fine Arts and the Philadelphia Museum of Art in 2007 with the generous support of 3,600 donors. (It is in the ars Medica Collection. Accession Number 2007-1-1)

13

Medical Education and Research at Jefferson Medical College

"*THE ESSENCE OF PATIENT CARE IS IN THE CARING FOR THE PATIENT*"[19]

FRANCIS W. PEABODY, M.D.

The New Year of 1990 came quickly after we returned from Frank's birthday celebration in California and settled back into our respective professional routines. As much as Frank and I appreciated our deepening personal relationship, there were continuing career pressures and various concerns with our children that never seemed to end. It was not surprising that before long our career goals seemed to collide. Frank resented my traveling; issues of trust arose whenever I was out of town for a few days at a time. Lack of trust seemed a throwback to my previous marriage. Frank had never seemed anxious before we were married about my entertaining authors while traveling, which I openly shared. Now I hesitated to talk about social responsibilities that were part of my position. I loved my role as an acquisitions editor and put a great deal of passion and energy into my work, just as I had always done in every position I held through the years. But my personal qualities were being negatively interpreted again and I became concerned the relationship I worked so hard to develop and sustain was being jeopardized. After

19 Dr. Peabody, *Teacher and humanitarian in a lecture to the Harvard Medical School graduates, 1926. This quote has been repeatedly published in the medical education literature ever since.*

eight exciting and productive years at the Davis Company with financial benefits we both enjoyed, I found it necessary to make a change.

Fortunately I soon found a challenging new opportunity created for me by Dr. Joseph Gonnella, who had recently been appointed as Dean of the Jefferson Medical College (JMC)[20] at Thomas Jefferson University (TJU), while continuing to serve as Director of the Center for Research in Medical Education and Health Care (CRMEHC) at the College. He invited me to join his team in the Office of Academic Affairs and the CRMEHC. There was no formal job description when I first arrived at the institution full time in December of 1990, but my position just seemed to expand and evolve according to the needs of the Dean's Office, project assignments, and my creative efforts within new programs. I was appointed as Senior Research Associate to consult with the dean, directors, and staff of the CRMEHC from a theoretical and clinical perspective and participate in development of new education and evaluation programs.

I already had a professional relationship with Dr. Gonnella and Mr. Jon Veloski, and knew quite a bit about Jefferson Medical College when I arrived on the Center City Philadelphia campus. I knew that Thomas Jefferson University was a private institution dedicated to advancing health sciences, education, and research and not a general liberal arts school. In addition to the Jefferson Medical College, one of the oldest medical schools in the United States established in 1824, there were professional schools of Nursing, Pharmacy, Health Professions, Public Health, and Graduate Biomedical Sciences established within the University.

On my first day at Jefferson and many days later, I was enamored by the great piece of art, *The Gross Clinic* painted in 1875 by Thomas Eakins for the celebration of the American Centennial that welcomed visitors to the Jefferson Medical College Building, its home since 1878. (The painting today is shared by the Philadelphia Museum of Art and

---

20 Jefferson Medical College is now known as the Sidney Kimmel Medical College. In 2014 Sidney Kimmel, President of Jones Apparel contributed 110 Million Dollars to Thomas Jefferson University for the Medical College.

the Pennsylvania Academy of the Arts.) Bought by alumni for the Medical College and widely considered Eakins' finest work, the huge dark painting depicts the surgeon with ungloved hands standing over the patient with a large open wound. Students and other observers including the artist are seen in the background. The principal subject of the painting, Dr. Samuel D. Gross, was one of the first graduates of Jefferson Medical College, where he became a charismatic professor and an internationally renowned authority on surgery. Considered the greatest American painting of the nineteenth century, the work is viewed also as a testament to Philadelphia's distinction in the medical and education fields. Throughout my tenure at Jefferson I was proud to be associated with this historic institution.

The original mission of the College was to "prepare patient centered clinically competent physicians." That mission was clear when I arrived at JMC and continues to this day. I learned recently that the College has prepared more physicians than any other medical school in the world, with more than 27,000 medical degrees awarded, and has more living graduates than any other school. The Jefferson University and Hospital System maintains various alliances locally such as with the Kimmel Cancer Center, and other education and health care facilities throughout the state of Pennsylvania as well as with the University of Delaware and its Health Science Programs.

The Research Center was divided into two sections, with Jon Veloski leading the medical education evaluation section and Daniel Louis leading the section on evaluation of health care outcomes. In 1970 as Associate Dean, Dr. Gonnella together with Mr. Veloski established the Longitudinal Study of Medical Students and Graduates, a computerized database system that tracks students from pre-admission through medical school courses to graduation, residency, and choice of career. It is the largest such database of medical education in the world. A similar tracking system was established for medical residents, who as postgraduates were admitted to specialty training at Jefferson. The Longitudinal Study has been very important in helping to answer questions about specific components of required and/or optional JMC programs and evaluating the outcomes of the overall medical school curriculum. In 1984, Mohammadreza Hojat, Ph.D., joined Mr. Veloski in maintaining the tracking systems and overseeing analyses of data and communication through publication. I worked closely with Mr. Veloski in the development of new research studies on outcomes of the program and short-term projects. Later I worked with Dr. Hojat on the development of studies on attitudes toward inter-professionalism and levels of empathy within nurse and physician students and practitioners, that have gained extensive international recognition.

Although the Center has been partially supported through the JMC administrative budget for program evaluation, it has been dependent on outside funding from individual contributors and private foundations, as well as associated institutions and various governmental and professional organizations for collaborative research projects. I was supported through a combination of institutional and other funding sources, such as the Division of Medicine, Bureau of Health Professions, Health Resources Services Administration (HRSA); the Division of Education section of the American Medical Association (AMA), the American Academy of Family Physicians (AAFP), American College of Physicians (ACP), and the Commonwealth of Pennsylvania.

Most of the Center staff members were statisticians or psychometricians with little or no clinical experience in health care; however, there were a few clinical faculty members who participated on a part-time basis in health care outcomes research. While my doctoral education and continued professional efforts emphasized program development and evaluation with focus on interprofessional curriculum, my many years of clinical practice and teaching in elite academic medical centers was a distinct benefit to the Center.

I was excited about the significance of the work being done at the Center on medical education in relation to the problems in the American health care system. Providing equal access to primary health care has been a problem for the nation throughout its history and continues to this day. Looking back through my own sixty-year professional life, the same problems we faced in the 1940s, '50s and on, we were facing in the 1990s when I arrived at JMC, and despite the many governmental initiatives and corporate efforts to modify our health care system, such as managed care, and improved medical education by expanding programs and increasing admissions, we continue to face the same problems: the high cost of health care; *the lack of access to primary care particularly for minority populations and in rural areas; the disparity in outcomes of medical care; and the unfavorable distribution of physicians, especially generalists.*

For example in 1971, the federal government, through Title VII of the Public Health Service Act, began supporting the training of primary care physicians when it recognized that segments of the nation's population had little or no access to affordable primary care. The AREA Health Education Centers (AHEC) were initiated in 1972 to address specialty misdistribution, particularly in rural areas. I am reminded of the award-winning television series from 1990 to 1995, *Northern Exposure*, that dramatically and humorously demonstrated the unique problems in rural areas and the contribution of young newly trained physicians supported by local, state, or federal government such as the National Health Service Corps (NHSC) in order to pay back medical school loans. In the beginning the program clearly demonstrated the difficult cultural adjustment of a young New York City physician who had just completed his residency in internal medicine as he sets up his practice in rural Alaska and interacts with the diverse population in this unique environment. Most medical students today graduate with significant debt, sometimes in the $100,000 range or more. All too often, despite their expressed interest in generalist careers, many new graduates decide to specialize and sub-specialize, in order to increase their income later and pay back their education loans.

In addition I have been reminded by Dr. Labadie that a major difference between medical and nursing education continues to be the focus of physicians on the "Rescue of Medicine" over health and the "medicalization" of health. As mentioned earlier, when Dr. Sherman and I were working together on the history taking component of our course and on our *Guide to Patient Evaluation*, we argued over the term universally used in medical textbooks, "medical history." I emphasized the difference in professional roles by insisting we use the term "health history," which brings in factors affecting daily living habits, such as diet, exercise, literacy and social relationships, mental, sexual and spiritual activities, all components of "Health" that nurses should consider when assessing health status. I joked by saying, "if we could only teach physicians to be nurses first, how much better health care would become." I won that battle in the book: it is "health history" and over the years many areas of medicine have slowly adopted the themes of "health promotion" and "prevention" and focus on "patient education for prevention."

The mandate to study these issues once again led to a request for proposals (RFP) announced in 1992 by the Health Resources Services Administration (HRSA), which stated:

> Medical schools and teaching hospitals should prepare many more physicians than now exist who will have the desire and the qualifications to render comprehensive, continuing health services including preventive measures, early diagnosis, rehabilitation and supportive therapy, as well as the diagnosis and treatment of acute or episodic disease states. (Politzer, Harris, Gaston, Mullan, Primary Care Physician Supply and the Medically Underserved. *JAMA* 1991 July3-Vol 266 No. 1. 3)

Jon Veloski shared the RFP announcement with me and we began to discuss the feasibility of Jefferson submitting a proposal. "Unfortunately it looks like the University of Washington is wired to get this grant," Jon said. "They have published in this area and have a record of developing creative programs for the rural areas of the northwest."

"But Jefferson has also been effective, what about Jefferson's Physician Shortage Area Program (PSAP) in Family Medicine?" I asked. "And you told me our Longitudinal Study was unique; we know how to collect, organize and analyze data," I said. (I had only been there a short while, but already I considered this school as my own.)

Howard Rabinowitz, M.D., Family Medicine faculty member and director of the PSAP program agreed with Jon, "We don't have a chance."

"But," I said, "You will never know if you don't try! As a collaborative program we would have a much better opportunity for national recognition. Who should we recruit?" I asked.

Jon called Dr. Barbara Barzansky, assistant director of the education section of the AMA (American Medical Association), and an old colleague I had also been introduced to by Jon at a meeting. He sent her a copy of the RFP. Barbara came to Philadelphia and we started to brainstorm together. I worked with Jon, Howard, and Barbara on the proposal. A few more partners were invited to participate. The final proposal we submitted was complex and thorough. To our amazement, we won the competition and received the contract to design and carry out a full national study of generalist physician outcomes of medical education.

The objectives of the research we conducted in collaboration with the AMA and the AAMC (Association of American Medical Colleges) and two private research partners were:

- to identify the variables in undergraduate medical education that best predict student choice of generalist careers (family practice, general internal medicine, and general pediatrics) and
- to formulate recommendations for both individual medical schools and public policy

To accomplish the objectives we developed and validated a series of questionnaires to:

1) gather information about specific characteristics of all active U.S. medical schools inclined to promote primary care for underserved populations
2) survey national samples of MD and DO (Doctor of Osteopathic Medicine) practicing generalist physicians
3) conduct guided site visits to selected schools with a high proportion of graduates becoming generalist physicians.

More than 12 papers were eventually published as a result of this study. The first paper published was an overall summary, while other papers examined individual variables within the students and/or the institutions that were considered to potentially influence the selection of a generalist career, such as:

a) financial support
b) rural or underserved mission)
c) presence of a family medicine department) and
d) length of family medicine clerkship.

In 1993 when we looked at possible curriculum variables, Problem-Based Learning (PBL) programs were thought to be more likely to produce graduates who select primary care careers. The use of PBL as a major part of the curriculum was relatively rare at that time, even though many schools did some case-based small-group teaching; less than a dozen schools (among 125 accredited schools in this country at the time) used PBL as the major instructional format. We were unable to isolate the independent effects of the comprehensive PBL curricula on medical students' choices of generalist careers because these programs were more likely to be located in medical schools that had a primary care or community-based mission. Nevertheless, it was clear that comprehensive PBL curricula embrace key features that have been shown to influence the choice of generalist careers, such as early exposure to generalist physician role models.

The Health of the Public Initiative

In addition to the federal government, various private corporations and non-profit community organizations made efforts to initiate and expand professional education programs to meet the health care needs of the public. One such effort was The Health of the Public Program, supported by the Robert Wood Johnson, Pew, and Rockefeller Foundations. It was a "Challenge to Academic Health Centers," which began in 1986 in six centers and expanded to more than 30 across the country when I came to Jefferson. The program was dedicated to advancing the "population perspective" in health care education through community partnerships, curricular reform, and collaboration among the health professions.

I was appointed as Coordinator of Primary Care and Community programs and served on the national Health of the Public Challenge Advisory Board. From that perspective I led the development of the Jefferson response to the Challenge, which we entitled JeffCARES (Community Action, Research, Education, and Service). This was an outgrowth of the Philadelphia Community Health Internship Program (PCHIP), a consortium of Jefferson and Philadelphia's five other medical schools that had created Bridging the Gaps (BTG) in 1991, an eight-week summer program sensitizing students to the problems of inner-city patients and providing awareness of community health issues.

While Thomas Jefferson University had a strong history of community-oriented activities, collaboration between disciplines and with community organizations, activities already occurring in the academic health center needed to be expanded and coordinated. In response to student interest and motivation, BTG provided medical and other health service professional students (nursing, pharmacy, physical and occupational therapy students at Jefferson) with an opportunity to explore their interest in primary care and community health service on interprofessional teams.

Originally initiated and coordinated by the University of Pennsylvania School of Medicine (SMUP) as their response to the Health of the Public Challenge two years earlier, the BTG program was also supported by a large group of smaller foundations and individual donors and expanded to include students of the other medical schools in Philadelphia. Students of the six institutions (University of Pennsylvania, Jefferson Medical College of TJU, Hahnemann Medical School, Medical College of Pennsylvania, Philadelphia Osteopathic Medical College, and Temple University School of Medicine) met together in weekly plenary sessions led by an inter-institutional faculty group to which I belonged, and were assigned as small interprofessional teams to various community partner agencies in our local neighborhoods. Students received a significant weekly stipend similar to those offered during the summer in basic science and hospital research labs. After the intensive community-based experience, the students were scheduled to present their work at an annual city-wide forum, as well as through a nationally distributed health action report.

The Problem of the Homeless in Center City Philadelphia

When I first moved to Center City Philadelphia I was made aware pretty quickly of the major problem of homelessness in the city. I was appalled to see the number of homeless individuals and families sitting, lying or walking on the narrow crowded streets asking for help. One day, on my way to work at F.A. Davis on Arch Street, I came face to face with the terrible problem of mentally ill homeless on the street. *People were scurrying about when all of a sudden, a strange human being came right up, looked at me and spit a huge mouthful of a partially chewed sandwich or something else right in my face.* Horrified, I stood for a minute, while no one walking by said a single word or stopped to help me clean myself off. I will never forget that day. I turned around and ran five blocks back to my apartment to shower, wash my hair, and throw everything I was wearing into the garbage or the washing machine.

TJU had long been concerned about the homeless of Center City, many of whom were found on the streets surrounding the University Hospital and campus. Historically, the homeless have been suspicious of the medical care system. They are reluctant to come to the emergency room until their problems are very serious because of the way they have usually been treated – which drives up the costs for conditions that in many cases could have been prevented.

During the summer of 1992 two Jefferson medical students, participating in Bridging The Gaps project with the University of Pennsylvania explored the issue of the homeless in Center City with the Homeless Project of Philadelphia Health Management Corporation. They took their concerns to the Dean, who asked me to work with the student council and a few interested family medicine and internal medicine faculty to arrange a meeting with the mayor's office to discuss the student concerns. The mayor informed us that the city was working with the sanitation department toward creation of a special service corps that could provide jobs for the homeless, where they would be in uniforms and trained to sweep and otherwise clean up the streets downtown. (The program was initiated very soon after and seemed quite effective.)

The city manager invited us to see an old factory building downtown within walking distance of TJU Hospital and campus that the city had in the process of rehabilitation in order to turn it into a homeless shelter in collaboration with The Salvation Army.

During the 1993 BTG internship, additional medical students at JMC interviewed homeless individuals in the Jefferson emergency room, on the streets surrounding the Jefferson campus, and at nearby community resource sites such as the Mercy Hospice and Family Center. Other internship students conducted a health needs assessment in the Ludlow community of North Philadelphia and worked at the St. Columba's Homeless Shelter, operated by Project HOME (Housing, Opportunities, Medical Care, Education), where Jefferson students had already established a small health clinic, JeffHOPE (Health, Opportunity, Prevention, Education). Paid summer internships provided these students with in-depth exposure to the challenges of public health initiatives and expanded their tolerance and empathy towards homeless individuals.

I worked to develop a Community Advisory Panel, inviting local non-profit community organizations in our neighborhood to the panel, including representatives of the Chinatown Development Corporation, Philadelphia Corporation for Aging, Philadelphia Health Management Corporation, Philadelphia Public Health and Education Departments, Diagnostic and Rehabilitation Center (DRC) – a mental health focused project, Project HOME, the Salvation Army, and the United Way of Southeastern Pennsylvania. They all wrote letters of support for our application to the Health of the Public Challenge, which was funded in 1995.

At the same time that I was actively directing this demanding project, my husband Frank, in his capacity as Associate Director of the United Way of Philadelphia, was working closely with the Salvation Army and with Sister Mary Scullian, Director of Project HOME, in the development of continuity facilities for transitional housing and job training for the homeless. Although we were not working specifically together, our communication was more mutually supportive since I was not traveling at this time.

We all, including students from the College of Nursing and the School of Allied Health, watched closely and found ways to participate as the Salvation Army Gateway Service Center for the Homeless was eventually opened successfully with greatly expanded opportunities for service. Soon, students, residents and volunteer attending physicians began to operate the JeffHOPE clinic at Gateway as well as at St. Columba's in West Philadelphia.

At the clinic a third- or fourth-year student teamed with a first- or second-year student to obtain a health history and conduct a physical exam and address the patient's chief complaint. They presented to the physician and together formulated a treatment plan. "*In addition to treatment, we educated shelter residents about how to use the health care system, how to find a primary care provider, and how to take more responsibility for their own health,*" said Lara Carson '95, a family medicine resident and founding member of JeffHOPE. Recognizing that clients have psycho-socio-cultural dimensions to their needs, students counseled them on drug and alcohol addiction (since many were chemically dependent),on housing, sexuality (for HIV/AIDS prevention), and potential educational and vocational programs. Guided by a social worker from the Department of Family Medicine, student teams worked with local agencies to coordinate much-needed services for the shelter residents, sometimes supported with Federal Work Study funds. For example, Salvation Army counselors collaborated with the students to develop training and job placement for recovering clients at the shelter. It wasn't long before the Philadelphia Culinary Institute started a special training program for employment in the food services network at the shelter, and Project HOME found transitional housing and maintained counseling services initiated at Gateway.

While it was tremendously satisfying for me to see this program successfully established and serve as a model for what is possible when students and professionals work together aggressively for the benefit of the community, my position at TJU continued to evolve. I became excited with a new curriculum challenge, **the Pennsylvania Generalist Physician Initiative**, its goal to substantially increase the number of generalist graduates of TJU by the year 2000.

Appointed coordinator of this program's Primary Care Curriculum Project, together with Dr. Gottlieb, the associate dean for academic affairs, I directed the activities of an interdisciplinary primary care task force in the development and evaluation of an enriched primary-care education at Jefferson.

Following the initial $150,000 planning grant we received from the Commonwealth of Pennsylvania, we were successful in obtaining a $1.5 million three-year continuation grant to implement the plans for generalist education. This allowed the diverse activities around Jefferson to find central coordination. Curricular planning became intense for the Initiative largely based on the findings of the various primary career outcomes research projects previously carried out.

As the *Director of the Pennsylvania Generalist Physician Project,* I was an active participant in the first-year medical student course, *The Life Cycle,* later entitled, *The Doctor in Health and Illness: Concepts and Practice of Comprehensive Medicine.* I was responsible for coordinating assignments of 225 first-year medical students to community physician offices, hospital units and clinics, as well as follow-up to community sites for clients with special problems: homeless shelters, mental health facilities, and an AIDS hospice.

Medical and Nursing Students Study Together

To prepare students for their initial experiences seeing patients at physician offices, clinics and in the hospital, I arranged with the School of Nursing to assist with a collaborative learning opportunity. The medical students spent several hours learning some of the basic skills they would need together with nursing students. The students rotated to "skills stations" in the Nursing School's learning laboratory dealing with "Universal Precautions" (ways to prevent the spread of infection in the hospital, such as hand washing, use of transfer forces, opening sterile packages, donning mask and gowns) and measuring Vital Signs: blood pressure, temperature, pulse and respiration. After watching videotapes and demonstrations by the nurses, students paired off to try out their newly gained techniques on one another. The surgical care program nurse coordinator and I developed a student study guide with the help of the physician infection control officer.

Before this lab experience we brought the students together in the classroom to talk about their respective program objectives and describe their career goals and interests. The subject of **Advanced Practice Nurse Practitioners** with expanded skills was shared. However, we had no idea how the students would react to the learning experience together. We decided to initiate a study of attitudes towards each other, by first reviewing the current literature on interprofessional learning for doctors and nurses. Of course, this was the subject of my doctoral studies and dissertation almost twenty years before. Dr. Hojat had been interested in exploring this topic with another colleague ten years earlier and they had created a survey questionnaire, however they were never given permission by administration to implement the survey. This time, Hojat and I decided to invite one of the nursing school faculty to help us update the literature and revise the questionnaire for assessing attitudes of both medical and nursing students. (I have to confess we never applied to the IRB (Institutional Review Board) for permission to administer the questionnaire for research purposes. Obviously with hundreds of studies done under the auspices of the Center for Research in Medical Education no risk to the students were determined generally.) We distributed the revised questionnaire to our large group of first-year medical students and the senior student nurse group together. The Attitude Survey was then distributed to the second-year medical and first year nursing students. Dr. Hojat analyzed the Data and together we wrote the first paper. The results of the comparison study were presented by Dr. Hojat at the AAMC Annual Meeting in Washington, and published in the journal *Academic Medicine.* I then presented the study results at the Isabel Maitland Stewart Research Conference at my Alma Mater, Teachers

College, Columbia University, in 2001. The paper was later published in the Journal *Evaluation and the Health Professions* in 2004.

One of the remarkable features of this work was that it was of interest to physicians and medical educators around the world. As a result of publication of the Attitudes study, our survey instrument has been translated into more than forty languages. Our studies in Philadelphia were subsequently conducted in Mexico, Italy, and Israel, and published in international journals.

I was also responsible for introducing a longitudinal maternity experience for first-year medical students that we entitled **Jeff MOMS (Maternity Opportunities for Medical Students) in** 1994 to meet the Pennsylvania Generalist Physician Initiative's goals for early patient contact and longitudinal experiences. Coordinated with the Life Cycle course, freshman students learned the role of a physician through a continuing experience with a pregnant woman in the OB/GYN clinic with the guidance and support of a certified Woman's Health Nurse Practitioner (NP) who worked in the clinic. I recruited this experienced NP and educator to assist me with development of a study guide for the students.

The role of the nurse practitioner was a topic of much discussion at Jefferson and considered important during curricular planning under the Generalist Initiative. In response to concerns related to the cost of health care in the United States, and to the inadequate access to care for those currently underserved, most health care reform proposals recommended that Advanced Practice Nurses serve a major role in primary care, focusing on health promotion, illness prevention, and management of common health problems. Even without government-introduced changes, nurse practitioners were being recruited to community-based health centers and managed care settings. The controversy of "independent versus collaborative practice" was a heated one then and continues seriously to this day. The Department of Nursing in the College of Allied Health Sciences at TJU, in conjunction with faculty of Jefferson Medical College, had just received state approval to implement a family nurse practitioner program focusing on a collaborative practice model in 1993. The Primary Care Task Force of the Pennsylvania State Generalist Initiative at TJU sponsored a dinner conference on the controversial theme in 1994 and invited several significant consultants as speakers for a panel, "*Nurses and Physicians: Collaboration or Competition*?"

The panelists were in agreement that collaborative practice was a mechanism to improve patient outcomes and a way to enhance the strength of each profession. However, the need for more research to evaluate outcomes for patients managed by nurse practitioners, independently or in collaboration with physicians, was made clear. In addition, the need to increase understanding among physicians of how nurse practitioners were trained and evaluated was also emphasized.

August 3, 1998
Dear Sylvia:

Writing this letter brings back wonderful memories of all the fun you and I have had in recent years writing these proposals. I cannot express in words my appreciation for all of the help you have given me, and more importantly, all that you taught me.

I can say unequivocally that were it not for you, we would never have completed the proposal for the $500,000 medical schools and primary care study, which has thus far yielded 12 publications. "They" said we were wasting our time, but you refused to listen. That award provided the momentum that led to the $400,000 managed care study, and certainly was a critical factor in our recognition as a national Center for Medical Education Research. The next step will be the UIME-21 Evaluation we have just submitted!

Sylvia, once again I can never thank you enough for all of your help and support with this proposal, I am looking forward to the next one.

Warmest regards,
Jon Veloski (with permission)

I am very proud of my accomplishments at Jefferson and what is even more important is that since my retirement I have maintained a close (tele-commuting) relationship with Dr. Hojat and Jon Veloski. I have participated on several significant studies through these years, especially on "empathy" in health care professionals, with the most recent publication occurring in 2011.

In June 1997, for the personal reasons described in chapter 14, it became necessary for me to leave Jefferson. Drs. Gonnella and Gottlieb invited the entire professional staff of the Dean's Office and the CRMEHC, as well as faculty of the first-year medical school course and partners at JeffCARES, to honor me on my official retirement from Jefferson Medical College and the University. A wonderful dinner was given for me in my favorite Philadelphia restaurant, "La Buca." My family came from New York to experience my "roasting" and see me open the gift: The Jefferson Bowl engraved:

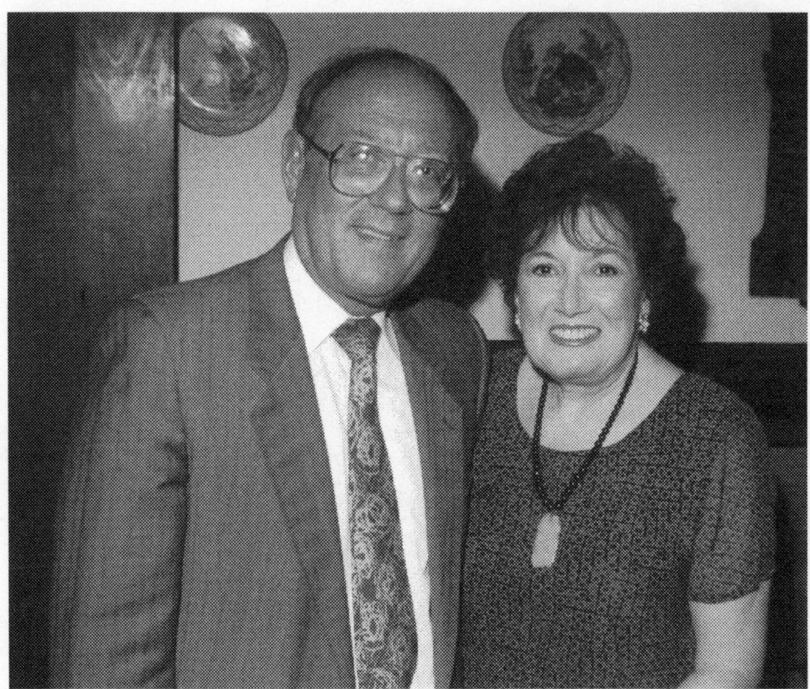

In1997, I took early retirement with Frank and a dinner was given in my honor by the Jefferson Medical College Deans **Joseph Gonnella** and **Jonathan Gottlieb**, at my favorite Philadelphia restaurant, La Buca. I also received a gift from the Deans of "T**he Jefferson Bow**l"**(13-008**) with the base inscribed:

In recognition of your enthusiasm and achievements in helping to transform our medical students into clinicians. 1991–1997

Health of the Public

An Academic Challenge

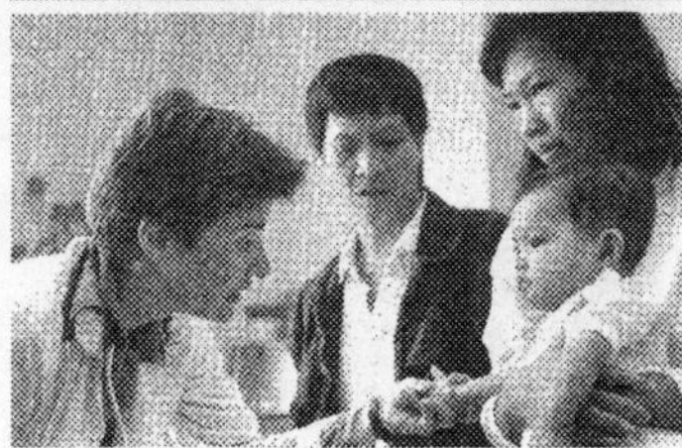

Supported by
The Pew Charitable Trusts
and
The Robert Wood Johnson Foundation
in collaboration with
The Rockefeller Foundation

JeffCARES
Community Action, Research, Education, and Service

"Americans expect hospitals and doctors to extend themselves as far as time and resources reasonably permit to address health needs in their communities. More should be done in carrying out preventive care, and in attempting to keep people free of serious disease.... Jefferson strives, as a private institution, to advance these societal objectives. As much as others may expect that commitment of us, even more so we expect it of ourselves."

Paul C. Brucker, MD
President, Thomas Jefferson University
Acting on Society's Needs
Thomas Jefferson University
Annual Report 1992

I was appointed **Coordinator of Community Health Programs** at JMC including the *Bridging the Gaps Summer Internship*, and *JeffCARES* Homeless projects all part of *The Health of the Public* collaborative programs with the other major institutions for Health Professional Education in Philadelphia. Brochures explain objectives, methods and multiple sources of funding through extensive grant writing.

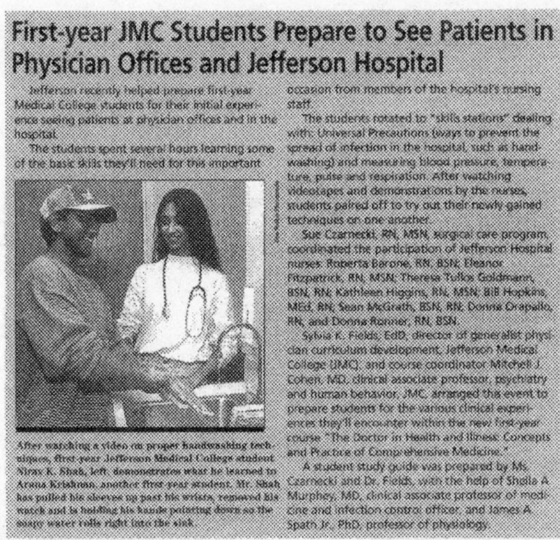

First-year JMC Students Prepare to See Patients in Physician Offices and Jefferson Hospital

Jefferson recently helped prepare first-year Medical College students for their initial experience seeing patients at physician offices and in the hospital.

The students spent several hours learning some of the basic skills they'll need for this important occasion from members of the hospital's nursing staff.

The students rotated to "skills stations" dealing with: Universal Precautions (ways to prevent the spread of infection in the hospital, such as hand-washing) and measuring blood pressure, temperature, pulse and respiration. After watching videotapes and demonstrations by the nurses, students paired off to try out their newly gained techniques on one another.

Sue Czarnecki, RN, MSN, surgical care program, coordinated the participation of Jefferson Hospital nurses: Roberta Barone, RN, BSN; Eleanor Fitzpatrick, RN, MSN; Therese Tulkos Goldmann, BSN, RN; Kathleen Higgins, RN, MSN; Bill Hopkins, MEd, RN; Sean McGrath, BSN, RN; Donna Orapallo, RN, and Donna Ronner, RN, BSN.

Sylvia K. Fields, EdD, director of generalist physician curriculum development, Jefferson Medical College (JMC), and course coordinator Mitchell J. Cohen, MD, clinical associate professor, psychiatry and human behavior, JMC, arranged the event to prepare students for the various clinical experiences they'll encounter within the new first-year course "The Doctor in Health and Illness: Concepts and Practice of Comprehensive Medicine."

A student study guide was prepared by Ms. Czarnecki and Dr. Fields, with the help of Sheila A. Murphey, MD, clinical associate professor of medicine and infection control officer, and James A. Spath Jr., PhD, professor of physiology.

After watching a video on proper handwashing techniques, first-year Jefferson Medical College student Nirav K. Shah, left, demonstrates what he learned to Aruna Krishnan, another first-year student. Mr. Shah has pulled his sleeves up past his wrists, removed his watch and is holding his hands pointing down so the soapy water rolls right into the sink.

Medical and nursing Students learn together as part of the **Pennsylvania Generalist Initiative** that I directed with Dr. Jonathan Gottlieb, JMC Associate Dean. It also included *JEFFMOM*S, a program where first-year medical students had a continuing care experience with pregnant women in the prenatal clinic and participated during the birth process, all under the supervision of graduate-level Nurse Practitioners.

This project gave impetus for studying medical and nursing student attitudes toward collaboration, as well as attitudes of practicing nurses and physicians. Dr. Mohammedreza Hojat and I created and validated the adapted **Jefferson Scale of Physicians and Nurses Attitudes toward Collaboration,** eventually used all over the world. Currently the issue is being studied among the nurses and physicians here in Savannah at Memorial Health/Mercer Medical School. (**(00-9) Dr. Hojat**)

My 60th birthday in 1994 was a wonderful weekend celebration in January for friends and family at the Ritz Carlton Hotel on Chestnut Street in Philadelphia**.** Here are images of **Frank and I**,(**A**); **my children and I**(**B**); **my brother-in-law Robert and sister-in-law Rozzie(C); my brother and his wife Marci and his children**: Eric (Amelia), Pamela, Carolyn, and Stephanie with her son Alex.(**D)** my dearest A**unt Sonia who supported and encouraged me all my life, and I. (**E),

I am seen here with my Jefferson colleague and friend **Jon Veloski with his wife Judy, a nurse who celebrated with me and my family.**

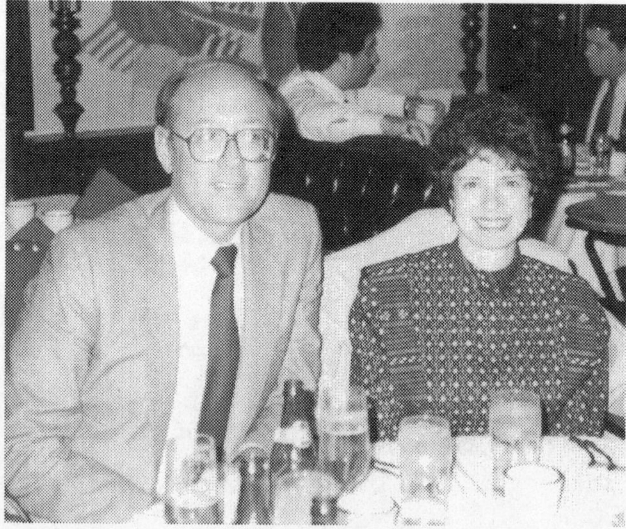

My editorial assistant at F.A.Davis Linda Weinerman Franklin is shown here at a previous dinner given by Dr. Gonnella. Unfortunately I could not locate a reproducible image with Linda and I together. She moved to Portland Oregon. Linda assisted me with the development of this Memoir for several years.

14

Family Joys and Sorrows: Moving South Again

"YOU HAVE BEEN A PROBLEM SOLVER ALL YOUR LIFE; YOU WILL FIGURE IT OUT"

ROBERT FAY, PHD

UNANTICIPATED RETIREMENT

On Sunday mornings, for exercise Frank and I would walk as far as the Benjamin Franklin Parkway to the Philadelphia Museum of Art and down Kelly Drive past Boathouse Row along the Schuylkill River. We would stop on the way back to pick up some fresh bagels and the Sunday *New York Times* to read with breakfast at home. Frank soon introduced me to a drive along our route, turning onto the highway and exiting near Schoolhouse Lane, where he formerly lived. There was an entrance there to Fairmount Park and a trail along a creek off the Schuylkill River. It was a crowded two-mile walk, shared with other walkers and some riding on bicycles or horseback. At the end was the charming historic Valley Green Inn where Washington slept one night; occasionally we would have brunch. We loved the opportunity to relax on a bench in front of the inn and watch the children feed the ducks in the creek. Writing about those days reminds me of how I really fell in love with Frank.

Once we moved further downtown, Frank started to play golf on Saturdays at a public course in New Jersey with our next-door neighbor Bob and his friends. Frank had told me several times when we were dating that golf was not very important to him anymore, but I was not so sure that was true then and I soon learned otherwise. I knew he had played all his life and was very good golfer, winning trophies he obviously valued. Sometimes he used to play together with his sister Ellen, dressed in matching outfits their mother had made for them. Unfortunately since leaving his position at the United Way of America, he could not afford a country club membership any longer. In those days it was a benefit often given to the most senior United Way executives in major cities to encourage their relationship with corporate sponsors, but Frank's position in Philadelphia at the time did not include such benefits. I did not realize how much he had missed the game until it became clear that playing golf again gave him something very positive in his life. I was certainly not a golfer. I had never had the time, money or inclination, although I did select golf during my freshman year of college to meet the physical education requirement. I think that was just part of my fantasy life; the Adelphi College campus was right next to the Garden City Country Club. Country club life was not in my family's history, and I held no such dream at that time.

Then suddenly a major personnel change was announced at the United Way offices. The Executive Director, Frank's close friend who had brought him to Philadelphia, was recruited to the Executive position in Los Angeles, where he had children and grandchildren. It was around the time of serious racial riots referred to as the "Rodney King riots." Four Los Angeles police officers were acquitted of charges in the savage beating of Rodney King in 1991 that was caught on videotape by a local resident. The riots lasted six days with significant looting and damage to private and public properties. Thousands of Los Angelenos took to the streets in violent display of protest. More than fifty people were killed and over 2,000 injured. Evidently major changes in community relationships and social programs were called for by the large black community and I believe the United Way president in Los Angeles, who had been in the position for many years, had chosen or been urged to retire.

As Associate Director for Community Programs in Philadelphia, and with previous experience in the city years before, Frank would be, I assumed, next in line for the Executive Director position. Frank submitted his application, but unfortunately John, the Associate Director for Development, the major fundraising leader, also applied for the position. A national search was now required, and a third candidate entered the competition. This individual had been very successful in raising corporate funds in a smaller city in upstate New York. Obviously in business affairs, raising the finances necessary takes precedence over spending the money for programs. While the Board and the community organizations administrators respected Frank for the way he collaborated with all factions, they gave the leadership position to the top fundraiser. I was terribly disappointed for Frank; he deserved the position but Frank did not express negative feelings. (Perhaps he was reminded of his own difficult experience as Executive Director during the school integration battles in Louisville, Kentucky, which was where his son was killed and his wife separated from him.) He might have even been relieved.

Once I met the new appointee, and learned he and his wife were going to move to the affluent Main Line suburbs instead of staying closer to the city lines, I sensed they were not expecting to be involved with the community who needed services. Frank was also uneasy when he realized he would be participating in all the evening events that called for leadership involvement, alone. The problems of Philadelphia, then the fifth largest city in the nation, with a large low-income and high-unemployment population, were very different from those of the new Director's former up-state city. Frank was not invited to consult about the differences. Within the year Frank admitted he was unhappy with the relationship; he recognized he was being pushed out. I tried to encourage him to look for another Director position in a smaller city outside Philadelphia, but his reaction was, "I've worked 40 years; I've had enough!" Those words became his mantra. He made it clear that he wanted to retire early and leave Philadelphia to fulfill his dream of living on a golf course and playing golf full-time. I did not want to hear about it.

Sure enough Frank came home one day and told me he had been called into the Director's office and given an offer to take early retirement. It was not a good offer, but Frank was ready to accept. He was not thinking about the financial impact for us or about my personal interests – he just wanted out. I encouraged him to consult with an attorney, which he did reluctantly. Eventually a three-year consulting contract was offered with reduced responsibilities and some benefits for him, but no health insurance benefit for Frank's first wife. I thought the compensation offered during the three years was insufficient, but Frank accepted anyway. He was satisfied. "I am tired and will have more time during the week to play golf," he said, but I was worried. I knew he had not accumulated enough funds for retirement other than his pension. With his obligations to pay alimony and health insurance to his ex-wife for life, it would be very difficult for us to give up my salary and live on our pensions; we did not have enough savings. But Frank was adamant about moving south at the end of the three-year consulting contract. I was definitely not ready to retire in three years, not emotionally or physically. I loved my ever-expanding role at Jefferson where I was completely immersed in the medical school curriculum and community activities. Meanwhile I had not been there long enough to accumulate significant pension benefits, and I was too young to receive Social Security income or Medicare. But Frank insisted on leaving early; I would have just three years to establish limited security for retirement.

Melissa, Alix and husband Ami Steinfeld (Move to 14-004)

Elizabeth and fiancé Mark before marriage.

Elizabeth and Mark and the whole family at wedding of Frank's daughter.

Andrew, Susan and Courtney, (granddaughter #2 at wedding of Frank's daughter).

Family Joy and Tragedy

The months went by quickly as our combined family expanded. When Frank's youngest daughter announced she was in a serious relationship with a young man and wanted to marry, we were happy for her. There was a lot of planning and unanticipated expenses, first for an engagement party, where we had a chance to meet the groom's family and then for the wedding. Mary had a good job in sales and thought our help would not be needed, but it never works that way; we would still have unanticipated expenses. She was in her late twenties and had colleagues at work and many childhood friends that wanted to see her marry. Weddings for Frank's other daughters were under some difficult circumstances so they had been small, but Mary wanted a "big elegant wedding." Since her fiancé was now out of the Marines and working for Marriott Corporation, they hoped to arrange a beautiful affair at a Marriott Hotel in Virginia about six months later. Two of my children were already married and I had two granddaughters, Alix and Courtney. I was glad that they would all be able to attend this wedding but I would have to cover the expenses.

About a month before the wedding, my Elizabeth (Liz) called me to tell me she was dating a "wonderful guy" and she was sure we would all like him. She wanted to bring him to Mary's wedding, and I was thrilled for her. At twenty seven, this was the first serious relationship for Elizabeth and she was right, Mark was a very bright sweet young man and handsome too. They both worked in banking, although with different large banks in New Orleans, Louisiana, and seemed to have many other interests in common. The night before the wedding ceremony, at the rehearsal dinner I noticed Mark was uncomfortable; he asked to leave the party early. When I asked Liz why, she explained that Mark had strained his back playing tennis several months ago and was taking muscle relaxant pills for the pain he was still having. The next day when I noticed his discomfort again he told me he had been hurting for more than three months, and just could not seem to get enough relief from the pain medication he had been given.

"Mark, that's a pretty long time after a tennis injury with no specific diagnosis, did you see an orthopedist?" I asked. When he answered, "no," I continued. "Have you been back to your primary care doctor?" He answered in the negative again, so I advised him to make an appointment with his primary care doctor as soon as possible when they returned home.

The wedding was everything Mary wanted; it was really lovely, everyone enjoyed the music and dancing and a great time was had by all, except Mark and Elizabeth. Mary even requested a Jewish hora, like she had seen at the Jewish wedding of Frank and I and at one of her friends. (This was the fourth wedding for Frank's children I had shared with his former wife. I was always cordial and friendly to her and her family, but Frank barely spoke to them at all, he was so bitter about her requested annulment and the constant demands she made of him for additional financial support. It never seemed to end.)

A few weeks later Elizabeth called me, crying hysterically. She and Mark were planning to get engaged, and were looking for a ring with thoughts of marriage a year later. But Mark had just returned to his physician as I had recommended. Blood work showed an anemia, which was unusual for a thirty-one-year-old male who had always been healthy. Then a chest x-ray followed and the results were devastating. Although not a smoker, Mark had an inoperable late stage lesion in his lung that had apparently metastasized. Mark had been briskly told, "There is nothing we can do for you. Go home, quit your job and travel as long as you feel you can."

"But what about drugs – chemotherapy?" Elizabeth had asked.

"There are no drugs for this type and stage of cancer – we just don't have chemotherapy that can make a difference," the doctor said.

"How long do I have?" Mark asked.

The doctor answered, "We really can't forecast with certainty, but probably nine months, maybe a year, maybe even fifteen months."

Elizabeth cried on the phone, "Mom, help me, what can we do? How can we get another opinion?"

I found myself crying with her, "Oh my God, I can't believe this is happening. Let me think. I will contact my friend Dr. Barbara Barzansky at the AMA, and ask her if she knows an oncologist in New Orleans." Barbara and I worked together on several Jefferson projects; I asked if she knew of anyone affiliated with Tulane or Louisiana State University School of Medicine she could recommend. Barbara told me she knew there was a new pulmonary oncologist from Sloan Kettering Cancer Center in New York City who had recently gone to the Oschner Clinic. She called his office immediately for me and the nurse called Elizabeth back personally, saying the oncologist would see Mark the next day if he was available, and to be certain to bring all the records possible. I was so grateful to Barbara; it gave Elizabeth and Mark some hope. After Mark obtained his records, he and Elizabeth went to Oschner Clinic the next day for the appointment.

The oncologist looked through all the records and offered to enter Mark into the lung cancer research study involving investigation of a new French drug, although theoretically the stage of Mark's disease was really past eligibility. I think the physician wanted to give Mark some hope. Unfortunately, Mark's health insurance company refused to pay for his treatment with the experimental trial drug. We did not give up. Oschner Clinic was self-insured and Elizabeth happened to have Oschner health insurance through her position at the First National Bank, which was next door to the clinic. The insurance representative there told Elizabeth that if she and Mark were married, she could put him on her insurance plan, but it would take thirty days to become effective. After the first thirty days of treatment the research grant would pay all the expenses. Unfortunately the cost for the first month of treatment would be $30,000.

Mark and Elizabeth decided to marry immediately and when an uncle of one of Elizabeth's friends, who was a judge, offered to marry them that weekend; they immediately accepted. I called my favorite New Orleans restaurant, Commander's Palace, to see if we could get a private room for a small reception on Saturday afternoon. It was Labor Day weekend, a traditional brunch was scheduled, and there were no private rooms available but a corner section of the dining room was reserved for our party of just the immediate family and a few very close friends. The Palace jazz musicians helped make the event special. Weddings are supposed to be happy and fun. This wedding was the saddest any of us had ever experienced.

Mark's family was devastated; his parents were in shock, they could not believe this was really happening. Neither could anyone else, Mark's mother, a devout Catholic, believed her prayers would intervene and save her boy's life. She told me that among her three sons, Mark was the jewel, an obedient child, serious about his school work, hard-working and ambitious. Our entire family had been so happy that Elizabeth had finally found love. Since it was a three-day holiday, I had also called the Royal Orleans hotel in New Orleans, explained the situation, and asked about a bridal suite for two nights; one just happened to be available.

On the Tuesday morning after the brief honeymoon, Mark started the chemotherapy treatment and I went to my old banker friend to ask for a loan to pay for the first month of treatment. At the same time Elizabeth went to the Oschner business office to see what special long-term arrangements could be made for the necessary charges. Mark went to his supervisor at his bank to ask for help. Three weeks went by without word from anyone so Elizabeth went back to the business office; she needed a copy of the month's charges. To her amazement the copy of the statement was clearly marked by a big stamp declaring "PAID." An anonymous donor had made the payment for Mark's treatment for the month. No one seemed to know who might have been the hero. There was a lot of postulating, but we never found out who had paid that bill.

After the first ten-week protocol of chemotherapy was over, Mark seemed to be doing very well, and he told Elizabeth that he felt better and wished they could get away for the Thanksgiving holiday. He mentioned the thought of playing golf with Frank. At that time my brother was living in Myrtle Beach, South Carolina, a destination with more golf courses than any other city in the country. I called my brother to discuss the possibility of our staying someplace near them for the holiday so Mark could have the opportunity to play golf with Frank. Norman invited us to come to Myrtle Beach and told us of a very nice furnished house one of their friends had available nearby.

We rented the house for Thanksgiving weekend and I made all the plane arrangements to Myrtle Beach. My sister-in-law made a wonderful turkey dinner and Frank took Mark to play golf for two days at the best clubs in the area. When Frank noticed how tired Mark became after six holes he urged him to skip the next hole and every other one after that. When they came back for dinner Mark was exhausted but very happy. Greens fees were about $100 for eighteen holes the first day; Frank said it was worth every dollar spent to see Mark so happy.

Back in New Orleans, everything seemed to be going well through the second round of chemotherapy and we were all optimistic. Then about six months after the protocol had begun Mark woke up one morning with his right eye all red and bulging. An immediate trip back to the Oschner oncology unit revealed the worst; cancer had spread to

Mark's brain. It was not a good omen; more chemo was in order. The additional chemotherapy seemed to sap all of Mark's energy.

After the wedding, Liz and Mark had moved into her apartment. It was on the second floor of a two-story building with a view of the water. Elizabeth had decorated it with charm and they were happy together. But Mark was getting increasingly fatigued as he managed to continue his work at the bank, leaving at noon to travel to the clinic for the chemo infusion and then returning to his job. Walking upstairs to the apartment was becoming painful. When Liz mentioned this to Andrew and Susan, they suggested Liz and Mark move into their two-story house in Destrehan, a close New Orleans suburb, with them. So, Mark and Liz gratefully accepted the invitation and moved into the master bedroom on the first floor, while Andrew and Susan moved upstairs to the extra bedroom next to Courtney's bedroom; she was now almost three. It was a very generous offer, especially since Elizabeth really needed the emotional support of her family as Mark continued to work, and take additional chemotherapy for a few months.

Unfortunately Mark became weaker and weaker and soon found it difficult to get up and leave the bed. He asked for and received sick leave. Liz continued to work as much as she could, but still managed to drive Mark for treatments. He stayed home alone with no more interest or energy except to be driven to the clinic for his treatments and then go home to watch TV or sleep. He seemed to have no appetite and was losing weight. It was close to the end of the year since the original prognosis had been made. I thought it was not good for Mark to be home all day alone, and advised Liz to look for someone to stay with Mark as a companion and prepare some food he might tolerate, but Liz said Mark refused to have any one. There was no hospice care available at that time in New Orleans, and Mark was still hopeful of remission.

Frank heard about the discussion and since his consulting position was flexible, he offered to go to New Orleans for a week and help with Mark. Although he was hoping for more chemotherapy, Mark was happy to hear Frank wanted to come and accepted Frank's offer. However, when Mark asked for heavier chemo, his oncologist said, "Mark, I'm afraid it is too dangerous, it will only kill you."

Elizabeth needed help. When Frank arrived she told him she was advised by the doctor to think about planning for the inevitable, that there was little hope Mark would last much longer. There was nothing else to do. "Call me if anything changes, but I don't think you should call 911 or take him to the hospital; for his sake, don't put him through more invasive procedures, try to keep him at home," the physician had said.

Elizabeth asked Frank to go with her to make funeral arrangements "Of course," Frank responded. During the week that Frank stayed, Mark seemed to be more alert, he ate some of Frank's preparations, they watched golf on TV, and went shopping for some new pajamas Elizabeth said Mark needed. Unfortunately, during the shopping trip Mark had become incontinent. He was devastated, but Frank took him to the men's room and helped Mark clean up as best he could.

After the week, Frank came home and I flew to New Orleans to help for the weekend. Liz took Mark to the clinic on Friday morning for a treatment while I stayed in the house and cooked a large pot of chicken soup and made a noodle pudding that is like bread pudding, which Liz told me Mark liked. When they came home Mark was exhausted, but he barely managed to eat a few spoonfuls of soup. "I'm too tired now, I'm going to lie down," Mark said and went into the bedroom.

Little Courtney followed him, "Mark, are you OK? Mark, are you OK?" Courtney asked and gave him a hug. She had fallen in love with Mark during the six months he and Liz lived with her family. Mark slept all evening and through the next day. Liz tried to get him up but he just refused.

On Sunday morning his brothers John and Matthew came and woke Mark up. Liz managed to get him to take some juice. I asked John to help Mark brush his teeth, and Matthew shaved Mark, while I gathered some clean linens. Then John helped me partially bathe Mark in bed and Liz helped me change the sheets. Mark was sitting up in bed looking pretty good when his parents arrived. They sat talking with him while I cleaned up the kitchen after lunch.

Suddenly, I heard Mark's father call me, "Sylvia, come right away. Mark said he was exhausted and wanted to sleep a little, but his eyes are closed; I don't think he's breathing!"

He was right. I could not feel a pulse or sense a breath; I knew he was going or gone. John turned him on this back and started pounding on his chest, "Call 911, call 911!" he cried.

"No John, he is at peace now, let him go," I said. Earlier that morning Liz had called the oncologist when she sensed Mark was close to the end. She had asked if he should bring Mark to the hospital.

"Liz," the doctor said, "keep Mark home, he is really better off at home. Why put him through resuscitation now? There is nothing else we can do for him, Liz, believe me I would be there pounding if I knew it could make him better."

I stopped John. I said softly, and then more firmly, "No, I will not call, Mark signed a DNR [Do Not Resuscitate] agreement, he does not want any special efforts if there is no hope for him. John, stop, let him go now, there is nothing more anyone can do for him."

Liz was in shock.

"Liz, come, just hold him and kiss him goodbye. He is at peace now." Liz held Mark. Mark's parents held him too. Everyone he loved was there. Susan had caught Courtney and taken her out of the house because we knew calling 911 was required even with a DNR. We did not want Courtney to be frightened by the noise of the fire engine and ambulance that would screech down the street.

Frank helped Elizabeth finalize the arrangements for the funeral mass, selecting pieces of religious literature they both thought represented the significance of this tragic premature death. Frank spoke that morning as though he was losing another son. We were all so grateful for his support. Over 400 people came to the wake and signed the Farewell book.

When Courtney, who is now twenty five, asked me recently how my book was coming along, I mentioned that I was writing about the sad loss of Mark. She told me she remembered Mark. Could it have been possible? She was only three years old. Later Courtney told her mother she remembered Mark watching her television shows with her.

We all remember Mark; how could we not remember this tragedy? It took months and months for Elizabeth to recover, maybe a year or more; she was a widow at twenty eight who barely had a chance to know her husband and to show him how much she loved him. (And to this day, as I write about Mark I find myself crying for Elizabeth's pain.)

About two years later one of Mark's friends introduced her to his friend Jeffrey, who happened to be a lot of fun, handsome, and Jewish too. The relationship clicked. Liz had her own beautiful dream wedding with all her friends attending. Jeff and Liz have been married now almost twenty years and given me the joys of my first grandson, Sam, now seventeen and about 6 feet tall, and my little princess, the star Rachel, granddaughter number three, who sang in the professional show *Annie* several years ago; she was the smallest orphan with the voice of a diva.

After Mark's death Frank and I returned to Philadelphia, he to his consultant role with the United Way, and I back to my meaningful educational activities at Jefferson. Frank was even more determined now to move south as soon as his contract was over.

Moving South Again

"Frank, if you insist on going south, it would be smart for us to move to my Condominium in Atlanta, on Chamblee-Dunwoody Road, just inside the Perimeter. The maintenance and mortgage payment is only $500 a month," I reminded him. The condo had three bedrooms, two and a half baths, and a large family room downstairs overlooking a lovely peaceful garden surrounding a creek. There was a small extra bedroom and full bath downstairs that Liz had lived in during high school. There was a dining room and living room with fireplace on the main level with sliding doors out to a deck overlooking the creek. The master bedroom and bath and second bedroom upstairs were perfect and the eat-in kitchen was ideal for the two of us, but unfortunately there was no golf course, just tennis that neither of us played.

Several months later we made a trip to Atlanta so Frank could see the condominium; it had been rented by a woman with two teenage children who had been considering buying it. Unfortunately she changed her mind, but it did not seem to make a difference, Frank was not interested. He said over and over again. "I want to live in a golf course community."

"Couldn't we just join a country club?" I asked.

"It is too crowded, the traffic is terrible, and I don't want to live in Atlanta." He kept up his mantra. "I want to live in a Golf Course Community! We returned to Philadelphia.

Reluctantly, I went along during holiday weekends and vacations over the next few years as we looked at golfing communities. We looked at one club after another in North Carolina, starting in Pinehurst, supposedly a golfer's paradise. I kept my negative thoughts to myself at first, but then I thought, "What would I do in Pinehurst?" It was not near anything other than golf. And it was cold, there was nothing I could find of interest. Chapel Hill, with its highly regarded state university seemed like a possible spot to me, but Frank's son had completed his degree in ornamental horticulture at Virginia Tech and had begun to work for Tom Fazio, one of the leading golf course architects in the world. Frank announced he wanted to live on a "Fazio" course. He did not like the old Fazio course in Chapel Hill. I was glad he did not want to live there when I realized they had snow in the winter. I had had enough snow in my life. I left New York fifteen years earlier because of snow and ice. "No mountains and no snow," I said.

Frank found a Fazio course he liked in Wilmington, North Carolina, but it was far out of the city, out in the boondocks, I thought. There was nothing nearby. I wanted to be closer to a university or large medical center. We visited a club in Wilmington that met my criteria and had two courses, one by well-known golfer and golf course architect Jack Nicklaus. Before Tom started working for Tom Fazio that would have been perfect as far as Frank was concerned, but not any longer; Frank wanted a Fazio course. We actually made two trips to Wilmington, because after the first trip when I said "no" to Frank's choice, he tentatively consented to my request, but later on the way back to Philadelphia, he changed his mind. He suggested we visit both golf communities again and I agreed, but after that visit Frank changed his mind again. I simply did not want to leave Philadelphia for the community he preferred in Wilmington. I thought about telling him to go where he wanted to go, and I would decide later if I would join him, but I truly did not want a permanent separation; I loved and respected Frank, but I needed his consideration of my needs too.

In 1994 the real estate market was not good in Philadelphia, or anywhere else. We had no idea how much we might be offered for our Philadelphia house at that time, and I did not want to sell my Atlanta condo until I knew where we would be going. I had only known work and school all my life, and never known the country club life; I had never really played golf, and had just recently started taking tennis lessons before I met Frank. Frank and I continued to argue over the isolation of some of the communities we visited. I made it clear we needed to be near a city with educational and cultural possibilities. I was not about to start commuting again to fulfill my life.

Frank finally wore me out with the suggestion we go further south, so we planned to look in Charleston, Beaufort, and Bluffton, South Carolina, and Savannah, Georgia, where his son was currently active. I knew a little about Charleston, Hilton Head, and Savannah, but not about golf course communities there. Late in December 1994 we started our search again, by first visiting Charleston. Frank did not like the Fazio course there; it was not a private gated community and seemed too commercial. He did not like the course on Kiawah Island, and anyway the homes there were quite expensive. Many were rental houses and there was an impersonal feeling about the place. We went to Hilton Head Island too where there were many golfing communities, one after the next. The roads were terribly crowded, and at most of the developments, including a new one with a Fazio course Frank liked, the homes were very expensive.

We then went on to Savannah and to The Landings on Skidaway Island nearby where Tom had recently completed the Fazio "Deer Creek" course. Driving over the drawbridge and Moon River (made famous by Johnny Mercer) was a lovely introduction to the island, where there was a state park and six golf courses at the private gated community.

When we entered the sales office for the Landings development we saw photos of a wide price range of homes. Some were smaller ones and older condominiums within our price range, but I did not want another condominium; they are often more difficult to sell over time. A few homes we saw the first day in the older section at the 25-year-old community were affordable, but with large dark wooded lots. It was dark so many older homes seemed unappealing; they needed updating. I was hoping to have something in stucco, light, newer, and prettier.

The Landings community was very attractive, with four clubhouses for dining, water everywhere, and forty miles of bicycle, golf cart and walking paths. Frank played golf on his son's Deer Creek course, the newest of the six courses at the development; he hoped we might find a home there. Unfortunately there were no small patio lots or homes available. All we saw were very large homes, many on huge lots; there was nothing we were shown that fit our budget. The Landings just seemed out of our reach.

We left the island and drove south to America's oldest city, St. Augustine, Florida, and stayed overnight; the city was charming. We had an appointment to visit a relatively new development on Route 17 along the Atlantic coastline that had only one golf course; the community itself was just starting, but the course was by Fazio. Yet, we knew immediately the costs were beyond our means. We then spent two days with one of Frank's old friends in their Ormond Beach development. His friends pleaded with us to move there, but I hated the place. We could afford it, but it seemed old and dilapidated to me in comparison to most of the developments we had seen, and anyway the one golf course was designed by some unknown architect; Frank would never have been satisfied. Time was running out and Frank was discouraged; we started back up Route 95 and during the drive made a decision to stop in Savannah again.

The Landings was the best place we had seen through all our golf travels. The Island was beautiful and Savannah had much to offer. There was a university and medical center close by, much Revolutionary and Civil War history, and the historic waterfront and downtown areas were charming. The Savannah College of Art and Design (SCAD) had been doing major restorations of historic warehouses, factories, and other disintegrating buildings into classrooms and dormitories that did not look like most college dorms. Walking the old Savannah waterfront was fun; there were all kinds of restaurants and shops to explore while watching big tankers float by, and the whole downtown was walkable.

The Landings community had more educational programs for men, women, and children golfers of all abilities than any of the other developments we had seen. It had dozens of tennis courts, two large outdoor and one indoor pool (later a second lap pool was added), and a large fitness center with all kinds of equipment and many scheduled training classes for all levels of fitness. It had four lovely dining venues, and two marinas including dry and wet docks for boat storage (not that we were boaters.) There was a charming Village Center with a small food market, a library, drugstore, hair dressing salon, several banks, brokerage offices, and a lovely Hallmark card and gift shop. Skidaway Island was everything we were hoping for. It was the right location, but we did not know if we could find the right home site within our budget.

I wanted to buy a lot, go home, put the house on the market, and return when it was sold to build a small house, but Frank was adamant: he was in love with the place and wasn't leaving. He had found his dream and he did not want to wait. It was cold and I was exhausted, the holiday was over, and we had to return to Philadelphia. I agreed to return to Savannah a month later to spend a few more days looking at small homes or lots to build a house, if we did not find a completed home. But, on the second day we found a strong possibility, a small stucco furnished "dream home" in Oakridge, one of the newer areas. The agent had not shown this house before because he thought we could not afford it, but he never told us that. When he realized we might leave without buying anything, he showed us a few potential building lots. The truth was we really could not afford the house unless I kept working, at least part time. I was tired and wanted to settle the issue now so I agreed to look inside the house. The house was on a corner surrounded by tall pines, moss-covered oak trees, and weeping willows in the back facing a small lagoon overlooking the 13th hole of the Oakridge golf course. There were three bedrooms and two baths on one floor with no stairs and it was decorated with fine English regency furnishings and beautiful floral window treatments the English owners were anxious to sell. The house was charming and seemed new; it had hardly been lived in. We hoped we might be able to buy some of the furniture, which would make it easier for Frank to move in after the closing. (We always knew we did not want to move any of our old Philadelphia home furniture, much of which had been rented originally, except for my small upright piano and the six beautiful English Regency dining room chairs I had found on sale in a wholesale factory store.) I gave in.

We had already agreed that I would continue to work in Philadelphia to complete the Pennsylvania State Initiative contract once our townhome was sold. I also knew I could continue to work long distance for Jefferson on special projects even after a sale. Actually I gave in for another reason. It was superstition! The address was 7 Skimmar Circle. I thought perhaps it was "meant to be." There was that old European superstition I had inherited from my mother. "Sk" were my two initials for Sylvia Kleiman and the "Mar" was for Frank's last name, Marzolf. Frank insisted we make a telephone offer to the owners, who were in England, before we left Savannah.

We had no concept of the actual cost of living and playing golf at The Landings, and no time to research appropriately. However, Frank would not be stopped, as he was determined to go back to Philadelphia with "a home at the Landings" to come back to, a home in a country club with a Fazio golf course. After some negotiating for the furniture, our offer was accepted. Within a few months Frank completed his employment contract and to my amazement, I had an appropriate offer for my Atlanta town house. The final profit enabled us to obtain a $50,000 golf membership in the Landings Club, entitling us to play golf on any or all of the courses. I would then have the incentive to learn to play golf.

Frank moved to the Landings on March 1, 1995. After the move-in, I returned to work in Philadelphia. It took us eighteen months to sell the house on Latimer Street for slightly more than our purchase price nine years before, and less than we had anticipated, all the time paying two monthly mortgages, insurance and taxes, and my commuting expenses, which were not deductible. In retrospect it was a foolish mistake at that time, but for Frank it was the right thing to do. Although I did not want to leave Philadelphia, it was more important to save this second marriage of almost ten years. Frank was "very happy and in paradise," he said. I hoped I would be happy too.

Unfortunately the commuting between Savannah and Philadelphia during the first two years was much harder than I thought it would be, and more expensive. I could not fly back and forth each week; it was too stressful. I left Savannah for Philadelphia early Monday morning on the 6 a.m. flight and then returned on Friday evening to spend weekends in Savannah. I then worked from the Savannah home during the following week and weekend. One of the problems was that there were no direct flights between Philadelphia and Savannah at that time. I usually flew on U.S. Air, but the flights were packed full and I had to change planes in Charlotte, North Carolina. The planes never seemed to leave on time and hardly ever arrived as scheduled; I often missed my connecting flight. It wasn't so terrible on Monday mornings, but my flight out of Charlotte for Savannah on Friday nights was the last for the day. All too often I had to stay overnight in a motel at the airport and several times, because there were large special events in Charlotte and no rooms left at the airport, I actually slept on the floor on rolled out bubble wrap behind the empty check-in counter with about 50 other passengers who missed their connections.

It was easier for me once back in Philadelphia. I was usually in my office by 10 a.m. Monday morning. When I left the house for work I always had to make certain the place was clean, neat and "picked up" because the real estate agent might want to show the house to potential buyers – not that there were many serious prospects during that first year. I was comfortable during the week. After calling Frank to share our daily happenings, I spent most evenings with my friends for home-cooked dinners or together at casual restaurants on Walnut Street or at the nearby Center City neighborhoods such as Chinatown, South Philadelphia, or sometimes suburban Manayunk. I was so busy all day at work, the week went fast.

I moved to Savannah late in July 1997 and made a new life for myself trying to learn to play golf and bridge, taking exercise classes, and making new friends through various group activities. I joined a women's book club that was part of the Landings Newcomers Organization. I read the daily newspaper and my old professional journals looking out over the lagoon behind our home on the golf course. The birds, the trees, the flowers, were everything I could not have imagined I would have in my life when I grew up in Brooklyn so many years ago. It was inevitable; I fell in love with my surroundings and the interesting people from all over the country and even the world who were my neighbors and friends. The Island is breathtakingly beautiful with so much plush greenery, water everywhere, and birds, wonderful birds of all types. (It reminded me of my exciting move from Brooklyn into the Meadowbrook Hospital Nurses Residence for my last two years in the Adelphi nursing program, and my appreciation for the birds surrounding my first house on Long Island.)

This was not just a retirement community. There were people of all ages including young professionals working in Savannah and over 1,000 children. I loved to explore the different areas selecting new routes on the island with its forty miles of paths for walking, cycling, and moving golf carts.

I had also started taking golf lessons privately and with small groups joining other beginners on the "Farm Team." We played nine holes together one day a week as a large group, and then on other days independently. Sharing the one golf cart with Frank was not a problem. Most women played at least two to three times a week, and on Sundays with their husbands. The Landings Country Club is a haven for men and women golfers with the largest number of active eighteen-hole women golfers of any other club in the country. Eighteen holes was too much for me; I only played nine holes, and despite the lessons, I was terrible. None of the women I played with seemed to mind. I appreciated the beauty of being outdoors in such a lovely environment able to understand the language during social events and descriptions of the different holes and strategies of play. But I am not a natural athlete, and not competitive in golf (or in bridge); my mind wanders and I can't concentrate. I think Frank was embarrassed when we were invited to play with other couples on Sundays. I don't know what he expected, but I could never imagine myself playing golf day after day as he and many others did. I had too many other things I wanted out of my life. In any event I was proud of what I was able to do, and I think my children were proud of my attempt to participate. I made it very clear, I was happy.

Frank had made many friends on the golf courses and I was starting to meet people through them. There were many clubs and non-profit organizations of possible interest to me. They were all looking for volunteers, but I was not ready; not until I stopped commuting would I be able to devote the time. We were invited to all kinds of cocktail parties and dinners, not just on weekends. I was learning that country club social life could be very busy as we often joined our new friends at music and theatre events downtown, including performances of the Savannah Symphony in the Civic Center. I thought I was back in Philadelphia at the Academy of Music, at half the price.

Elizabeth and Jeffrey Laufer meet and marry three years later. Here is my immediate family at the wedding, Granddaughter #1 Alix Sara is the junior bridesmaid and #2 Courtney Danielle, is the flower girl.

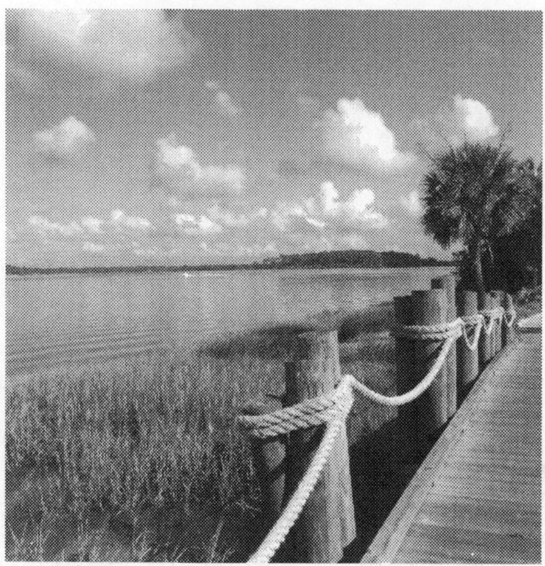

Frank and I explored potential retirement options on the east coast and discovered Skidaway Island. Here is a lovely scene of the inter-coastal waterway near the home we eventually purchased at the Landings.

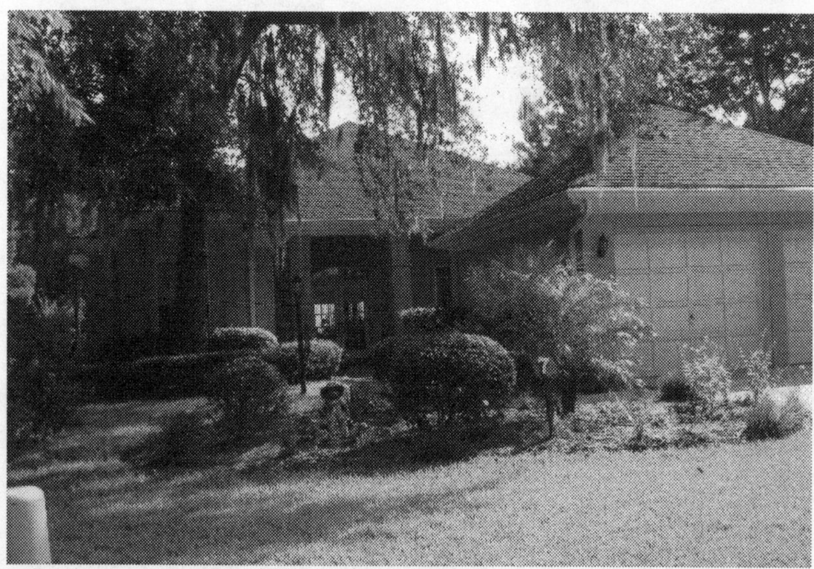

Our new small patio home on a lagoon with a view of one of the golf courses at the Landings, 1995.

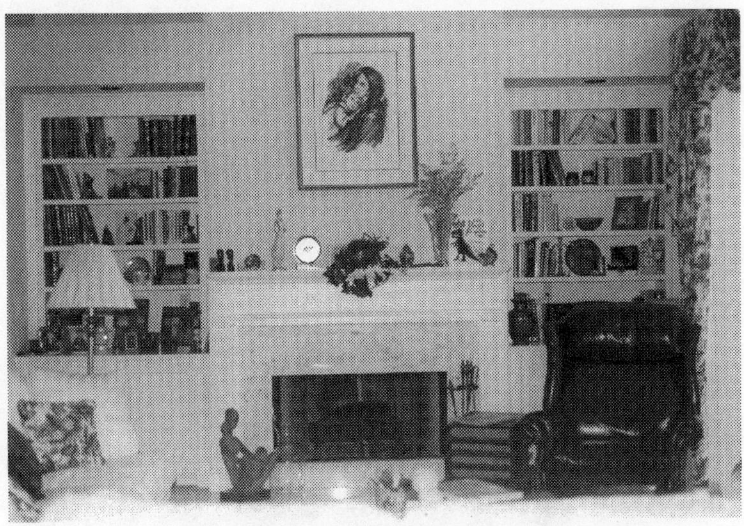

The interior of our home overlooking the water with much room for our books and collections. The piece of Art (Mother with child) over the fireplace was a gift from my children on my 60th birthday.

Courtney Danielle preparing for dance recital.

My first grandson, Samuel Mathew, born March 23, 1998 son of Elizabeth and Jeffrey Laufer.

My third granddaughter, Rachel Emily, born October 16, 2000, daughter of Elizabeth and Jeffrey Laufer.

"The Marshes" Main Community Facility

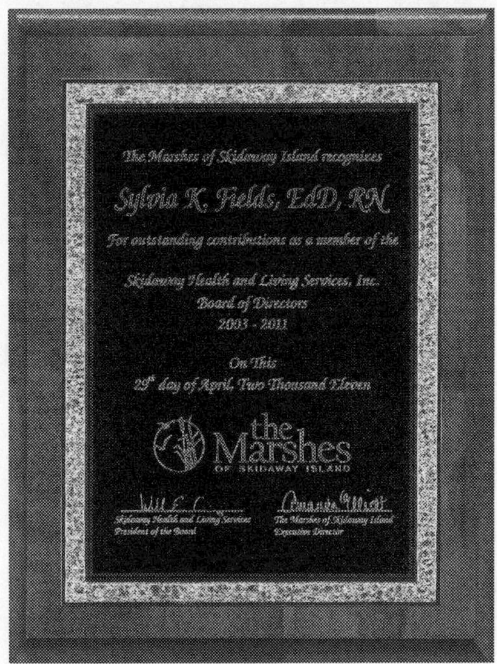

The Skidaway Island Health and Living Services

Board Appreciation plaque for 10-year service.

15

Volunteering for Community Service: Visiting Family Heritage Sites: 100 Years of Teachers College Nursing

Planning a Long Term Care Facility on the Island

One day while I was still commuting to Jefferson, I saw a small ad in the weekly Island magazine inviting Landings residents who were interested in developing a Continuing Care facility on the Island to come to an evening meeting at the local Presbyterian Church the following week. I showed it to Frank and told him I was interested in view of the different experiences our mothers had had: my mother's negative experience in Philadelphia and Frank's mother with a very positive experience in Sacramento. I was particularly concerned about the quality of nursing care in these facilities. At Emory University we had had a graduate program to prepare gerontological nurse practitioners, but had to close the program due to lack of interest; this was evidently a national problem. Nursing "homes," even those offering skilled nursing care, would not pay the salaries demanded by graduate level nurses. A new professional role for administrators did not require a nursing background; the MBAs and MHAs were running the show across the country in hospitals, nursing homes and rehabilitation centers.

Frank decided to come with me to the meeting. We did not know anyone there, but after personal introductions and many questions for consideration, the leader asked us to form committees, have meetings, and return together in two weeks. In view of my part-time status, I volunteered for the program committee, but declined the request to chair the committee. Frank found himself chairperson of the hospital affiliation committee. Janet Kuhn, who volunteered to chair the Program Committee, was a former nurse faculty member in pastoral nursing at Villanova University close to Philadelphia. We later met at her house, just around the corner from our home, with a few more volunteers to share ideas. I wrote everything down we discussed and formulated a program circulated to all the interested parties, and everyone agreed with the plans for projected services. Frank set about contacting the CEOs of the two hospital systems in Savannah: Memorial Health University Medical Center and St Joseph's/Candler hospitals. His committee tried to get the two systems to cooperate and share strategies for hospital relationships, but unfortunately after several meetings they were never able to agree. (The two systems were urged to collaborate in the development of a Cancer Research and Treatment Center, but were unable to accomplish that mission either, when state and federal funds from Tobacco Monies were not offered even when the two systems agreed to collaboration. To this day there are two separate Cancer Centers for this small city.)

It was decided that once there was a developer in place and the initial plans and funding were approved by the necessary governmental groups, the facility administrator and the medical director could restart discussions with the hospitals. Nothing else occurred then that needed Frank; I knew he was relieved to step back. About a year later an Atlanta corporation pursued purchase of the land, obtained initial start-up funding and slowly proceeded with plans for construction of a continuing care community that would include about 200 independent, assisted living, and skilled nursing care units. I was asked to serve on the Board of Trustees all during the financial development, but it was not until the year 2002 that construction was finally initiated and 2005 that the first residents began to move in.

"I know that by keeping her nose in the books, she is going to be a reader.

If she's a reader, she could be a writer. She could be a doctor.

She could be anything."

—A Reach Out and Read Parent

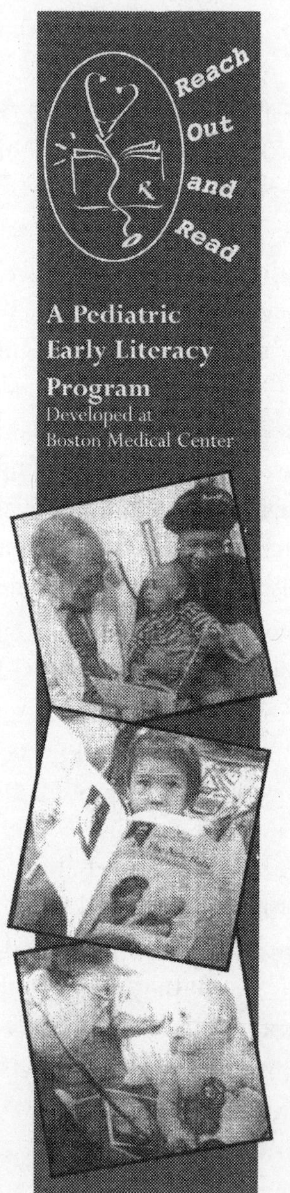

Reach Out and Read brochure.

The One Hundred Club and Early Literacy "*Born to Read*" and "*Reach Out and Read*"

Years earlier, in 1998, the wife of one of Frank's golfing partners, a retired orthopedic surgeon, had invited me to join an organization called "The One Hundred," a community group supporting the Backus Children's Hospital of the local non-profit Memorial Health University Medical Center. The members, mostly women residents of the Landings, but with some men, such as Dr. Tom Clark, a retired pediatrician, raised funds through raffles and various social events and then distributed the funds according to the hospital's requests. I volunteered for the Education Committee because I had seen articles in the Savannah news about the fifty percent high school dropout rate among Savannah public school students. Tom and I were especially concerned with the need to focus on early childhood education.

Dr. Patricia (Patty) Shapiro, the chair of the Education Committee, brought to our attention an early literacy program called "Reach Out and Read" that had been started at the Boston City Children's Hospital in 1989. Since she was about to return to full-time medical practice, Patty asked me to be co-chair and gather more information about the program. The American Academy of Pediatrics had officially endorsed the Reach Out and Read model of early literacy and Scholastic Publishing Company had just published the first Reach Out and Read Book Catalog, offering children's books at significant discounts to Reach Out and Read programs. At that time there were fewer than 500 medical center programs across the country and less than one million books had been distributed.

I also heard about another early literacy program that the Savannah Public Library was interested in establishing in collaboration with the health professions. When Patty resigned her chairperson role I took it over and arranged a meeting with the library's Director of Children's Services, who was looking for financial aid to develop a "Born to Read" program; we decided to work together.

Our Born to Read program with the Public Libraries centered on new mothers in the Memorial Hospital before discharge and involved distribution by volunteers or nursing assistants of a free new culturally sensitive small book entitled *Read to Your Baby and Your Baby Will Read to You*, along with personal guidance about the importance of communicating with the baby and later reading to promote child development. The One Hundred group agreed to support the purchase of the books and a very practical gift of an erasable refrigerator magnet that had emergency phone numbers and space to write in the dates of necessary follow-up examinations for mother and baby. When the infants born at Memorial were brought to the Well Baby Clinic at Memorial Hospital for health supervision, immunizations, and preventive education, Reach Out and Read took over. At that time there were very few infant and children's books that included minority characters, but we worked with several publishing houses that furnished us with new culturally sensitive, age-appropriate books for our clinic population. The books were given to the parent at every visit starting at six months of age by the treating physician or nurse practitioner along with anticipatory guidance toward verbal communication with the infant. By the time the child was five years of age, if he or she was brought to the clinic regularly according to recommended health promotion and immunization appointments, up to ten books could be owned. Unfortunately, among the primarily low-income families who came to the clinic, these books might be the only books in the home.

In addition to purchasing the books at wholesale cost, The One Hundred funded a part-time position for an administrator to organize and oversee volunteer services, maintain the supply of selected books for free distribution, and facilitate a collection process for used books from the community. A bookcase and small tables and chairs were also provided by The One Hundred for the clinic waiting room, where the slightly worn used books collected were on the shelves waiting to be read to children by volunteers, or older children. The used books could be taken home when requested by the parent or child. Later when the program was receiving accolades, I wrote a grant request in response to an RFP from the CVS Pharmacy for additional funds to bring the Reach Out and Read program to the Chatham County Health Department Child Health Clinic, which was successful. The Reach Out and Read program at Backus Children's Hospital of Memorial Health continues to this day, with the One Hundred providing $25,000 annually.

In view of my involvement with the early literacy projects, I had been asked to join the Savannah Literacy Council, which worked to recruit volunteers to support reading skills for all ages in Chatham County: school age to senior citizens through the public school and library systems. Our education committee also wanted to introduce the early literacy programs to primary care hospital residents and attending community physicians in Savannah and the surrounding counties.

Working with Dr. Martin Greenberg, chair of Pediatrics at Memorial Medical Center, we developed a continuing education lectureship at the Hospital Auditorium that included an evening supper and lecture with a special award to an outstanding child health advocate nationally.

In collaboration with the Savannah College of Art and Design, an award was developed by Professor Dorothy Spradley, SCAD faculty member, and our One Hundred Award Committee members May Poetter, SCAD professor of foundations (and mother of the SCAD president, Paula Wallace), Barbara McLaughlin, President of the One Hundred, and myself. The award created was a magnificent bronze sculpture of two parents lifting up their infant and toddler to the sunlight. The mayor of Savannah attended the program and read a Savannah Proclamation honoring our organization and the Reach Out and Read Program. The first award was given in early 2000 to Dr. Barry Zuckerman, Professor of Pediatrics and Public Health at the University of Boston School of Medicine and Chief of Pediatrics at Boston Medical Center. With colleagues he had developed the Reach Out and Read program in 1989, which has subsequently been established by volunteer organizations at many medical centers across the country.

In 2013 there were 5,000 Reach Out and Read programs in the United States and six and a half million books distributed to four million children. Of course this is only one of many programs that attempt to improve early literacy in this country; the needs are still overwhelming for many of our low-income children. I was sad to see an article on the front page of *The New York Times* Review of the Week section, just this week, sixteen years since we established the Reach Out and Read and Born to Read programs here in Savannah addressing part of the problem. Walter Dean Myers, an author of books for children and young adults including *Monster*, and the previous Library of Congress National Ambassador for Young People's Literature, and his son Christopher Myers, an author and illustrator of books for children and young adults including *Harlem* and other collaborations with his father, asked "Where Are the People of Color in Children's Books?" Of 3,200 children's books published in 2013, just ninety three were about black people, only fifty seven were about Latinos, and just forty eight were by them, according to a study by the Cooperative Children's Book Center at the University of Wisconsin. These authors (Myers father and son) abhor the study results:

> Through the books they read, children can explore and hopefully find characters they can identify with, and potentially begin to find their own identity. When children cannot see and learn about characters in books that look and perhaps live as they do, they cannot sense that they are important.

This is a tragedy for all children, especially for children of color from low-income families. As the authors emphasize, "There is work to be done."

Telecommuting from Savannah for Jefferson Studies

In addition to my community activities in Savannah, by telecommuting to Philadelphia I was able to continue to work on various critical medical education evaluation topics for JMC Center for Research. Concurrently our Jefferson research expanded to include a continuing series of studies on the levels and impact on patient outcomes of "empathy" in health care professionals according to our Jefferson definition.

The 1999 report titled *To Err is Human: Building a Safer Health System* by the Institute of Medicine estimated that between 44,000 and 98,000 patients die annually from avoidable medical errors. This report attracted a great deal of attention by the public and the medical profession. By working at home, I was able to participate in a sponsored curriculum project at Jefferson Medical College that focused on better preparation of third-year medical students related to the issue. Following my literature review and pursuant to a needs assessment and a pilot program developed by faculty that included a plenary session and workshops, our team was able to develop a knowledge and attitude survey instrument as a pretest-posttest for *a one-day interclerkship program for medical students on medical errors and patient safety.* The results of the full study were not published until 2007, but there was clear evidence that the knowledge, attitudes, and beliefs of students were changed by the one-day educational program.

I continued involvement in several other important medical education curriculum projects while living in Savannah, including a *Review of Medical Education Research Centers for the Department of Health Resources and Services.* What made all this work more fun for me was that I was able to recruit some of my Savannah friends like Gail Andrus, whose husband was one of Frank's golfing friends and whose daughter Jenny had become my protégée at Jefferson Medical College. Gail helped with literature review and secretarial work needed for the projects, offering financial benefits we appreciated. I do not know how I could have done everything I did without her help. During the years, Jenny not only graduated from JMC with high honors, she completed an ENT residency and surgical fellowship training in laryngology at Boston University.

Traveling Our Family Heritage Routes

As the years moved along, Frank and I kept hearing from friends and family about their international travels; we were particularly anxious to see Europe. It was in 1998 that Frank told me about a trip some of his golf partners were taking on a special tour of Scotland, the birthplace of golf, and I encouraged him to participate. It was clear to me that golf was more than a hobby; it was in his blood. The golfers would play 36 holes each of four days on different historic Scottish courses. When I asked Frank whether the wives were going along, he told me that only the men were on the trip. I did not mind; Scotland was not on my "must see" list. Frank did go and had a wonderful time bringing home special objects reflecting the courses he had played. It turned out that the other wives who were devoted golfers joined their husbands at the end of the intensive all male golfing week for touring the country together. I was somewhat disappointed when I learned I had not been invited to participate, but it was just as well, I was not an 18 hole golfer like the other wives and I knew it would have been much too expensive for me to join the group.

Several months later my cousins Jerry and Joyce in California asked if we were interested in touring France on a budget with them for two weeks by bus. I was quick to say, "of course." Frank was also excited about this trip; one of his grandmothers was of French heritage, her surname was "Fontaine." It was a remarkable experience, although there were a few difficult days; it is impossible to satisfy everyone. Unfortunately we were assigned to a hotel in the suburbs of Paris, which meant traveling each day with the group back and forth on the bus within Paris and outside. Not everything turned out according to the brochure, but I have some remarkable memories of the places we visited and the people we met. Starting and ending in Paris, we visited the famous Louvre Art museum, where a special museum guide spent what seemed like an hour describing the *Mona Lisa*. On permanent display since 1797, the painting was acquired by King Francis I, for France. We learned it was the "best known, most visited, most written about, most sung about, and most parodied work of art in the world." Given its reputation I was surprised it was as small as it was. Following the guide along and standing with 50 other members of our group to hear about the history and fine details of other paintings and sculpture was not as much fun as we expected and very tiring. Of course, my cousin's wife, Joyce, an established professional artist with a Master of Fine Arts Degree from the University of California, Long Beach, was thrilled with all the details presented in the history of the works to which we were introduced.

One day we visited the *Palace and gardens of Versailles* ten miles outside of Paris. The French chateau that was the royal residence of French King Louis XIV was the central part of the governmental complex until the revolution in 1789. I loved the elegance and opulence of the Palace with its magnificent furnishings, but it all seemed to upset Frank. "No wonder there was a revolution, people were starving," he said. With all the walking through the city and tourist sites he started having pain in his legs.

He was anxious to make the next stop on the trip southwest to the commune *of Lourdes in the Hautes Pyrenees.* When he was a student at Notre Dame University Frank had heard of the stone grotto with a statue of the Virgin Mary at Lourdes. I think it was the subject of the movie *Song of Bernadette* about poor fourteen-year-old Bernadette Souberoux who in 1858 saw visions of the Blessed Virgin Mary and described miracles of healing and hope that occurred. We were told six million pilgrims each year come to visit Lourdes from all over the world. What we saw that day was literally thousands of sick and handicapped people in wheelchairs and on stretchers trooping through the grounds with their transporters to experience the perceived holiness and healing of the waters. For me the whole scene was terribly depressing and commercialized. Yet, we decided to buy a small bottle of the healing water to take home to our neighbor John Burns, a lifelong smoker who was dying with lung cancer. Tragically he passed away several months later, but he and his wife Pat had been most appreciative of our small gift. Then two years later, to our shock, John's wife also became ill and eventually died of lung cancer. I did not remember her smoking, but ironically we had the same birthday and I am an avid non-smoker. It is still painful for me to think of Pat. That was more than ten years ago.

California Family Dr. Jerry & Joyce Weiss with Frank and I on Tour of France, overlooking Monte Carlo.

There were several other well-known and fun tourist places we visited in France including *charming Nice and exciting Monte Carlo.* Frank and I were overwhelmed at the Giverny home and garden of the famous artist Claude Monet. By far the most meaningful experience was the visit to the gravesites of our young soldiers who gave their lives on the beaches of Normandy during the World War II invasion by combined British, Canadian, and American armed forces. Although I was only ten and a half years old in June 1944, I remember those scenes from the newsreels we saw at the Saturday movie matinee, and then the films produced about the war through these many years showing the "D Day" invasion. My young cousin Alfie was only 19 when he was killed in Belgium and later buried in Normandy, but I was not able to see his grave there with the Jewish star above. After the war his father, my Great-Uncle Bill, who had brought my mother, her father, brother, and great-grandmother to this country after World War I, had Alfie's remains brought back and buried in the family plot in Cedar Grove Cemetery in Flushing, Queens, New York.

We were both exhausted after the trip to France, and as happy as Frank had been for the first five years at the Landings, he started to become depressed again about his diminishing golf skills. Having been recognized as an excellent golfer all his life he was now in his 70s and his physical condition was changing. His golf game was not what it had been before and no matter how many lessons he took, or how many times he altered his golf swing, he could not seem to improve; there were many younger and stronger men at the Landings who were now his competition. He lost interest in socializing with some of his golfing buddies and other friends we had made together. It did not help that my bridge game and golf had not improved very much, but I did not suffer over my limitations and decline; I just kept making more friends.

To my disappointment, I learned that Frank had started smoking again along with several of the other men on the golf course. His feet were bothering him and he requested a flag for his golf cart, which allowed him to drive up closer to the green. He had been considered pre-diabetic when we moved to Savannah, advised to restrict his diet, exercise, and lose a few pounds. I watched his diet as best I could most of the time, especially since I was always struggling to not gain weight, but when he insisted on biscuits and gravy for breakfast at his favorite diner, I could not stop him. He did not want to walk with me for exercise, refused to use my treadmill when the weather was bad, and said he did too much exercising on the golf course. Frank was supposed to check his blood sugars and we had obtained the necessary supplies. But he resented my interest in his condition and when I asked about the results, he kept saying, "it's OK."

Slowly Frank was becoming more depressed as he had been before we left Philadelphia five years before. I thought he needed a change so when his sister Ellen asked us to join her and her husband Bill and their daughters on the west coast of Ireland for a week, we accepted the invitation. Frank's niece Mary and her husband, an executive for the new Intel headquarters in Ireland, lived with their seven children, including an adopted boy from India, in Portland, Oregon. They had just finished building a wonderful new five-bedroom stone home in Ballyvaughn overlooking Galway Bay. Mary and her husband were terrific people, and we were lucky to be the first guests in their Irish home, even before the younger children arrived for their summer vacation. The family fun started for us when Mary picked us all up at the airport. It was a wonderful time: each day was great, laughing and joking and enjoying everything we saw or ate, the shopping for Irish souvenirs and kibitzing nightly over different beers with the locals in nearby pubs. It had always been a great experience being with Ellen and Bill when we visited them and Frank's mother in Sacramento. I loved all of them and their eight children.

Several years before, Frank had received an invitation to visit the Marzolf Winery in Alsace-Lorraine, where apparently his father's family had originally immigrated from on the way to the United States. Frank did not know of this family, but supposedly according to the invitation and enclosed list there were 1,000 Marzolf families around the world, who must have been related somehow. Before we left for Ireland I learned about a perfect way to visit the winery after Ireland while we were in Europe. We would fly to Paris from Ireland and take the train to Nancy where we could pick up a barge trip on the Rhine to Strasbourg. On the way the barge was to stop in the town of Colmar, which was close to the winery in the hills of the ancient village of Gueberschwihr. Evidently we would have the afternoon free in Colmar to visit the winery. I made the arrangements through our local travel agency on Skidaway Island. Does anything ever go straight? There was a major hitch.

Unfortunately when we arrived in Nancy we learned that the motor of the barge was out of commission. The barge would need to be towed through the canal but it could not be towed with the passengers on board. We were given a choice to get our money back, but there were no other trips they could offer us; it was the middle of August and we were stranded. The leader for the tour operator, Abercrombie-Kent, told us the trip could be continued if most of the passengers agreed to sleep and eat our breakfast and dinner on the barge, getting off onto three small motor boats to drive through the canal from each town to the next. The barge could then be towed without the passengers to its destination each day. It sounded crazy but most of us accepted the deal rather than have to find our way back to Paris, which was already packed with tourists. Our barge trip turned out to be a fun adventure: off the barge, on the boat, off the boat, on the bus to town, guided tour of the town, lunch, back to the boat, off the boat, back on the barge for dinner. The bar on the barge was always packed; and there were freshly baked croissants, rolls, pastries with omelets and other breakfast specialties each morning; appetizers and cocktails each evening before and then dinner entrees and desserts paired with fantastic wines with every meal, only to be topped with after-dinner cordials, cheeses and fruits. The lunches in town were individually chosen, but the variety and quality of each meal was as amazing as the next.

There had been a lot of walking on cobblestone streets in Ireland and in all the towns we visited during the barge cruise, so Frank had much difficulty with his feet. Sometimes he chose to stay back on the boat rather than joining the group going ashore with lunches specially prepared for those who stayed on the boats. We had made friends with a California couple on the barge. The wife had some medical problems and also stayed on the boat during the lunch breaks. Once we reached Colmar, she and her husband chose to take a taxi with us from Colmar to the charming historic 13th-century village. It was a marvelous experience meeting this young Marzolf family and touring the winery. The husband did not speak English and none of us spoke French, but the young mother and her two children, ten and 12, spoke enough English; we managed very well. We tasted every wine they had and bought as many bottles as we could carry. Then they gave us extra Marzolf labels to take home with us to share with all the children. The Marzolf wine was actually like champagne but could not be called champagne because it was not from the Champagne region of France.

Our San Diego friends had never been to Philadelphia, so six months after we arrived home we arranged to meet them in Philadelphia for a historical tour and then proceeded to New York City by limousine for a few days, where my daughter Melissa was able to get us a two bedroom hotel suite for the price of two single rooms. We brought back fresh bagels and juice, and made fresh coffee in the suite for breakfast every morning. Then we played bridge in the suite in between running to dinners and theatre. They were great fun to be with and we planned to meet them the following year in their home town of San Diego. Unfortunately about six months after we returned from New York, we learned that the wife had died. We never made it to San Diego. We never learned what was wrong with her either, but about a year later we received a marriage announcement from him in San Diego. Life moves on.

I will never forget those magnificent weeks in France, Ireland, and Alsace, where Frank was able to learn all about his Catholic heritage, his mother's Irish background and his father's French and German background, more than a century before. I envied Frank and decided I wanted to visit and learn more about my own parents' Jewish background. My mother had written about her early life during World War I in a Carpathian Mountain town in Hungary named Sighetu and in the capital, Budapest. I knew very little about my father's home city in Munkács; he had left as a teenager, and never spoke much about his early years. I discussed a possible trip with Frank, but he said he did not think he could manage the walking, so I asked my brother. He turned me down due to his precarious health situation. Finally, my mother's nephew Irving and his wife Ruth expressed interest. He had been born in Hungary, but came to the U.S. as a toddler; he remembered nothing. Although she was born in the United States, Ruth's family came from the same area as my mother's family so she knew places of interest for both of us; meanwhile we both did some research and I offered to make our travel arrangements independently with my local Four Seasons Travel agency in Savannah, who had arranged the Abercrombie and Kent travel to Ireland and facilitated the barge trip on the Rhine to the Marzolf winery. We could never have found a pre-planned tour that would take us to see specifically what we wanted to see. Meanwhile Ruth did some more research to identify a few restaurants, museums, and historical monuments that would be of special interest to us.

Our personal guide, who spoke all the necessary languages, and an individual driver picked us up at the Budapest airport for transfer to the

Intercontinental Hotel to check in and enjoy coffee and pastry while we reviewed the plan originally made for our two-week visit, beginning with three days of touring in Budapest, a beautiful city on the Danube. There was so much to see on both sides of the river, in Buda and Pest; much old and some new. In addition to the museum of Hungarian history we were particularly impressed with the Museum of Contemporary Art. Since we were looking at our Jewish heritage, visiting the famous historic Doheny Street Synagogue with its museum of Judaica and the outdoor memorial to Wallenberg, the righteous Christian who helped save Jews during World War II, was particularly meaningful. I remember my mother telling me about her life in Budapest during World War I when my grandfather and my aunt's husband had been drafted into the Hungarian Army in 1914. Grandma and my aunt received a small benefit from the Hungarian government because their husbands were in the service, but it was not enough, so through some other family members they found work rolling cigarettes for the black market. Mother and her sister with two infants lived in a tiny apartment near the famous grand synagogue. From her description I believe I recognized the old apartment building across the street in the back of the temple that could probably seat about 1,000 in prayer. The temple museum was magnificent. Two young female university students took us through the beautiful building and explained the significance of the museum holdings, including many pieces that had been salvaged from other Hungarian synagogues destroyed by the Germans. I was impressed to learn that these students were majoring in Jewish Studies in the public university, but not surprised that they were also being trained for potential jobs in tourism. Shopping in Budapest was marvelous. It seemed to focus on the fine hand-painted Herend porcelain pottery. Ruth and I fell in love with a magnificent nude female bust that came in two sizes, as well as some smaller unusual serving pieces. Ruth and Irving were able to ship their purchases home to New York, but I carried my smaller, well-draped porcelain lady home in my arms. She sits regally and erotically on my fireplace mantelpiece.

The food everywhere was wonderful, but one night was particularly magnificent. By telephone from New York Ruth had made the reservation for us for dinner one evening at Gundel, the most famous and expensive historical dining place in the country from the turn of the 20th century. As we waited for our traditional (although not kosher food), we took pleasure in the beautiful art on the walls by famous Hungarian artists and listened to Gypsy musicians playing marvelous traditional Hungarian music I had heard all my life growing up.

When World War I was over in 1918, my mother and her family returned from Budapest to Sighetu in northern Hungary, although it was then declared as Czechoslovakia and later Romania. Most of the Jews who stayed there were killed by the Nazis or taken to the German-run Polish concentration camps by 1945. Among the few survivors of the camps was Nobel Peace Prize winner Eli Wiesel. My mother knew of his family, and we heard that the city had put up a plaque honoring him on the wall of his former home in Sighetu. We wanted to see the town, having heard that after World War II it was turned back over to Romania. Among the few other camp survivors from Sighetu and known by Ruth and Irving, and by my mother, was Dr. Gisella Perl, whose husband and son did not survive the slaughter. My mother's sister (Irving's mother) was a schoolmate of Gisella's before she left Sighetu for medical school in Vienna in the 1920s. She became an obstetrician/gynecologist and later returned home to practice medicine with her husband. Deported to Auschwitz in 1944, she was assigned as physician to the camp inmates and saw the most terrible suffering inflicted on them by unbelievably inhuman Nazi camp leaders and physicians, particularly Dr. Mengele. Her book, *I was a Doctor in Auschwitz*, describing what she had experienced, was published in 1948. I believe a documentary film was also produced. It is a nightmare of cruelty that no reader could believe. In her book Dr. Perl described how she was saved from death by a priest after a suicide attempt following the horrors of Bergen-Belsen. He helped her to finally heal as much as possible with the help of nuns in a convent and then by his friends in Paris. Eventually she was able to come to New York, where she studied and prepared to practice medicine at Mt. Sinai Hospital in New York City. Ruth had worked for her in her office while she was in graduate school at Columbia, and had met Irving through his mother, who, like my mother, had become Dr Perl's patient. Years later she retired to Israel and ultimately passed away.

After having read her book and knowing her full story, it was important for us to try to see if there were any remnants of the former large Jewish community. We understood the synagogue still stood in Sighetu and the cemetery was open where some ancestors might have been buried, although of the many Jews who had lived there before the war, most were killed or deported to labor camps; we knew of no family member or other Jews who returned permanently. We left Budapest driving north to Nyiregyhaza, a large city in Hungary with a population over 100,000 just inside the border, where a monument to Holocaust victims was erected in 2004. We were also compelled to visit Auschwitz in Poland, but I had another mission first; I wanted to see where my father came from, which was now across the Hungarian border in Ukraine. Auschwitz would wait until we had seen Sighetu and then Munkács (now called Mukachuva).

As we drove north in Hungary we were impressed with the roads and the beauty of the scenery. Stopping along the way for lunch in a roadside inn we appreciated the explanations by our guide of the previous years before independence from communist rule, the attempt at revolution that left many Hungarians dead and scars on the buildings in Budapest, and about the final success and changes in the country as the result of the democratic government. On the drive north the guide talked about the differences in the economic situations in Hungary, Ukraine, Poland, the Czech Republic and Slovakia following the breakup of the Soviet Union. We had a lovely dinner and stayed overnight in a very nice hotel in Nyíregyháza. In the morning we left early after a good breakfast, driving east to Sighetu; we did not need visas to enter Hungary or Romania.

The drive through the mountains was as beautiful as my mother had described. When we arrived we drove around the town, and, sitting in the dining room of a small hotel overlooking the Town Square for lunch, watched the people. There were teenagers dressed in jeans and American sneakers just as in the United States; gypsy women in long colorful skirts and men in black hats and pants with colorful vests. Along the road into town we saw many gypsies riding in horse-driven carts, and their small thatch-roofed houses decorated with all kinds of colorful art. A local guide took us to see the Jewish cemetery; it was overgrown and hard to read the monuments as we looked for the names of our family members, *Berkowitz* and *Heisler,* but could not find any we were able to read. I have photos of the cattle crossing the unpaved dirt roads on the way back to Hungary.

We returned to the hotel in Nyíregyháza, had dinner and stayed overnight again. The next morning we started out going further north to reach my father's home town Mukachuva, a much larger city now in the Ukraine. One of my second cousins, an Auschwitz survivor our extended family brought to the United States in 1946 and who now lived in Los Angeles, had learned from my cousin Jerry about my planned trip. He had returned there soon after he was released from Auschwitz before entering the United States and years later had visited with his children to show them his former home. He knew there were still some camp survivors in the city, so he sent me the name of one of his camp mates and asked me to try to find her and give her $50. I knew one of my father's nephews had survived and returned after the camp; my mother and father had been able to visit him and his family in the early 1960s, but I was uncertain if any of them were still there or even alive. We thought one of his great-nieces had been able to get to Israel, but I did not know if anyone from our family was still alive. My father was able to bring another one of his nephews who survived Auschwitz to the United States in 1946, but I knew he had been ill and passed away in the 1980s, and with my father and mother gone, I had lost contact with his family.

A visa had been required for us to go across the border to the Ukraine, but when we got to the border, the visas were not enough. We waited for hours to enter the dilapidated run-down city where they charged us $25 USD each for health insurance just to ride around the city a few hours. Our guide told us there was no approved hotel in the city so we could not stay overnight. We had to look for ourselves for some kind of remnant of the Jewish presence in the city. The city looked terrible, the roads were filled with potholes, and the buildings were falling apart. Some animals were being led through the roads, while others just seemed to be roaming the streets; there were only a few old cars.

Suddenly I saw a Hebrew word on one of the buildings, and asked the driver to stop. At that moment a woman came out of the building. I got out of the car and stopped her. I did not speak anything but English and a few words of Yiddish, so I showed the woman the paper with the names Helen _____ and my cousin's name Steve Mermelstein, and Auschwitz. With the help of our guide, who spoke Ukrainian, I made her understand I was from the United States and looking for Helen, whose surname name I have since forgotten. She became all excited and told the guide she did know Helen and Mermelstein, and would cancel the taxi that had just arrived for her. She said she would take us to Helen if afterwards, our driver could take her home. He agreed and she got into our car to show the driver where to go. It was not far. It turned out that all the synagogues in the city had been destroyed by the Germans or the Russians. The building I found had been purchased by an American Jewish organization to serve as a synagogue and a community center and that a rabbi came monthly from Kiev to teach classes to children and adults about Judaism, which the Communists had not previously permitted. They baked challah and matzos and brought kosher food for the Jewish community, which was fewer than one hundred people at the time. There were also other efforts to help Jews who wanted to go to Israel to find relatives there.

We found Helen, an elderly woman, who was so happy to meet us and extremely grateful when I gave her the $50 and the note from Steve. Evidently she received a small pension from the government and lived in a studio-like apartment with a tiny kitchenette and bathroom in a downtrodden building with chickens and dogs running around outside. The government checked everyone's mail and stole any cash or checks inside, so my cousin wrote to her but could not enclose money. Helen wanted to serve us tea but she was embarrassed because she did not have any sweet cake to offer. She ran to her next-door neighbors to ask if they had anything to share with her for us. Her neighbor came back with Helen and in pretty good English welcomed us and invited us into their larger apartment to have tea and cookies. They were really happy for Helen to have guests; evidently she had no surviving family members, and this family was very important in her life. The neighbors were a younger family who I believe owned the house they were all living in, but they were struggling because jobs were difficult to find in the city. Theirs was a larger apartment decorated pretty well; they were not Jewish; actually there were no religious icons of any kind. After the tea, Helen wanted to take us to see the Jewish Community Center that had been recently fitted with a mikvah, so that the religious bathing rituals of Judaism could be introduced for conversion, etc. We promised to return after a short visit to the Center, which was very interesting; then we took Helen back home and all visited together. We learned that the husband was an engineer, but did not have a job. He repaired TVs and computers; the mother was a pediatrician working for a government health center, and the oldest child, a daughter, Irenka, who spoke English fairly well, had recently finished medical school, but did not have a job. There was a teenage son in the family who also spoke English, and was very computer savvy.

We had a wonderful afternoon with all of the family, exchanged e-mail addresses, and started a friendship that lasted a few years. It was amazing how we communicated online. I tried to find a medical program that Irenka could enter in the United States to improve her education and eventually earn an American medical license, and sent her an in-depth computer program to help her improve her English language reading and speaking skills. I communicated with every kind of Ukrainian-American organization I could find that might be able to bring her to the States, but I could not afford to send her the papers and fare for a tourist trip. Then new problems arose in the family with the grandparents and the ownership of the house they all lived in. It was complicated and eventually Irenka got a job in Kiev and we lost contact.

But back to our original trip, after we left Mukachuva we returned to Budapest for a few more days of touring in and outside of Budapest, enjoying the food, the shopping and the music. We then took the train to spend a few days touring in Warsaw, where we saw remnants and a monument to the Warsaw Ghetto as well as the other various historical and art museums. We then went to Krakow – Kazimierz (a historical district in Krakow), where we found an active synagogue and a very nice hotel and restaurant established by some returning Jews. I am not sure why we were given a tour of some historical creative art in a huge salt mine in Krakow, except that it was near the most important part of our trip, the State Museum Auschwitz-Berkenau in Oswiecim, Poland. It is impossible to describe in words my feelings about our experiences there. A few Jews who survived the Holocaust tried to return to Poland, but I don't know how many were really successful. Even though the economic situation was far better in Poland and Hungary than the Ukraine, I never felt comfortable as a Jew in any of these countries.

I cannot forget what I have read, seen, and learned about intolerance as a result of this trip, particularly the way the Jews have been treated during my own lifetime around the world. I cannot forget that had my parents not left Europe soon after World War I, they might have been victims of the Holocaust. I cannot give up thinking, once again

"There, but for the grace of God, go I.

Budapest, Wallenberg Memorial outside the famous Doheny Street Synagogue. Armed with moral courage and Swedish "free" papers, Raole Wallenberg saved as many as 100,000 Hungarian Jews from death close to the end of WW II in Hungary.

List of other "Righteous Ones" who helped save other potential victims in Budapest.

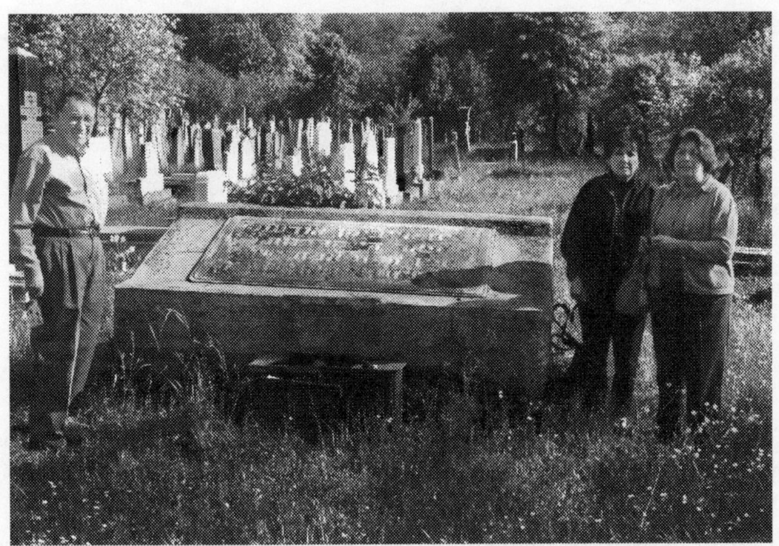

Visiting Jewish cemetery in author's mother Frieda Berkowitz's hometown Szighet in Carpathian Mountains (now in Romania), with my cousins Ruth and (Irving Heisler deceased).

Synagogue stands but no Jews remain in Szighet.

Wall plaque on former home of Nobel Peace Prize winner Elie Wiesel in Szighet.

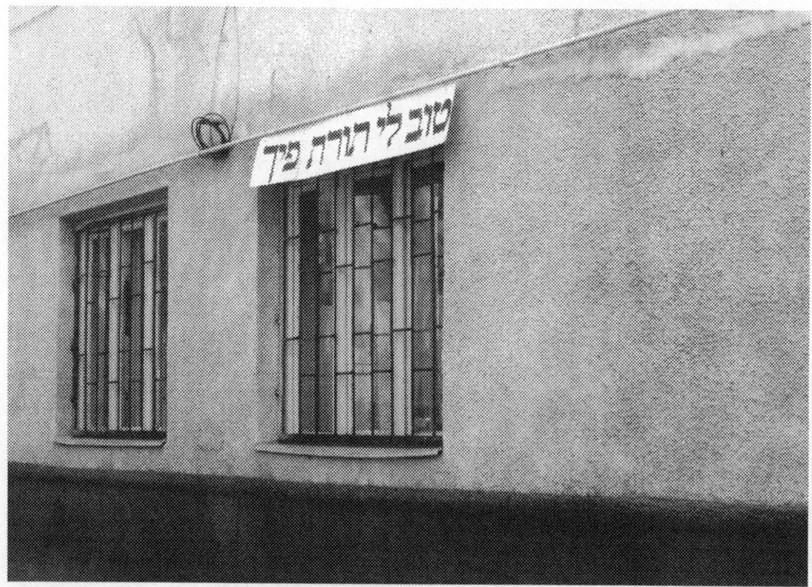

New Jewish Community Center in my father's hometown, in Munkacs Ukraine.

Crematorium at Auschwitz Concentration Camp, Poland

Warehouse Dormitory at the Crematorium.

Teachers College 100th Anniversary Reunion with Emory Faculty, Dr. Ruth Yurchuck, and Dr. Leah Gorman. Faculty member and T.C graduate Rose Dilday, MS, attended the reunion with us but did not appear in the photo.

Teachers College 100th Anniversary Reunion with Dr. Georgie Labadie, (my doctoral advisor and friend) and her husband Dr. Robert Labadie.

16

The Savannah Health Mission: 1996-2006

"First Be, Then Do"

Miles "Chip" Goldsmith, MD, F.A.C.S

The Early Years

It was April 1996 when Dr. Chip Goldsmith, after hearing a sermon at Christ Church one Sunday, was inspired to do something about a problem he faced in his medical practice every week at the Georgia Ear Institute in Savannah. The sermon was not about health care, but Chip knew it was directed to him and the medical professionalism he valued. It seemed that every week more and more of the patients referred to him at the Institute needed medical and or surgical treatment, but had no health insurance and could not afford to pay out of pocket for care.

I did not know Dr. Goldsmith at that time, but I was well aware of the problem of inequality in access to health care through the professional and public literature and media I followed regularly. The problem existed and persisted during the 20th century throughout the nation, certainly when I first entered the health profession early in the 1950s. People died without access to care even when it was available for those who could afford private care, had access to public health clinics and services or had government positions that included health benefits such as teachers, police, and others.

However in Savannah, many citizens worked for small local companies at minimal pay, or at part-time or seasonal jobs in hospitality, construction, landscaping, agriculture, home health care, etc., or in the arts with no health benefits, and could not afford the cost of a private medical office visit. Diabetic complications, sky-high blood pressure, untreated kidney disease, and pain that made work impossible forced them to the emergency room. They also could not afford the drugs, specialty care, or expense of surgery prescribed there. Ineligible for Medicaid and too young for Medicare, too many, particularly those with pre-existing conditions such as hypertension, cancer, COPD, or diabetes, were falling through the cracks.

Small businesses could not afford to provide insurance; large corporations might offer insurance, but the employees could not afford their share of the cost. A truck driver complained that his company offered him insurance at $360 a month, but there were office visit co-pays, a $1,500 deductible, and an annual limit. Meanwhile individual insurance was "off the charts," especially for those with pre-existing conditions; the primary cause of bankruptcy was medical bills.

In 1996 there were about 35 million uninsured in this country – and as many as 50,000 in Chatham County (the base of Savannah) and the immediate surrounding counties. The cost of health insurance and medical care was estimated to have quadrupled over the previous ten years. The challenge over whether health care was a right of citizenship or a privilege for those who could not afford to pay for it eventually led to political conflict across the country in the national elections of 2008, then in 2010 congressional development of the Affordable Care Act (ACA) modeled after the state law in Massachusetts. Meanwhile for the most part the ACA, commonly referred to as "Obamacare," was upheld by the Supreme Court. This issue of inequality in access to health care for those who lived in rural areas, were poor, or had darker skin all too often led to unnecessary deaths. There was no doubt in Dr. Goldsmith's mind in 1996 that it was unethical for the most advantaged country in the world not to meet the basic health care needs for all its citizens. So Chip recruited professional nurse colleagues at the Ear Institute, Ann Hallock and Antha Grady, to explore free clinics he had heard about in other states where physicians and nurses volunteered to care for working citizens without insurance. ***Then they did something about it*!**

With contributions of a small group of Savannah's spiritual, educational, and political leaders, the *Savannah Health Mission* was born. People lined up outside the Georgia Ear Institute on Thursday evenings, and most of the time they were taken care of that night by Dr. Goldsmith and/or other physicians, such as Dr. Steve Rogers, full-time Memorial-employed board-certified anesthesiologist and pain specialist also certified in family medicine. Mostly through word of mouth other employed Memorial physicians and several retired physicians were recruited. Dr. Shaun Franklin, attending physician in the department of Family Medicine, started to bring her third-year medicine clerks and some residents to the clinic for experience. Laboratory tests and X-rays were arranged at Memorial Hospital, and referrals were made to the hospital clinics and cooperating physician specialists in the community for evaluation. While there were no charges for primary care at the evening clinic, follow-up fees were negotiated in critical situations through the patient services office at Memorial. Most of the specialists who either came to the clinic to see special cases or accepted our referrals are acknowledged at the end of the memoir.

The Savannah Mission functioned early on as a legally incorporated non-profit organization, supported through contributions from individuals, churches, community organizations such as the Savannah Foundation and others led by Dr. Goldsmith and an all-volunteer board of directors, composed of various community leaders or benefactors. There were no charges to the Mission from the Ear Institute or the Memorial Hospital for space, utilities, housekeeping, and lab work. Liability insurance for the Board members was paid through the Mission budget. No governmental funding was offered or requested. Volunteer physicians and nurses were covered for liability through their independent or employing institution liability policies by state law. Volunteers who were not employed elsewhere were covered by a Georgia State Good Samaritan Ruling, and legal, accounting, and computer services were contributed.

Some prescription pharmaceuticals were contributed, and volunteers assisted patients in accessing drugs free or discounted through Med

Bank (an independent non-profit organization established to assist uninsured patients with their prescription drug needs) or directly through pharmaceutical company patient assistance programs that were being introduced across the country. Mission expenses were therefore kept to a minimum, and patients were charged no fees. However with no paid medical staff there were significant limitations in the services that could be offered by the all-volunteer professional groups. The line-up outside the Ear Institute grew longer and the extent of Savannah's uninsured became more obvious.

By the year 2000, as the demands for mission services and personnel increased significantly, the volunteer coordinating nurses left the hospital and Mission for graduate study towards nurse practitioner training. The Mission Board decided to employ a part-time executive director, and began the search for a licensed professional nurse with administrative experience.

Meanwhile, my husband Frank and I were facing a serious financial challenge. Our investment accounts were sliding and our future at the Landings was threatened. Frank declared we could not afford to live at the Landings any longer.[21] He wanted to move, but he had no idea where we might move to. I definitely did not want to move. I had moved enough and I loved the Landings and all the friends I had made. I told Frank I would get a part time job; I love to work, I am not afraid. I had been earning extra money through the years in Savannah by virtue of collaborative projects at Jefferson Medical College. However, it was apparently not enough. It was OK with me, I had no babies anymore and I had worked all my life just as every other woman in my family had done.

I read the job description in the *Savannah Morning News* and decided to explore the employment opportunity. Frank was still not happy about the idea, as he believed we needed to move, but he still had no idea of where to move. I was determined not to move again, I wanted to stay where we were in Savannah. I loved our home and the life we had entered.

---

21 I did not know of the full financial significance of our living costs at the Landings, especially his golfing expenses.

I knew Shirley Johnson, the nurse on the Mission Board responsible for recruitment to the director position. I had worked with Shirley through the Shepherd Lectureship project at Memorial Hospital the year before. Shirley knew well how creative, passionate, and energetic I was and suggested I visit the Mission one evening soon. I was excited about the opportunity. Having worked for years so effectively in collaboration with physicians I thought I knew "how physicians think." After visiting the clinic just one evening I was able to identify the most significant problems; I felt confident in my ability to take on the challenge and Shirley agreed.

She recommended me to Dr. Goldsmith. I was invited to interview with the Board members where I described my philosophy of patient care and social commitment to the importance of quality and equality in access to health care, as well as my extensive experience in grant writing. After all, the most important part of my job at first would be to raise enough money to pay myself a salary. I would need to recruit more volunteer and retired physicians and nurses for the Thursday night clinic. I don't know that anyone else applied for the job, but I got it and was appointed Executive Director. A news article describing my appointment was published and I was interviewed on the radio, which attracted a few more volunteers and some cash contributions.

In October, 1999, I watched as 30 or more adults and children gathered outside the Ear Institute waiting in the cold autumn air for the ENT patients within to exit the building. Only then could the new patients with specific or generalized health complaints enter through the side door, sign in, and wait to be called for an interview and hopefully some treatment. It was a depressing sight; I told the Board I thought it was inhumane. But what was even worse was the knowledge that there was sometimes no physician available when the patients lined up and possibly only one or two physicians on the way at 5:30 or maybe even 6 p.m. There was one Hospital employed professional nurse, who came after work and volunteered to conduct examinations for patients, although she was not a certified nurse practitioner. There were very few masters-prepared and certified nurse practitioners in Savannah at that time and they were already employed in physician offices or at a community center. I tried contacting the local Nurse Practitioner organization, and attended their meetings and continuing education conferences in order to try to recruit some volunteers for our evening clinic. But, I had no luck as everyone was already overworked. There were some volunteer generalist physicians but no regularly scheduled providers. Some nights when Dr. Goldsmith or Dr. Rogers were not available and no other volunteer physician appeared we nurses tried to determine patients' needs, however most of the patients needed more than we could provide. Often a trip to the ER was recommended or return to the Mission in hopes of finding additional physicians the following week.

According to the established system non-medical professionals interviewed everyone on the line to generally verify financial eligibility for the clinic; essentially it was no insurance coverage. Retired volunteer nurses attempted to uncover patient complaints and triage for severity of needs. Some patients were treated for simple problems with over-the-counter drugs, while others were given donated sample prescription drugs according to protocols established. It was getting colder outside; clearly we needed an indoor waiting area with seating protected from the elements, so I brought the line into the lobby of the Medical Education auditorium next door to the Institute, handed out numbers and searched for chairs. We needed both to develop a system for establishing appointments and to formalize a system for physician and nurse recruitment and scheduling. I had a lot of work to do. I had my own theme to share so I had book marks and prescription note packets printed up with: "Love Thy Neighbor as Thyself." What could be more ecumenical?

It was very important to review and expand the fund-raising activities. I wrote an article about the clinic for the local Skidaway Island weekly newsmagazine. As the lines outside became longer I set out to recruit more volunteers, first from the people I knew on Skidaway Island. Several retired physicians, nurses and teachers among my bridge friends, my golf friends, my book club friends, and my Jewish Women of the Landings (JWOL) friends responded.

a free
healthcare
clinic

Savannah Health Mission Brochure.

Most professional volunteers came to clinic after their normal work schedule during the day, so we served casual supper during the clinic hours starting at 5:30 after the ENT patients completed their treatment. Some did not think food was necessary, but I believed strongly that we needed to provide food for volunteers. I sent letters on Mission stationery (which listed the distinguished members of the Mission Board) to the various local restaurants and caterers in Savannah emphasizing that the food was offered for the ten to 15 volunteers at the clinic each week, not the patients. Two JWOL friends, Janet and Anna, agreed to orchestrate contributions of suppers each night. They arranged to pick up prepared food each week from contributing restaurants or with the help of other friends, actually prepared the food themselves. We ate a lot of pizza, deli sandwiches, lasagna, manicotti, and stuffed shells. Sitting down together for the light supper offered in the small kitchen of the Ear Institute, professionals and non-professionals were family, chatting away and sharing stories and some nights even jokes, especially from Dr. Steve Rogers; he was a hoot. We became friends and colleagues as we cared for and about the patients we served. Sometimes, we did not finish the clinic service until 9 p.m. The clinic prospered, due in part to all our many generous friends who donated their time, talent, and money.

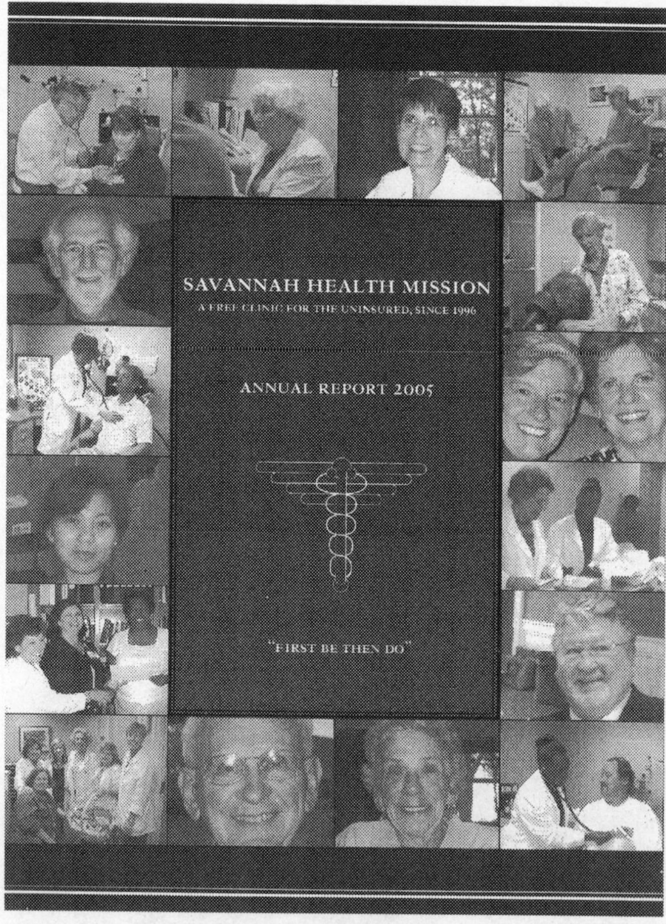

Mission Newsletter Annual Report 2005

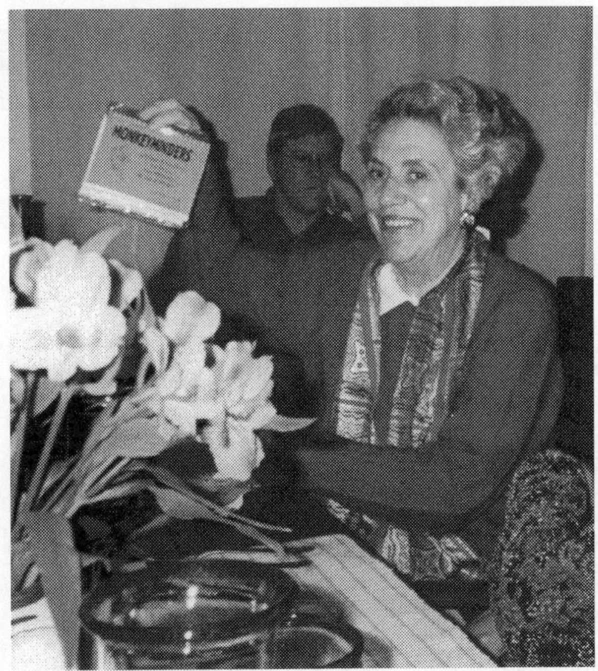

Susan Cohen, Pharmacy Assistant for the Mission.

I needed someone to help obtain and organize donated drugs and I hoped one of the pharmacists at the hospital would help out, but the director indicated they were understaffed and he could not find anyone to volunteer. When I could not find a retired pharmacist or pharmacy student to help us, I appealed to Susan Cohen, a retired chemical engineer who had taken bridge lessons with me. "Susan," I said, "you told me you were bored and needed a challenge. Well, chemists work with formulas, and drugs have formulas, you can become the Mission pharmacist." She looked at me as though I was crazy. "It is really interesting and I don't need a registered professional pharmacist. Come down Thursday night, meet community volunteers, the doctors and nurses and some of the patients and observe the operation. When you see the disorganized cartons of contributed drugs you will understand what needs to be done first and recognize the contribution you could make. Many of the pharmaceutical companies are offering assistance to low-income citizens and they particularly wanted to help those who are working and trying to help themselves." Susan liked the idea of doing service and making a difference for the community, as we all did. She came to my office the next afternoon and I showed her one closet I had organized and the storage room filled with boxes. She looked at the disorganized mess of donated drugs that had accumulated in the storage room and started to work cleaning out the shelves by discarding outdated contributions. She agreed to go with me to buy a workman's rolling tool storage cart at Sears Roebuck so we could bring supplies and our commonly ordered drugs for immediate care. She spent hours studying the uses for each drug in our supply and organized them on the rolling cart we bought. Susan then applied to the various pharmaceutical houses for information about their free patient drugs, and kept meticulous paper and computerized records of what was ordered and what was received and distributed to individual patients. During the afternoons patients came to our office so that Susan could help them to complete the necessary financial information on the application forms and ensure each patient's signature. Every company's forms were different and more confusing than the next. (Susan had emigrated to the United States after World War II from Slovakia, having survived the holocaust, hidden by the nuns in a Lutheran Orphanage. Later under Communism she was educated as a chemical engineer.) She showed much empathy for our poor sick patients in her accented English and they all appreciated her interest, patience and caring. In return Susan appreciated the small hourly salary I managed to offer her; she found special meaning in her life through the appreciation she received from all the professional and volunteer staff as well as the patients.

Susan was invaluable, as was Myrna Doerfler, a retired accountant who became the clinic's bookkeeper. (I think she was making up to me for the accidental rib fractures I sustained when she took her foot off the brake on a windy day while driving our golf cart on the Marshwood course.) Two years later when Myrna's vision began to fail and she required special treatments, Theresa Sullivan, another bridge buddy of mine, took over as bookkeeper, bringing her husband Joe Morgan with her to the clinic. Joe found a new community interest by organizing and maintaining the clinic charts and supplies, and guiding patients through the admission process. While some of our tasks could be accomplished by volunteers, not all allowed the same degree of flexibility as others. There were several teachers, social workers and counselors like Carol Bowen and Mollie Stone, (the wedding cake maker) who came often and couples who volunteered together; i.e., Anne and Ziggy Hudson and Jacquie and Joel Spevack, who came fairly regularly like the Hudsons, two retired Armstrong faculty who had been volunteering since the clinic was first established. I cannot begin to tell how much all these volunteers contributed, and how much I appreciated their support and friendship.

I realized we needed a currently licensed professional part-time nurse with the time and flexibility to work some regular daytime hours to help me answer the phone, respond to phone messages, and triage by interview prospective patients over the phone. The nurse needed to be capable of providing general medical information to callers and scheduling specialty appointments, as well as assist some physicians with procedures on Thursday evenings during clinic hours. It was necessary for me to expand my grant writing in order to raise additional funds to support this position. We were receiving many referred patients from the health department, various physician offices across the county and the expanding J.C. Lewis Homeless Facility.

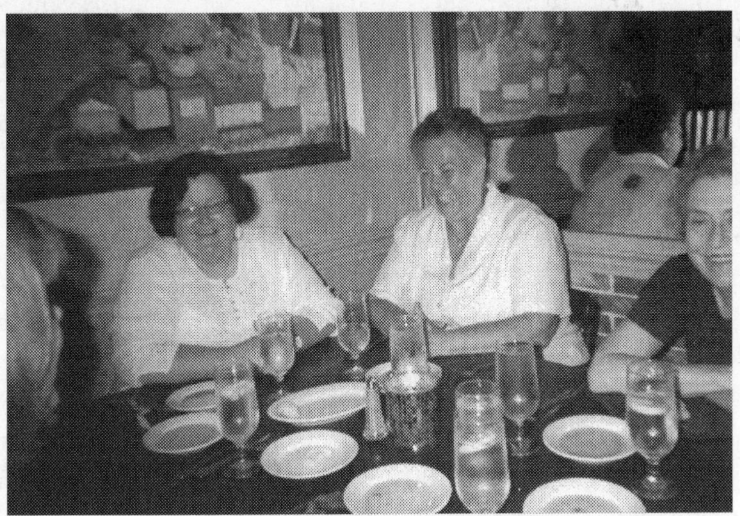

Staff; Zellie, RN & Veronica Reitz

Volunteer Nurses Louise Quirk and Anne Lyon raise funds with 9 Hole Golf Tournament. (Courtesy of Louise)

I am not sure how it happened but one day Veronica Reitz showed up to volunteer. Veronica was not a licensed nurse, but she was a certified home health aide with years of patient experience, and a "jack-of-all trades." Finding the right nurse to work our diversified part-time hours was not easy but often Veronica could help out. Several nurses came and went until finally Zellie Wise joined the Mission staff, as part-time Nurse Facilitator. Zellie, who had completed her BSN degree, also had a good sense of humor and was fun to work with. Having these two individuals on board made every day exciting.

As a result of the networking that was occurring, volunteers appeared from various sources. Steve, a minister counseling AIDS patients in a Methadone Clinic, needed a licensed Neurologist or Neurosurgeon to document the mental and physical limitations of one of his patients in order for the patient to obtain authorization for Medicaid assistance. I was able to recruit John, a member of my monthly Couples bridge group at the Landings, who had recently retired as chairman of the neurology department at Columbia University Medical Center in New York City, to come to our Mission and conduct the required neurological assessment without an office visit fee. His letter, on our stationery affirming the disability of this patient was accepted by the Social Security Department. The patient's medical expenses for the cocktail of anti-viral drugs and the Methadone were then covered. In appreciation, Steve offered to come to the Mission office and help input patient treatment data into our computer during clinic. There were several other volunteers who helped enter patient care data including Gail, a golfing partner of mine and Elizabeth Sprague, one of our Board Members.

Through the efforts of our Board members many new volunteers were recruited and all kinds of fund-raising activities were spawned. For example Paula Reynolds was an established real estate broker on Skidaway Island I knew who had graduated from medical school years before, but left a residency to raise her children and was now continuing her education toward a Master of Public Health Degree. I asked Paula to join our Mission Board. She had told me that most Real Estate brokers or associates were independent entrepreneurs and only those with years of experience were able to afford private health care insurance. "They know the problems of the uninsured," Paula said, and she arranged a lottery that was promoted by brokers throughout the region. She knew how to fund-raise. Paula and her colleagues solicited many fantastic prizes and travel deals that generated several thousand dollars over a short period, all for the benefit of the Savannah Health Mission.

John Porter, another Board member and financial consultant, asked me to speak to the Skidaway Island Rotary Club in order to get their financial support. I received so much enthusiasm John recommended I join the Club. I did not know much about Rotary International before I joined, but I soon learned about the magnificent work of the organization internationally and the fun activities we developed locally; my activities and financial contribution benefitted both organizations, for Rotary not just locally, but special projects regionally like a library in Haiti and second-hand medical equipment collected locally and distributed internationally. I was particularly interested in the world-wide efforts for Polio eradication and support we provided for a local Post-Polio group. Since our mission budget could not readily support my membership, and although my personal finances were very limited I agreed to contribute my own funds. Our Mission and several other social agencies I supported, such as "Safe Shelter" for abused women, benefitted from the black tie annual dinner dance and Mardi Gras event sponsored by Rotary, where fun gambling took place in Plantation Club at the Landings. A whole new life opportunity was opened for me. Before long I was speaking to Rotary groups all over the city, and participating in various volunteer activities supported by our chapter, especially at DeRenne Middle School, where we were partners in trying to help improve the outcomes of the public school education. In a program on Careers, I introduced several classes to medicine and nursing and other diverse new medical careers. I had fun partnering with Phil, one of the other Rotary members as we taught finances to several classes in the Junior Achievement program. Unfortunately the after-school hours of computer tutoring for individual students were often frustrating, but that is another story.

As a Rotarian with a medical background I took foreign students studying at Armstrong Atlantic State University (AASU) under Rotary Scholarships (GRSP) to meet fragile premature babies on the neonatal unit, older children with life-threatening diseases at the Memorial Children's Hospital and their families at the Ronald McDonald House for a holiday party and gift giving. The students were introduced to critical medical situations and life experiences they had never had before or might never have again. One year I received a beautiful letter from the parents in Sweden of one GRSP student expressing deep appreciation for the meaningful learning experience their son had received with an eight-year-old victim of leukemia scheduled for transplant who we learned later did not survive.

Recruiting new Board members was an ongoing dynamic process. Fortunately as year-long terms ended, we were able to attract new members, who often came enthusiastically with innovative ideas for increasing funds and expanding activities. Alice Jepson (Mrs. Robert Jepson) was a tremendously positive influence; she taught me and our team how to increase income by encouraging new contributors with the challenge of matching contributions. Alice participated in every event, contributing whatever she could and always hanging in to help clean up at the end. This beautiful and elegant woman became my friend and supporter. She and her husband continue to stand out as models of generosity for our city through significant contributions to the arts, education, and health care, especially for our clinic while I was involved.

Alice Jepson, Board of Directors member

Robert & Alice Jepson: significant contributors
(From the archives of Telfair Museums: Courtesy of Katherine Alt)

When Father Joe Smith, who had facilitated a regular monthly continuing contribution of $500 to the Mission left our Board to move to another parish outside our county, I was worried St. James Church might not continue the contribution, so I approached the rabbi of Mickve Israel Reform Synagogue (the third oldest Jewish synagogue in the U.S., established in 1733 where I was a member,) for the opportunity to address the congregation. He arranged that address for Thanksgiving Day, when all the downtown spiritual centers rotate worshiping together. It was Mickve Israel's turn and the chapel was packed with congregants and guests from the entire downtown Savannah historic district. Although not the tradition for most Jewish services, on this occasion, the hats were indeed passed, and the contributions certainly came in. Following the service and my presentation there was a lovely reception with sweets given by the Sisterhood of the temple. After that event Rabbi Belzer became a regular member of the Mission Board along with Reverend John Anderson, Memorial Hospital chaplain, to provide spiritual partnership.

There were many other volunteers who helped us develop ways to assist patients with specific problems requiring medical specialists. The dental hygienist examined the patients with mouth and/or dental complaints and consulted with Dr. Gerald Kramer, our volunteer dentist. He provided her with a protocol for prescription drugs (antibiotics and/or analgesics,) for patients with infections and/or pain and made referrals to other cooperating dentists for extraction and/or treatment on extended financial plans.

We were able to recruit other specialist physician volunteers who came to the clinic periodically for patient evaluation and follow-up or who agreed to see some patients in their offices. There were several orthopedic and plastic surgeons who were willing to take patient referrals from our primary care medical group, and because so many of our patients were diabetics, we developed an agreement with local podiatrists for free or regular discounted podiatric care. I made arrangements with the Georgia Eye Institute to provide examination space and technical assistance one afternoon each month to volunteer ophthalmologist, Dr.

Hank Croci. Upon his referral, our diabetic patients and others with significant retinal problems were able to receive follow-up treatment by specialists arranged under financial plans at the Georgia Eye Institute.

Many of our female patients needed assessment and preventive care such as mammography and/or Pap smears. Dr. Frank Collier retired OB/GYN and his wife Patricia, a retired Women's Health Nurse Practitioner, (who in the 1970s had been a student of mine in the graduate program at SUNY Stony Brook) came to help each week. Since our Ear Institute ENT examination tables were unsuited for GYN exams the Colliers were given space down the hall where the Residents held their GYN clinics during the day. Some patients with serious problems were referred by Dr. Collier to the GYN Residents clinic. Patients needing Mammography were referred to the County Health Department Facility or South Coast Imaging, where my friend Dr. Patty Shapiro was the director.

Health education and prevention was a major theme of our Mission and the Colliers provided as much education as they could. However, patients requesting specific family planning support were for the most part referred to Planned Parenthood.

Crisis and Opportunity

The salary I earned working part time at the Mission helped ease our financial stress at home, at least for a while. I was optimistic; I thought we would be OK, until my husband Frank's emotional health deteriorated further. The day he came in from a round of golf and announced that he would not be playing in his regular games with his old pals, because he was no longer good enough, was the beginning of the end of his happiness at the Landings. He went downhill physically and emotionally. Frank was depressed, his diabetes progressed, he labored just to walk, and against my wishes he smoked openly on the back porch.

Sometimes when he might have been playing golf, Frank sat inside and played solitaire. He decided that he could not live at the Landings anymore; he found it too debilitating to be in this environment without the ability to enjoy it as he once had. He was determined to move. And at the end of 2002, after seventeen years together, including conflict the last two, although we both knew we loved each other, Frank moved to Virginia near his daughters. ***He moved without me, while I could not move with him.***

I took it hard, I cried and cried and before he left I begged him to reconsider. But I was angry and hurt. Golf had become more important to him than my welfare. I had moved with him to Savannah, giving up a position at **JMC** I loved and our friends and happy life in Philadelphia. It had meant a significant decrease in the potential pension I would have received in three more years. I asked my primary care physician for a psychological referral. My normally low systolic blood pressure shot up over 200, requiring hospitalization for a few days. I thought I was really having a heart attack, but a stress test showed my heart was OK.

My lawyer said, "Sell the house, you can't afford to live there alone." But I was determined to stay. I went to see Dr. Fay, the psychologist I was referred to. I told him the story of my life, and how successful I had been professionally, but what lousy luck I had in my personal life. "What can I do? I am almost seventy years old. I don't have enough money to stay here alone. What will I do?"

Dr. Fay responded with the message I had heard more than twenty five years before**.**

"Sylvia, you have been a problem-solver all your life, you will figure it out."

I had learned that you have to decide which of your life goals cannot be compromised. I had devoted all my life to caring for others, including my husbands, my children, and my parents. I had committed to providing quality patient care, and for all of my professional successes, I could not do for the husband I loved what I had spent my career teaching to others. I could not get him to listen to his doctors, to eat with his health in mind, to stop smoking, and I could not get him to enjoy exercise and music in our beautiful home and its lovely surroundings. He was just too depressed to be able to be happy around me.

I went home and I looked around. I thought about my work at the Mission. I felt good about what I had achieved there in the few years, and who I had become as a result of my life's work. This life and this home was where I was happy and I could not give it up. In order to start my life over again as a newly single woman, I poured myself into the Savannah Health Mission.

I believed in Dr. Goldsmith's theme, "First Be, Then Do." I had loved and lived my theme, "Love Thy Neighbor as Thyself." And I knew I had to fulfill my dream, "To be what we are and to become what we are capable of becoming is the only end in life."

I had many ideas to increase the Mission income so I could double my earnings and I prepared a plan to develop the activities necessary for my objectives that did not encroach on the daily medical practice at the Georgia Ear Institute. I told Dr. Goldsmith about my personal problems and asked for his support in changing my position to a full-time one, so I could refinance my house. I had worked for fifty years and I had never missed a mortgage payment. I had borrowed and I had paid back all those fifty years.

At the same time I needed to refocus and expand our program for our patient population with what I believed were important health maintenance services. It was not enough for our patients to receive medical attention; we needed to really focus on *prevention and education.* The Board agreed, and with their backing I convinced Memorial to provide us with $25,000 of financial help annually and more physical assistance in terms of referrals for specialty care.

I dreamed up a project that could be established at the clinic during the day as well as in the evening, and I wrote more grant applications including a major request to the national Episcopal Foundation with the support of the local bishop of the Savannah Episcopal Church. I called the project: **Project HOPE: *Health, Opportunity, Prevention, and Education.***

The Foundation responded positively. What we really needed to do was teach our patients to change their debilitating behaviors and avoid the conditions that brought them to us in the first place. Project HOPE was a special personalized wellness project that taught health, nutrition, exercise, and even non-traditional methods of prevention such as meditation. Smoking became our target; funds were allocated for special stop smoking activities. I refused to give patients free drugs unless they agreed to follow our stop smoking guidelines. I made arrangements for our patients to participate in Memorial's fitness program that was open all day; a few did. I was the role model of health promotion. "You only have one body, you can't abuse it, you must take care of it, if not you who else?" I cried. We did exercises together in the chair. "Let's move" and when it was quiet we marched those patients who could through the halls of the hospital in the evening for exercise. We also helped pay for transportation to the clinic in the evening when transportation was a problem. Specialists were brought in to provide alternative techniques. Different weight loss programs were reviewed, but we used the model of Weight Watchers Inc. Patients learned to read food labels, recipes were shared, and low-cost healthy meals were prepared together. We encouraged healthy snacks of fresh fruit and vegetables, and we had a lot of fun in the process during the program.

At the end of a twelve-week program we had a graduation "SPA" event. One of our clinic patients who had studied massage therapy came to give chair-side back massages for relaxation and pain relief. Another clinic patient who completed a pedicure program came with appropriate equipment to give pedicures. Lancôme Cosmetics representatives at Belk's Department Store whom I befriended gave facials and applied make-up and distributed samples of products. We shared special healthy treats. It was a wonderful evening everyone enjoyed. Graduation Certificates were given. Then at the end of the year, I was very surprised when Savannah Health Mission was honored by The United Way with a beautiful plaque as "Community Organization of the Year." I brought the plaque back to the Ear Institute for Dr. Goldsmith. He was the one who deserved to be honored: "We Did Something!"

The first week of May 2006 was the third Robert Wood Johnson Foundation "Cover the Uninsured Week" to emphasize our national crisis in health care. The Mission celebrated a decade of helping the uninsured with a marvelous celebration on May 7th in the Savannah Civic Center to thank all the volunteers and contributors who had sustained Chip's vision. Sonny Dixon of WTOC hosted and Ben Tucker and students from the Savannah Arts Academy Orchestra and Chorus provided music. A silent auction was held to increase the funds raised to keep the Mission alive.

Fran Levow organized a large group she and I recruited of "Celebrity Chefs" among Savannah's medical profession and highly regarded caterers dressed in contributed white jackets and tall chef hats offered the most elegant gourmet food and served their specialties. Alice and Bob Jepson contributed wine from their California winery and Alice stayed with us until the end of the party helping to clean up. It was a marvelous event, and we raised a several thousand dollars for the clinic programs.

Meanwhile the problem of access to health care was the main topic of political discussion all over the country. Massachusetts had recently passed an innovative health care plan to cover almost everyone, based on proposals that called for an individual mandate to purchase insurance, with government support for citizens not eligible for Medicaid or Medicare, and unable to pay a reasonable premium amount. This was exactly our clinic population so I was invited to join a community panel of medical experts for a discussion at the main Chatham County Public Library on Bull Street on "Health Care and the Uninsured." The auditorium was packed. I spoke about my many years in health care and how so many were unable to be helped. I described how the problems we currently had were the same problems we had throughout the twentieth century, except that then, many more people had died, not just from wars, but because they did not have access to preventive health care or treatments we have available now, although if you are poor, live in a rural area and your skin is shaded you don't have the same opportunities to live healthy.

More creativity on this complex problem was called for during the 2008 presidential election that focused on the more than 50 million people without access to health care, amid escalating health care costs. The Affordable Care Act (ACA) developed by Congress under the model of the Massachusetts Act was introduced and later signed by President Barack Obama in 2010. Citizens are no longer denied insurance for care because of preexisting conditions, the children of those with insurance are covered under their parents' policies up to the age twenty six, and workers do not have to give up their health insurance when they wish to change their jobs. The debates have continued despite the constitutionality of most of the components of the Act being upheld by the Supreme Court. There is still much to do, but it is better than what we had before. I do not understand the thinking of those who object to the provisions of the Affordable Care Act. In the long run those people who are now able to get insurance for health care are for the most part now able to work and maintain their health.

We helped a lot of people who came to the Savannah Health Mission. For example, we helped Jan S of Wilmington Island, who became uninsured at fifty three, when she needed health care most. Her story was described in the *Savannah Morning News*. After a midlife divorce with accompanying loss of health benefits, she was seriously depressed and losing her vision from uncontrolled diabetes and hypertension. Working as a housekeeper, she could not afford the physician office visits, nor her necessary drugs and supplies. After she was referred by her physician to Savannah Health Mission, we were able to provide medical supervision and help her with her prescription drugs. Jan became part of Project HOPE, to learn as much as she could about how to live successfully with her chronic illness. With all the teasing and kibitzing that went on with our group, Jan began to join in; she started to laugh. She was challenged and remarkable. The weight came off slowly but it did not take so long for the blood pressure to drop. Meanwhile her vision loss stabilized. Within the year she was back to creative painting, and her art was soon displayed at a downtown gallery. In a little while she had hope and enthusiasm for living again.

After my husband Frank became ill and depressed and left Savannah in 2003, I found significant personal satisfaction in my work with the patients, staff, volunteers, and board members of the Savannah Health Mission who had all become my friends. Eventually our clinic merged with another clinic in Savannah that could offer daytime hours. I worked to effect a seamless merger and then voluntarily relinquished my position to the director of the other clinic and stepped aside. Today, it is not unusual for me to go into town and meet one of our former patients, who always manage to say thank-you for the caring way they were treated. I am reminded not how exhausted we were at the end of the evening, but how much we felt appreciated.

Acknowledgements for Savannah Health Mission at the Georgia Ear Institute 1996-2006

On behalf of all the patients who received care at the Mission, Thank you to all the following

Board of Directors

M. Miles Goldsmith, III, MD, FACS (President); Don L. Waters, ESQ (Treasurer); Shirley Johnson, RN, MSA (Secretary); Jo-Beth Allen; Rev. John G. Anderson; Rabbi Arnold M. Belzer; Ray Gaskin, MD; Hugh Hale, III; Alice A. Jepson; Lester B. Johnson, III, ESQ; Mimi S. Jones; Hon. Jack Kingston; J.C. Lewis, III ESQ; Barbara M. Murphy; John E. Porter, III; Paula Reynolds, MD; Stephen Rogers, MD; Tom Scardino; Father Joseph Smith; Elizabeth C. Sprague; Sylvia K. Fields, EdD, RN (Executive Director)

Clinic Staff

Zellie Wise, RN, BS

Susan Cohen, MS Pharmacy Assistant

Jane Seeker, Clerical Assistant; Carol Bowen, MS, Counselor

Nancy Gallagher, RDH; Director Dental Service,

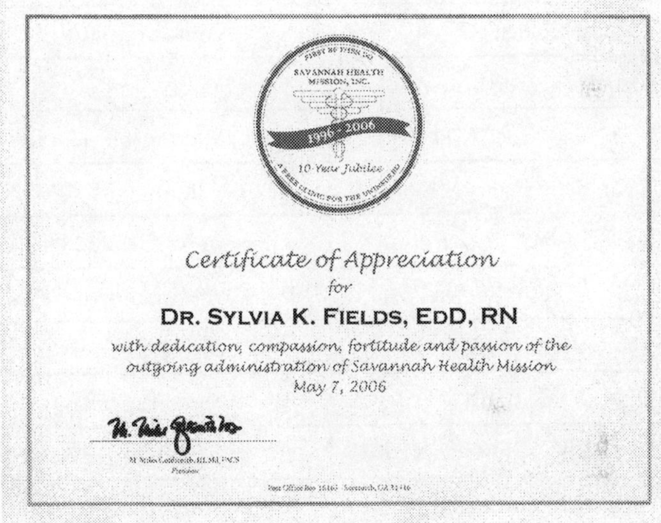

SAVANNAH HEALTH MISSION, INC.

1996 – 2006

10 Year Jubilee

Certificate of Appreciation

for

DR. SYLVIA K. FIELDS, EdD, RN

with dedication, compassion, fortitude and passion of the outgoing administration of Savannah Health Mission

May 7, 2006

I receive appreciation plaque at the 10th Anniversary Dinner Celebration

Volunteer Medical Staff	Volunteer Nurses and Medical Assistants
Stephen Allen, MD	Virginia Dooley, RN
Cindy Carter, MD	Frances Dotton, RN, PHD
Frank Collier, MD	Judy Hobson, RN
Patricia Collier, RN, NP	Anne Lyon, RN
Nicholas V. Costrini, MD	Louise Quirk, RN
Henry Croci, MD	Sally Perkins Johnson, RN
Kimberly Crute, MD	Shirley Johnson, RN, MSN
Charles "Chad" Foster, MD	Beverly McCamman, RN
Shaun Franklin, MD	Wayne McHowell, RN
Ray Gaskin, MD	Jerlyn Moore, RN
M. Miles Goldsmith, III, MD, FACS	Sheila Page, RN
Ann Hallock, DNP, ANP	Gail Quinn, RN
Donna Knight, PA	Ann Scott, RN
Joseph Nettles, MD	Nancy Tesinsky, RN
Jeff Oberdick, NP	Cynthia Weber, RN
Lorraine Pare', MD	Charmaine West, RN
Stephen Rogers, MD	
Tomoral Sams, DMD	
Irwin Streiff, MD	

Non-Medical Volunteers		
Cheri Acree	Louise Howard	Peter Paar
Anna Barbo (food coordinator)	Ann & Sigmund Hudson	Marion Paquin
Janet Basseches (food coordinator)	Safi Ingram	Doug Powelson (IT)
Myrna Doerflier (Bookeeper)	La Wanda E. Johnson	Veronica Reitz
Theresa S. Morgan (Bookeeper)	Lee Kulbreth	Rev. Steven Schulte
Keith Douglass	Gail Levasseur	Joel Spivak
Linda Fidler	Susan Lokey	Jackie Spivak
Mary Friday	Wilson Miles	Elizabeth C. Sprague
Jean Giblin	Becky Milmine	Mollie Stone
Justin Goldberg	Joseph Morgan	Debbie Usher
Joe Green	Barbara Murphy	Claire Waters
Carlton Hodges, CPA, (Accountant)	Donna Miliatedes	

Community Health Providers Who Accepted SHM Patients In Their Offices		
Stephen Acuff, DDS	Philip Flexon, MD	Mark Murphy, MD
Joseph Alpert, MD	Lloyd S. Goodman, MD	Robert Rollings, MD
Roy P. Baker, MD	Juha Jaakkola, MD	Matthew Rosenthal, DMD
James Bazemore, MD	James Judy	Julia Routhier, DDS
Randolph Bishop, MD	Mark Kameleson, MD	Ray Rudolph, MD
Tucker Brawner, DPM	Woo Kent, MD	Tomoral Sams, DMD
Nicholas V. Costrini, MD	Diana Kim, DDS	C. K. Scala, DPM
Dale Daley, MD	Gerald Kramer, DDS	Patricia Shapiro, MD
Frank Davis, III, MD	James A. Lindley, Jr., MD	Steven Shapiro, MD
William Degenhart, MD	James Robert Logan, MD	John Spellman, MD
Mathew Deich, MD	Alan Lord, MD	Anthony Sussman, MD
H. Clark Deriso, MD	Julia Mikell, MD	Edward J. Whelan, III, MD
Kevin Kickison, DDS	Jackson Morgan, DDS	James A. Yeckley, MD

Image of Florence Nightingale reflects her historical importance and title often given “Mother of Professional Nursing. ” Also known as “The Lady With the Lamp” who led the development of high-quality nursing care and saved many lives during the Crimean War. http://www.loc.gov/pictures/item2004672058/

17

Research and Scholarship: Return to Nursing Education

"Let us never consider ourselves finished nurses – we must be learning all our lives."

Florence Nightingale

Research and Scholarship Award

One dark cold rainy October evening in 2003, more than fifty years after I started the nursing program at Adelphi University, I was honored as I accepted the *Research and Scholarship Award* from the Nursing Education Alumni Association (NEAA) of Teachers College, Columbia University, and was inducted into the T.C. Hall of Fame. Over a twenty-five-year period I had earned my BSN and three graduate degrees from Columbia while teaching and raising three children. My career had been exciting and productive, and I had lived an adventurous and meaningful life up to that time. I had retired from my full-time position at Jefferson Medical College but I loved my work, so I had maintained a research interest by telecommuting. However, I thought my academic career was probably coming to an end.

At that October ceremony my accomplishments over the years were acknowledged, including the most recent story of my role at the Savannah Health Mission. Many of my former colleagues, known leaders of the nursing profession who had also received their graduate degrees from T.C., were there that night. I had invited my New York family members daughter Melissa and Ami Steinfeld and closest long-time friends Rebecca and Louis Fierro and Millicent and Lenny Kramer, as well as in-laws Rob and Roz Fields to witness the award ceremony. I was glowing, and not just from the wine; everyone there was very proud of me too.

During the presentation my doctoral dissertation was noted as the foundation for a life-long commitment to interdisciplinary and interprofessional education, research, and collaborative service in the community. Jon Veloski, Director of Medical Education research at Jefferson Medical College, a long-time colleague and friend, along with his wife Judy, a University of Pennsylvania graduate nurse, had contributed to the award recommendation by Dr. Keville Frederickson, Chair of the NEAA Awards Committee.

Jon wrote, *"Dr. Fields continues to serve as a role model for interdisciplinary professional education and practice as she currently leads a free health care clinic for the uninsured and consults on educational evaluation projects…her career reflects her courage and commitment to reach beyond nursing's boundary to design new approaches to nursing (and medical) education, scholarship, and research."*

What excited me most about his recommendation however was his next statement, *"Sylvia's work at the Savannah Health Mission belongs to that long and honorable tradition of nursing education that began with Florence Nightingale. I believe that Sylvia's leadership in the Mission provides an important example of how nursing, social service and medicine can be united in a fruitful partnership. It springs from the true compassion and knowledge of active citizens, and thus points to what is best in our American society."*

Of course, I cannot really accept Jon's comparison of me to Florence Nightingale, but it certainly excited me that October evening, and all the years later, because I knew intuitively then that the award was not the end of my career. It was the beginning (I was not finished then and I am not finished now!)

Florence Nightingale, well educated by her father through the Classics, known as the "Lady with a Lamp," and the "Mother of

Professional Nursing," was my professional idol through all these years. Her courage in entering nursing against her father's wishes as I had done when I was just sixteen stood out in my mind, although I was nowhere as educationally prepared to make a difference as she was. She knew the lives and work of the ancient Greeks and Romans, translated the works of Plato and others, and defined good moral character and virtue as attained through *Education*, not technical training, as the foundation of overall human success, happiness and the welfare of the community[22] (According to my mother, I did not even know how to sew a button on straight.) But I had goals like Florence, and I was willing to keep working my way up.

Florence has been credited with political action, using her contacts as she aimed for improved sanitary practices in hospitals, public health facilities, and formal education for nurses. Her many efforts to promote public health, especially through the collection of significant outcome statistics and secular nurse education, became a model for the United States and the rest of the world. Perhaps Florence should be best recognized, however, for her role in promoting continuing and expanding education. "***Let us never consider ourselves finished nurses – we must be learning all of our lives.***"[23]

---

[22] (Lachman, V.D., "Strategies Necessary for Moral Courage" OJIN: the Online Journal of Issues in Nursing Vol. 15, No.3, and Manuscript 3. DOI; 10.3912/AJIN.Vol 15.No.03.Man.03).

[23] Nightingale, F. (2012) Florence Nightingale to her Nurses. (Originally published in 1914) Forgotten Books. Retrieved from www.forgottenbooks.org.

Dr. Christine Coughlin (Secretary of Teachers College Alumni (2003) presents me with the Teachers College Columbia Alumni Award for Scholarship and Research [24] 2003.

NURSING HALL OF FAME

Teachers College Columbia University

2003

In Recognition and Appreciation
of your Extraordinary Contribution to the Nursing Profession

Sylvia K. Fields

Inducted at the Awards Ceremony on October 2, 2003 in New York City

Diane Jons-Mancino, President
Nursing Education Alumni Association

I am admitted to Teachers College Columbia Nursing Alumni Distinguished Hall of Fame 2003.

---

[24] October, 2003 Christine Coughlin EdD, RN was Chief Nursing Officer/Vice President Patient Care Services, New York United Hospital Medical Center. Currently she is Associate Professor College of Nursing & Public Health Adelphi University, Garden City, NY

Alix Steinfeld graduates from SUNY at Stony Brook 2002.

ARMSTRONG STATE UNIVERSITY[25]

Five years following the Research and Scholarship Award Ceremony, not too long after the original Savannah Mission merged with another free clinic in town and I was unemployed, a TV advertisement by the Robert Wood Johnson Foundation caught my eye:

"A Shortage of Nursing Faculty Predicts a Serious Shortage of Professional Nurses for the Immediate Future."

The doors were being closed; applicants to nursing programs across the country were being placed on waiting lists because there were not enough qualified nursing faculty to teach in the classrooms, on the hospital floors, in our schools, or in our community centers, and few were in the pipeline forward, the commentary said. It was 2008.

25 Formerly Armstrong Atlantic State University

This was happening just as the country was debating and the nursing profession was preparing more action to address our nation's most pressing health care challenges: *access, quality, and cost.* Students were not entering graduate programs in nursing to be prepared for teaching. In fact, few graduate programs were being offered in nursing for teacher preparation. Most nurses were entering graduate programs at the master's level to prepare for advanced practice roles as clinical specialists, nurse anesthetists, nurse practitioners, and nurse midwives.

This was by no means the first time I had heard this plea for more faculty, but it was the first time I was not already employed or completely involved with other independent professional obligations. I thought to myself – ***they need me***. ***Why not return to teaching?*** I am available. I might be able to teach one or two courses. But then I hesitated, maybe not – it had been almost 30years since I last taught a course in nursing – yet, why not? I had stayed active in community health care practice at the Mission and was an avid reader who maintained my continuing professional education through the American Nurses Association (ANA) and various sources of public and professional health-related literature.

I called the office of the Department of Nursing at the nearby Armstrong Atlantic State University (AASU) to explore the feasibility of returning to nursing education after almost 30 years. I asked about part-time teaching opportunities, and was told by the secretary that although she did not think there were any part-time positions open, she was certain the chairperson would want to meet me. She insisted on making an appointment for the following afternoon.

The next day I was in the department chairperson's office sharing my curriculum vitae and being interviewed. I learned there were no part-time positions available until the spring, but they were desperate for a faculty member with my qualifications now. Before I knew it, I had called Teachers College for my transcripts. When I called Adelphi, I joked as I spoke to the secretary in the Registrar's office, "I was there from 1950 to 1954. Do you still have my records or were they archived some place because you thought I would be long gone?" The secretary laughed and responded, "Of course, we have your records. We told you when you first came here in 1950 your education would last you your lifetime!"

I had not discussed the terms of an appointment at our first meeting, so I thought I should ask the Armstrong chairwoman about my title and salary. I had been associate professor at SUNY and full professor at Emory University. My last professorial salary at Emory where I also had the responsibilities of Director of the Undergraduate Program had been about $35,000, but when I moved to F.A. Davis Publishing in private industry I started with $50,000 plus an annual bonus. It was 1982. My next academic salary was as Research Associate at Jefferson Medical College, where I was largely supported by research grants. When I left my full-time position after seven years I was earning the equivalent of $65,000 annually.

The AASU Nursing Director told me she hoped she could give me the title of Associate Professor, and the full-time position available was budgeted at $50,000 for ten months. It was the best she could do. I was aware that new baccalaureate graduates were started with salaries between $40,000 and $45,000. That was a long way from the $3,000 I earned when I started with my B.S. at one of New York's most prestigious hospitals in 1954. I was sure I was overqualified, certain my academic credentials and history of research and publication were well beyond that of the any of the faculty. I learned the National League for Nursing Accreditation visit was scheduled to assess the program in January 2009. No wonder I was being pressured to join the faculty and come on board so quickly. There was the evidence for the faculty shortage I described earlier. Nurses in clinical practice were earning much more than faculty (and nurses, especially the associate degree and most baccalaureate students, were for the most part not learning how to teach).

I asked the director for a week to think about it; she gave me three days. I thought I might do better at Georgia Southern or the University of South Carolina at Beaufort, but I understood well the nature of faculty appointments and budgets. I had maintained my Georgia license since my Emory appointment in 1978, but I was not licensed in South Carolina, and I knew the process could take as much as six months.

Meanwhile the commute to Statesboro was probably at least one hour and a half, while Armstrong was only about twenty minutes away. I did not want to start looking for something else. It was mid-July and the next semester would be starting in mid-August. I also realized the income was important for me; I accepted the offer.

I received all my transcripts by express mail and within two weeks I was appointed to a temporary full-time associate professorship at Armstrong Atlantic State University College of Nursing in Savannah, Georgia. A few weeks later I was teaching in three undergraduate courses, *Evidence-Based Nursing Research* and *Health Assessment Skills Laboratory* during the day-time hours, and *Professional Role Development: RN to BSN* in the evening to undergraduates in the upper division curriculum. The following semester a graduate course in *Health Policy* was added to my evening schedule. Meanwhile, I was turning seventy five years "young."

Fortunately, I was able to team teach with other faculty members during the first semester, but after that I was pretty much on my own, although two young faculty members were particularly supportive to me. (Michelle and Pam became like daughters to me.)

I was starting all over, teaching in courses where the science was not just reorganized, it was updated and expanded from what I had last known and taught in the 1970s and 1980s. Fortunately the curriculum was pretty much defined; all the previous course outlines were described in detail in three-ring binders held in the department office. Required textbooks had already been ordered and were in the College bookstore. Course outlines described the goals, objectives, evaluation methods, and grading policies. Content outlines were fairly specific but fortunately there was flexibility and creativity allowed in the teaching methods.

The required use of technology for communication was sometimes more confusing than I thought necessary and online class conferences proved an ongoing challenge for me. This was certainly more difficult because of my years, but particularly due to the generational and background differences within the pool of diverse students. In addition, the contentious political scene surrounding health care in the country made the environment for teaching more stressful.

Meanwhile I had maintained long distance activities with Dr. Hojat and Mr. Veloski on curriculum and research projects at Jefferson, particularly on "Empathy in Health Care Providers." As the first semester gave way to the second, I began to recognize a lack of empathy in this new breed of students, as well as in some practicing nurses, faculty, and physicians I encountered, while health care for the uninsured was being debated in the public and professional press. I was hearing negative comments about uninsured patients not taking prescribed diet and exercise instructions or prescription medications, or returning for follow-up care, and even worse.

It was a matter of blaming the victim. This issue became the impetus for a new research study using the Jefferson Scale of Empathy in Health Care Providers.

Professional Role Development: RN to BSN

I needed to rethink the significance of my own basic and advanced nursing education and reflect on what was important in the current world role for professional nursing. My small student group in the RN to BSN course was a "mixed bag." Some students had just recently completed the two-year associate degree and had little or literally no clinical experience, while a few students had multiple years of diverse clinical experience but poor understanding of science they had learned years before. All had very little academic background beyond the minimal requirements. in the social sciences and humanities: history, economics, human development, music, art, or literature. Only one or two had a full understanding of what to expect from the course, how they would change as a result of the course, or what they planned to do after they earned the bachelor's degree. Some students were considering continuing on toward the master's degree leading to nurse practitioner certification. Few spoke about teaching when asked. Many were holding jobs – without higher goals or interest as professionals beyond a slightly increased salary. These students were also required to take the evidence-based research course, although I never heard of any specific interest in research at the beginning of the course, or at the end. How their practice would change after completing the BSN program was nowhere in their sight, although the issues related to advocacy for health care reform and changes in nursing practice with the introduction of advanced practice nursing appeared often in the public press. Clearly the barriers to this practice needed discussion in the course, and the mandate for graduate education was there.

Since I had been involved in the 1970s with the early acceptance of the concept of advanced practice, and had participated early on with development of innovative strategies for teaching and evaluation in the nursing assessment course, also introduced during the current RN course, I was interested in learning how the roles of advanced practice nurses were actually moving ahead in primary care, especially during the current politically contested health care reform environment. The role of the graduate level nurse practitioner in the community seemed fairly well accepted now by consumers of preventive health care and the majority of hospitalized patients, as well as other health professionals across the country, but there have definitely been barriers. Acceptance within the medical profession varies significantly, affected by the political divide in relation to economic issues, including access to health insurance, expansion of community health centers, and reimbursement by government funding for medical and nursing care under Medicaid and Medicare. State legislators, influenced by the medical societies, have certainly limited the ability of nurse practitioners (NPs) to provide service to the extent of their capabilities through independent practice. Just recently Connecticut became the 18th state in the nation to allow independent practice for certified nurse practitioners (with three years of experience in collaboration with physicians). In most cases NPs work in large collaborative practices, except in more rural areas.

As of May 2014, the number of previously uninsured Americans who gained health insurance under the new public options rose approximately to 12 million, while the percentage of Americans who were uninsured (although they were interested in insurance) decreased from 18% to 13.4% of the eligible population.

In 2004, the American Association of Colleges of Nursing (AACN) had adopted a position statement concerning the future of advanced practice nursing education. A target date of 2015 was recommended as the time when master's preparation for advanced practice nurses would be replaced by doctoral level education. However, it is clear, the 2015 target date has come and gone; it will not be met. Significant economic changes in the country since that proposal was announced have resulted in budget downturns at all institutional levels, especially for higher education. The funds are not there to support doctoral education as a requirement for practitioners, particularly due to the increase in the population needing primary care; a rapidly aging population, the growing incidence and earlier onset of chronic disease, new health care reform agendas, as well as the shortage of physicians entering primary care, and the projected severe shortages of nursing faculty has made it clear that nursing education cannot produce the required numbers of advanced practice nurses even at the master's level, certainly not to require the doctoral degree by 2015, especially when most nurses today are still entering the profession at the minimum level of the associate degree. While the Doctor of Nursing Practice (DNP) degree is being explored at many large academic medical centers across the country, their ability to attract paying students for primarily online courses and to develop new professional positions that meet the proposed objectives is questionable. I have not met many nurses with that level of professional education and experience working in Savannah. Meanwhile there has been a long history of vigorous and organized resistance from the medical profession in my state of Georgia to allow advanced nurse practitioners, nurse midwives, and nurse anesthetists to practice to the full scope of their education, training, and experience. I understand there is a perceived source of conflict between primary care physicians and advanced practice nurses, except in rural and low-socioeconomic areas where physicians often resist accepting patients when government supported health care does not meet their expectations for reimbursement. In my state the governor has refused to expand Medicaid despite the millions without health insurance.

Developing Creative Learning Experiences

Although I needed to develop my own creative teaching strategies for the professionalism course in relation to specific objectives, the previously established outline for the course did include at least one required text, the best-selling general leadership volume, *The Seven Habits of Highly Effective People*, by Stephen R. Covey. I wished I had been more familiar with Covey's work before I started teaching, but I was certainly glad the reference was there for me. Students had the paperback; I had found an audiotape of the author reading the book and was able to use clips relevant to the theory to stimulate discussion and create written assignments directed for those in nursing roles for individual classes. Students also contributed personal stories from their own working experiences that helped illustrate concepts and gave relevance to the theory presented throughout the course.

The course outline also first included an early overview of Florence Nightingale during the Crimean War and the history of professional nursing. I was reminded of Jon Veloski's previous comments for my award in 2003 about the contributions of Florence Nightingale, and reflected on her writings in her primary text *Notes on Nursing: What It Is and What It Is Not.* So, early in the course, my students and I watched the classic TV movie I had found on DVD, *Florence Nightingale*, starring Jaclyn Smith, Claire Bloom, and Timothy Dalton, to reflect on the background and qualities that made Florence unique. The students all loved the movie, which I found on Netflix; they all planned to buy the DVD to show to their families and friends. The cover of the DVD included the overview comment, "Into a violent world of men, one woman brought mercy." This reminded us of how the profession of nursing is so often implicated with the tragedies of war. Such was the case with Clara Barton as well, who traveled behind lines to work as a battlefield nurse during the American Civil War and then organized the American Red Cross. (The world-renowned American poet Walt Whitman also served as an unofficial nurse during that war.)

We then discussed fictional characters in literature and other media, including Nurse Catherine Barkley, a lead character in Ernest

Hemingway's *A Farewell to Arms* during World War I, and Major Margaret J. "Hot Lips" Houlihan, the strict but passionate head nurse in the movie and then on the iconic TV series *M*A*S*H* set during the Korean War. We also discussed the true story of the courageous nurses stranded on Corregidor in the Philippines early in World War II. We began a discussion of how the media has represented nurses over the years, some real and others fictionalized, occasionally with admiration, but often negatively, especially with sexuality and humor.

There were positive comments about Nurse Carol Hathaway played by Julianna Margulies in the long-running NBC drama *ER*, who was considered a good representative of our profession: modern, practical yet compassionate, and of course the on and off love interest of Dr. Doug Ross, George Clooney. On the negative side was the representation of Nurse Ratched, the fictional but iconic nurse from Ken Kesey's novel *One Flew over the Cuckoo's Nest*, a frightening, seemingly omniscient and omnipotent caregiver famously played by Louise Fletcher in the 1975 movie version, who inspires violent sabotage and revenge in her patients. She won an Oscar for her role and a reputation that has been carried forward into our general vocabulary. The discussion became more heated when more recently *Nurse Jackie* from the long-running TV series was brought up. I only watched one show; I did not appreciate the ethics of her behavior, and I am surprised the series has withstood the condemnation from the ANA and other professional associations. Most medically focused TV shows, however, attract audiences.

In *Florence Nightingale Today: Healing, Leadership, Global Action* (Dossey, Selanders, Beck & Attewell, 2004), the authors interpret her biographical data and personal writings to link her teachings to contemporary nursing theory. They recommend that if nurses everywhere would use Nightingale for inspiration, each could make a difference in the state of our health on various levels. "The goal of a healthy world is only possible through leadership and global action by well-educated (and courageous) nurses today." Meanwhile just this summer, Hawkins and Morse (The Praxis of Courage as a Foundation for Care, *Journal of Nursing Scholarship,* 2014; 46:4, 263–27) call for the return of the concept of "Courage" (that had somehow disappeared in the literature), to the original framework and terminology that defines Nursing Theory.

I was very saddened when I learned that Dr. Maxine Greene, educational theorist, model teacher, philosopher, and author, had died recently at ninety six years. Every student who took one of her courses at Teachers College Columbia University loved her; I was one of those lucky students. She was a tremendous influence on my professional development as an educator. *The New York Times* identified Dr. Greene as "one of the most important education philosophers of the past 50 years" and an "idol to thousands of educators," a woman regarded by many as the spiritual heir to John Dewey.

I thought once again about Dr. Greene in relation to her educational philosophy and theory course I took: *The Arts and American Education,* where she stressed the importance of the humanities (the arts: imaginative literature, music and art) as preparation for all the professions. This was a multidisciplinary examination of social, racial, gender, and sexual issues that I was able to apply while teaching at SUNY Stony Brook in the 1970s and then to the role of the professional nurse in my version of the course: *Professional Role Development: RN to BSN.* Now in the 21st century the course had the same objectives but some different strategies that were just as meaningful. The course took an in-depth look at the history of nursing and current philosophy and theories of professional nursing through the arts. We covered wars and economics, and considered the surrounding social and political events of the time. For example, now my students were assigned to independently read the novel or view the film, *The English Patient*, the story of an unusual episode during the African campaign of World War II, about the British, Germans, and a badly burned pilot that focuses on a very "hot" love affair between *The English Patient*, who was not really English (but a Hungarian count) and the wife of a British secret agent. The empathetic and skilled Canadian nurse Hana manages his severe pain as she cares for the dying patient in a severely damaged war-torn Italian villa. Several other characters play strong roles in the story. I provided a study guide to support online and in-class discussions relating to the history of the times and the diverse characters that were designed to stimulate critical thinking. *The English Patient* is a complicated story that explored complicated situations. Some of the questions I posed for my students were: *What qualities made the nurse in the story human? What skills did she demonstrate that made her a professional? How would you have behaved if exposed to the same situations?*

In terms of different cultures in this country, there was also the movie *Gran Torino,* directed by Clint Eastwood that dealt extensively with the immigrant Hmong people in Minnesota after the Vietnam War (Students brought this very interesting and challenging film to my notice in the Research Course, when I added a current Nursing Research study focused on this group to one of the course examinations.)

In addition to all the media utilized in the course, a trip to the Telfair Art Museum was promoted through distribution of free tickets I was able to obtain as a museum member. The objectives were:

- to sharpen skills of observation as part of the professional nurse's role;
- to examine works of art including portraits, landscapes, and stories as though we were examining a patient;
- to assess certain strengths, identify limitations, and look for specific elements in the face, eyes, skin, speech, positioning, behavior, backgrounds as preparation for the nursing process: assessment, planning, carry out interventions, evaluation of specific findings and outcomes; and
- to search for the artists' meanings. What and how did the painting make you feel?

Most of all, I wanted to emulate ***Dr. Greene when she emphasized that education was to open our minds, to challenge preconceived ideas, to think outside the box, and to find "meaning" in our own lives.***

It disturbed me to learn that not too long after I left Armstrong the RN-BSN program became a completely online program. I don't think I would have been able to support such a change. **Nursing is not like any other academic program; it is a relationship between individuals**. I believe that students learn best when they can interact directly together with the teacher and classmates. I believe the teaching can be most effective when the teacher can learn who the students are as people, discover where they are intellectually, and discover what he or she can do to help students grow. We may have a syllabus that provides a basic score and melody, but with each interaction together there is improvisation against that disciplining background. Students continually add to the outline what they bring from their own life experiences. With exceptions, of course, online education is likely to be a "one-size fits all endeavor…a monologue and not a real dialogue" [26]

I know the teacher can respond to students via e-mail and establish chat rooms and discussion boards, but without eye contact and sensitivity to unspoken thoughts and moods, enthusiasm may be difficult to achieve. How can the teacher adjust the course in a fluid and meaningful way for all students when they do not know each other?

My patients and my students have made me who I am. We have nurtured each other. I can't help but think that learning online makes intellectual life more sterile and abstract for students, particularly for the young student, and for the teacher, lonely.

Evidence-Based Research

There was much more I needed to learn during my return to academia particularly during the *Evidence Based Nursing Research Course.* Early in the course as we reviewed the *Ethical and Legal Considerations in Research,* I was reminded of reading the memoir of Dr. Gisela Perl, *I Was a Doctor in Auschwitz* and then of my visit to Auschwitz in Poland. I do not think my background as a Jew made these experiences any worse than those for men or women of other faiths. World history, literature, and cinema, true or fictional, are filled with horror stories of man's inhumanity to man: torture, murder, cruelty. It continues daily in the news for the whole world to hear and see. Just yesterday we learned of the assassination of another journalist in the Middle East. During this

---

26 (http://www.nytimes.com/2012/07/20/opinion/the-trouble-with-online-education.html?_r=0). 334-345

course I wanted to read portions of Dr. Perl's book to my students, but I held back. Dr. Perl's specific details are too horrible to describe here; my brief explanation to the class was sufficient. One movie stands out for me, *Schindler's List.* It tells two sides of the story, which I also saw at the Wallenberg Monument outside the Doheny Street Synagogue around the corner where my mother lived during World War I.

It was during the Nuremberg Trials following World War II that this issue of *Ethics and Medicine* first received attention. When the U.S. Secretary of State and Secretary of War learned that the trials for war criminals would focus on justifying the atrocities committed by Nazi physicians as "medical research," the American Medical Association was asked to appoint a group to develop a code of ethics for research that would serve as a standard for judging the medical atrocities committed by physicians on concentration camp prisoners. The first trials were known as the Doctors Trials, and 20 of 22 plaintiffs were physicians. Most were found guilty and sentenced to death.

The Nuremberg Code, first established in 1947, and its definitions of the terms *voluntary legal capacity, sufficient understanding, and enlightened decision* have been continually evolving in setting ethical standards in research. The code required informed consent in all cases but made no provisions for any treatment of children, the elderly, or the mentally incompetent. Other international standards followed, particularly the Declaration of Helsinki, adopted by the World Medical Assembly in 1964 and then revised in 1975. In the United States, federal guidelines for the ethical conduct of research involving human subjects were not developed until the 1970s.

The ethics of investigation and experimentation were not considered, and there were few safeguards especially for the most vulnerable in society. We reviewed in class one well-known tragedy: the 40-year Tuskegee Syphilis Study. Initiated in 1932 by the U.S. Public Health Service in African-American men in the small rural college town of Tuskegee, Alabama, the study was conducted to determine the natural course of syphilis. Information about an effective treatment was withheld from the subjects, and deliberate steps were taken to deprive them of treatment. Many died and syphilis was spread unnecessarily. Years later the study was reviewed and found unethical and eventually President Clinton apologized to the descendants of those who died prematurely.

Despite the supposed safeguards provided by the federal guidelines, some of the most atrocious examples of unethical research studies took place in the U.S. as recently as the 1990s and some abuses probably continue to this day. For example there is the contemporary story recently uncovered and published in 2010 as *The Immortal Life of Henrietta Lacks,* the mother of HeLa cells. Rebecca Skloot wrote the remarkable story of cancerous cervical cells removed by a physician researcher from a poor African American tobacco grower patient for study without her knowledge in the 1950s in the colored ward at Johns Hopkins Hospital in Baltimore, Maryland. Although scientists are using the progeny of the cells for research to this day, neither the patient nor her family were informed. She died prematurely of complications of her disease, which was common at the time. Neither Henrietta nor her family ever received compensation while millions of dollars have been generated for various research/treatment activities.

In 1973 the Department of Health, Education, and Welfare published the first set of proposed regulations on the protection of human subjects in research studies. The most important provision was a regulation mandating that an institutional review board (IRB) functioning in accordance with specifications of the DHEW, review and approve all studies involving human subjects. This certification was important when I later needed to approach the IRB at AASU and the two hospital systems in Savannah for permission to conduct a study with students and hospital nurses.

The federal government developed an online continuing education program leading to certification that is available for all individuals participating in research studies as researchers or reviewers; students in research are usually required to complete the program for certification as well. According to my Research Course outline, all the students enrolled in the course were required to complete the certificate program. It was all as new for me at that time as it was for my students. I needed to complete the course and obtain certification as well. Understanding the ethical principles involved was important, and three ethical principles were identified as relevant to the conduct of research involving human subjects: the principles of *respect for person, beneficence, and justice.* The theme was Protection of Human Rights:

1. Self-determination
2. Privacy and dignity
3. Anonymity and confidentiality
4. Fair treatment
5. Protection from discomfort and harm

These terms have also become important in recent years through the administration of health care in this country, not just research, under what are known as HIPAA (Health Insurance Portability and Accountability Act) Laws.

Measuring the Outcomes of Nursing Care

When I returned to teaching in 2008, evidence-based nursing research was not just "theory"; it was very much alive and well all over the world, and the literature was extensive. I had a great deal to learn about what was going on. I was particularly impressed by the amount of quantitative work that was taking place. The quality and quantity of professional nursing care was being measured and the value of education made a difference; the baccalaureate degree was important in terms of life/death outcomes of patient care, as was being determined by Dr. Linda Aiken, RN, and her team at the University of Pennsylvania and elsewhere.

I was learning right along with my students as we shared the journal articles about the Aiken studies and others relating to specific nursing problems and outcomes of nursing intervention. (Nursing Research was not taught in the BSN program when I was a student, and I had never taught Nursing Research in the past. My own research had been primarily Educational Program Evaluation Research.) I had to relearn the quantitative and qualitative basics myself, but I remembered the 1965

ANA position that recommended the baccalaureate degree in nursing as the minimal educational requirement for licensure as a registered nurse. The statistics were much simpler in those days. Unfortunately, that recommendation went nowhere; now we have the evidence of why the improved education through the BSN makes a difference. Unfortunately the quality of education nurses have been receiving since the associate degree programs replaced the diploma programs have not met the needs of nurses during the expansion of the nurse's role in primary care and community health. The original proposal for this replacement by Dr. Mildred Montag at Columbia University had intended replacement to lead to a technical role, not a professional role, which had always been intended to require the baccalaureate degree at a minimum. There were to be separate licensing examinations, but they were never developed. Today more than 60% of practicing nurses in the workforce across the United States are associate degree graduates. It is recommended that 80% should have a minimum of the baccalaureate degree.

It was very exciting to see how far nurses had come in working with teams and large data bases to show that the time nurses spent with patients and the quality of their education made a difference in relation to morbidity and mortality outcomes. Dr. Aiken's work was published in top-ranked professional journals for physicians as well as for nurses, economists, and health policy makers. The public press quickly recognized the implications.

"Better ratios of nurse staffing and better educated nurses shorten the length of hospital stays and decrease complications leading to improved morbidity and mortality outcomes." In other words, the more educated the nurses are who are taking care of you in the hospital, the faster you will heal, the less pain and complications you will have, the earlier you will be discharged, and the longer you will live.

And I believe, through my personal experience and the research I have been involved with on interprofessional attitudes and empathy, when physicians and nurses work as a team demonstrating respect for each other, patients heal better and live longer.

Fulfilling the Faculty Role in Nursing

Although I had not considered the other professional responsibilities in addition to classroom teaching that usually came with faculty appointment when I accepted the position, there was no way I could get out of committee assignments. I was soon assigned to the Program Evaluation committee, which made sense since program evaluation was a major theme in my graduate studies at Columbia University. Fortunately it only met monthly, and the months went by quickly without my having any serious additional written assignments. I was expected to creatively expand course development while struggling with student evaluations for all my courses, which had to be done online, so I was not eager to assume additional responsibilities.

Back in the 1960s at Columbia University I had been inducted into Sigma Theta Tau, the honor society in Nursing, but as a graduate student, commuting to Long Island, I had little time to be actively involved. So when I joined the faculty at Armstrong I thought I should become an active member in the chapter at AASU to participate with my new colleagues. I did hesitate when asked to serve as vice president for the organization, but finally accepted as long as I was not obligated to run for president the following year. I needed any free time to work on my "memoir."

When I was asked to organize the annual lecture with dinner I hoped I could arrange to have the event at the Marshes, the long-term Continuing Care Center where I was still a member of the Board of Directors and known as the "conscience" of the Center. One of the other faculty members arranged for a former colleague to lecture on "Universal Health Care" in Canada since she served as a Nurse Attorney with the Canadian Health Care System.

I had always maintained membership in the American Nurses Association and I was glad to have the opportunity to meet other nurses outside the Armstrong faculty by attending the local Georgia Nurses Association meetings. I fantasized about getting involved politically with the state legislature to promote the acceptance of the expanded role for nurses in public health and the federal proposal for "Increasing access to Health Care." I promised myself that as soon as my "memoir" was finished I would return to active membership with GNA.

Mentoring Young Faculty in Research Methodology

I recognized soon after I arrived at Armstrong that very few young faculty members had experience with research and publication, so I offered to help. I had been involved with several studies on empathy in medical students and nurses through my Jefferson Medical College relationship and it seemed appropriate to initiate a study among students at Armstrong when I heard faculty express concerns with the lack of empathy demonstrated in some students and hospital nurses.

One of our previous Jefferson Medical College studies showed that levels of empathy in medical students decreased once the students entered the third year, where they experienced intense patient contact and were under the supervision of the medical residents. It was hypothesized that underlying the decrease in empathy among the students was the fatigue and apparent cynical attitudes of residents and attending physicians based on the issues surrounding the economics of health care.

I formed a small group with three interested faculty and we used the Jefferson *Scale of Physician Empathy* as a prototype to develop a research proposal. Dr. Hojat, the Director of the Longitudinal Studies at Jefferson, wanted to validate the questionnaire for all health provider students, not specific to any one discipline, so generalized verbiage was utilized to revise the scale.

We hypothesized that empathy would decrease during the fourth semester when nurse students experience in-depth patient contact and are under the supervision of clinical nurse mentors, who might be similarly fatigued as the medical residents after working twelve-hour shifts. In collaboration with Jefferson's Center for Research in Medical Education and Health Care (CRMEHC), we planned to compare the scores on levels of empathy of baccalaureate nursing students and the clinical nurse mentors. Our research team presented the proposal to the Armstrong University IRB, and with their approval, we proceeded to the IRB at the two hospital systems: St. Joseph/Candler and Memorial University Medical Center/Mercer Medical College.

At Memorial, our study quickly received approval by the IRB when no risks to the participants were identified. Practicing nurses were recruited as mentors and a strategy for distribution of Consent, Demographic Forms, and Empathy Scales was determined in the hospital. The Armstrong faculty team then scheduled the distribution of the appropriate forms and scales to the first-year Armstrong students. Subsequently the following year, the Scales, etc., were sent to the same cohort, now second-year fourth-semester students, just prior to graduation. All the forms returned from the hospital nurses and the students were sent by Federal Express to the CRMEHC at Jefferson University for statistical analysis.

We anticipated creation of three papers from the data for publication. The first was to validate the new Scale for students with no specific health profession identified. The second paper would eventually represent a qualitative descriptive review of written comments on the submitted scales in response to several specific questions, and the third would be specific to the comparative study of the students and their assigned clinical nurse mentors. I had hoped one of the other faculty members would serve as Principal Investigator and start the writing process for the first paper in order to receive first author credit in the title, however no one volunteered. I ended up summarizing the analytical response and writing the first paper; it took me more than a year to complete the work. I was exhausted.

After critique and editing, "*Measuring Empathy in Health Profession Students: Adaptation of the Jefferson Scale of Physician Empathy*" was finally published in July 2011 in the *Journal of Interprofessional Care.* The new form of the Empathy Scale for health profession students was subsequently used by Dr. Hojat and others in a comparative study with Pharmacy and Medical students at Jefferson Medical College.

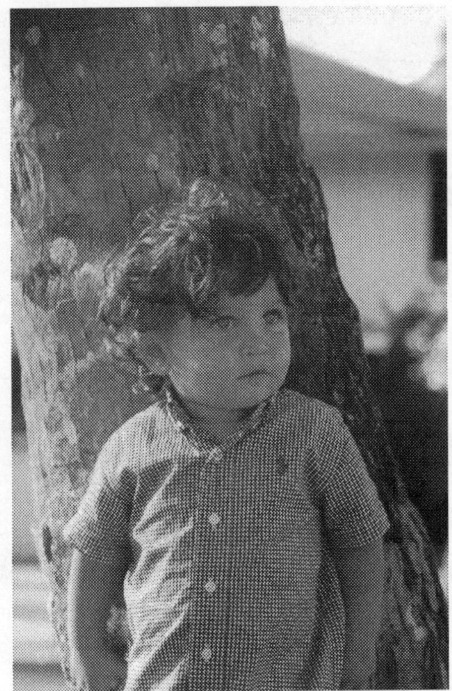

Second grandson, Jonathan Zackary Fields, born June 26, 2008 to Andrew and Shelly Fields.

Fourth granddaughter, Gabriella Madison, born November 12, 2010, to Andrew and Shelly Fields

My three children, Melissa, Andrew and Elizabeth surprised me with a gathering for my 75th birthday at the Ritz Carlton Hotel, Amelia Island. January, 20, 2009

With my granddaughter Rachel Emily at my birthday event.

With Millicent Rubenstein Barton Kramer my dearest friend since the fourth grade in Brooklyn and life in Old Bethpage, Long Island.

18

Finding Love in the Sunset of My Life

MY FAMILY AND PERSONAL LIFE

I started to work on this memoir early in 2003 as a form of therapy soon after my husband Frank left Skidaway Island in severe depression. Finding confidence again I vowed to set aside at least five hours each week to write up for publication stories of my early years, unique education, and continuously evolving career. I prepared an initial outline and recruited my friend Doreen to help, mostly to put on paper what was happening in the world around us during those years to stimulate my memory. At first it all seemed to come easily; I could see the scenes in front of me as though it was just the day before. But then each day, life seemed to interfere. I was distracted, so maintaining the original writing contract became impossible. The days, weeks, months, and years flew by as I was busy with managing the Mission full time; tutoring 7th and 8th graders at DeRenne Middle School; and riding out the difficult development and construction phase of the ***Marshes***. That was a long difficult effort before it was completed and ready to admit residents in 2005. All the time I was also still consulting with various educational research projects at Jefferson Medical College. My Curriculum Vitae just kept expanding.

Deep inside, I was lonely. I had been hoping to meet someone to restore my faith in the possibilities of romance, partnership, and maybe even marriage again.

As the result of the serious economic recession, maintaining my personal finances in order to stay in the home I loved was a challenge. I had shared half of the value of our home with Frank out of my retirement savings, and I hoped to find a way to increase my income; professional financial counseling didn't help much. It all seemed downhill. My attorney told me again to sell the house: "You can't afford to live at the Landings."

As much as I adored my children, I did not want to move to New Orleans. Then, on August 29, 2005, Hurricane Katrina, a category 3 storm made landfall in New Orleans with 127-mph winds. Failure of the levees left the city flooded and much more. Called by FEMA the most catastrophic natural disaster in the history of the United States, Katrina devastated coastal areas of Louisiana and Mississippi and beyond. My daughter Elizabeth's ranch house across the street from the 17th Street Levee in the Lakeview area of New Orleans next to Lake Pontchartrain was underneath eight feet of water for three weeks. The family was uprooted, moving first to Florida, next to Baton Rouge, and then Houston, Texas, before life in a trailer back in New Orleans.

Jobs were lost, the children's schooling interrupted, everything treasured was destroyed, including one of the three beautiful hand-painted Chinese cabinets I had shipped home from Shanghai China 20 years before. It took more than two years before Elizabeth and her family were able to return to a partially refurbished home they had purchased around the corner to replace the destroyed ranch, and another two years before reconstruction and any sense of normalcy returned. Fortunately, my son Andrew's home was not damaged as seriously, and his family was able to move across the river to the west bank of New Orleans while his partially flooded Old Metairie house was being refurbished.

Following the disaster, Gerry, my children's father who had been evacuated to Melissa's small New York City apartment temporarily, returned to New Orleans. He was seriously ill and had no financial resources, which only added to the children's stress. He did not live very long. In a way his death was a relief for all of us. He and I had never been able to have a civil conversation since our divorce more than twenty five years earlier, despite the many long-distance family gatherings for birthdays, holidays, weddings, births, and other milestones that were supposed to be joyful.

Somehow, with the courage of our convictions, through all the triumphs and setbacks in our lives, my children and grandchildren have persevered along with me. Bruised but not defeated by what life has thrown our way, we have demonstrated our resilience; we are a family of survivors. As I look back on my achievements, it is with great pleasure that I have had the opportunity to see my children weather the storm and watch my grandchildren grow into young adults, already making their own mark on the world.

In 2008, I learned Frank was very ill in Virginia. I tried to reach out to him a number of times before but he refused to see me or accept my help. My children loved Frank and tried to maintain contact with him and his children after he left. I know he appreciated all our concerns for him, but unfortunately he would not assume any responsibility for his own deteriorating condition; he continued to eat poorly, smoke heavily, and bemoan his fate.

Late in 2009, when he was too ill to continue to live independently, he gave up his apartment and moved in with one of his daughters and her family in Charleston, S.C. Unfortunately, it was too late; no one knew he had developed inoperable lung cancer.

Melissa visited Frank one weekend the following March and was disturbed to see how much weight he had lost. She called me immediately: "Mom, Frank looks terrible, I can barely recognize him. He is really sick. I know he refused to see you before, but maybe he is ready to change his mind. He asked about you and was surprised you were working so much. I think he would like to see you again. Would you visit him? Charleston is not that far from Savannah."

I agreed. "We had many wonderful times together. I loved Frank, and have truly missed him. Ask him if he will see me now." His daughter asked if I would be willing to visit Frank at her home. His health had deteriorated further and he was now under Hospice Care. He had asked to see me. She said he was only expected to live a few more weeks. I agreed to visit that weekend and called Melissa to see if she could return to be there with me. Fortunately she was able. I had no idea what to expect, but I did not want to visit Frank alone. When I drove up to the house they were all sitting outside on the front porch, Frank and Mary smoking. I did not recognize him.

Frank always had a full face and an easy smile, with thick dark eyebrows and short gray hair that flattered him. Now his hair was sparse and white, his eyes deeply sunken, and the brows thinned significantly. It was hard to talk; I did not know what to say. His granddaughters, one a senior in high school and the other a sophomore, came home from a youth group meeting at church and filled me in on what they were doing. Mary's husband John grilled hamburgers and hot dogs outside on the back deck. The girls set up several different salads on the buffet and asked what we wanted to drink. When everything was ready, John called us inside to the family room to eat. The dining room had been converted into a hospital room for Frank, who said he did not have any appetite and wanted to lie down to rest. The rest of us went into the family room for a casual dinner. I don't eat beef or hot dogs any more so I placed a few spoons of salad on my plate and began to nibble. I really had no appetite either. Everyone was drinking beer, wine, or Coke, but I had no desire for any of them. I asked if I could make a cup of tea and Melissa joined me.

A lot of news about the rest of the family was shared while we were eating, but afterwards I went in to check on Frank. He woke up and asked me to sit down on the chair next to the bed; he hesitantly reached for my hand. "Sylvia," he said, "thank you for coming. It is good to see you. You look wonderful. I am so sorry you have to see me like this. Can you stay for a while?" I told him I would stay the night, but I had to leave early because I had student assignments to check and return on Monday. He started to dose off holding my hand, but when I gently pulled my hand back, he awoke, held on and said, "Tell me, did they ever finish the Marshes?[27] Is Bill Goldsmith still alive?" Bill was a friend (now in his 90's) we had met at the first meeting of the continuing care project in 1996, and had been involved as an engineering consultant in developing the Marshes. I told him Bill and his wife Barbara had moved to a senior living facility near their son in Atlanta. He asked,

[27] The CCRC on Skidaway Island where I was on the Board

"Are you still working at the Health Mission?" I told him the clinic had merged with another clinic where they had their own space for a full-time mission during the day. "Tell me about your work now," he asked. I described the courses I was teaching and told him about how much I had learned since returning to teaching, and about still working with the Jefferson team on research projects. Frank suddenly said, "Sylvia, I am sorry. I need to apologize to you. I know how stupid I was now. We could have worked it out. It was my fault. Please forgive me. I loved you, and we had a wonderful life together. Please forgive me." He started to cry. I continued to hold his hand, and struggled to hold back my tears, but all I could say was, "I'm sorry too, I loved you." I said very little after that, and kissed the top of his head. I did not know what to say. I could certainly not tell him I had met someone three months ago and was enjoying my time with him,

"Can't I get you something to eat or drink?" I asked, "How about your favorite drink, a Manhattan?" He laughed, "OK." I called John in, but quickly Frank said, "No, I can't tolerate alcohol anymore." I stayed and Mary brought out the old photo albums I had brought with me. The girls came in to look at the photos they had never seen. We laughed at how we looked on some of our great trips abroad.

I went home on Sunday after breakfast, reliving the seventeen years we had been together. Even though I resented retiring early from Philadelphia because it affected my retirement pension and made me have to return to work to stay in my house, I have been so grateful to Frank for bringing me to Savannah. I think about it a great deal. Thank heaven I had the courage to stay when he insisted upon leaving.

Frank died two weeks later. I did not return for the funeral. I wrote to his sister in California expressing my sympathy and regrets for not being able to save Frank. She sent me a tape of the memorial service she had arranged a few months later in a Catholic church in Sacramento and a card printed in his honor.

Meeting the Renaissance Man

A few months after I began my second year at Armstrong, in the fall of 2009, Kathryn, the recruitment hostess at the Marshes where I was still on the Board, initiated a conversation with me about one of her new clients she thought I should meet. "He is a recently widowed physician who placed a deposit on one of the independent living cottages at the facility. He really seems nice, and I understand that he is a physician who teaches medical students at Memorial Hospital and directs the cardiac rehab unit at Candler." I was intrigued. Kathryn told me his name and promised she would arrange an introduction soon. "So far he has not been able to sell his large house in order to move into the cottage he has reserved, so he is not preparing to move yet," she said. Several weeks passed before I heard his name again, although not from Kathryn.

When I arrived with my colleagues to the Memorial Health/Mercer Medical School IRB [1]meeting to present our Armstrong research proposal on "Empathy in Nursing Students and Their Clinical Nurse Mentors," to Dr. Richard Leighton, Chairman of the IRB Board, two members of the Board who had reviewed the proposal were complimentary as they introduced us and recommended approval. I was nervous when I made my presentation. The rest of my team and I were asked to step out of the room while the full Board voted.

It did not take but a few minutes until we were called back into the meeting room. We learned the research proposal had been unanimously approved by the full Board. It was then that I recognized his name. Dr. Leighton was the widower Kathryn had spoken about. It suddenly dawned on me I had actually met him once before. Dr. Leighton had been one of the volunteer chefs at the 10th anniversary of the Savannah Health Mission in 2006. He was very quiet and shy that day, and I was so busy I hardly spoke with him. His wife was still alive then. (Evidently she had developed a reoccurrence of her cancer and had died a few months before in March 2009.) Now, I knew his changed marital status and his academic qualification as a cardiologist and educator. It was quite coincidental, I thought. My first master's degree was in Cardiovascular Nursing at Columbia University with clinical experience at Presbyterian Hospital in New York City. Later I found out he was a resident in Cardiology around the time I was working on my Master's Degree. And that he liked to cook and had at one time taken a course in French cooking in Paris. Clearly, we had mutual interests to explore; we were both educators, and I understood he liked to cook; I liked to eat heart-healthy food and always wanted to learn the secrets of fine French cooking.

In the meantime, as vice president of Sigma Theta Tau (STT), I had arranged the annual Dinner/Lecture at the Marshes around the Thanksgiving holidays. The president of STT at Armstrong had invited one of her Canadian colleagues from home to lecture on the Canadian Health Care System following the dinner. I decided not to wait for another introduction. I checked the Landings Phone Directory and called Dr. Leighton to invite him to the STT Dinner/Lecture. Michelle, one of my young colleagues had worked with him at Candler Hospital Cardiac Rehab: "Sylvia, he is the nicest doctor I have ever known in my whole life."

Dr. Leighton seemed pleased about the invitation. I can't say it was love at first "sound or sight," but I came away with a good feeling after our very brief first phone conversation. We had never actually had eye contact during the IRB meeting. Now he made me feel at ease in inviting him. That evening as he entered the main floor from the elevator at the Marshes, several other nurses who evidently knew him were smiling and anxious to greet him. I was behind the registration table and could tell he enjoyed the attention. I thanked him for coming and walked with him to the "cash bar" to buy him a glass of wine. I then had him sit with Michelle and me for the buffet dinner, but I had to run around to greet nurses at the other tables, so we did not have much time to talk alone. Although he did not say much that night, he listened. He has a very pleasant subtle sense of humor. We walked to the lecture hall and sat together. I was really glad the lecturer had great slides and presented very well.

After the lecture, Michelle and I introduced Dr. Leighton to some other Armstrong administrators, faculty and STT officers as we walked together to the exit. He thanked me for the invitation and said he hoped we would have another opportunity to meet; so did I. I was nervous, would he actually call me? I could not tell what he was thinking. He knew I lived at the Landings and was on the Marshes board. I had not known his deceased wife, who apparently had been an eighteen-hole golfer. That meant she was a good golfer, while I am only a nine-hole not-so-good golfer. My mind raced as always, thinking of possibilities! Would he be satisfied with me as a potential golfing partner? I doubted it. For sure I should warn him, or he would be disappointed! Later, I was so relieved when he told me he really preferred to play tennis, although I wouldn't do very well with tennis either. However, later we did play golf together several times and I was not so bad…so I told myself.

(I will have to work on my golf as soon as my book is finished.)

A few days after the lecture I received a handwritten thank-you note from him. It was very nicely penned, better than most other physicians' handwriting I had tried to decipher. I was really excited when he invited me to the Marshes Formal Holiday Black Tie Event a week later. As a board member I was already expected to attend, but I was really glad to be invited. I hated the idea of driving up and making an entrance there alone. I was also glad it was a black tie affair. To me, every man looks more attractive in "black tie" formal attire.

I was nervous, for it had been a long time since I had had "a date." It was ages since I had been to a formal affair. I struggled to decide what to wear to the party, but when my friend Julie offered me a few choices from her wardrobe, I selected one dress I thought was more interesting than anything in my own closet. Unfortunately it was a little tight, and I knew I would need help with the zipper, so once I had finished fixing my hair and makeup, and I had the dress on, I called Joy who lived across the street to come over and help zip me up. We made it just in time for Joy to get back home when my doorbell rang; my date had arrived.

I guess I looked pretty good in the low-cut black cocktail dress. Dr. Leighton exclaimed "Wow!" when I opened the door. This time the wine was complimentary, and we had a few more than at the previous event. As always at the Marshes, the food was fantastic and the music was great.

It was a wonderful surprise to learn that Dr. Leighton also liked to dance just like me, for after reading, dancing is my favorite pastime. The music was perfect and we did not miss one dance; I could not lose the smile on my face all night. Somehow during an intermission in the music, we were able to enjoy the dinner and get in a few words about our families. It was weird to learn that our three children were all about the same age; he had two sons and one daughter, while I had two daughters and one son. Each of his children was within a year of my children.

Later after we came back from the party, I had to call Joy again to come over and unzip me. I was smiling from ear to ear.

Getting to Know the Renaissance man

The more time we spent together, the more personal and professional interests we discovered we had in common. I told him about my other research projects at Jefferson and the development of an international group expanding the studies of Empathy related to patients with diabetes and other problems.

Known by colleagues and friends as "Dick," Dr. Leighton was a distinguished Academic Professor of Cardiology, and had been Dean of the Medical School at the University in Toledo, Ohio. Since his retirement he has maintained some of his professional activities here in Savannah, mainly his enthusiasm for teaching medical students as a Tutor in the problem-based curriculum for the Cardiac, Pulmonary, and Renal units and interest in the ethical and legal aspects of medical research, by serving as Director of the IRB at Memorial Health/Mercer.

Early on I was taken with Dr. Leighton's modesty and sense of humor. I could not help noticing that while he dresses conservatively, he also sports not a Rolex, but an inexpensive Mickey Mouse watch. One clue that there was a fun future in our relationship, came on my birthday a few months after we met. He surprised me with a Minnie Mouse watch. Minnie is dressed as a nurse and one hand tells the hour holding a thermometer.

I cannot call him "Dick." Somehow that name just does not fit. I asked him if everyone called him "Dick." He responded with, "My mother called me 'Richie." I asked if I could use "Richard." I believe it fits him perfectly, since Richard is a king's name, much more dignified and appropriate for this man of many interests and diverse skills, I consider a "Renaissance Man." Not only does he play tennis and golf but he swims early in the morning three times a week, and rides his bike with a physician friend on Saturday afternoons. Trim and fit, he is very attractive to me. I wish I could be as active as he, although I manage to exercise daily while power walking and listening to country or classical music on my Walkman. I vary my routes around this beautiful Island or the weather is not complying, I use the treadmill in my house in front of a television set tuned in to whatever news stories, drama, or lecture of interest I can find.

A few months into our relationship, after hearing more about my Jefferson and Armstrong "Empathy" studies, Richard gave me an interesting book I had not heard of, *The Age of Empathy: Nature's Lessons for a Kinder Society* by Frans De Waal published in 2009. De Waal is a Dutch biologist and psychologist at the Yerkes Primate Center of Emory University and the director of the Living Link Center at Emory. He explored the concept of empathy in various animals as well as questions about empathy in humans. In 2007 *Time* magazine selected him as one of the world's most influential people. With all the terrorism going on in the world, Richard and I are not so sure this is the Age of Empathy, but the topic continues to capture my attention in both the professional and personal arena.

Recently Richard introduced me to the Great Courses of the Teaching Company, fascinating DVDs about various topics; history, philosophy, literature, science etc. We started with one course on the beginning of our civilization. I found it fatiguing to just watch the tapes, but I discovered that watching while on the treadmill, I was learning about the Big Bang theory and evolution with every step. Much of this scientific information wasn't known when we were in school years before.

When the next catalogue arrived, I realized here was an opportunity I could not deny myself.

I had asked so many questions over the years about the history of my religion, but was never really able to take the time to study seriously. There is a bookcase in my house filled with books addressing different Jewish related themes, (fiction as well as non-fiction) that I had picked up while browsing in book stores or received as gifts from my parents, or children when they entered adulthood. For the most part however, all I had usually done was browse. As soon as I saw the next teaching Company catalogue with several products on religion I knew I needed to order one of the courses on the history of the Jews, "**Between Cross and Crescent: Jewish Civilization from Mohammed to Spinoza**" given by a professor at the University of Pennsylvania, David Ruderman. There it was, "Spinoza" the source of the poster on my office wall with the bird on the beach and his quotation that is the source of philosophy for which I have an interest. Dr. Ruderman's course has fulfilled my need for answers about where my people came from, the diverse journey taken through the centuries, and the significance of it all. This also brings me to another topic Dr. Richard and I have appreciated sharing. The differences and similarities in our religious beliefs have also been a topic for much discussion. Dr. Leighton has a Methodist background and of course I am Jewish. There are actually few differences in what we believe in; our values and beliefs are similar. Neither one of us is really into prayer services, and sermons. What we both enjoy is the music — sacred music in the temples and as well as classical music in the theatres, concert halls, and other venues. Richard has joined me for traditional Jewish New Year Rosh Hashanah and Yom Kippur evening services and I have accompanied him for special programs at his Methodist church.

Richard had belonged to a *Couples Book Club* with his wife for several years, so when he asked me if I would be willing to join, I accepted. It turned out there were a few members of the club I knew from Rotary Club which made it easier to fit in. The book to be discussed for my first club meeting was an epic historical war and romance novel that chronicled the rise of Mustafa Kemal Atatürk, "Father of the Turkish

Nation," entitled *Birds Without Wings*, by Louis de Bernières in 2004. It was a great story, but long, so we decided to share the reading. I read the first five chapters the first week and then explained the story to Richard after dinner one night. Then Richard took the book and read the next five chapters. We continued alternating chapters telling the story and then discussing what we thought was going on until the book was finished, just before the month had passed. It was a lot of fun and it was clear we both enjoyed not only the book's history and romance but being together and sharing dinner. There is so much diverse literature, professional and non-health-care-related, that comes into our homes we also share much of the rest of the reading. We peruse the *Wall Street Journal* and *The New York Times* and also share magazines such as the *New Yorker, Harpers, Smithsonian, Time*, and others. Richard tends to scan and then select sections he thinks will interest me and I take longer on the non-professional, more public readings, filtering for what I think he has missed. As a result Richard and I always have a great deal to talk about.

Taking Cooking Classes Together

When we first met, we dined out often but it wasn't long before we started taking cooking classes together and then began to experiment with cooking at home, usually in Richard's larger and much better equipped kitchen, but not always. We both enjoy cooking that derives from other geographical regions and cultures, but Richard is much more precise and proficient than me. While on sabbatical for six months in Paris thirty years ago, he found the time to take a course in gourmet French cooking. As a result, he is quite meticulous and artistic in his food presentation. When following a recipe, Richard tries to have every ingredient measured and poured or chopped out, while I am much more prone to improvising – a remnant of my early nursing career. If I don't have every single ingredient listed on the recipe and I don't think it is critical to the flavor, I will settle for some substitute.

We even started inviting friends to share our home cooked meals of what we have recently learned. One year we hosted a wonderful dinner for almost forty guests as a fundraiser for Hospice where Richard is on the Board and invited two musicians from the Philharmonic to play. It was a big hit. Fortunately we were able to find help for prepping, serving and cleanup. We decided "once a year" for the big event was enough, especially while I have been working on this manuscript.

With a common interest in fine art we both have belonged to the Telfair Art Museum for many years. However, Richard is a member in the "Directors Circle" enabling us to attend openings of new exhibits and to meet distinguished artists. Meanwhile we have started to collect the fascinating new digital art of our mutual friend, Reverend John Anderson, a former pastor at Memorial Hospital and former member of the Board at Savannah Health Mission. In addition, wherever we travel we enjoy visiting the local art museums.

Our Mutual Love of Dancing

I think it is amazing how we both love to dance and constantly receive compliments when we're out on the floor. Maybe it is because of Richard's white hair that makes people comment. They must recognize our ages and think it is unusual that we can expend so much energy while dancing. Evidently the joy we are having shows. Once in North Carolina our friends took us "clogging" for the first time. We sat there observing how much the dancers were enjoying themselves until I could not wait any more. The music got to me, so I stood up and started, and in a minute Richard had followed me. We were moving along pretty swiftly, both of us smiling and laughing like always. When we stopped a gentleman came up to us and said, "You two really know what you're doing. [He must have been kidding!] How long have you been married?" I laughed, but Richard said, "We're not married!" "Oh, so how long have you been dancing together?" We both looked at each other, smiling. Richard hesitated and then looked at his watch, and replied, "Oh, about ten minutes." (I broke up laughing.) Another weekend while we were taking a cooking course at Jekyll Island, Georgia, there was dancing during dinner Sunday evening. Of course we were up there enjoying ourselves, surprised no one else in our group joined in. At the end as we were leaving, a young couple came up to us. The woman looked at Richard with tears in her eyes and said, “Can I hug you?” Surprised as we were, Richard said, “Sure.” And she put her arms around him and hugged, holding on for several minutes. With tears in her eyes and a Latin American accent she said, “Seeing you two dancing like my parents used to do back home brought back such wonderful memories.” I asked where home was and she said, “Cuba, but it is a long time ago.” We had to tell her that we had been to Cuba for the first time just six months before, and we had danced almost every night at dinner. We had also received compliments there, and I couldn’t figure out why, except that we were obviously having such a good time. And perhaps, at an age when enjoying dancing is probably not so common.

Music in Our Blood

We especially appreciate all types of music: classical, pops, blues, country and some spiritual and religious sounds of our youth. We both took piano lessons as children and have pianos in our homes; although Richard has a more interesting small baby grand and can remember some of the Chopin he learned. My piano is much smaller and needs a serious tuning.

We enjoy attending Philharmonic orchestra and chamber music performances and concerts here in Savannah and at various other musical festivals. It was only a few months after we met that Richard asked me if I would like to attend the Spoleto Music Festival in Charleston, South Carolina. I had not been there for many years so he planned the trip, selecting the music, the theatre, and the restaurants. It was a wonderful few days. We repeated the trip the next two years and fell in love with the young cellist, Alisa Weilerstein. I was so enthralled at seeing her passionate playing live, I had to buy all her CDs. I predicted she would be very successful. Well, sure enough, the next year she won a $500,000 MacArthur "Genius" award. We have become like groupies following our other favorite musicians. Last June we followed magnificent creative violinist Daniel Hope and remarkable pianist Wu Han from the Savannah Music Festival to the Aspen Music Festival in Colorado. As I wrap up this memoir, I write while listening to my favorite artists on CDs or listening to *NPR Performance Today*; I find tremendous "wellness" listening to music And on top of all of that is our mutual love of opera. We manage whenever possible to enjoy the Metropolitan Opera Saturday afternoon movies in HD, usually with our friends, The Clarks, followed by dinner.

Traveling Together

During the past five years Richard and I have traveled overseas together in the study of food and cooking and in relation to national and world affairs to some incredible and exotic places neither one of us had visited before, such as Easter Island, Cuba, and recently to Iran with the Council of World Affairs. Each one of the trips has been unique and exciting. In Cuba, in addition to dancing every night, and enjoying the rum drinks, we visited a cigar factory and although always a nonsmoker, I took a few puffs on a famous Cuban cigar—the same kind my father used to smoke before his gastric ulcer created bloody havoc and almost killed him. I just felt like I wanted the experience once, just briefly. I will never have to do it again. We drove downtown in one of the historic American convertibles from the 1950s. I was thrilled to find someone in the Jewish Temple and Senior Center who knew my family who had come to Havana after WWI, when because of the quota restrictions they could not get into the United States. I had last seen the children of that family in 1960.

We especially enjoyed the local art, poetry and music during our travels, particularly in Buenos Aires, where we attempted to learn the tango; and in Mendoza where we sampled the famous wine, rode horses and learned how to make empanadas. In Valparaiso and Santiago, Chile, we were introduced to the fascinating collections of art, sculpture, and books in the homes of Nobel Prize–winning poet Pablo Neruda. We could not resist buying some of Neruda's romantic poetry, which we adore.

> "You and I are the land full of fruit. Bread, fire, blood,
> and wine make up the earthly love that sears us."

Our most recent trip was to Iran where we were citizen diplomats. It was a wonderful lesson in history of the Persian Empire, archeology, culture, and current Islamic politics. We understand a little bit better the difference between the Sunni and Shiite and perhaps the objectives of the Islamic Regime in Iran with its prohibition of alcohol, but cannot fathom why we were unable to dance just a few steps to the beautiful Persian melodies for strings. Visiting Persepolis, the Carpet Museum, and other museums and monuments, magnificent mosques, beautiful Persian gardens in the desert, and the Shah's Palace, were particularly remarkable learning experiences. Being welcomed and greeted so warmly everywhere by beautiful children and young university students was heartwarming. "Now the history of civilization all seemed to come together with the Big History from the Teaching Company."

Through our work, Richard Leighton and I have both been fortunate to choose professions that have allowed us to use our knowledge and expertise in the service of others. It has now been more than five years of partnership and they have been wonderfully successful and happy fulfilling years for both of us. We are as excited today about our professions as we were as beginning students and educators. As one can readily see, finding the Renaissance man has absolutely enriched my life and I am certain extended it. Richard says the same about my impact on his mortality. We are fortunate to be able to maintain good health into our ninth decade, have so many friends, and take pride in the accomplishments of our children and grandchildren. We appreciate being able to live on this beautiful island, and to keep our minds active and positive through the work we both enjoy.

P.S. It turned out Iran was not our last trip abroad' WE RETURNED TO CHINA a few months ago. After writing earlier about my trip to China for my 50th birthday in 1984, when Richard, who had a similar trip in the 1980s, learned about a possible new visit to see how China had modernized today, we both could not resist the temptation. It was another amazing experience. We prepared for the trip with another Teaching Company Great Course, Dr. Richard Baum's, "The Fall and Rise of China." Too much to write about, we traveled mostly by new hi-speed trains across the country and through the mountains in three and a half weeks. We were impressed and amazed at the new construction of massive new cities. This time few bicycles to see, but mostly large automobiles: Mercedes, Lexus, BMW, not always able to speed along the new highways due to the sheer numbers of vehicles. We traveled miles and miles, viewing all kinds of temples, mosques, museums learning the history and spiritual backgrounds of the diverse major and minor religions. We made friends among the residents, dancing alongside our elderly Chinese compatriots, who were excited to learn how old we were and how far we had traveled and accomplished so much at our age. We rode the cable cars half way up and then climbed the famous large mountains earning medals for our accomplishments. And then there was the new Dam on the Yangtze River; a magnificent site to experience. I have included several images for your reference.

Dr. Richard Leighton and I traveled to my first **Academic Cardiology Meeting, Phoenix, Arizona**, January, 2011. I met several of his former professional colleagues and we played golf with his friends Sandy and Arnie.

We traveled independently to **Argentina, Chile and Easter Island, 2013**. Here we are on Easter Island in the middle of the Pacific viewing some of the many hundreds of "Moai," ancient remains of historic "Gods" of local tribes.

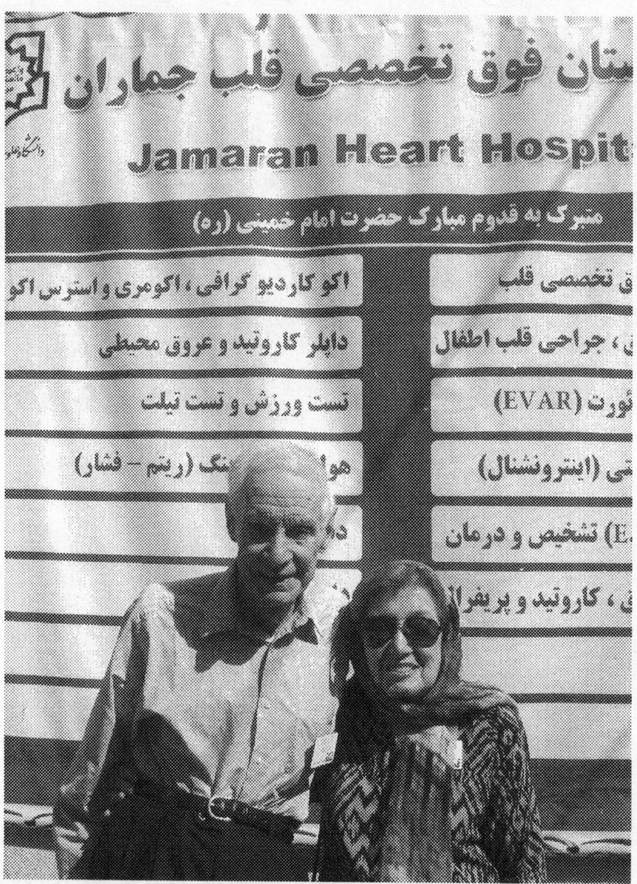

We traveled to **five cities in Iran** as **"Citizen Diplomats" with the Council of World Affairs April 2014**. Here we are in front of the Heart Hospital outside the home of the Supreme Ayatollah in Tehran. Later we visited remarkable archeological remains of ancient Tehran, Persepolis and Isfahan.

In September 2014, we attend the **wedding in Puerto Rico**, of the daughter of Dr. Leighton's Cardiology Trainee of forty years ago. *Here I am, wearing the elegant Iranian scarf I bought in the spring during our Iranian trip.*

Dr. Richard Leighton and I make a **return visit to China**, **June 2015** after thirty years and view multiple world heritage sites including X'ian where we experienced the amazing Terra Cotta Warriors, and museums honoring Confucius. We won medals for climbing mountains: seen here at the top of Hua Shan Mountain. Later we spent three days on Yangtze river cruise viewing the new Dam.

19

My Legacy

Looking Back
Past Accomplishments
Described in My Memoir

A. *Innovative and accelerated RN to BSN Programs.* When asked recently what I believed was my greatest accomplishment in nursing, I thought for a long time. Finally I wrote, perhaps it was development of accelerated opportunities to enable graduates of diploma and associate degree programs with clinical experience to earn the baccalaureate degree and move on towards graduate degrees in nursing education or clinical practice, thereby enriching the professional nursing workforce.

B. *Development of Interprofessional Learning Opportunities in Nursing and Medicine. 1)* Doctoral Dissertation: A National Survey of Interprofessional Education Opportunities for Baccalaureate Nursing Students: 1975-1977; 2) Development of Interprofessional Textbooks for Physicians and Nurses; 3) Development of Interprofessional Courses for Nursing and Medical Students; 4) Development of Interprofessional Research Opportunities; 5) Development of Community Based and Continuity Learning Experiences that encouraged entry to Primary Care Specialties for students at Jefferson Medical College, Philadelphia, PA

C. Perhaps my greatest contribution is as a *role model for continuing education* throughout my career and my enthusiasm for returning to education of nurses in the sunset of my life.

All through my life there have been individuals who helped me move forward. I acknowledge many of these individuals at the end of this book. If not for the support I received I would not have been as successful professionally as I have been. There would have been no funds for graduate study, no awards or acknowledgements received, no role modeling for me to emulate. Unfortunately the kind of help I received is not always available for young colleagues today. When I returned to academia in 2008 I decided to "do something" about that limitation for my colleagues at ASU.

Since research and publication often leads to recognition that is rewarded with salary increases, promotion, and/or tenure awards, I wanted to help my new young friends accomplish those goals. With the help of my Philadelphia partners, I brought the *Jefferson Scale of Physician Empathy* to Savannah in order to provide my AASU colleagues with the opportunity to be actively involved in a new study. Subsequently three faculty colleagues participated with me in a new study of "empathy" in nursing students. The first paper proposed was published in the *International Journal of Interprofessional Health Care* in July 2011. Although I played a significant role in the preparation of the first manuscript, after publication I stepped aside in order to work on this memoir. We planned two additional papers utilizing the data we had collected and I am pleased to report that work is in progress on a new interprofessional study expanding the student population and utilizing the adapted Jefferson Scale for health provider students.

I appreciate comments below about our activities together.

> **Dr. Pamela Mahan wrote**, *"Sylvia has been a tremendous mentor for me in doing empathy research. The knowledge and passion Dr. Fields has for her work is extraordinary. I feel privileged to know and to have been allowed to work with Dr. Fields on the empathy study."*

Mr. Jeff Harris added his thoughts, *"I want to say that, when I first met Dr. Fields, I was, frankly, surprised that I was meeting her, as I was (and am) in awe of her background. When I was invited to participate in an empathy study with her, I could not believe my good fortune. Dr. Fields has had a major impact on my nursing career. For that, I will always be grateful.* Jeffrey W. Harris

****

I am happy to include another quotation in my honor by my friend Julie Heintz here in Savannah.

Julie Heintz, RN, BS, BSN, Clinical Quality Control Consultant; Memorial University Medical Center, Savannah Georgia

"President John Quincy Adams once said,
If your actions inspire others to dream more, learn more, do more and become more, you are a leader."

"*When I read this quote, Dr. Fields comes to mind. She has taught and inspired countless women and men to become leaders in the nursing profession she has helped to pioneer. She proves hard work and perseverance is the pathway to success. Her career explained in this memoir, as a nurse, educator, scholar, mentor and accomplished leader has truly been an amazing journey, not only for her, but for all of nursing. I am proud and honored to call her my mentor and friend. This is a sincere thank you for inspiring me to continue my education and further my nursing career." Julie Heinz*

In response to the request from the newly established Memorial Health System Nursing Research Council, I have been serving as advocate, consultant, and mentor in development of *Evidence Based Nursing Research Studies* at Memorial University Medical Center in Savannah where I already serve voluntarily as a community member on the Institutional Review Board. Our new study "*Attitudes of Physicians and Nurses toward Collaboration*" using the Jefferson scale at Memorial University Medical Center" is progressing.

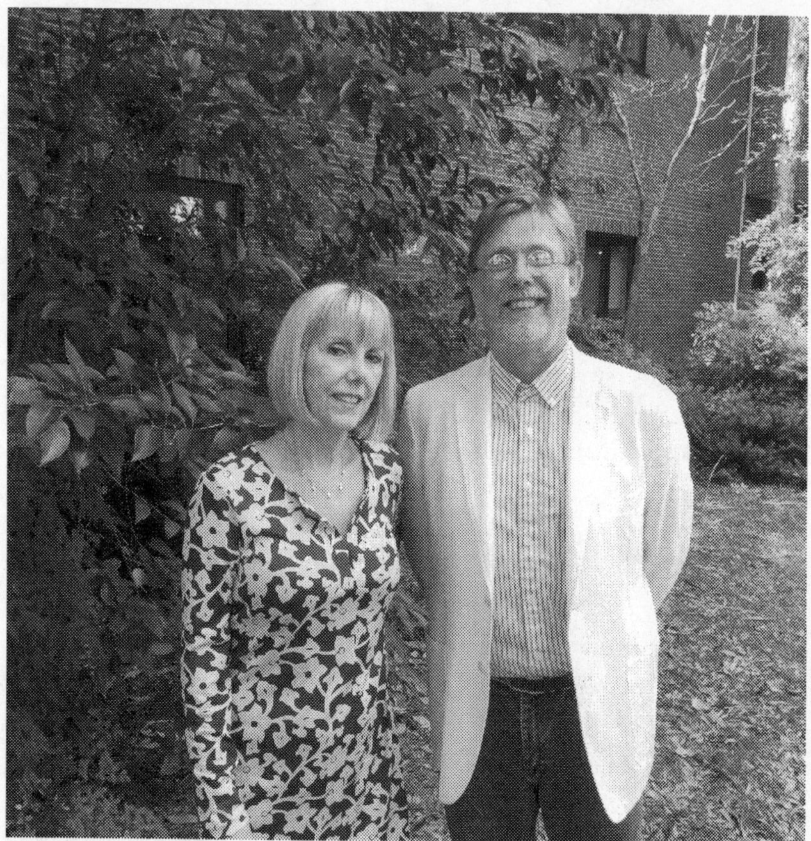

Jeffrey Harris, RN, MS and Pamela Mahan, PhD., R.N. who conducted with the author an initial study of empathy in Armstrong Nursing Students, "*Measuring empathy in healthcare profession students using the Jefferson Scale of Physician Empathy: health provider-student version.*" Published in the *Journal of Interprofessional Care*, July 23, 2011.

THE JEFFERSON SCALE OF PHYSICIAN EMPATHY (JSPE)

Measuring Empathy in Medicine and the Health Professions

Center for Research in Medical Education and Health Care

Jefferson Scale of Physician Empathy Brochure

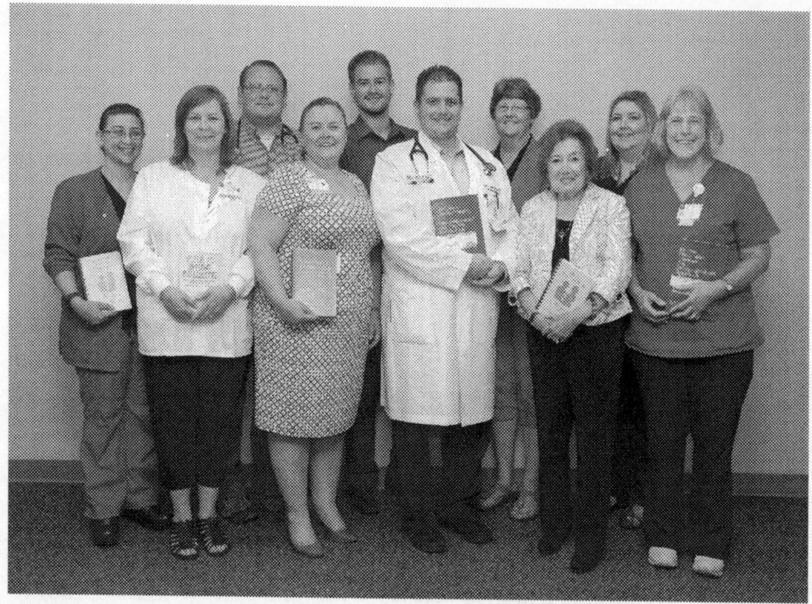

Memorial Health Nursing Research Council July 2015.Study of Nurses and Physicians Attitudes toward Collaboration at Memorial University Medical Center/Mercer University School of Medicine, using the *Jefferson Scale of Attitudes toward Physician-Nurse Collaboration*.

MY VERY PERSONAL LEGACY

Gabriella's first birthday.

Sam and Rachel, 2011

Jonathan at six, 2014

Gabriella at four, 2014

Sam had his Bar Mitzvah in Touro Synagogue, March 2011.
My entire immediate family participated.

Sam, recent photo, 2015 (almost six feet tall; "a future attorney")

Rachel had her Bat Mitzvah in Touro Synagogue, October 2013

Alix, Technical production manager CNN News 2015 NYCity.

Courtney's graduation from University of Arizona 2013. She received the BA majored Communication and Leadership. She was elected President Alpha Delta Pi Sorority and received "the Power of One Award."

Courtney Danielle traveled the country visiting colleges as leadership trainer for national Alpha Delta Pi Sorority

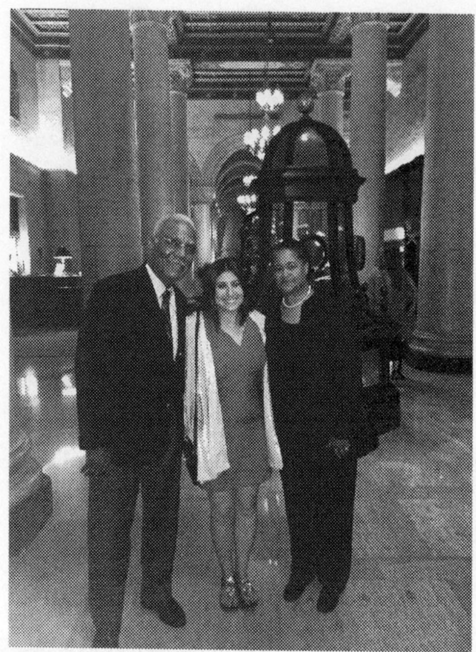

Courtney with my dear friends Drs. Georgie & Robert Labadie while visiting the University of Miami during Spring 2015.

20

Epilogue

I have often been asked by prospective students, "What can you learn in nursing school that will get you through the rest of your life?" I know how to answer that question. I have been a strong advocate for the potential of a professional nurse; most of all I know what it has meant for me. I've been a professional nurse for more than sixty years and I know how my nursing education and lifelong professional experiences have enabled me to keep moving on – to continue to deal with and overcome all kinds of problems in living.

Nursing has been more than an education for a job; it has been a lifelong commitment to human compassion and continuing learning. Year after year, the Gallup polls identify nursing as the most ethical profession. There is no more noble or rewarding a profession or standard of personal conduct than to understand human behavior well enough to become a coach, and teacher, and to be able to effectively react in a crisis and provide comfort to those in need.

As long as I have been a nurse, I have been explaining to people what nurses do.

I explained to my parents what I was learning in nursing school, I explained to my patients how I would be caring for them, I explained to my students what I would be teaching, I explained to physicians what nurses are capable of doing, I explained to administrators what nurses should be doing, and I explained to legislators what nurses must be doing. And much of the time they listened.

But the time came for me to explain it again, this time in a comprehensive package to a world where the American health care crisis is on everyone's radar, where the roles of health care professionals have changed dramatically and will need to continue to change, and where nursing has advanced to the forefront of health care reform.

Nursing, as it was once known, is hardly recognizable. A nurse is a nurse is a nurse is just not true. Long gone are the women in starched white uniforms and caps who moved almost invisibly through the hospitals. And hopefully sooner rather than later, the wildly inaccurate stereotypes of nurses as sex kittens, dumb blondes, and evil tyrants will disappear. Today women and men with humanistic education, specialized technical training, and advanced degrees in distinguished looking laboratory jackets, or in colorful scrubs, are integral members of interdependent health care teams that permeate our entire health care process. This includes primary care centers, hospital acute care units, palliative care in community hospice centers or at home. Nurses are conducting independent and collaborative interprofessional evidenced-based research around the world. Nurses are officers of corporations and leading major Foundation Boards. They are senators, representatives and other legislators among governing agencies; and officers in the Armed Forces; presidents of universities; and on official committees developing policies and programs that benefit all of us. These are nurses today!

Has this wonderful growth and diversity in the field of nursing interfered with one's ability to understand who nurses are and what nurses can do? I must clarify the differences; the title "nurse" is not one-size-fits-all. Not only does our current national shortage of nurses and nurse educators convince me that students may not be able to see the dynamic opportunities available to them, but the public's lessening confusion about the expanded functions of the highly knowledgeable nurses on whom they depend convinces me that it's time to update the story of nursing for everyone's sake, including the medical profession. And how best to accomplish this but to start with what I know and tell my own personal story.

I have spent my professional life practicing and advancing the responsibility and credibility of the nursing profession through leadership positions in nursing education and community health. In addition, as a doctorate-holding nurse clinician and educator I have been able to apply my diverse background to the education of medical students and physicians. My professional efforts and accomplishments have been acknowledged in publications, with honors and awards.

It has been a long and difficult journey from that small Brooklyn apartment where I looked out the window at a brick wall, slept on a sofa bed across from my brother, and cared for family members who were Holocaust survivors. All I wanted was a room of my own, and an adventure. I received all of that and much more, including support and encouragement from my family and children, who somehow survived me and are stronger as a result. I appreciate all the friends, colleagues, teachers, patients, and students throughout the years who strengthened my resolve to live the adventure of my life as a humanist.

Every time I drive over the bridge to the beautiful island I live on, where I am surrounded by tall pines, waving palms, and majestic oak trees covered with Spanish moss, lots of birds, and friends from all over the world. I pinch myself and think how lucky I am that I searched for adventure and became a professional nurse, a member of the most ethical profession in the world.

And, I am particularly grateful today for the true love I finally found, my best friend and soul mate Richard (Dick) Leighton, The Renaissance man, who accepts me as I am.

In the past, when I told my stories, friends, students and strangers always said, "You should write a book!"

Alas!

Everything is Possible

Sylvia Kleiman Fields

The Florence Nightingale Pledge

"I solemnly pledge myself before God and in the presence of this assembly, to faithfully practice my profession of nursing. I will do all in my power to make and maintain the highest standard and practice of my profession.

I will hold in confidence all personal matters committed to my keeping in the practice of my calling. I will assist the physician in his work and will devote myself to the welfare of my patients, my family, and my community.

I will endeavor to fulfill my rights and privileges as a good citizen and take my share of responsibility in promoting the health and welfare of the community.

I will constantly endeavor to increase my knowledge and skills in nursing and to use them wisely. I will zealously seek to nurse those who are ill wherever they be and whenever they are in need.

I will be active in assisting others in safe guarding and promoting the health and happiness of mankind." –Florence Nightingale.

Armstrong Atlantic State University
Department of Nursing
Pinning Ceremony Class of 2008

Sylvia K. Fields Publications

BOOKS:

Sherman, J.L. and **Fields, SK.** ***Guide to Patient Evaluation***. Flushing, NY: Medical Examination Publishing Company, 1974 ***American Journal of Nursing,*** **"Book of the Year" Award - 1974; 2nd Edition, 1976; 3rd Edition, 1978; 4th Edition, 1982; 5th Edition, 1988 International Editions** (Japanese, Spanish, Chinese-Unofficial.)

Fields, SK. and Yurchuck, R.M., **Nursing Examination Review and Study Guides: 1984-1986,** Garden City, NY: Medical Examination Publishing Company: ***Adult HealthNursing, Women's Health, Child Health, Psychiatric Mental Health***

BOOK CHAPTER:

Fields, SK, Savard M, Epstein, K. **The Female Patient.** In:Douglas, P. (ed)

Cardiovascular Health and Disease in Women. Philadelphia, PA:WB Saunders;1993:3-21.

PEER REVIEWED JOURNAL ARTICLES:

Fields, SK, Mahan, P, Harris, J, Tillman, P, Maxwell, K, Hojat, M.

Measuring empathy in healthcare profession students using the Jefferson Scale of Physician Empathy: health provider-student version. ***Journal of Interprofessional Care,*** July 23, 2011.

Aronson C, Rattner S, Borden C, **Fields SK,** Gavin J, Veloski J.J. Cross-sectional assessment of medical and nursing students' attitudes toward chronic illness at matriculation and graduation. ***Acad Med*** 2008: 83,10 (Suppl.) S1-S5)

Moskowitz E, Veloski JJ, **Fields SK,** Nash DB. Development and evaluation of a one day interclerkship program for medical students on medical errors and patient safety. **Amer J Med Quality**.2007, Jan-Feb;22 (1):13-17.

Veloski JJ, **Fields SK,** Boex JR, Blank LL. Measuring professionalism: A review of studies with instruments reported in the literature between 1982 and 2002. ***Acad Med.*** 2005; April;80(4):366-70.

Fields SK, Hojat M, Gonnella JS, Magee M. Comparisons of nurses and physicians on empathy: An operational measure and preliminary psychometric data. ***Eval & the Health Professions*** 2004 March 27(1):80-94.

Hojat M, **Fields SK,** Gonnella JS. Empathy: An NP/MD comparison ***The Nurse Practitioner*** 2003; 28 (4): 45-47.

Hojat M, Gonnella JS, Nasca TJ, **Fields SK, et all.** Comparisons of American, Israeli, Italian and Mexican physicians and nurses on the total and factor scores of the Jefferson Scale of Attitudes Toward Physician-Nurse Collaboration. ***The International J Nurse Stud.*** 2003.May; 40(4): 427-35.

Hojat M, Nasca TJ, Cohen MJM, **Fields SK**, Rattner SL, Griffiths M, Ibarra D, Alcorta-Gonzales AA, Torres-Ruiz A, Ibarra G, Garcia A. Attitudes toward physician-nurse collaboration: A cross-cultural study of male and female physicians and nurses in the United States and Mexico. ***Nursing Research,*** 2001; March-April. Vol 50(2):123-128.

Hojat M, **Fields SK,** Griffiths M, Cohen MJM, Plumb JM. Psychometric properties of an attitude scale measuring physician-nurse collaboration. ***Eval & Health Profess.*** 1999 June; 22(2):208-220.

Hojat M, **Fields SK,** Rattner SL, Griffiths M, Cohen MJM, Plumb JM. (1997). Attitudes toward physician-nurse alliance: comparisons of medical and nursing students. ***Acad Med.*** 72(10): S1-S3. Presented at the RIME conference AAMC annual meeting, November 1997.

Xu G, **Fields SK**, Laine CA, Veloski JJ, Barzansky B, Martini CJM. (1997). The relationship between the race/ethnicity of generalist physicians and their care for underserved populations. ***Amer J Public Health.*** 87(5): 817-822.

Fields, SK, Veloski, JJ, Barzansky, B. Rattner, S. (1996). PBL and primary care career choice: a complex relationship. ***Acad Med.*** 71(9):939-940.

Gottlieb JE, **Fields SK**, Hojat M, Veloski JJ. (1995). Should half of all medical school graduates enter primary care: perceptions of faculty members at Jefferson Medical College. ***Acad Med.*** 70:1125-1133

Xu G, Rattner SL, Veloski JJ, Hojat M, **Fields SK,** Barzansky B. (1995) A national study of the factors influencing men and women physicians' choices of primary care specialties. ***Acad Med.*** 70:398-404.

Xu G, Veloski JJ, Hojat M, **Fields SK**. (1995). Physicians' intention to stay in or leave primary care specialties and variables associated with such intention. ***Eval & Health Prof.*** 18 (1):92-102.

Martini, CJM, Barzanski, B; Veloski, JJ, Xu, G, **Fields, SK**. (1994). Medical school and student characteristics that influence choosing a generalist career. ***JAMA.*** 272:661-668.

Fields, SK. (1976). Nurses earn their B.S. degrees on the job.***Nursing Outlook.*** 3:21-25.

Wieszorek R, Pennington, E, **Fields, SK**., (1976). Interdisciplinary Education: A Model for the Resocialization of Faculty. ***Nursing Forum.*** XV:52-60.

NON-PEER REVIEWED ARTICLES:

Rothman N, Arcangelo V, **Fields SK**, Gottlieb, J. (1994). ***Physicians and Nurse Practitioners in Primary Care: Collaboration or Competition.*** Thomas Jefferson University Health Policy Newsletter. Vol.7(3). September.

MULTI-MEDIA LEARNING PROGRAMS:

1974 Series on Health Assessment Techniques. Westinghouse Learning Systems

1975 Series on Clinical Anatomy & Physiology. Westinghouse Learning Systems

1976 Series on Hypertension. Westinghouse Learning Systems

Special Research Reports:

1975-1977 **Fields, Sylvia Kleiman.** *The Concept of Interprofessional Collaboration in Baccalaureate Nursing Education Programs: A Descriptive Survey.*

Unpublished Doctoral Dissertation: Columbia University 1977 (Dissertation Abstracts)

2000- 2001 **Fields SK** Federal Funding for Medical Education Research in the 1990's: What Have We Learned from the Three Medical Education Research Centers (MERC) Cooperative Program? An Evaluative Analysis**. *Contract Report submitted to BHPr, HRSA, DHHS.* March 2001**.

Selected References

American Nurses Association. (2015). Code of Ethics for Nurses with Interpretive Statements. 2nd Edition. Silver Springs, MD: Nursesbooks.org.

American Nurses Association. (2015). Nursing: Scope and Standards of Practice. 3rd Edition. Silver Springs, MD: Nursesbooks.org.

American Nurses Association. (2003). Nursing's Social Policy Statement – 2nd ed. Silver Springs, MD: Nursesbooks.org.

Antler, J.(1997). The Journey Home: How Jewish Women Shaped Modern America. New York, NY. Shocken Books Inc, Toronto. Random House of Canada LTD, New York. The Free Press; a division of Simon & Schuster Inc.

Benner, P. Sutphen, M., Leonard, V., & Day, L.(2010). Educating Nurses: A Call for Radical Transformation. Stanford, CA: Jossey-Bass.

Benson, E. R. (2001). As We See Ourselves: Jewish Women in Nursing. Indianapolis, IN: Center Nursing Publishing.

Buchanan G., Bretherton, T. (2008). Safety in Numbers: Nurse-to-Patient Ratios and the Future of Health Care. New York. Cornell University Press, Sage House.

Collins, F.S. (2006). The Language of God: A Scientist Presents Evidence for Belief. New York, NY. Free Press: a division of Simon & Schuster Inc.

Cook, E.T. (1913). The Life of Florence Nightingale Vol 1 & 2. London, England. Macmillan and Co. LTD.

Convey, S.R. (2004). The 7 Habits of Highly Effective People: Powerful Lessons in Personal Change. New York. Free Press: A Division of Simon & Schuster Inc.

D'Antonio, P. (2010). American Nursing: A History of Knowledge, Authority, and the Meaning Of Work. Baltimore: The Johns Hopkins University Press.

Dawidowicz, L. S. (1975). The WarAgainst The Jews 1933 – 1945. New York: Holt, Rinehart and Winston.

Dossey. B.M. Selanders, L.C., Beck, DM, Attewell, A. (2005). Florence Nightingale Today: Healing, Leadership, Global Action. Silver Springs, MD: Nursesbooks.org.

Evslin, B. (Ed) The Spirit of Jewish Thought. (1969) New York, N.Y.: Grosset & Dunlap, Inc. LOCCC 68-10736

Fields, S. K. (1977). The Concept of Interprofessional Collaboration in Baccalaureate Nursing Education Programs: A Descriptive National Survey. Unpublished Doctoral Dissertation, Columbia University.)

Finkelman, A., & Kenner, C. (2010). Professional Nursing Concepts: Competencies for Quality Leadership. Sudbury, MA: Jones and Bartlett Publishers.

Goldsmith, C, Ice, D. (2007). Moon Shadows: Reflections of Life in the Low Country. Hong Kong. C & C Offset Printing Co. LTD.

Horrigan, B.J. (2003). Voices of Integrative Medicine: Conversations and Encounters. St. Louis, MS. Churchill Livingstone.

Howe, I. (1976). World of Our Fathers. (With assistance of Kenneth Libo) New York & London: Harcourt Brace Jovanovich.

Johnson, S. (2015). What Would Florence Do? A Guide for New Nurse Managers. Silver Springs, Maryland: Nursesbooks.org.

Lader, L (1973). Abortion II: Making The Revolution. Boston: Beacon Press.

McGrath, E.J. (1959). Liberal Education in the Professions. N.Y. Teachers College, Columbia University

Nightingale, F. (1980). Notes on Nursing: What it is and what it is not. Edinburgh, London and New York: Churchill Livingstone.

Norman, E. M. (1999). We Band of Angels: The Untold Story of American Nurses Trapped on Bataan by the Japanese. New York: Pocket Books.

Perl, G. (1948). I Was A Doctor In Auschwitz. Salem, NH: Ayer Company, Publishers, Inc.

Pinar, W.F. (Editor) (1998) The Passionate Mind of Maxine Greene. Bristol Pa.: Falmer Pres, Taylor & Francis Inc.

Ruderman, D.B. (2005). Between Cross and Crescent: Jewish Civilization from Mohammed to Spinoza. Chantilly, Va. The Teaching Company

Scannel-Desch, E. & Doherty, ME. (2012). Nurses in War. New York: Springer Publishing

Sherman, J. L., & Fields, S. K. (1988). Guide To Patient Evaluation: History Taking, Physical Examination and the Nursing Process. New York: Medical Examination Publishing Company.

Skeet, M. (1980). Notes on Nursing: The Science and the Art. Edinburgh, London and New York: Churchill Livingstone.

The New York Times. (2007). The New York Times Guide to Essential Knowledge, A Desk Reference for the Curious Mind. New York: St Martin's Press.

Wiesenthal, S. (1969-1998) The Sunflower. New York: Shocken Books.

Acknowledgements

It is impossible to recognize here all the individuals who helped me through the years to develop as the person and professional I became, but there are a few who deserve credit. I have already dedicated this volume to my parents and children who lived their lives along with mine. Then there are the teachers over the years that helped me to accomplish my learning needs and supported me personally. Two stand out in my memory: Mrs. Weiner, history teacher and advisor at James Madison High School along with Mrs. Quinn, RN, my teacher in the Home Nursing Course Mrs. Weiner recommended I take to complete my academic credits for graduation. She recognized my innate qualities and guided me towards professional nursing. It would be a very different book had these two women not played such important roles.

At Adelphi I must recognize Dean Margaret Shay who recruited me and supported me throughout my four difficult years in the nursing program. Some of the Adelphi faculty members stand out. Certainly if Dr. Atlas, chemistry instructor during the first semester had not gone out on a limb to save me for nursing, I would not be here today. I appreciated him then but I never had a chance to thank him after I completed the program; I do so today. A few other teachers are still in my memory for the support they offered when I ran into trouble, specifically Justina Eisenhower. I did thank her again and again enthusiastically when she placed the Adelphi pin on my new white uniform the evening before graduation.

Prior to my experiences at Teachers College, some very elegant women stand out among the distinguished mentors I had during my early teaching days, i.e., Ruth Sleeper, Director of Nursing at Massachusetts General Hospital and president of the National League for Nursing and Edythe Alexander, Director of Nursing at Lutheran Medical Center in Brooklyn, New York and author of multiple editions of the award winning textbook, "Principles of Operating Room Nursing."

Years passed and much has happened so it is difficult to remember most faculty I knew at Columbia University, with the exception of those I had a relationship with over time, more than one semester. I can fondly remember over the twenty years of my education at Teachers College: Mildred Montag, Maxine Greene, Frances Reiter Kreuter, Elinor Lambertsen, all have passed away. But the most significant one is of course, the dearest and longest friend, not just while I was a student, but throughout all these years as well, Dr. Georgie Labadie. I said it before and I say it again, without Georgie I would never have completed my doctoral dissertation and without her support during the last two and a half years, I would not have completed this manuscript. Thank you Georgie and thank you Dr. Robert Labadie, and Richard thanks you both for being there for me too.

Although Ellen Fahy was not one of my instructors at Columbia, she definitely took on the role of advisor, mentor and supporter at SUNY, Stony Brook as did Jacques L. Sherman, Jr. MD, my co-author of "Guide to Patient Evaluation." My life changed significantly as a result of these two individuals, who unfortunately did not live to see this book become a reality.

The question arises, who, in addition to Dr. Labadie specifically helped me with this manuscript. **I must first recognize Carolyn Zalesne**. It was 2008 and you were the editor of a newsletter for a group, called '*The Jewish Women of the Landings*." I was a member of the group, although not very active. You heard that I had returned to teaching nursing, more than ten years after retiring from an adjunct position at Jefferson Medical College and moving to the Landings of Skidaway Island with my golfing husband. I had recently retired as well from a position at The Savannah Health Mission. It was your idea to prepare an article for the December (Chanukah) edition of the JWOL Newsletter by interviewing me personally. Brilliantly, you tied my" rekindling of my nursing career" at Armstrong to the lighting of Chanukah candles, candles that are supposed to only last a brief time, but that burned for eight nights. You focused on how long a career should last. Mine has certainly taken many twists and turns.

Obviously, this book is evidence that there is no need to consider limitations to a career, certainly not in my mind.

After the article appeared and we both were awarded with suggestions from readers, "You should write a book," we set out to do so. Carolyn, you offered to help and we sat and talked and you wrote many notes. But it was time for another teaching semester for me and I had four courses to teach. I could not concentrate. You had other interests as well so neither one of us was anxious to continue. It is hard to believe that more than seven years have passed. I finally finished, although certainly not alone. The story is much different than what it might have been had we finished together in 2009. ***Carolyn, I want to thank you for your contribution.*** *I am certain you will recognize some of your early efforts within these pages and I am sorry it took me so long to get my act together.*

Although she has requested no accolades, my former golfing partner and academic enthusiast **Doreen Higgins** needs to be acknowledged next. For years, while I was telecommuting to Jefferson on special research projects, Doreen helped me by copyediting various papers I was preparing at home. Later when I started teaching at Armstrong she helped me correct the English grammar within my student papers, and evaluate the Research Posters the students generated. In the meantime I began to think about writing my memoir: *Again, Students and colleagues kept saying, "You should write a book."* My original idea for this memoir was to focus on the decades I have lived from the beginning in the 1930s and tie as many of my personal experiences to the associated world events during that time. Doreen reviewed the brief outlines I offered within each decade and accepted the various references texts I shared. She added other references and proceeded to prepare brief 1-2 page introductions to each of the decades covering a broad list of topics we thought might be related. Then I started adding my current reflections on the past events. The system did not work; there was simply much too much unrelated content that could not be easily integrated. I thought I would need a wheelbarrow to carry the completed manuscript to the publisher if I included everything. I needed to change the outlines and limit general information prepared by Doreen to only what was directly relevant to my experiences. Doreen's role in copyediting therefore became primary. ***Thank you Doreen, for helping me right up the end.***

When I realized early on I needed more help, I was reminded that my former assistant editor at F.A. Davis twenty five years ago might be able to help me. **Linda Weinerman Franklin** was now editor-in-chief of "First Books," a small publishing company in Portland, Oregon. We have maintained our personal friendship, through divorce and remarriage ever since Philadelphia, including corresponding visits between Portland for me and Savannah for Linda. I am tremendously grateful to you Linda, grateful that you never completely gave up on me after I sent my first few drafts. I know you spent hours and hours over months trying to help me organize the voluminous outpouring of my Memoir. All this was while you were maintaining your full time position. I am sorry you could not see me through to production Linda, but had you not provided the bulk of organizational guidance I would not be here today. I believe we are still friends! **Thank you Linda Weinerman Franklin**

Along the way several other individuals responded to my request for help with typing components of the manuscript. One of those individuals was **Joy Howard**, friend and neighbor who with her husband Pat, helped me with various personal needs around the house that made it possible for me to devote attention to my writing. In relation to this manuscript however, Joy typed for me; tedious, boring, requiring careful attention and patience. And then she was here for emergencies; Joy zipped me up and out" the night of my first date with Richard Leighton for the black-tie-dinner dance at the Marshes. **Thank you Joy and Pat Howard for your friendship and support.**

It was at a family wedding in Jacksonville a while back that I reunited with **Karen Gelhaar** after many years and remembered she was a free lance writer/editor. After learning I was struggling with the book I was writing, Karen offered to help anytime I needed help. It took almost two years but I finally decided to take up her offer a few months ago. They have flown by. **Thank you sincerely Karen for all your encouragement, support and editorial assistance**. It has not been easy for either one of us, since you are in Atlanta and have recently gone through a terrible personal tragedy. I am so sorry. Thank you Karen for you definitely helped move me along to this day.

Peter Lonergan, BA, MA: World Wide Camera. Thank you, Peter for all your patience and assistance in facilitating the reproduction and transfer of the images for this Memoir. You deserve a medal.

Rabbi Robert Haas. You were fairly new to our congregation, Mickve Israel Synagogue (established in Savannah Georgia in 1733) and I had not met you. I called to make an appointment to meet with you and talk about my book. I believe you were trying to get to know the members, perhaps others like me who are not very active. I even sent you a file with the not quite completed manuscript at your request, although I doubted you would have the time to struggle through my long story. In any event you convinced me you should visit me in my home, and you came. I'm not sure what I was thinking of, but I guess I wanted some approval for what I had written about Judaism and my struggles with faith. I worried about Spinoza who I had adopted for the theme of my text and the commandments, (after the first ten) that I might not have been obeying. More than a year passed; we never spoke much during the few times I came to temple, but recently I read some of your words in the Savannah Morning News relating to care for the homeless, and I recognized those words, there was no question they influenced my life from the beginning. With your permission I am repeating them here.

"According to our sages, helping those in need is equal in importance to all of the other commandments given to us by God. As Jews, we believe it is our obligation to donate our efforts toward the betterment of the world, and there is no greater way to fulfill this obligation than assisting those people who are struggling in life. May god give us the strength and fortitude to continue to perform …acts of loving kindness, throughout our lives." (Savannah Morning News Sunday November 15, 2015) **Thank you Rabbi Haas, I guess you did read my manuscript.**

Richard F. Leighton, M.D., thank you for coming into my life and this memoir, although I wish it had been earlier. If only I could be as organized and thorough as you; the book would have been completed well before you arrived, but it would never have been the same book. I hope my readers understand what a "gem" I found in you, and how much I appreciate your love and your contribution, not just to this Memoir, but to my life.

And to **Adriane Pontecorvo** and staff of Archway Publishing, thank you sincerely for your patience and support during this project.

The Cover Artist

M. Miles "Chip" Goldsmith, M.D., F.A.C.S.

"First Be, Then Do."

The water color Painting "*Mystic River*," on the cover of this book was a gift of the artist to the author of this "Memoir." A self trained professional artist, known as "Chip," Dr. Goldsmith, was born and raised on the "Isle of Hope" just outside Savannah Georgia, one of the pristine island communities which punctuate the inland waterways of the low country. An honors graduate of the University of North Carolina and it's Medical College in Chapel Hill, Dr. Goldsmith is the region's only fellowship trained 'Neurotologist," specializing in management of disorder of the ears and hearing problems. He is Clinical Associate Professor, Department of Surgery, Mercer University.

Known for his commitment to community health and social welfare, Dr. Goldsmith established the Savannah Health Mission, a free clinic for those without health insurance at the Georgia Ear Institute. (1996-2006.) The author, in her capacity as Executive Director of SHM worked closely with Dr. Goldsmith. His theme, "**First Be, Then Do**" clearly inspires service that brings meaning to our lives.

In recent years Dr. Goldsmith has been continuing his community service by volunteering to help children and adults with hearing problems in developing countries. Here he is seen examining a young boy in Belize.

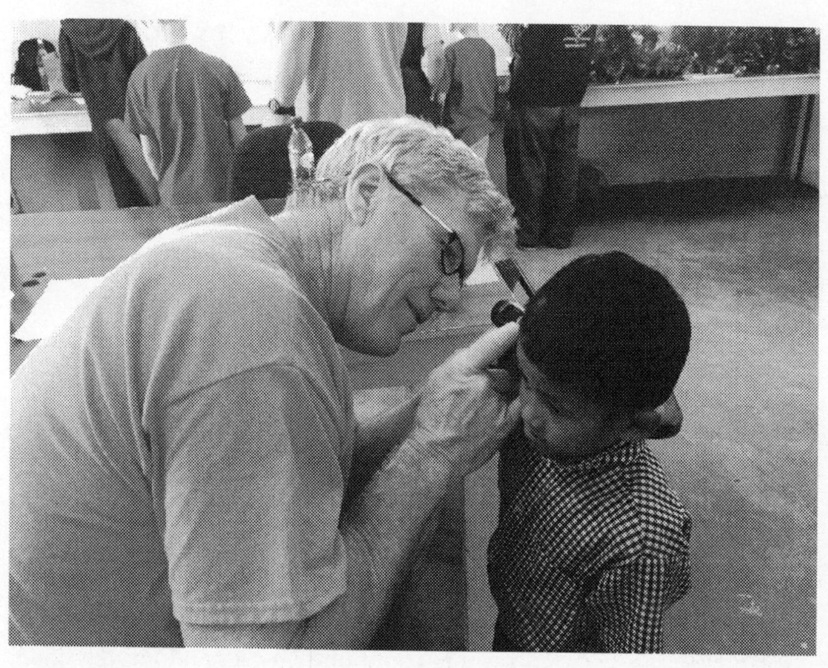

Printed in the United States
By Bookmasters